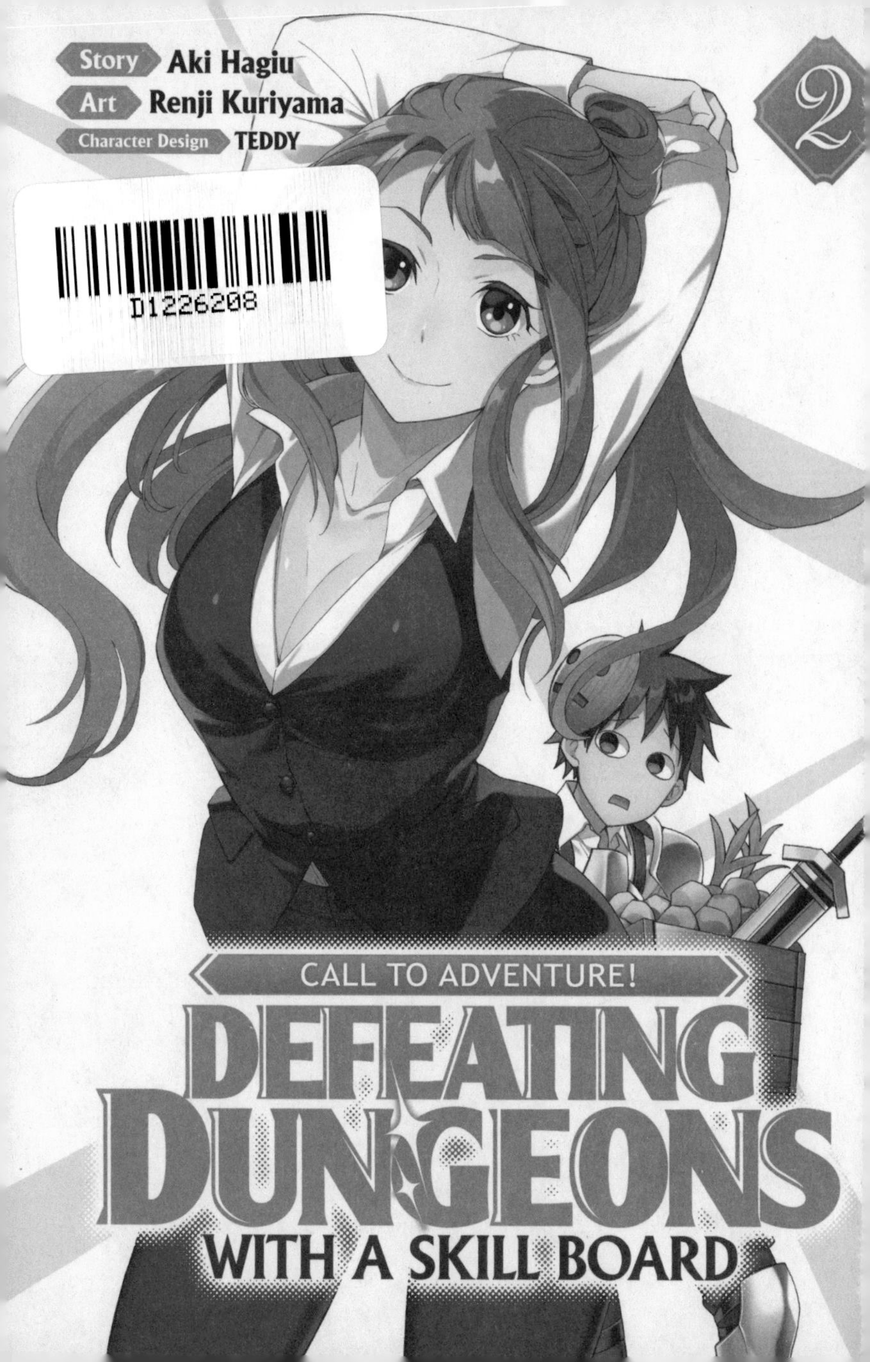
Story Aki Hagiu
Art Renji Kuriyama
Character Design TEDDY
2
CALL TO ADVENTURE!
DEFEATING DUNGEONS
WITH A SKILL BOARD

2

CONTENTS

Chapter 6   003

Chapter 7   035

Chapter 8   072

Chapter 9   104

Chapter 10   128

Chapter 6

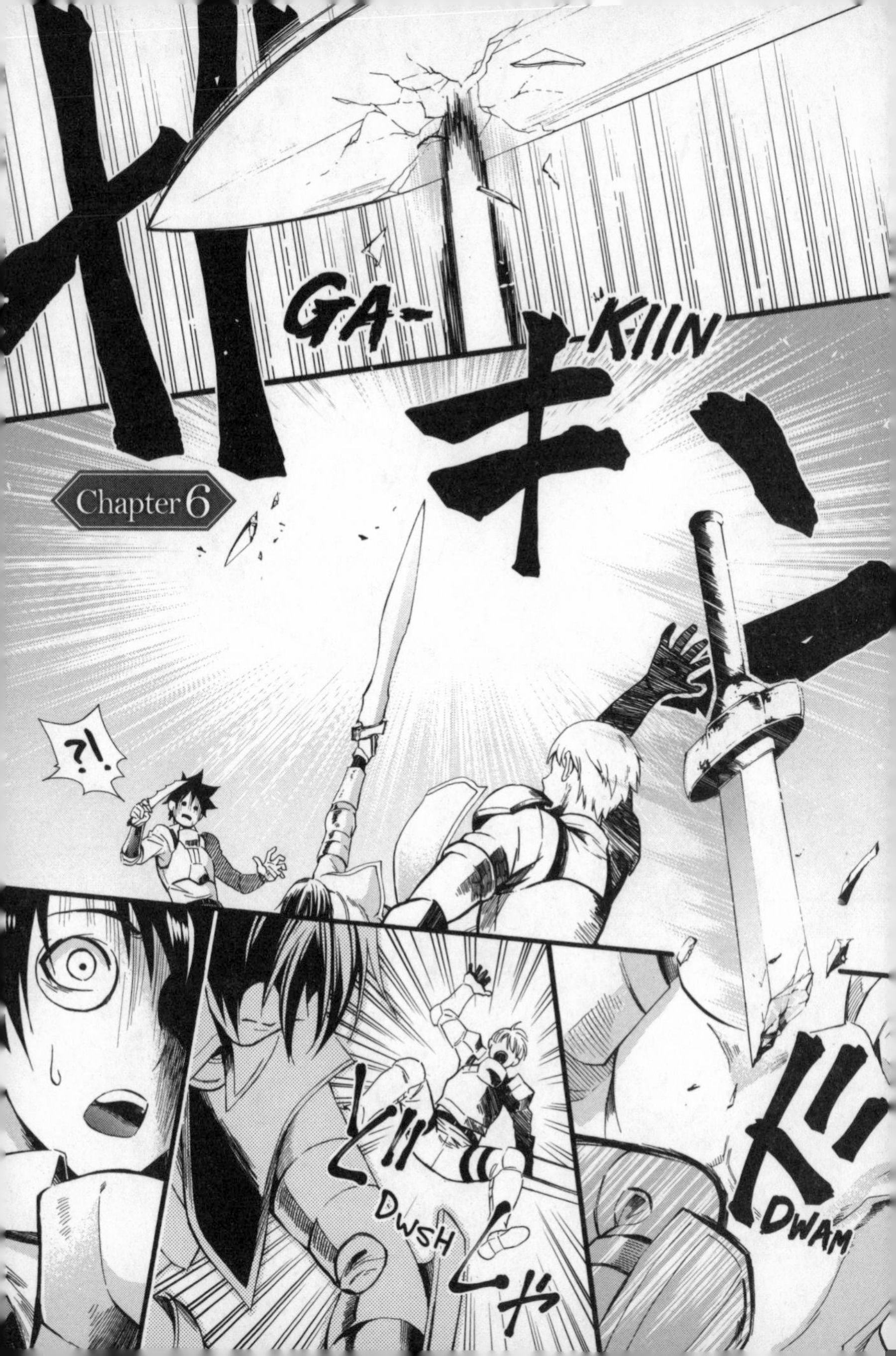
GA-
-KIIN
?!
DWAM
DWSH

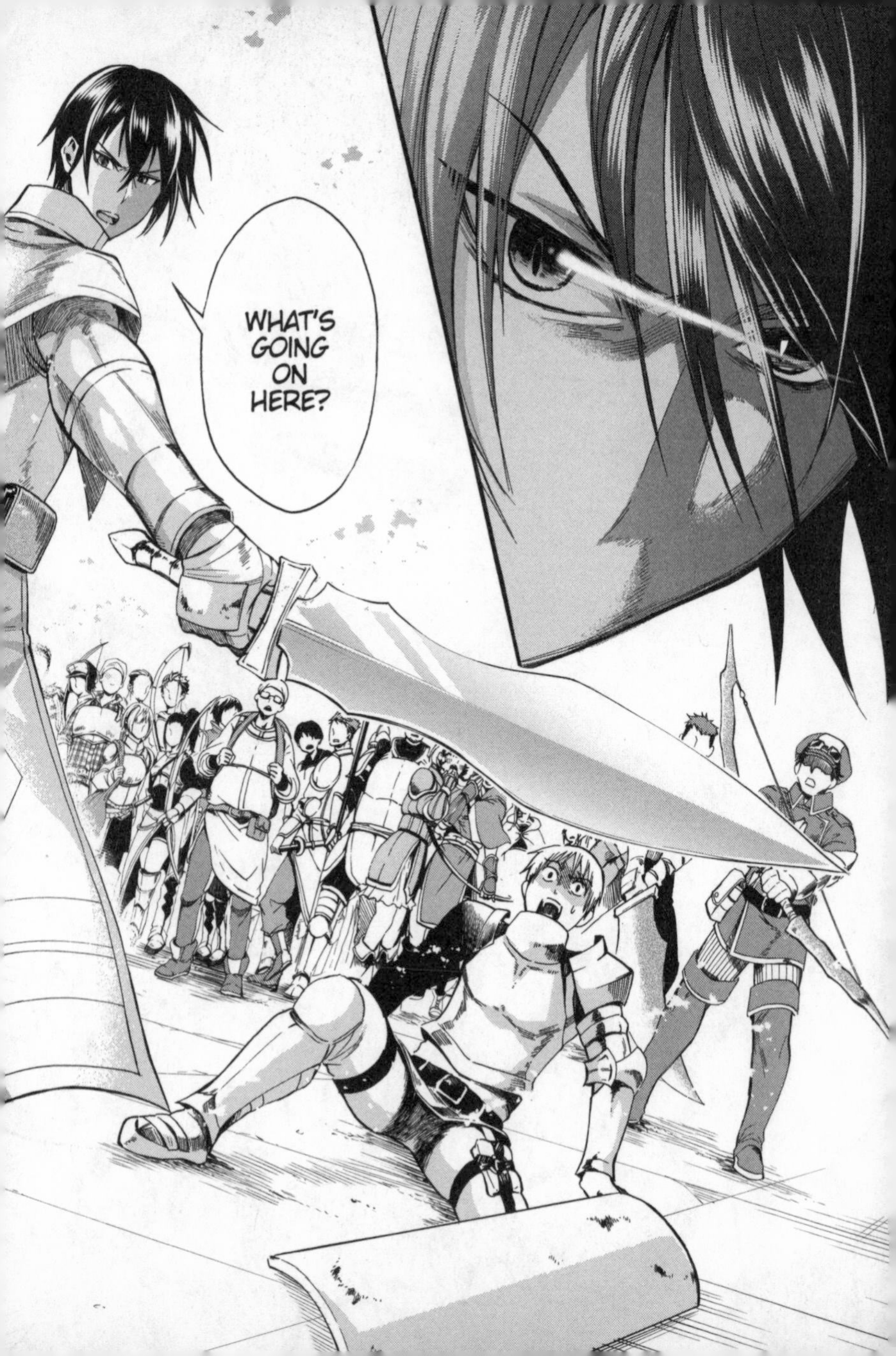
WHAT'S GOING ON HERE?

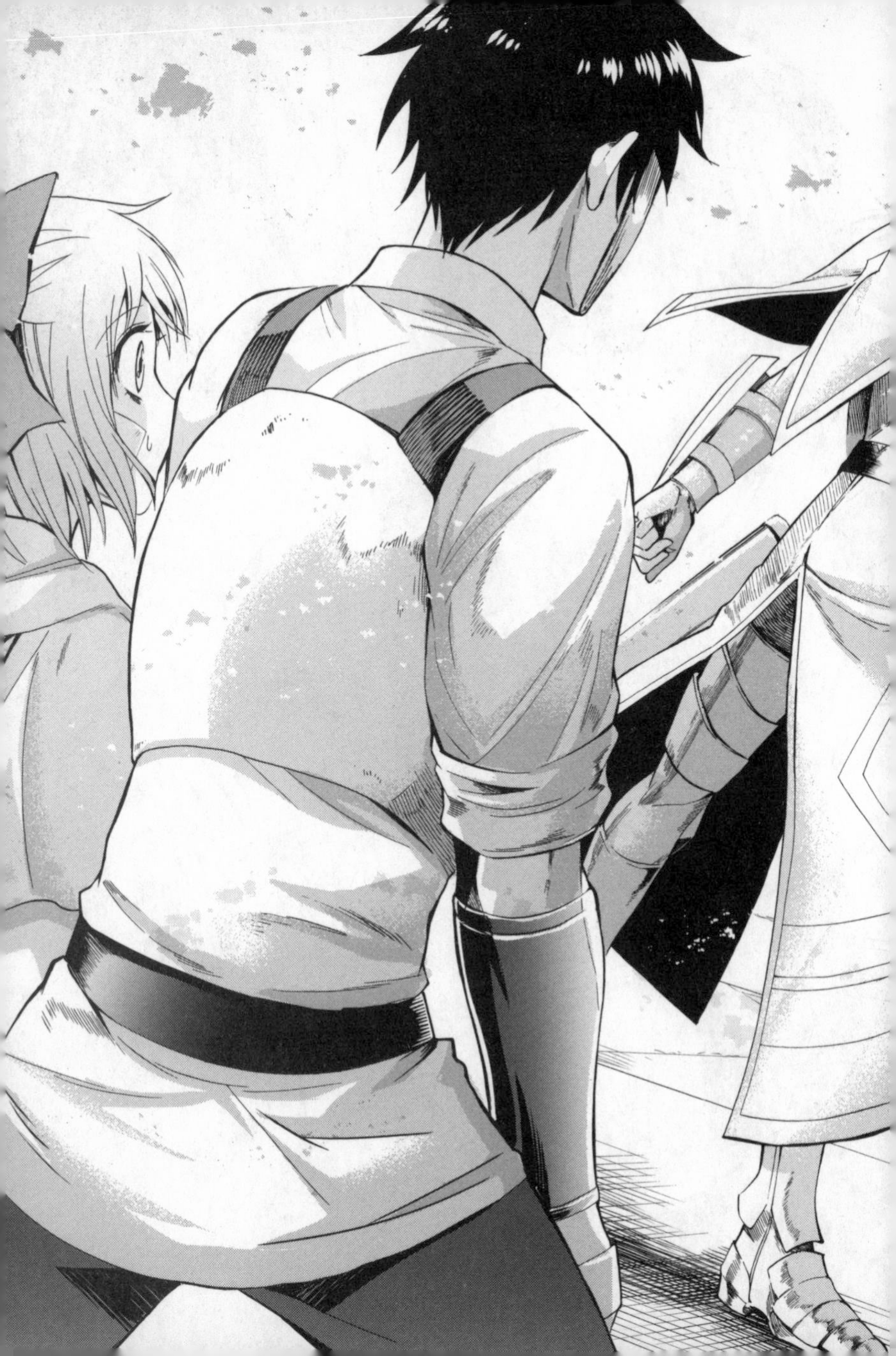

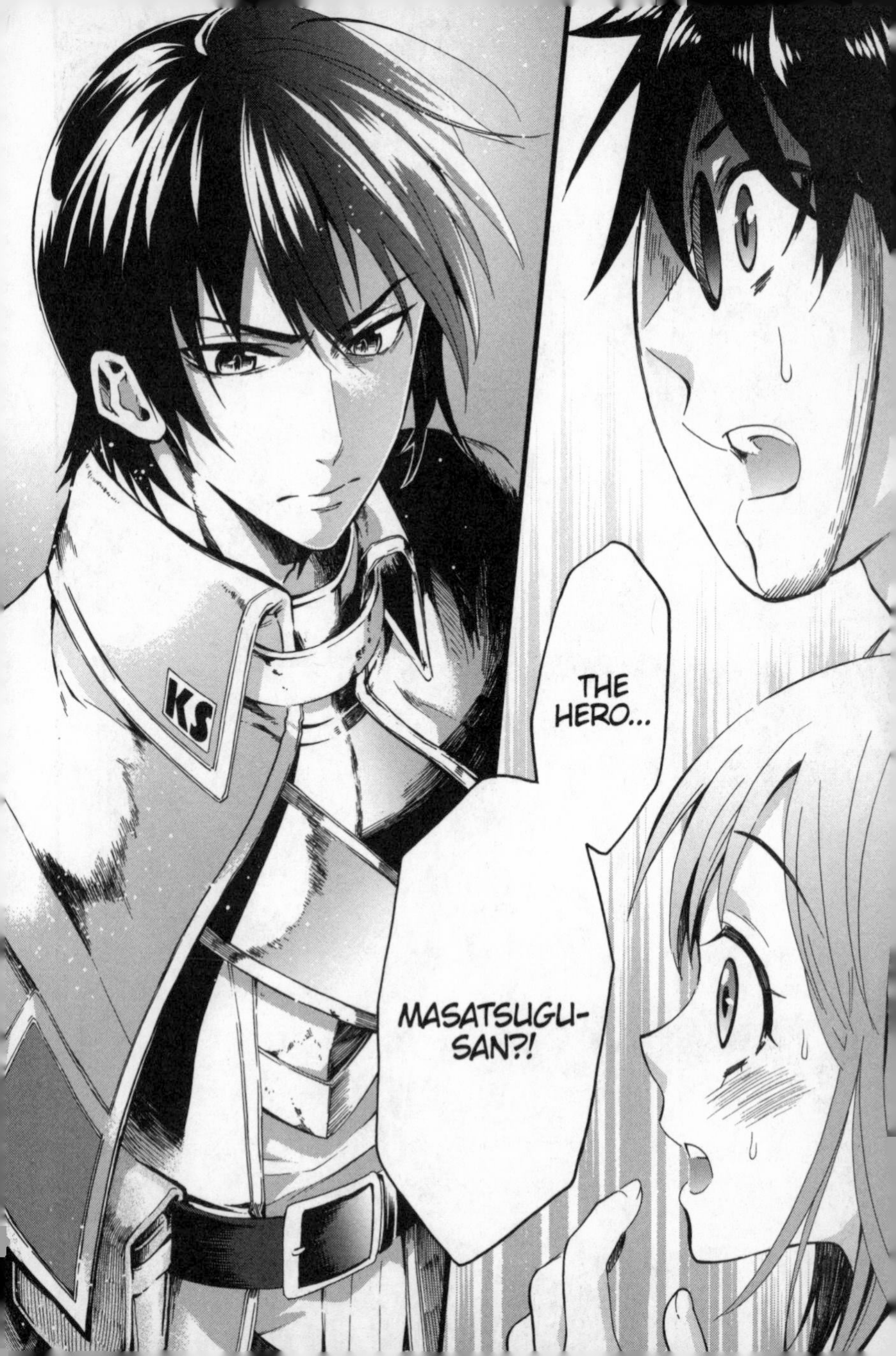
THE HERO...
MASATSUGU-SAN?!

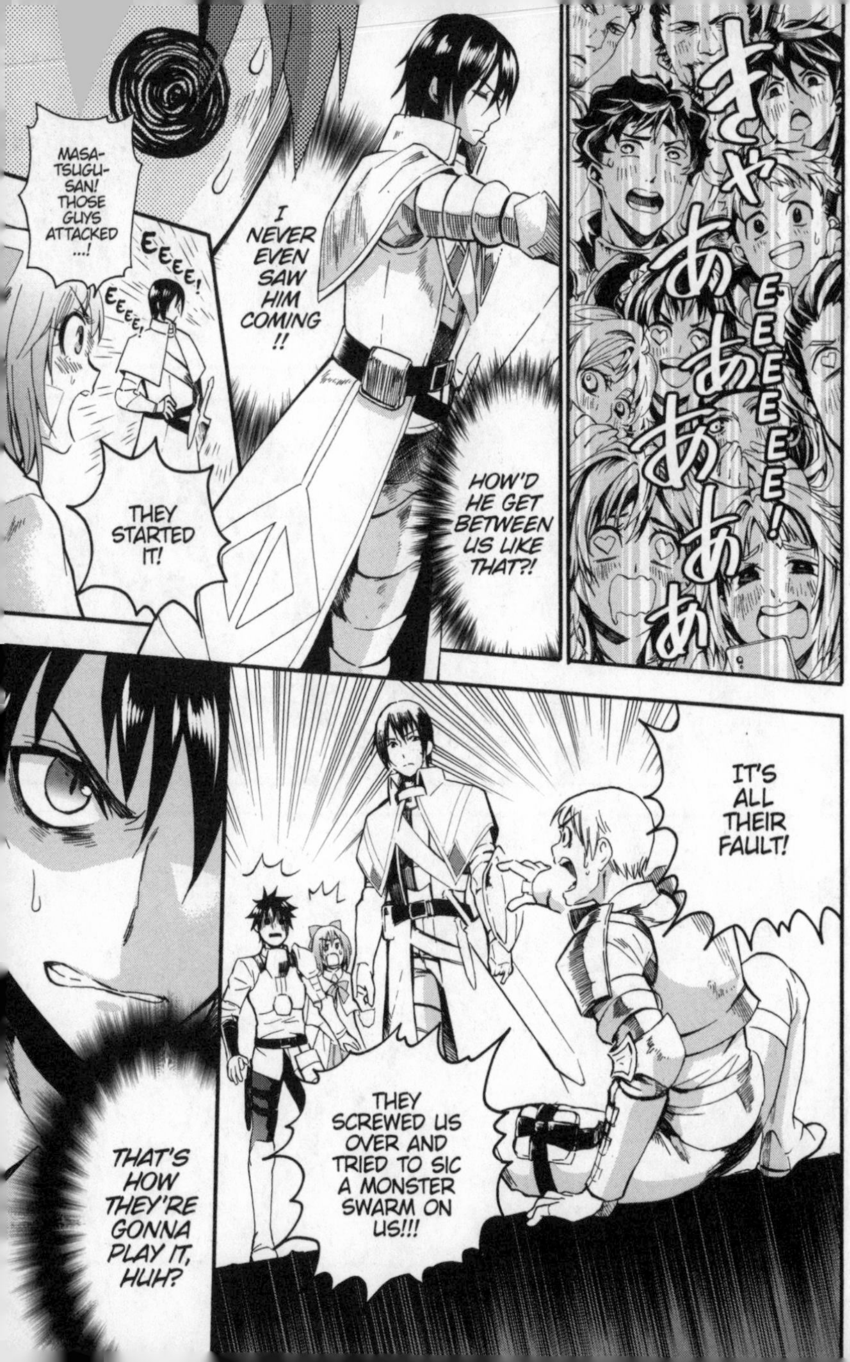
きゃああああああ
EEEEEE!
I NEVER EVEN SAW HIM COMING!!
HOW'D HE GET BETWEEN US LIKE THAT?!
MASA-TSUGU-SAN! THOSE GUYS ATTACKED...!
EEEEE!
EEEE,
THEY STARTED IT!
IT'S ALL THEIR FAULT!
THEY SCREWED US OVER AND TRIED TO SIC A MONSTER SWARM ON US!!!
THAT'S HOW THEY'RE GONNA PLAY IT, HUH?

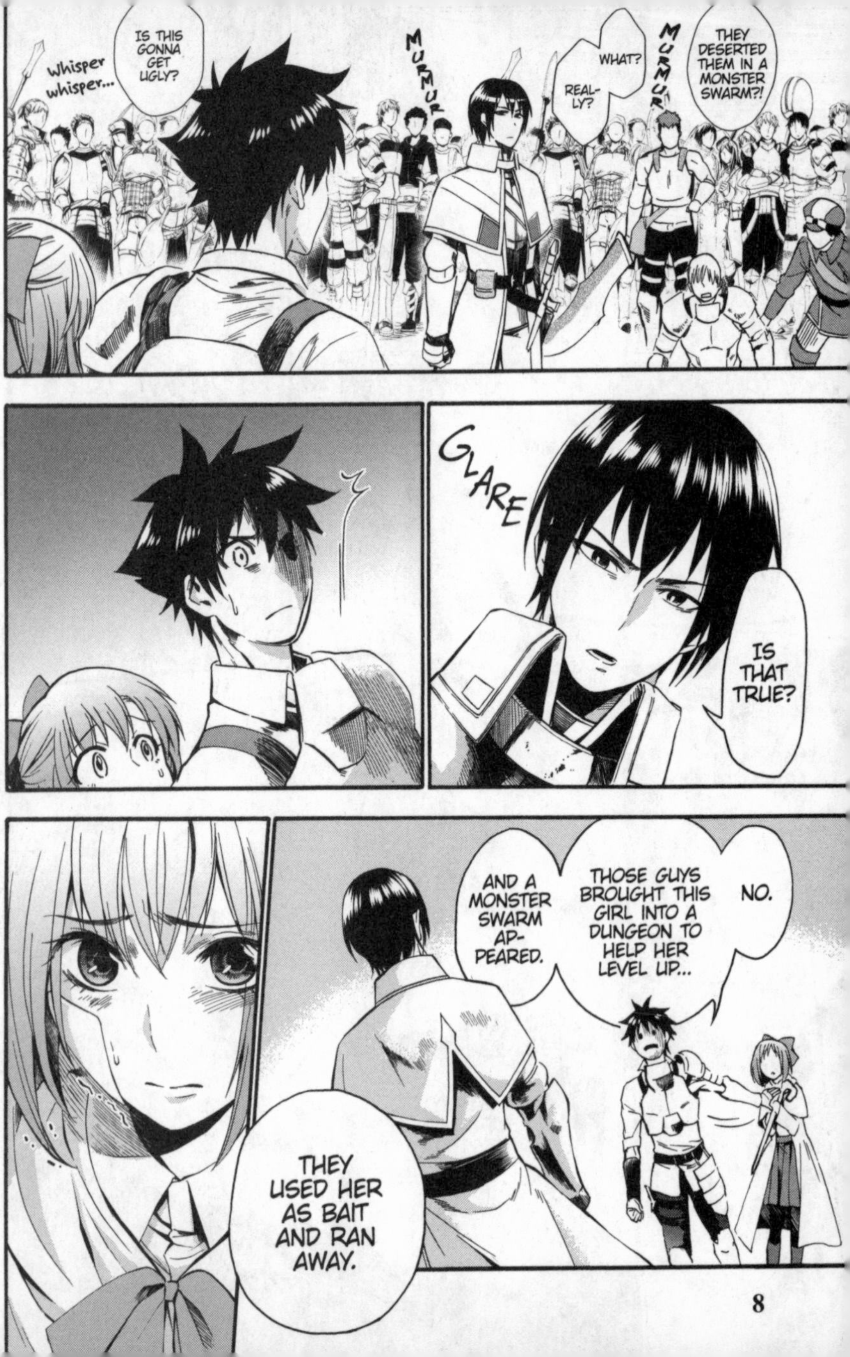
THEY DESERTED THEM IN A MONSTER SWARM?!
MURMUR
WHAT?
REAL-LY?
MURMUR
IS THIS GONNA GET UGLY?
Whisper whisper...
GLARE
IS THAT TRUE?
NO.
THOSE GUYS BROUGHT THIS GIRL INTO A DUNGEON TO HELP HER LEVEL UP...
AND A MONSTER SWARM AP-PEARED.
THEY USED HER AS BAIT AND RAN AWAY.

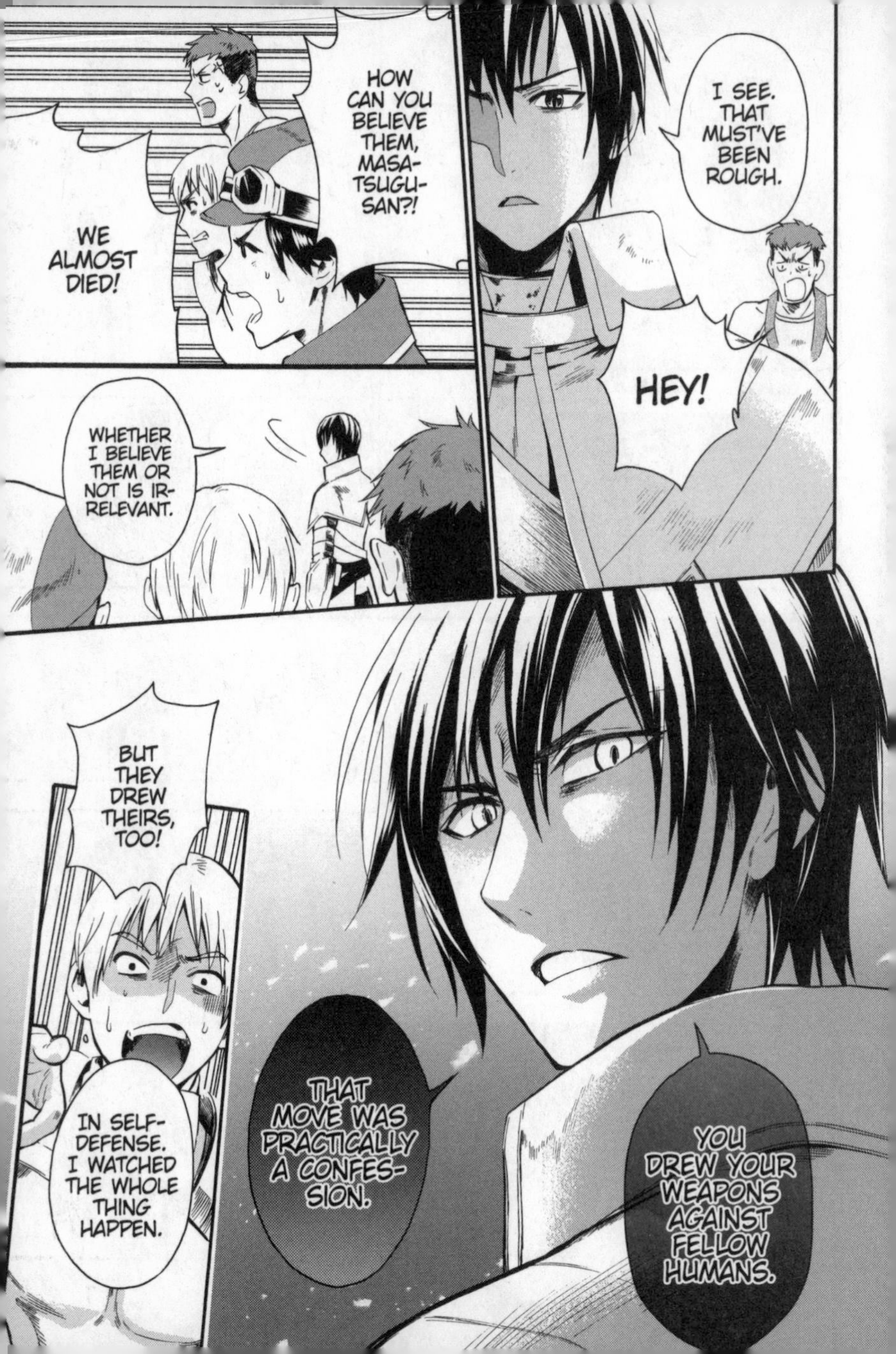
I SEE. THAT MUST'VE BEEN ROUGH.
HEY!
HOW CAN YOU BELIEVE THEM, MASA-TSUGU-SAN?!
WE ALMOST DIED!
WHETHER I BELIEVE THEM OR NOT IS IR-RELEVANT.
YOU DREW YOUR WEAPONS AGAINST FELLOW HUMANS.
THAT MOVE WAS PRACTICALLY A CONFES-SION.
BUT THEY DREW THEIRS, TOO!
IN SELF-DEFENSE. I WATCHED THE WHOLE THING HAPPEN.

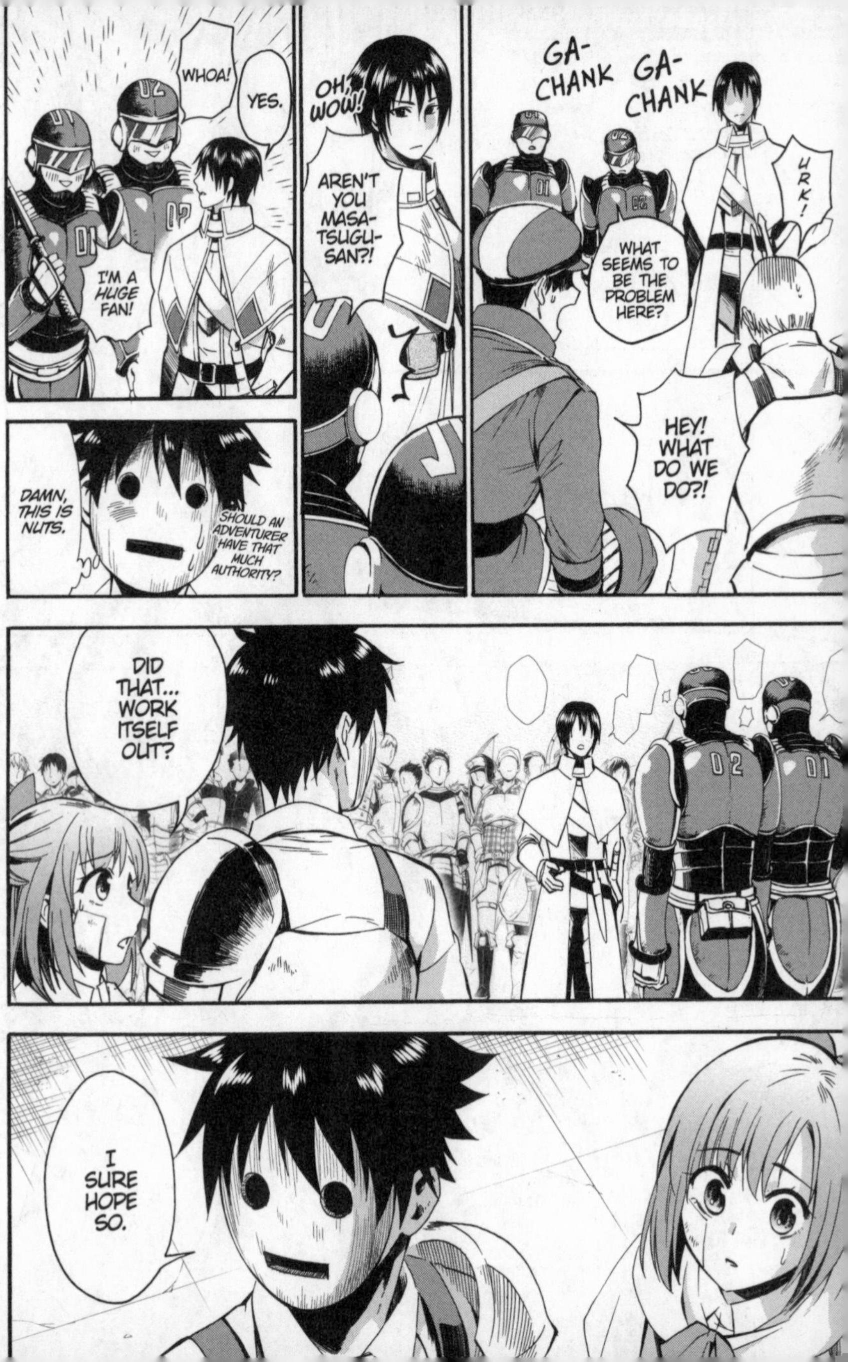
GA-CHANK GA-CHANK
URK!
WHAT SEEMS TO BE THE PROBLEM HERE?
HEY! WHAT DO WE DO?!
OH, WOW!
AREN'T YOU MASATSUGU-SAN?!
WHOA!
YES.
I'M A HUGE FAN!
SHOULD AN ADVENTURER HAVE THAT MUCH AUTHORITY?
DAMN, THIS IS NUTS.
DID THAT... WORK ITSELF OUT?
I SURE HOPE SO.

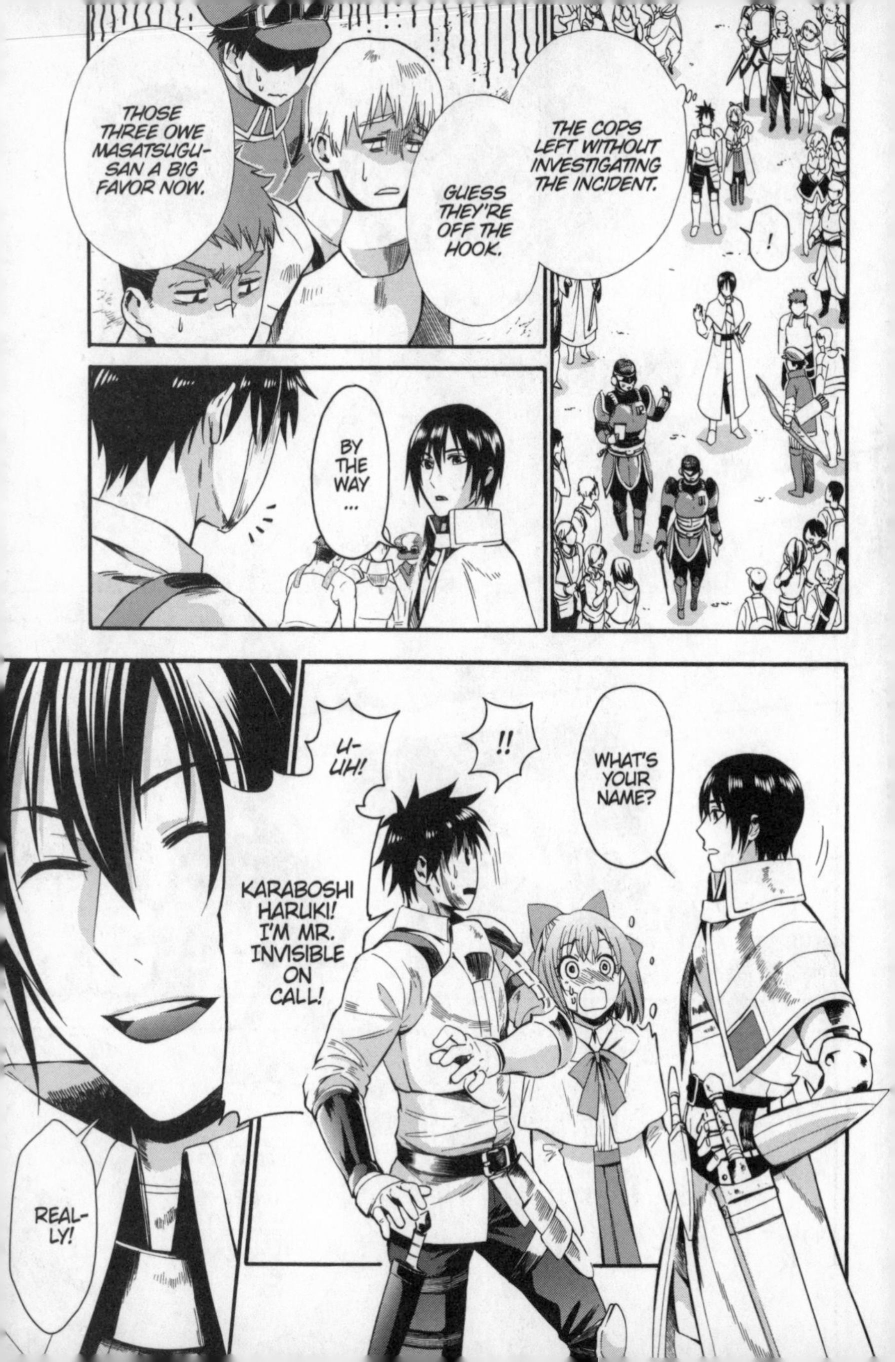

!
THE COPS LEFT WITHOUT INVESTIGATING THE INCIDENT.
GUESS THEY'RE OFF THE HOOK.
THOSE THREE OWE MASATSUGU-SAN A BIG FAVOR NOW.
BY THE WAY ...
WHAT'S YOUR NAME?
!!
U-UH!
KARABOSHI HARUKI! I'M MR. INVISIBLE ON CALL!
REAL-LY!

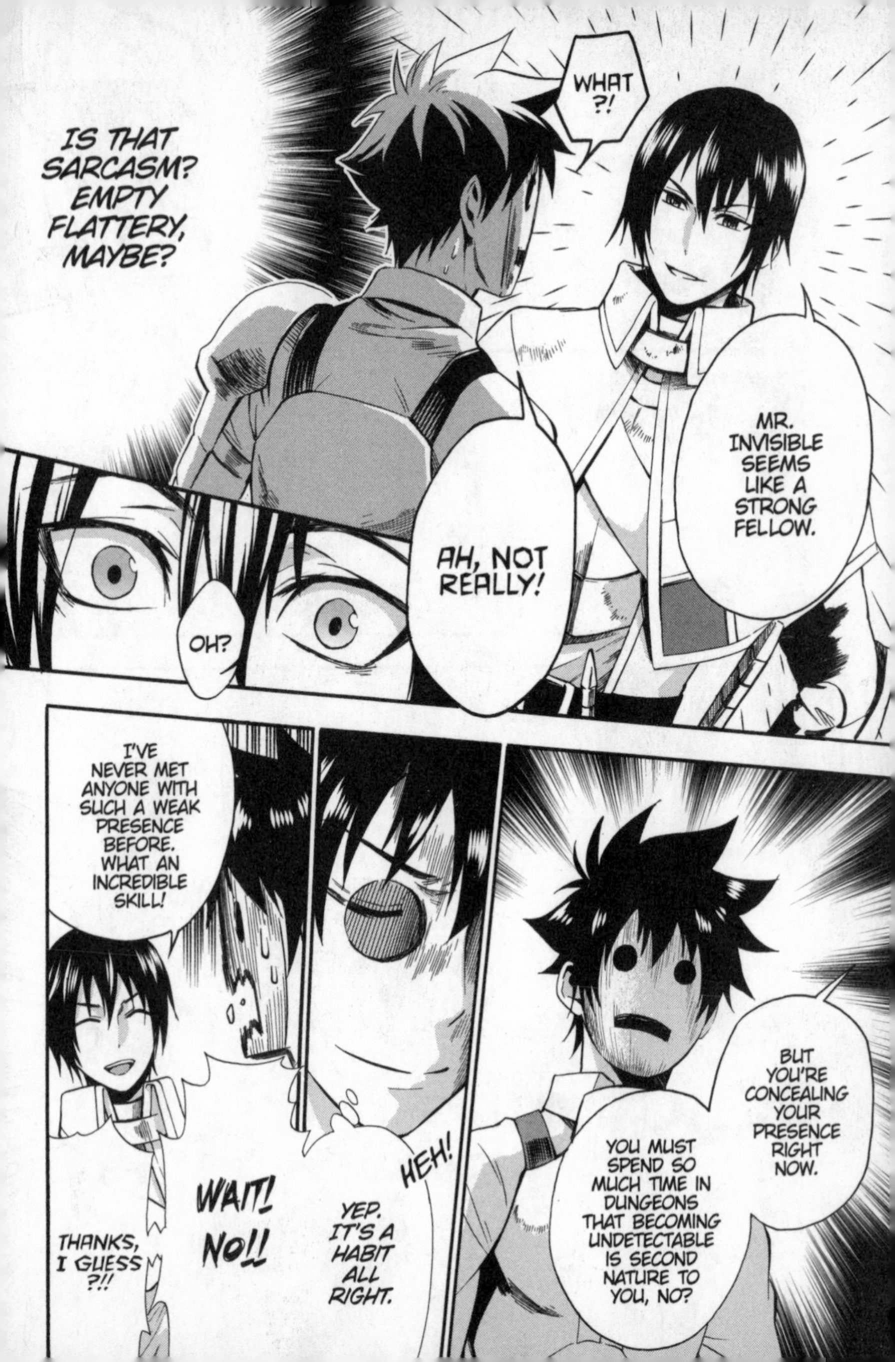

MR. INVISIBLE SEEMS LIKE A STRONG FELLOW.
WHAT ?!
IS THAT SARCASM? EMPTY FLATTERY, MAYBE?
AH, NOT REALLY!
OH?
BUT YOU'RE CONCEALING YOUR PRESENCE RIGHT NOW.
YOU MUST SPEND SO MUCH TIME IN DUNGEONS THAT BECOMING UNDETECTABLE IS SECOND NATURE TO YOU, NO?
HEH!
YEP. IT'S A HABIT ALL RIGHT.
I'VE NEVER MET ANYONE WITH SUCH A WEAK PRESENCE BEFORE. WHAT AN INCREDIBLE SKILL!
WAIT! NO!!
THANKS, I GUESS ?!!

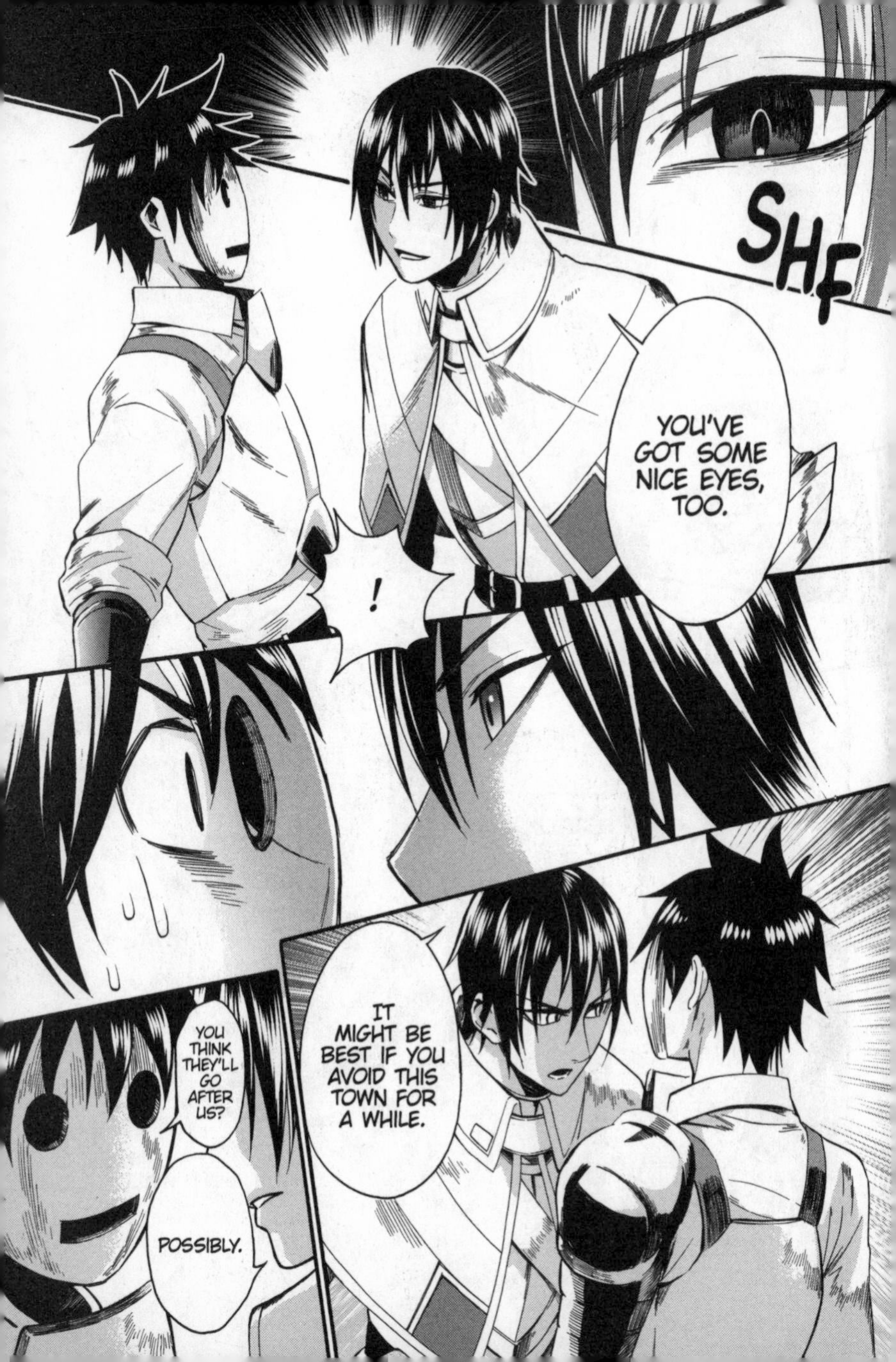
SHF
YOU'VE GOT SOME NICE EYES, TOO.
!
IT MIGHT BE BEST IF YOU AVOID THIS TOWN FOR A WHILE.
YOU THINK THEY'LL GO AFTER US?
POSSIBLY.

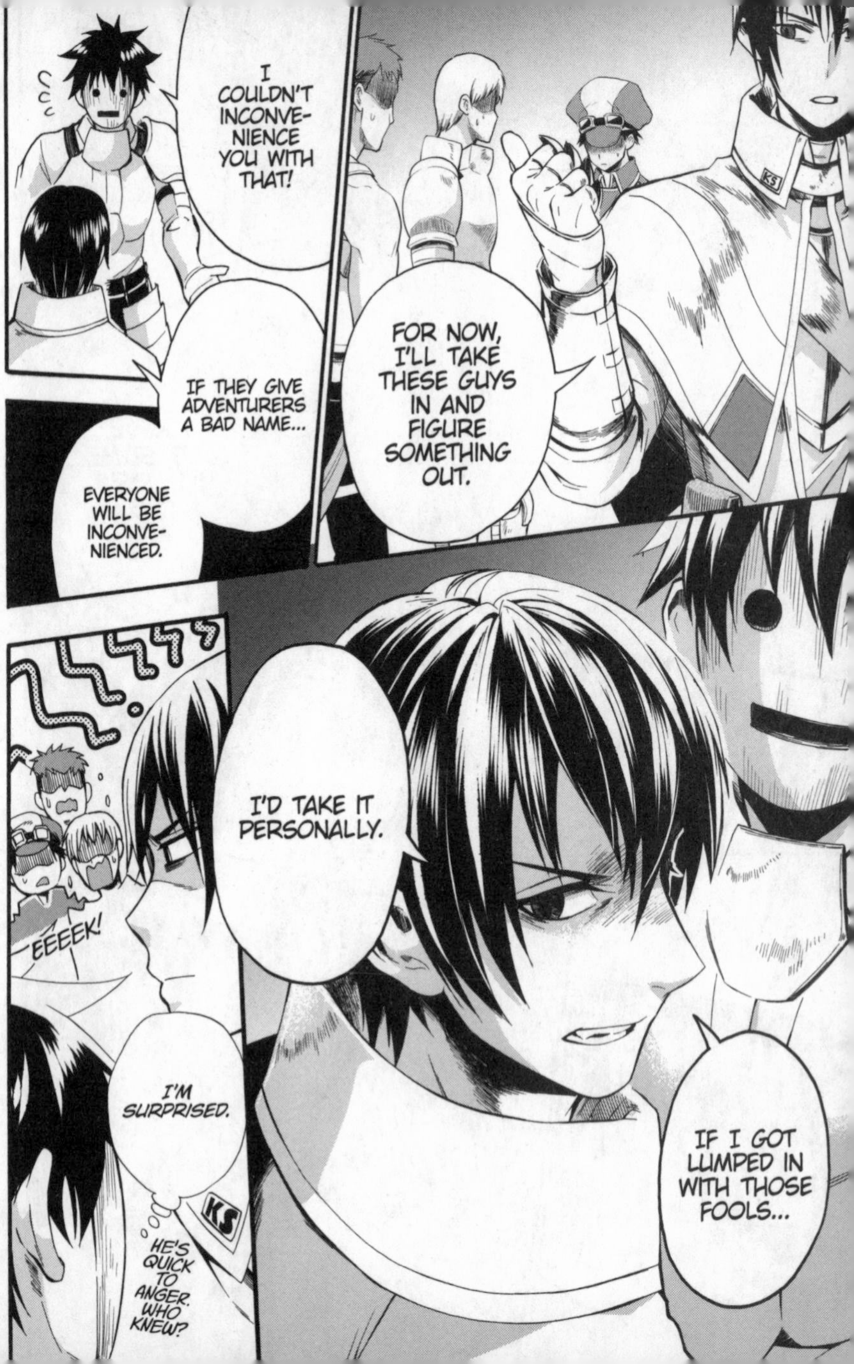

FOR NOW, I'LL TAKE THESE GUYS IN AND FIGURE SOMETHING OUT.
I COULDN'T INCONVENIENCE YOU WITH THAT!
IF THEY GIVE ADVENTURERS A BAD NAME...
EVERYONE WILL BE INCONVENIENCED.
IF I GOT LUMPED IN WITH THOSE FOOLS...
I'D TAKE IT PERSONALLY.
EEEEK!
I'M SURPRISED.
HE'S QUICK TO ANGER. WHO KNEW?

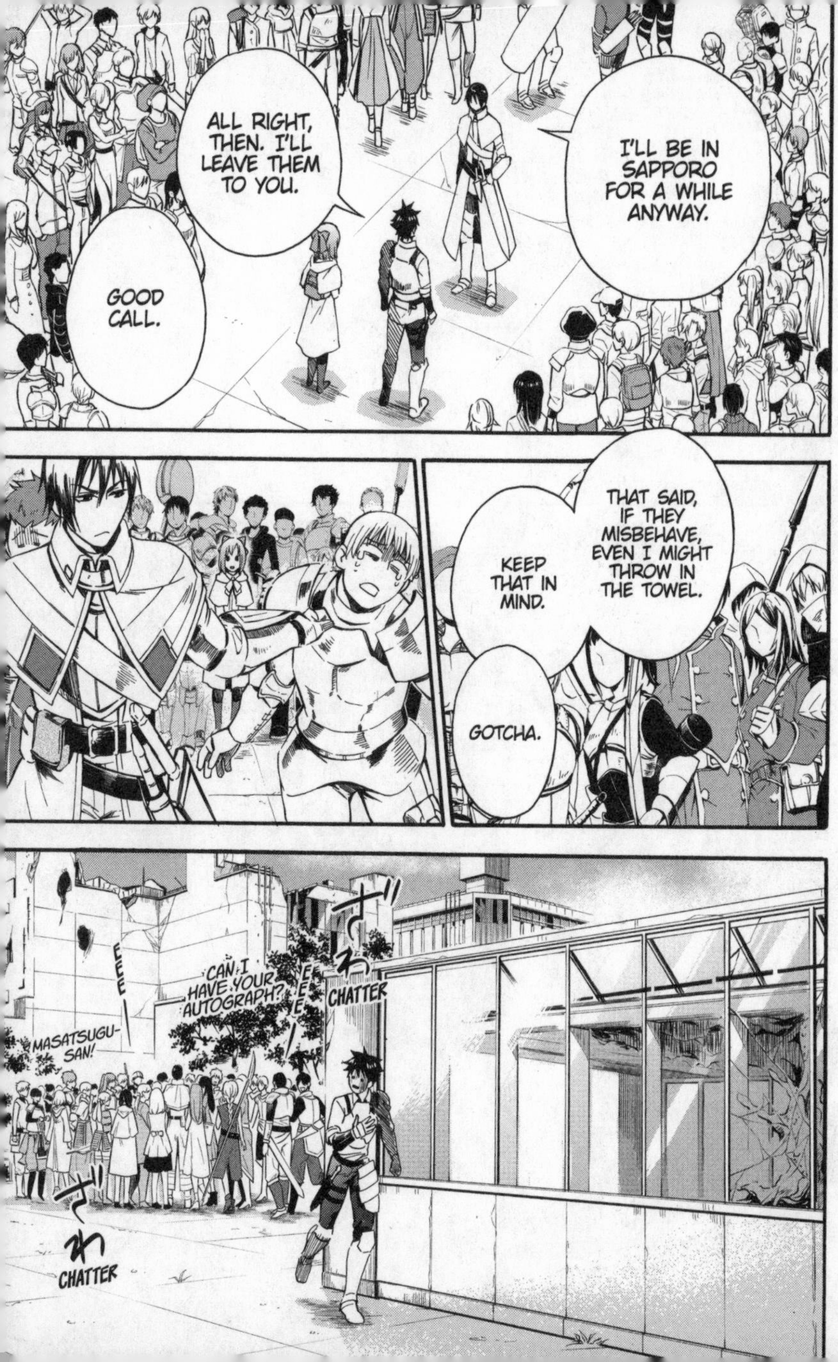
I'LL BE IN SAPPORO FOR A WHILE ANYWAY.
ALL RIGHT, THEN. I'LL LEAVE THEM TO YOU.
GOOD CALL.
THAT SAID, IF THEY MISBEHAVE, EVEN I MIGHT THROW IN THE TOWEL.
KEEP THAT IN MIND.
GOTCHA.
ざわ
CHATTER
EEE-!
CAN I HAVE YOUR AUTOGRAPH?
EEE-!
MASATSUGU-SAN!
ざわ
CHATTER

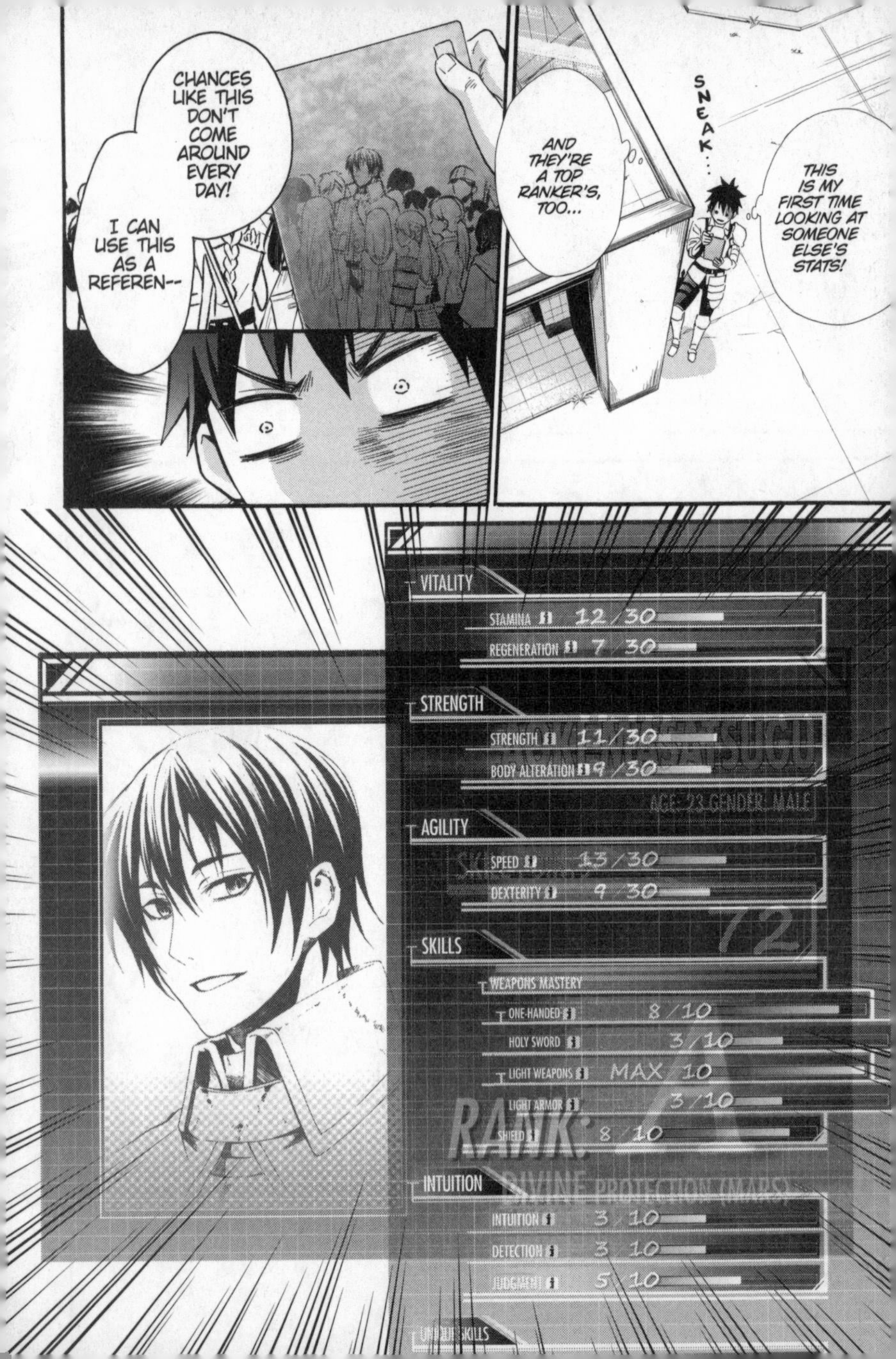
SNEAK...
THIS IS MY FIRST TIME LOOKING AT SOMEONE ELSE'S STATS!
AND THEY'RE A TOP RANKER'S, TOO...
CHANCES LIKE THIS DON'T COME AROUND EVERY DAY!
I CAN USE THIS AS A REFEREN--
VITALITY
STAMINA 12/30
REGENERATION 7/30
STRENGTH
STRENGTH 11/30
BODY ALTERATION 9/30
AGE: 23 GENDER: MALE
AGILITY
SPEED 13/30
DEXTERITY 9/30
72
SKILLS
WEAPONS MASTERY
ONE-HANDED 8/10
HOLY SWORD 3/10
LIGHT WEAPONS MAX/10
LIGHT ARMOR 3/10
RANK:
SHIELD 8/10
INTUITION
DIVINE PROTECTION (MARS)
INTUITION 3/10
DETECTION 3/10
JUDGMENT 5/10
UNIQUE SKILLS

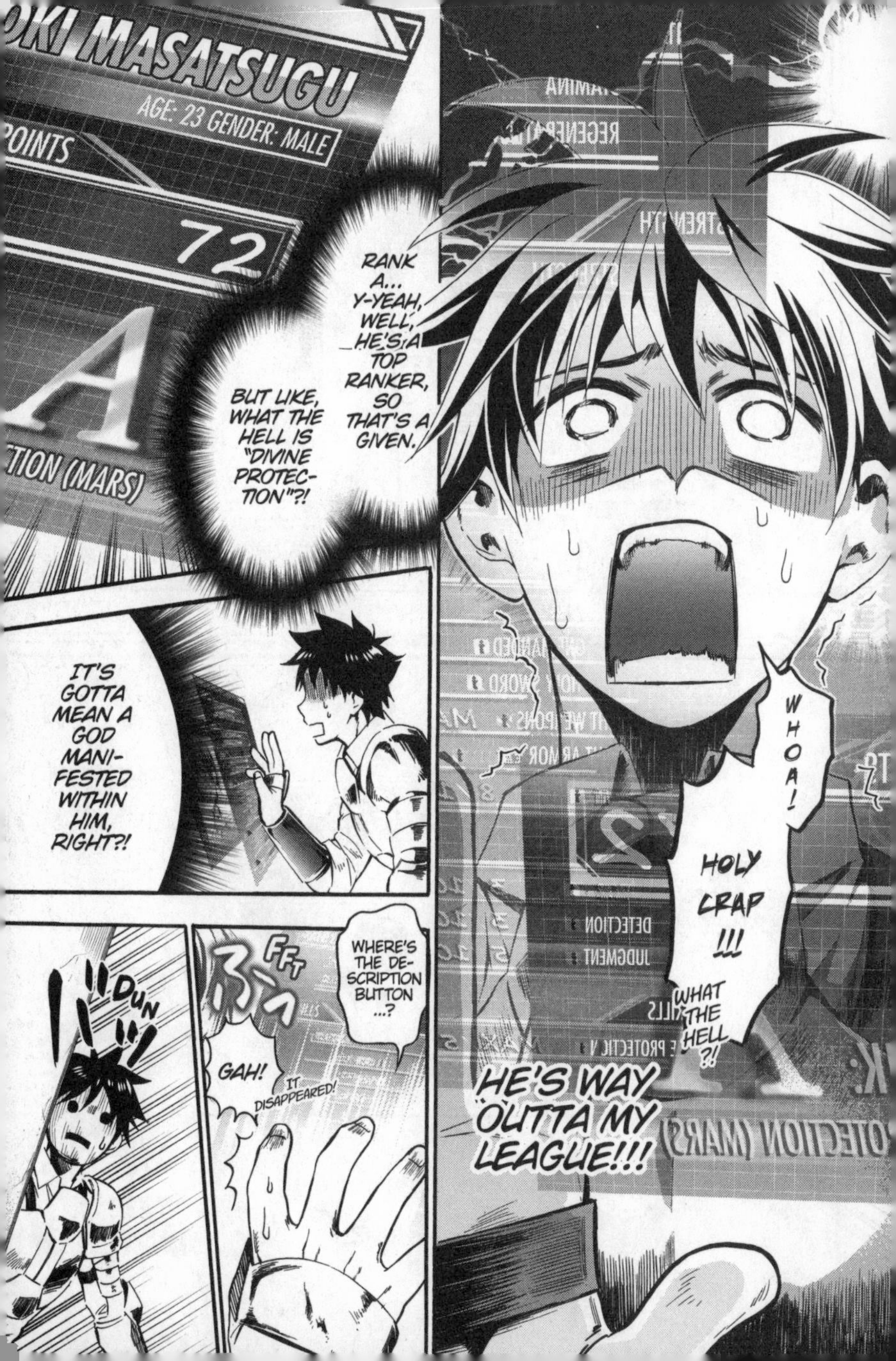
WHOA!
HOLY CRAP!!!
WHAT THE HELL?!
HE'S WAY OUTTA MY LEAGUE!!!
OKI MASATSUGU
AGE: 23 GENDER: MALE
POINTS
72
A
TION (MARS)
RANK A... Y-YEAH, WELL, HE'S A TOP RANKER, SO THAT'S A GIVEN.
BUT LIKE, WHAT THE HELL IS "DIVINE PROTECTION"?!
IT'S GOTTA MEAN A GOD MANIFESTED WITHIN HIM, RIGHT?!
FFT
WHERE'S THE DESCRIPTION BUTTON...?
GAH!
IT DISAPPEARED!
DUN

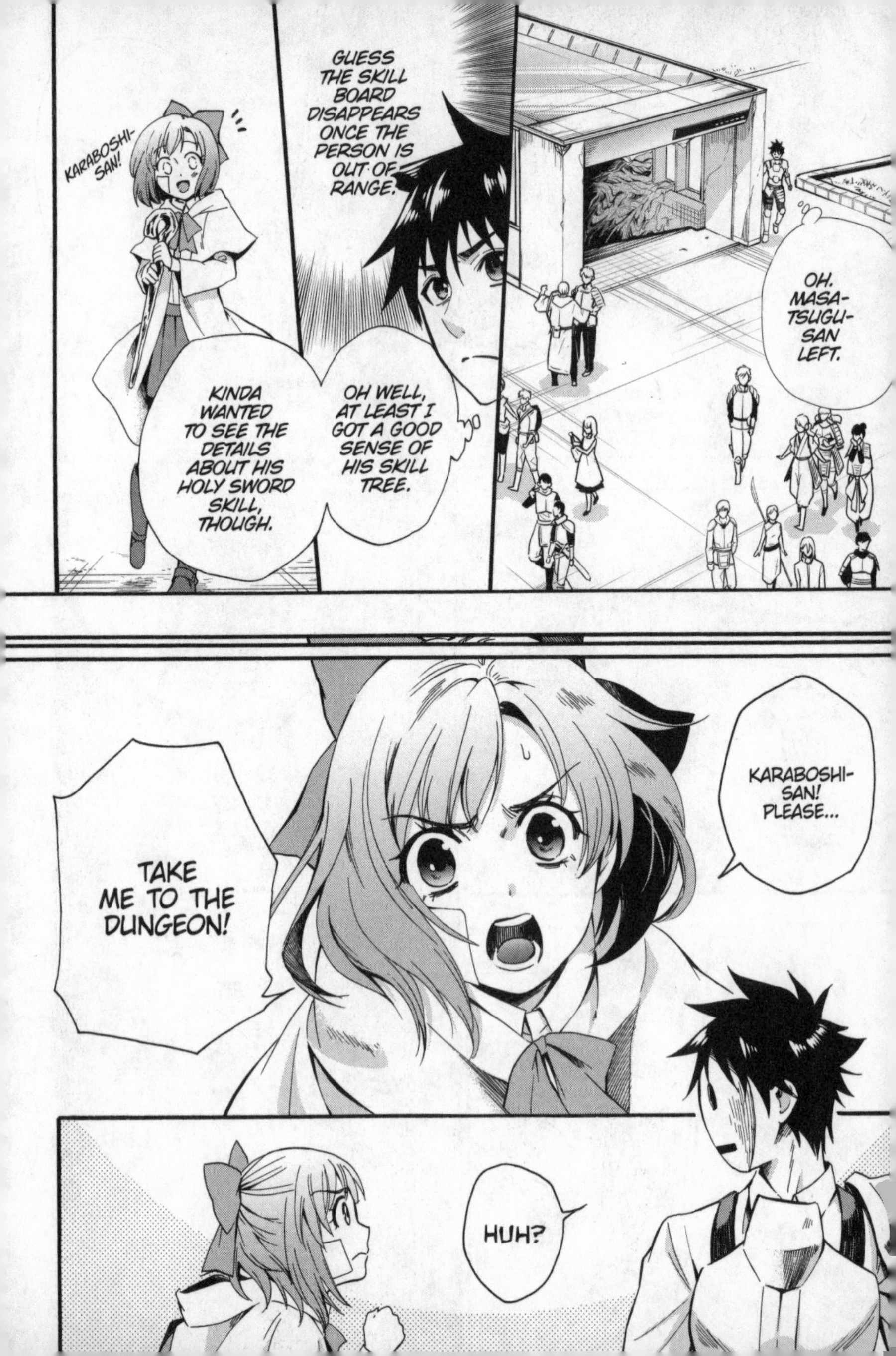
OH. MASA-TSUGU-SAN LEFT.
GUESS THE SKILL BOARD DISAPPEARS ONCE THE PERSON IS OUT OF RANGE.
OH WELL, AT LEAST I GOT A GOOD SENSE OF HIS SKILL TREE.
KINDA WANTED TO SEE THE DETAILS ABOUT HIS HOLY SWORD SKILL, THOUGH.
KARABOSHI-SAN!
KARABOSHI-SAN! PLEASE...
TAKE ME TO THE DUNGEON!
HUH?

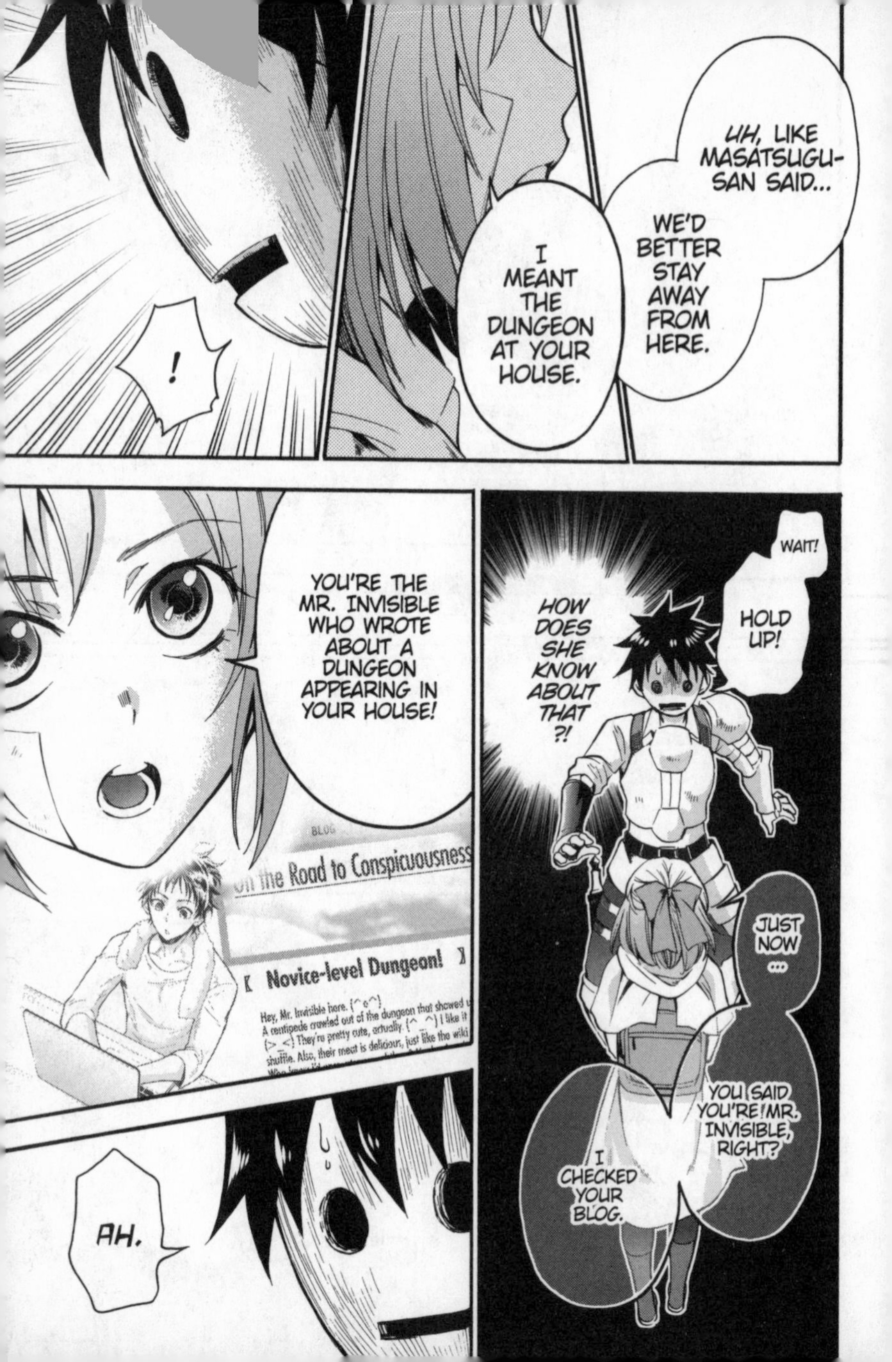
UH, LIKE MASATSUGU-SAN SAID...
WE'D BETTER STAY AWAY FROM HERE.
I MEANT THE DUNGEON AT YOUR HOUSE.
!
WAIT!
HOLD UP!
HOW DOES SHE KNOW ABOUT THAT?!
JUST NOW...
YOU SAID YOU'RE MR. INVISIBLE, RIGHT?
I CHECKED YOUR BLOG.
YOU'RE THE MR. INVISIBLE WHO WROTE ABOUT A DUNGEON APPEARING IN YOUR HOUSE!
BLOG
On the Road to Conspicuousness
【 Novice-level Dungeon! 】
AH.

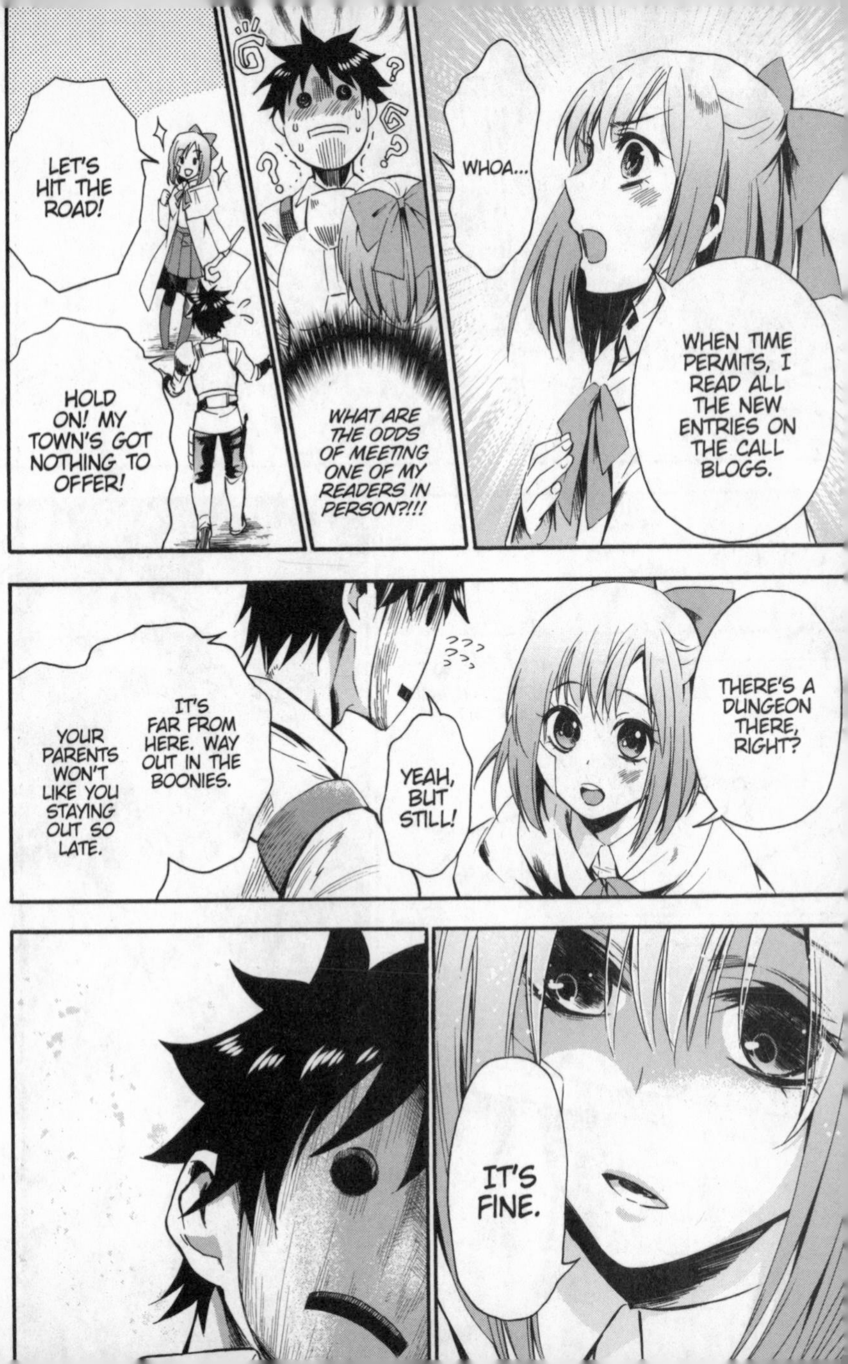
WHOA...
WHEN TIME PERMITS, I READ ALL THE NEW ENTRIES ON THE CALL BLOGS.
WHAT ARE THE ODDS OF MEETING ONE OF MY READERS IN PERSON?!!!
LET'S HIT THE ROAD!
HOLD ON! MY TOWN'S GOT NOTHING TO OFFER!
THERE'S A DUNGEON THERE, RIGHT?
YEAH, BUT STILL!
IT'S FAR FROM HERE. WAY OUT IN THE BOONIES.
YOUR PARENTS WON'T LIKE YOU STAYING OUT SO LATE.
IT'S FINE.

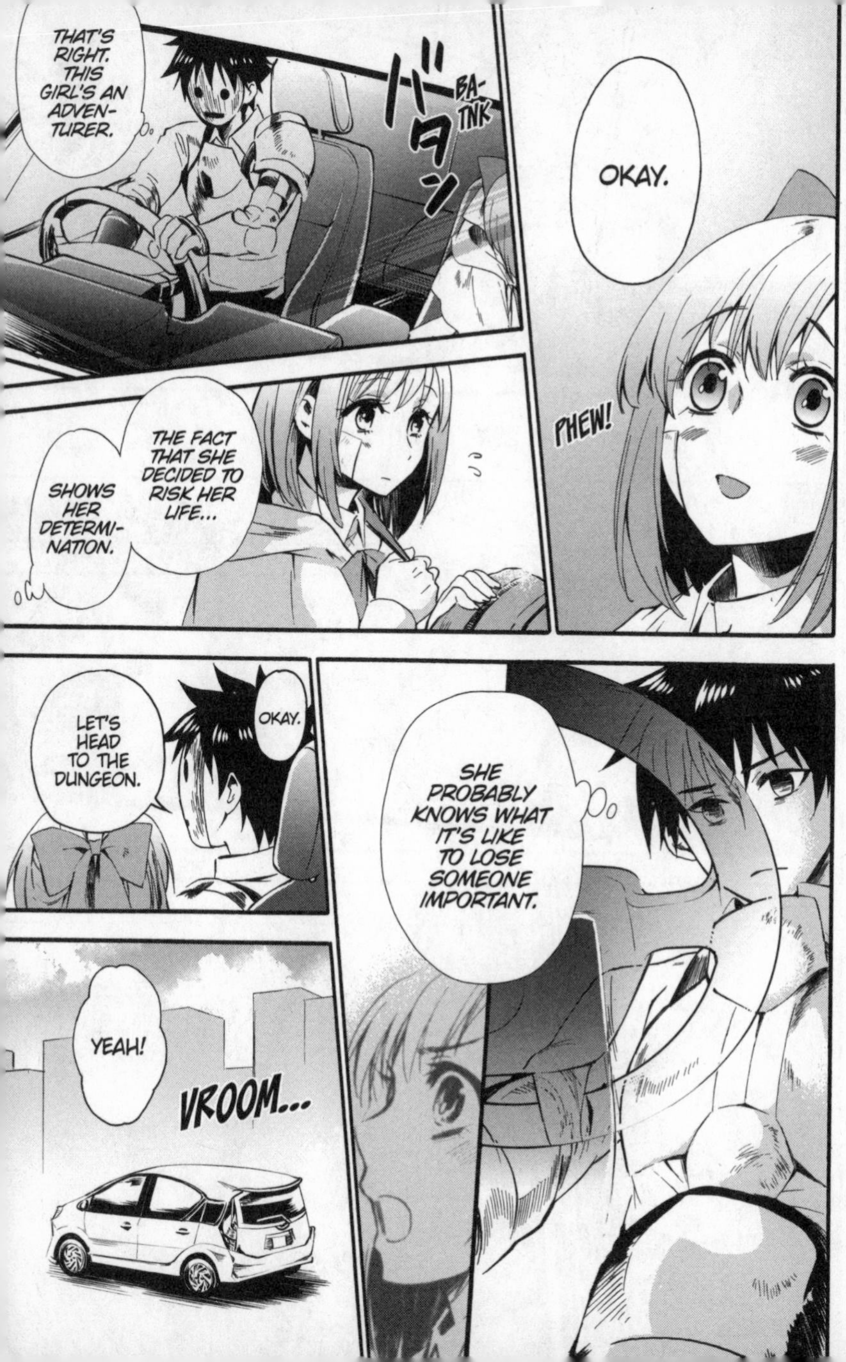
OKAY.
PHEW!
BA-TNK
THAT'S RIGHT. THIS GIRL'S AN ADVENTURER.
THE FACT THAT SHE DECIDED TO RISK HER LIFE...
SHOWS HER DETERMINATION.
SHE PROBABLY KNOWS WHAT IT'S LIKE TO LOSE SOMEONE IMPORTANT.
OKAY.
LET'S HEAD TO THE DUNGEON.
YEAH!
VROOM...

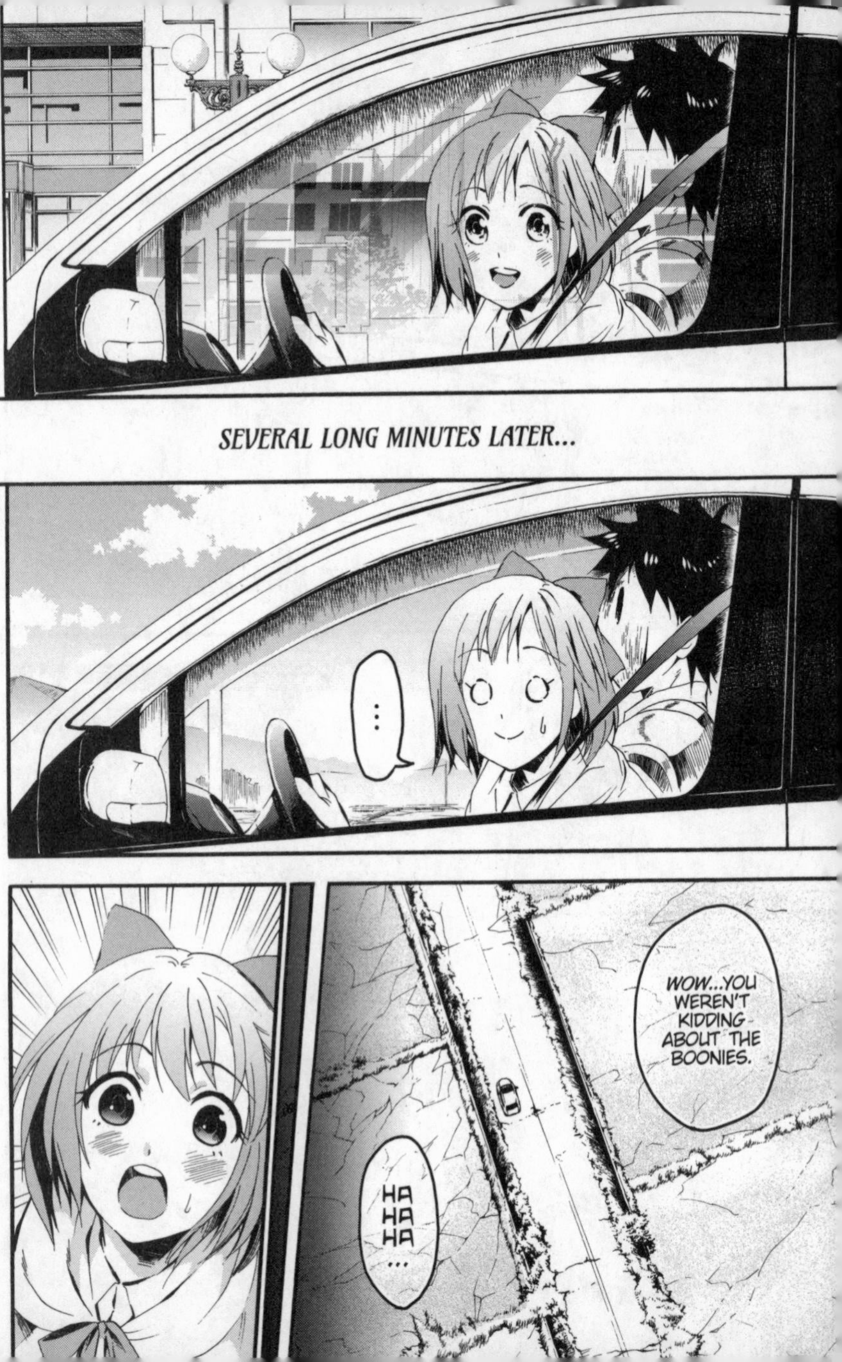
SEVERAL LONG MINUTES LATER...
...
WOW...YOU WEREN'T KIDDING ABOUT THE BOONIES.
HA HA HA ...

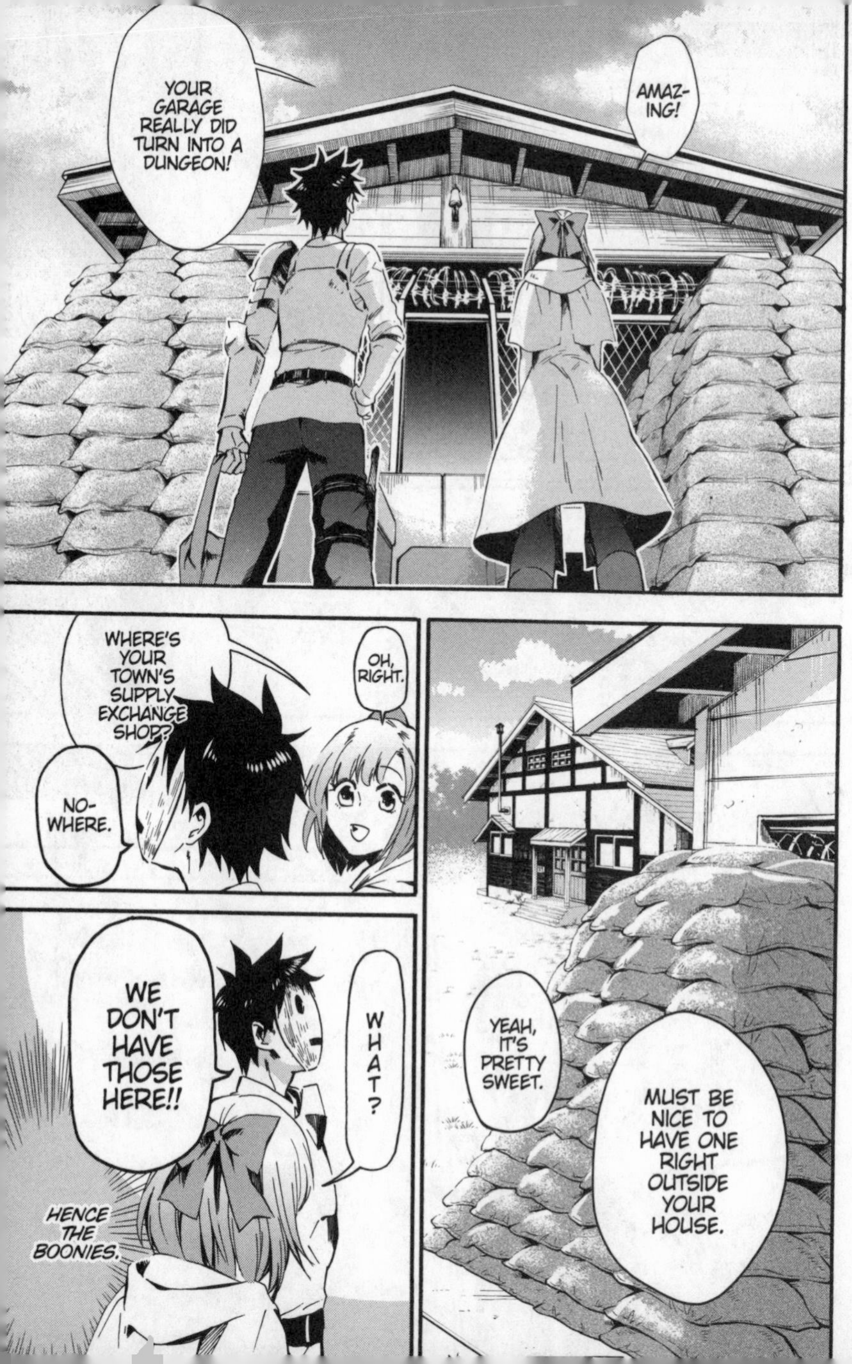
AMAZ-ING!
YOUR GARAGE REALLY DID TURN INTO A DUNGEON!
MUST BE NICE TO HAVE ONE RIGHT OUTSIDE YOUR HOUSE.
YEAH, IT'S PRETTY SWEET.
OH, RIGHT.
WHERE'S YOUR TOWN'S SUPPLY EXCHANGE SHOP?
NO-WHERE.
WHAT?
WE DON'T HAVE THOSE HERE!!
HENCE THE BOONIES.

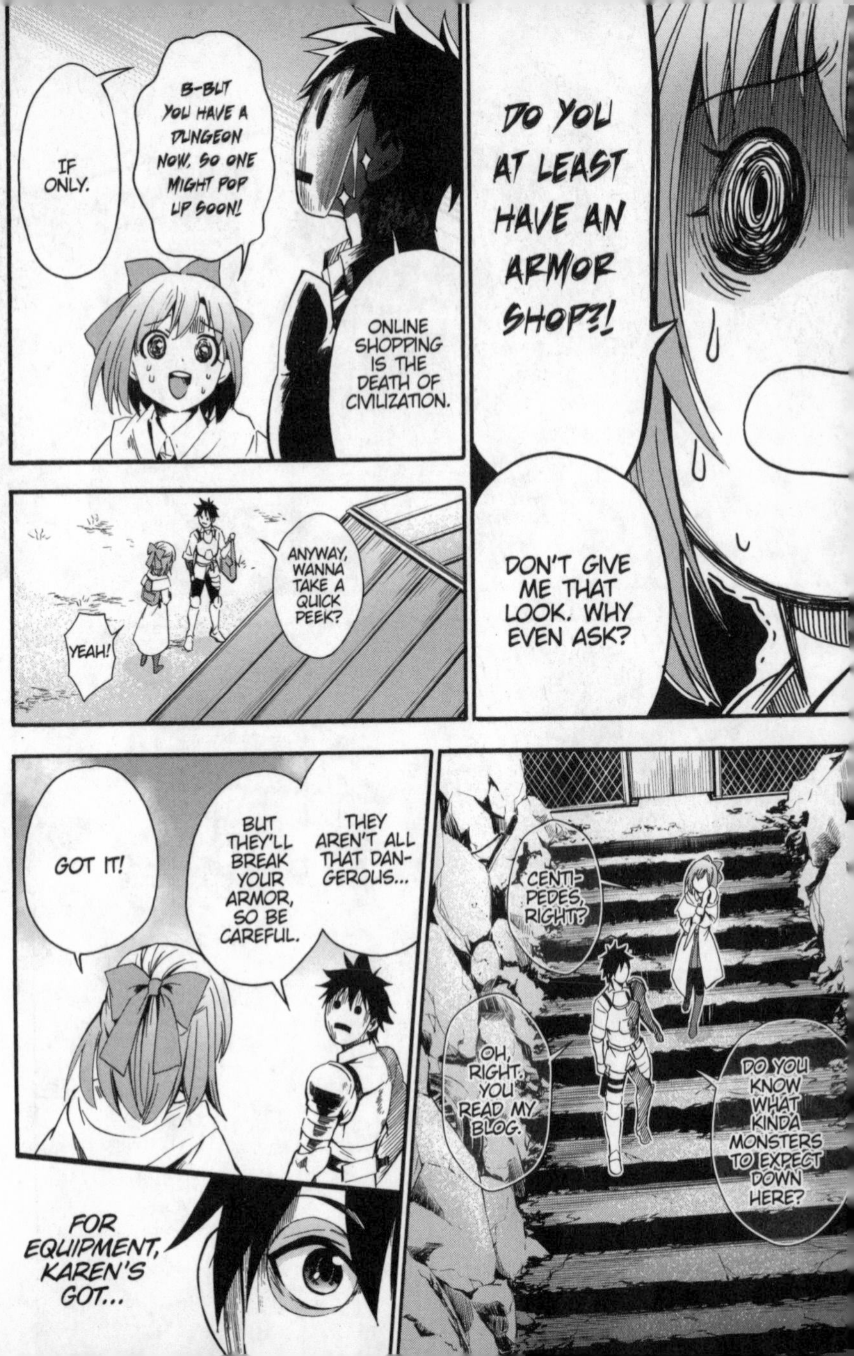
DO YOU AT LEAST HAVE AN ARMOR SHOP?!
DON'T GIVE ME THAT LOOK. WHY EVEN ASK?
ONLINE SHOPPING IS THE DEATH OF CIVILIZATION.
B-BUT YOU HAVE A DUNGEON NOW, SO ONE MIGHT POP UP SOON!
IF ONLY.
ANYWAY, WANNA TAKE A QUICK PEEK?
YEAH!
DO YOU KNOW WHAT KINDA MONSTERS TO EXPECT DOWN HERE?
CENTI-PEDES, RIGHT?
OH, RIGHT. YOU READ MY BLOG.
THEY AREN'T ALL THAT DAN-GEROUS...
BUT THEY'LL BREAK YOUR ARMOR, SO BE CAREFUL.
GOT IT!
FOR EQUIPMENT, KAREN'S GOT...

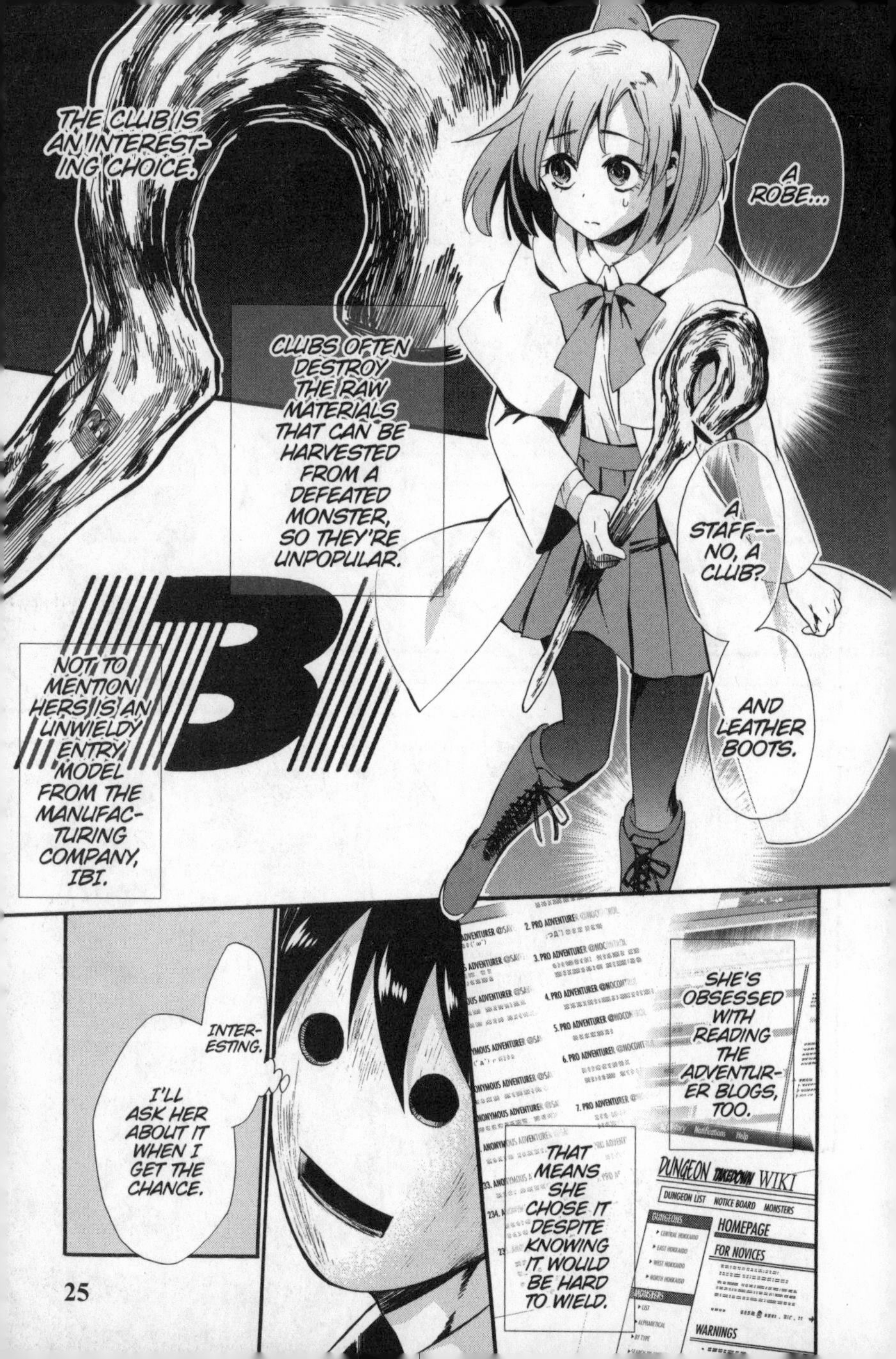
A ROBE...
A STAFF-- NO, A CLUB?
AND LEATHER BOOTS.
THE CLUB IS AN INTERESTING CHOICE.
CLUBS OFTEN DESTROY THE RAW MATERIALS THAT CAN BE HARVESTED FROM A DEFEATED MONSTER, SO THEY'RE UNPOPULAR.
NOT TO MENTION HERS IS AN UNWIELDY ENTRY MODEL FROM THE MANUFACTURING COMPANY, IBI.
SHE'S OBSESSED WITH READING THE ADVENTURER BLOGS, TOO.
DUNGEON TAKEDOWN WIKI
DUNGEON LIST NOTICE BOARD MONSTERS
HOMEPAGE
FOR NOVICES
WARNINGS
THAT MEANS SHE CHOSE IT DESPITE KNOWING IT WOULD BE HARD TO WIELD.
INTERESTING.
I'LL ASK HER ABOUT IT WHEN I GET THE CHANCE.

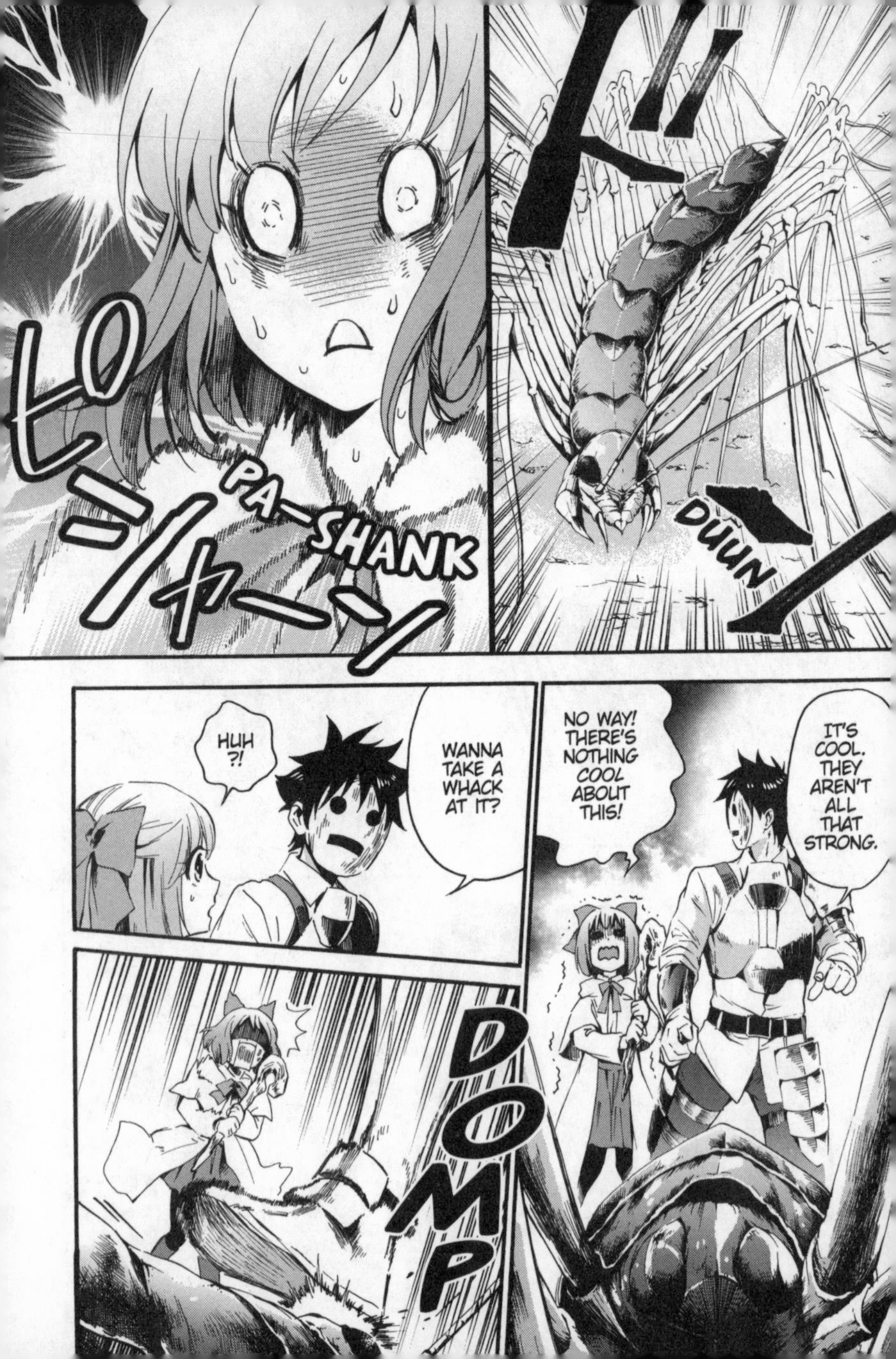
DUUN
ピシャーン
PA-SHANK
IT'S COOL. THEY AREN'T ALL THAT STRONG.
NO WAY! THERE'S NOTHING COOL ABOUT THIS!
WANNA TAKE A WHACK AT IT?
HUH?!
DOMP

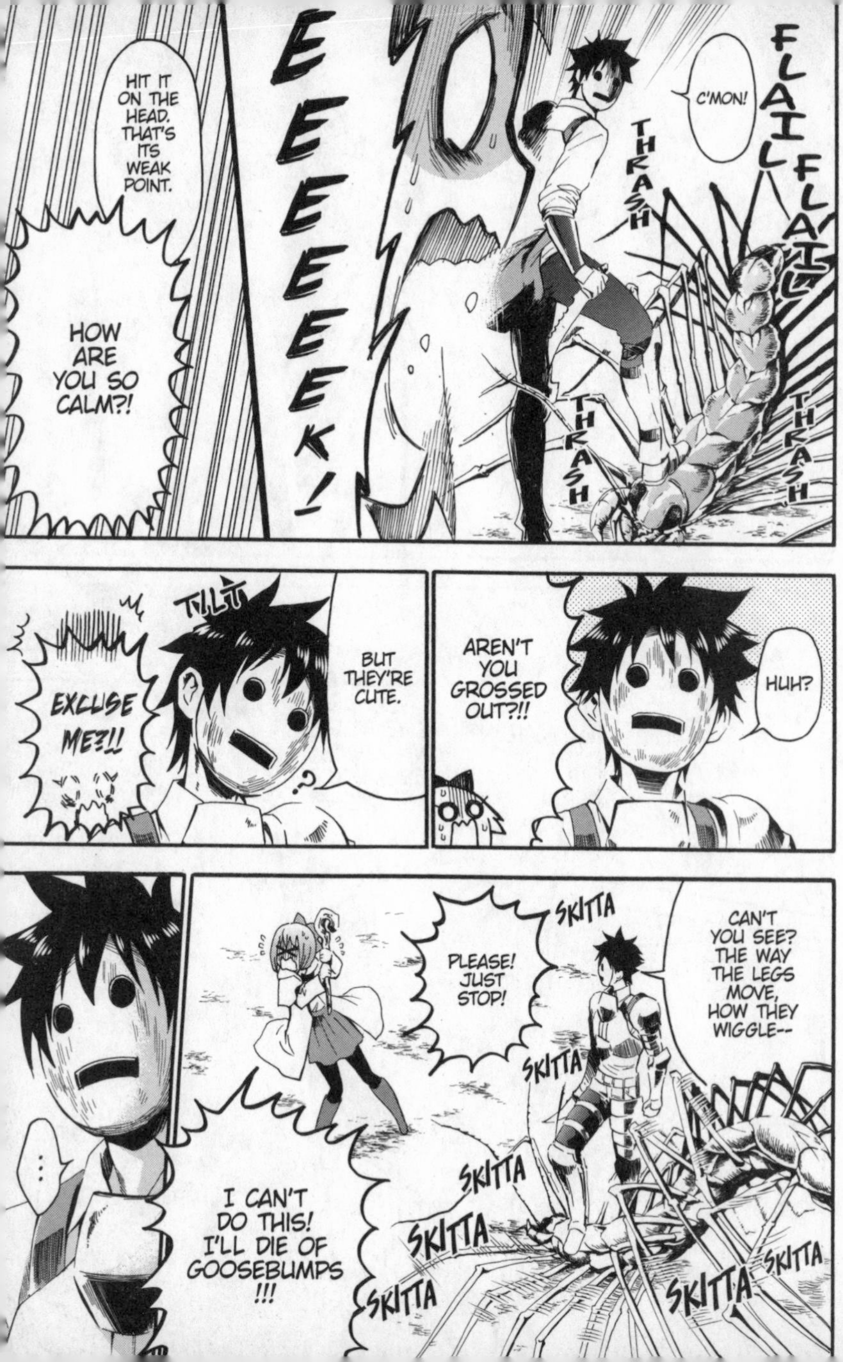
FLAIL FLAIL
C'MON!
THRASH
EEEEEEEK!
HIT IT ON THE HEAD. THAT'S ITS WEAK POINT.
HOW ARE YOU SO CALM?!
THRASH
THRASH
HUH?
AREN'T YOU GROSSED OUT?!!
BUT THEY'RE CUTE.
TILT
EXCUSE ME?!!
CAN'T YOU SEE? THE WAY THE LEGS MOVE, HOW THEY WIGGLE--
SKITTA
PLEASE! JUST STOP!
SKITTA
SKITTA
SKITTA
SKITTA
SKITTA
SKITTA
I CAN'T DO THIS! I'LL DIE OF GOOSEBUMPS!!!
...

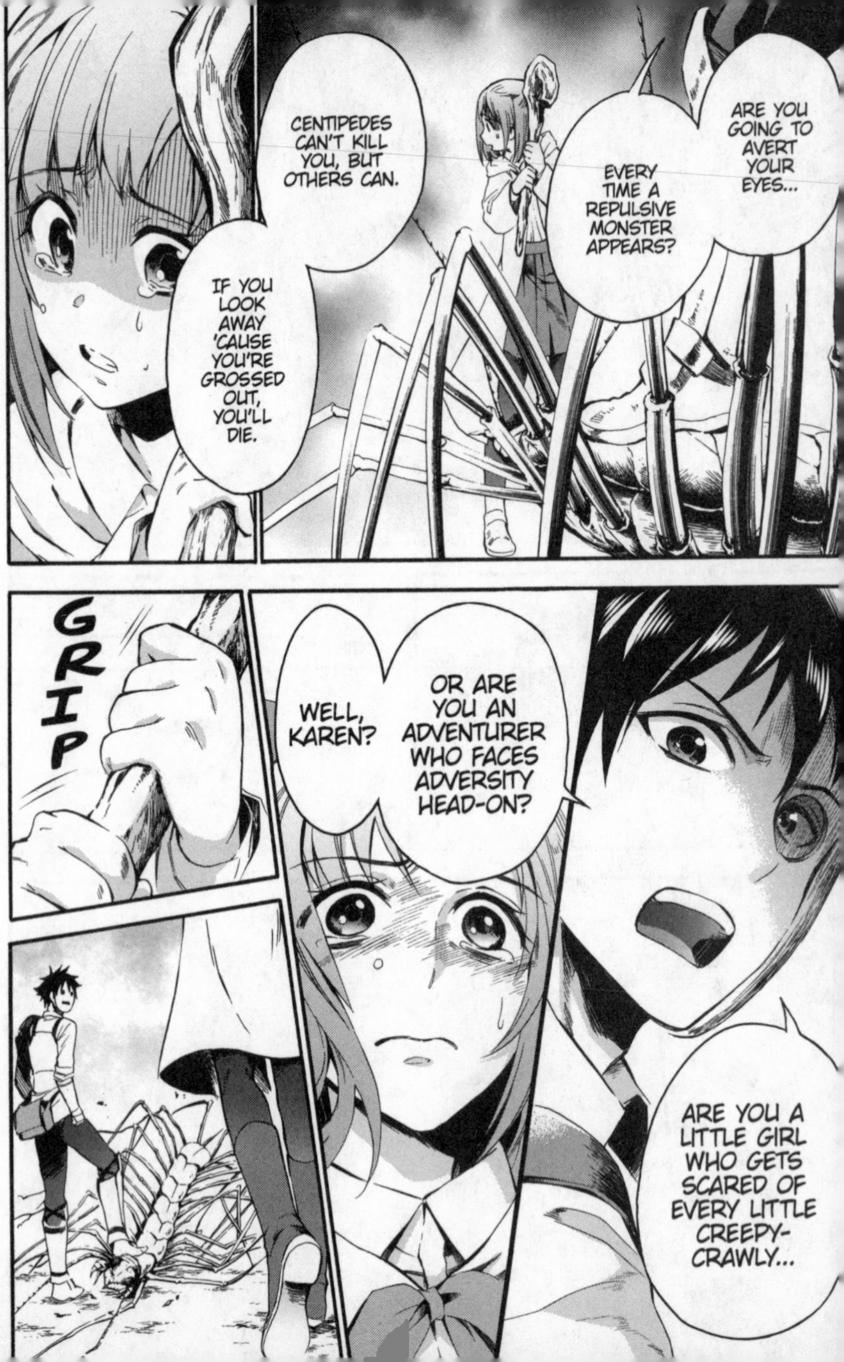
ARE YOU GOING TO AVERT YOUR EYES...
EVERY TIME A REPULSIVE MONSTER APPEARS?
CENTIPEDES CAN'T KILL YOU, BUT OTHERS CAN.
IF YOU LOOK AWAY 'CAUSE YOU'RE GROSSED OUT, YOU'LL DIE.
ARE YOU A LITTLE GIRL WHO GETS SCARED OF EVERY LITTLE CREEPY-CRAWLY...
OR ARE YOU AN ADVENTURER WHO FACES ADVERSITY HEAD-ON?
WELL, KAREN?
GRIP

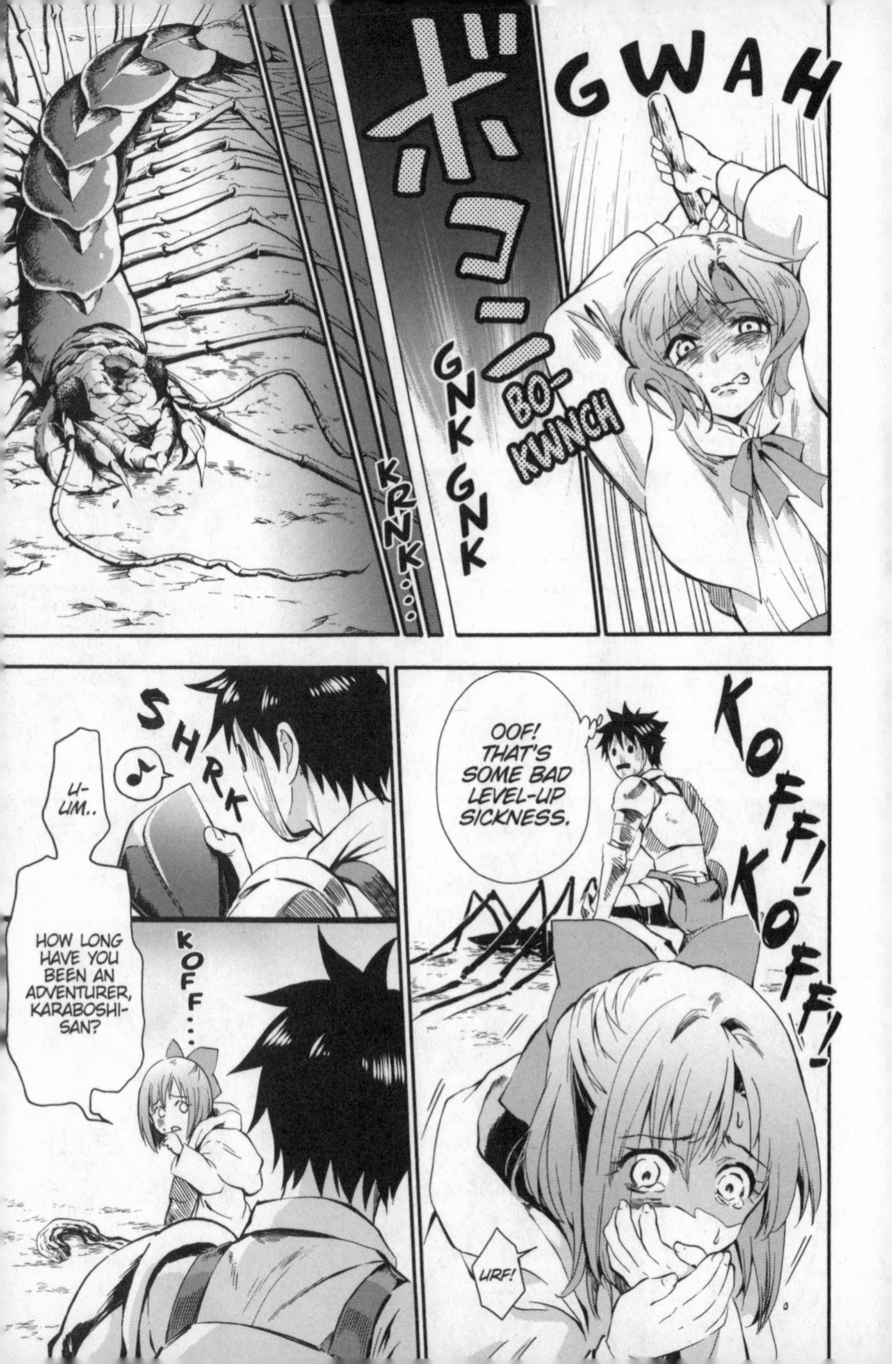
GWAH
ボコー
BO-KWUNCH
GNK GNK
KRNK...
KOFF! KOFF! KOFF!
OOF! THAT'S SOME BAD LEVEL-UP SICKNESS.
URF!
SHRK
♪
U-UM..
HOW LONG HAVE YOU BEEN AN ADVENTURER, KARABOSHI-SAN?
KOFF...

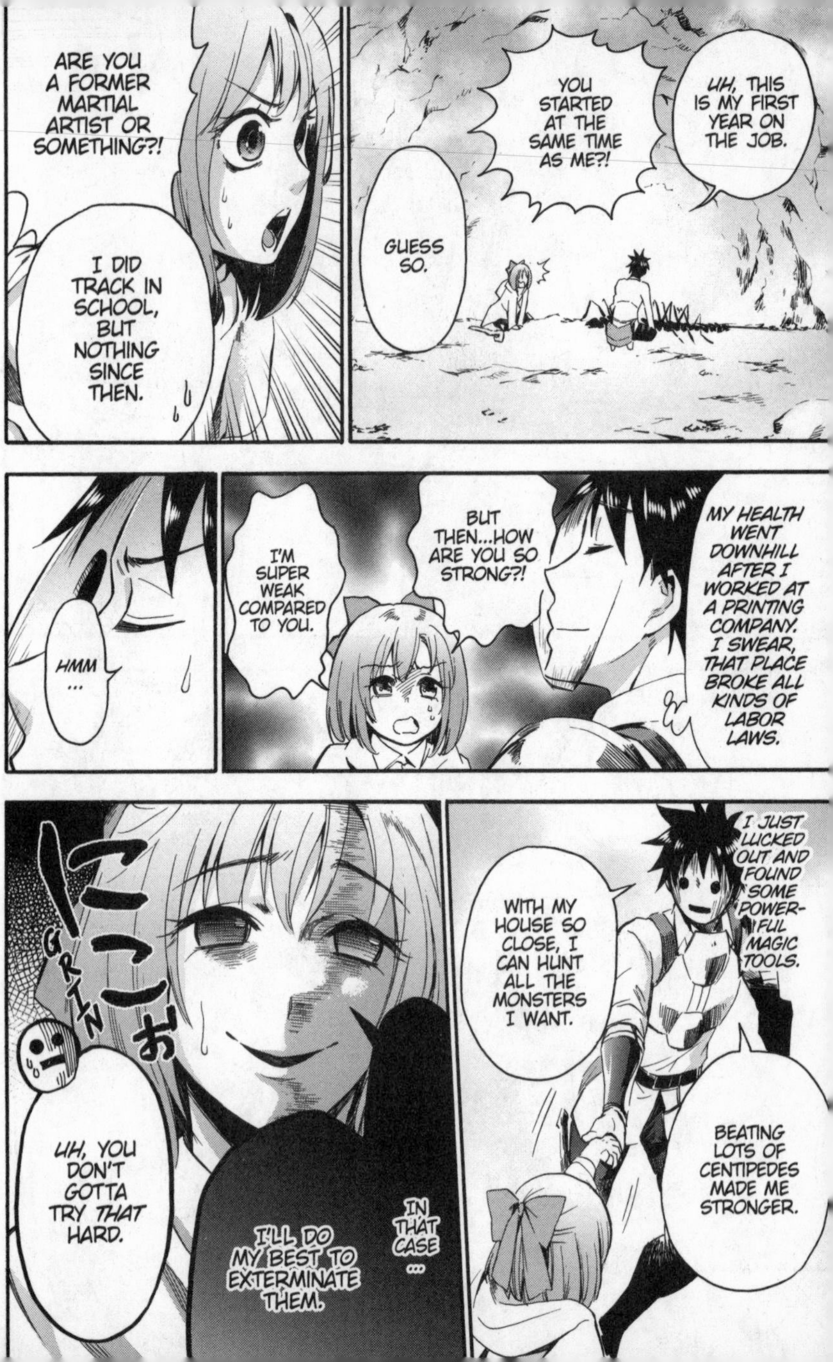

UH, THIS IS MY FIRST YEAR ON THE JOB.
YOU STARTED AT THE SAME TIME AS ME?!
GUESS SO.
ARE YOU A FORMER MARTIAL ARTIST OR SOMETHING?!
I DID TRACK IN SCHOOL, BUT NOTHING SINCE THEN.
MY HEALTH WENT DOWNHILL AFTER I WORKED AT A PRINTING COMPANY. I SWEAR, THAT PLACE BROKE ALL KINDS OF LABOR LAWS.
BUT THEN...HOW ARE YOU SO STRONG?!
I'M SUPER WEAK COMPARED TO YOU.
HMM ...
I JUST LUCKED OUT AND FOUND SOME POWERFUL MAGIC TOOLS.
WITH MY HOUSE SO CLOSE, I CAN HUNT ALL THE MONSTERS I WANT.
BEATING LOTS OF CENTIPEDES MADE ME STRONGER.
IN THAT CASE ...
I'LL DO MY BEST TO EXTERMINATE THEM.
にこぉ
GRIN
UH, YOU DON'T GOTTA TRY *THAT* HARD.

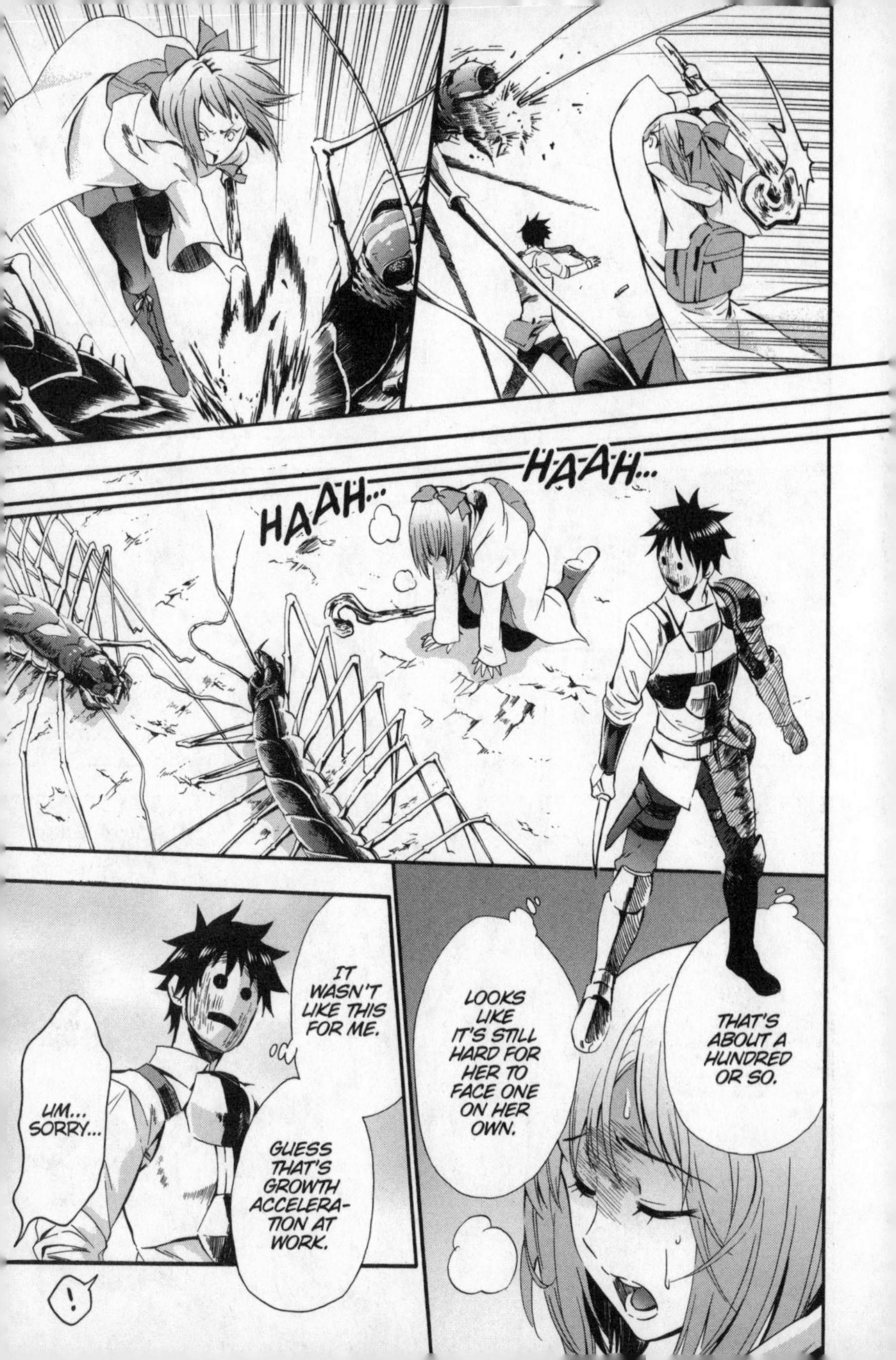

HA-AH...
HAAH...
THAT'S ABOUT A HUNDRED OR SO.
LOOKS LIKE IT'S STILL HARD FOR HER TO FACE ONE ON HER OWN.
IT WASN'T LIKE THIS FOR ME.
GUESS THAT'S GROWTH ACCELERA-TION AT WORK.
UM... SORRY...
!

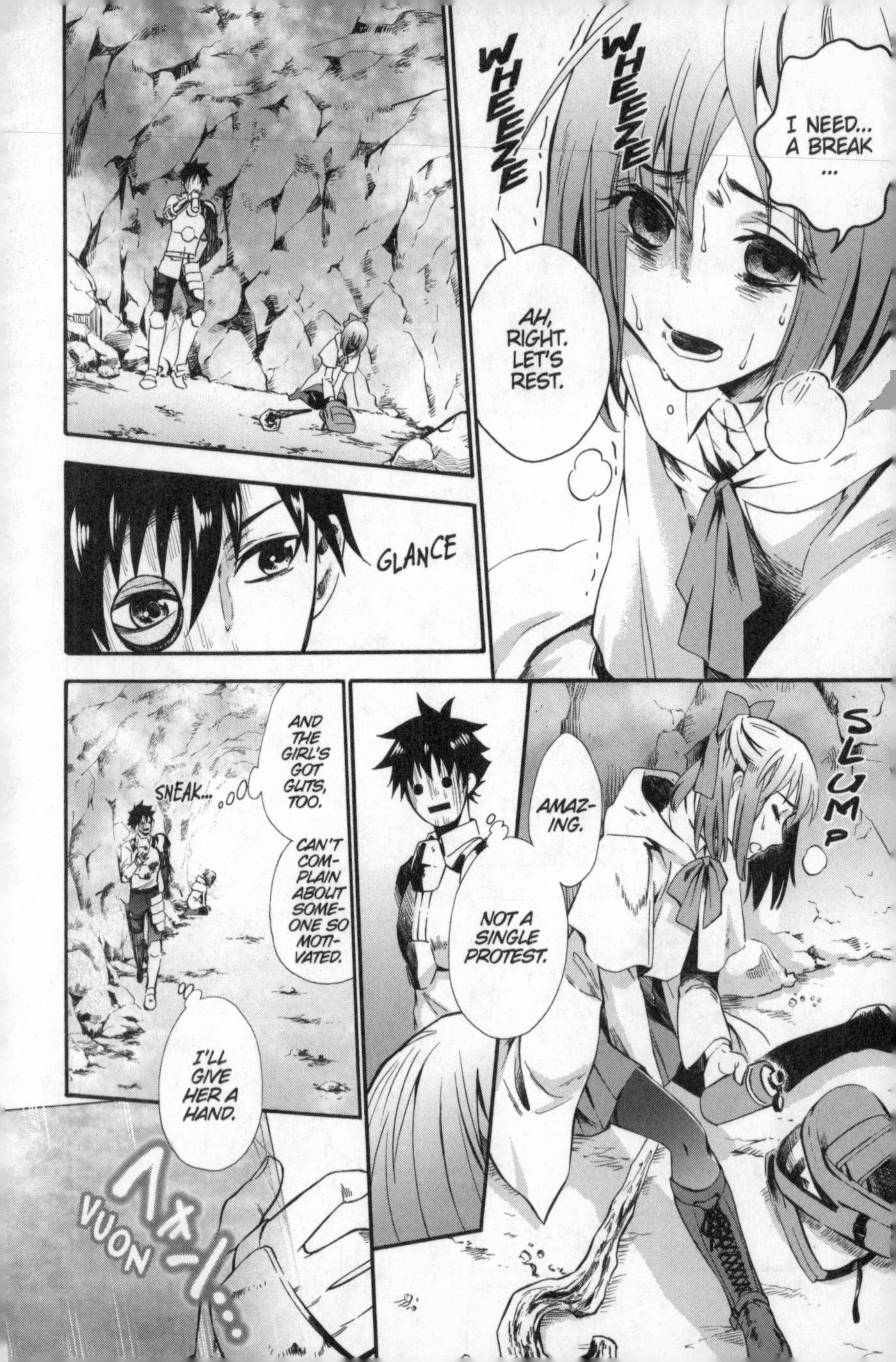
I NEED... A BREAK ...
WHEEZE
WHEEZE
AH, RIGHT. LET'S REST.
GLANCE
SLUMP
AMAZ-ING.
NOT A SINGLE PROTEST.
AND THE GIRL'S GOT GUTS, TOO.
SNEAK...
CAN'T COM-PLAIN ABOUT SOME-ONE SO MOTI-VATED.
I'LL GIVE HER A HAND.
VUON

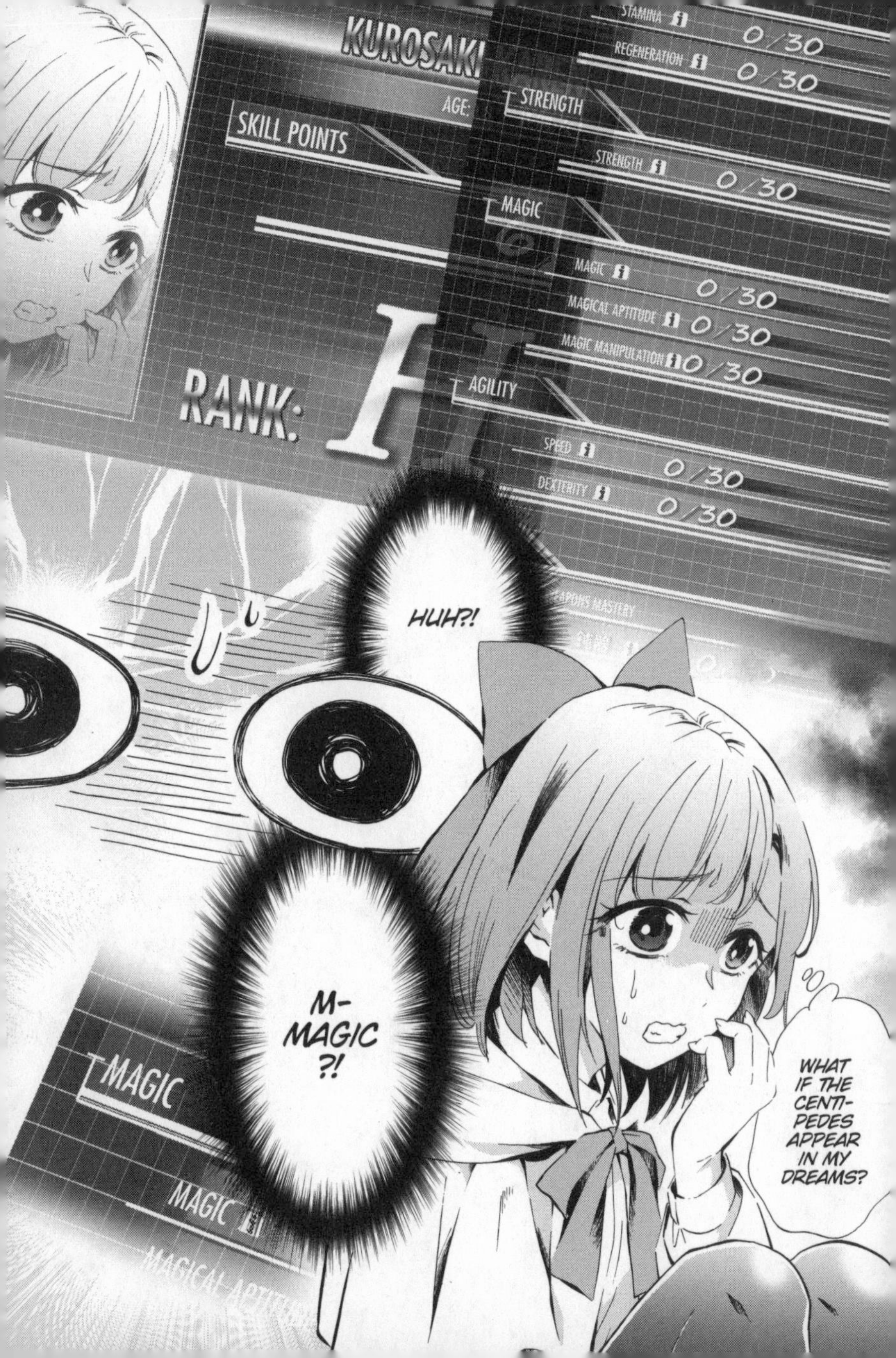
STAMINA
0/30
REGENERATION
0/30
STRENGTH
STRENGTH
0/30
MAGIC
MAGIC
0/30
MAGICAL APTITUDE
0/30
MAGIC MANIPULATION
0/30
AGILITY
SPEED
0/30
DEXTERITY
0/30
KUROSAKI
AGE:
SKILL POINTS
RANK: F
HUH?!
M-MAGIC?!
WHAT IF THE CENTIPEDES APPEAR IN MY DREAMS?
MAGIC
MAGIC

CALL TO ADVENTURE!

DEFEATING DUNGEONS WITH A SKILL BOARD

2

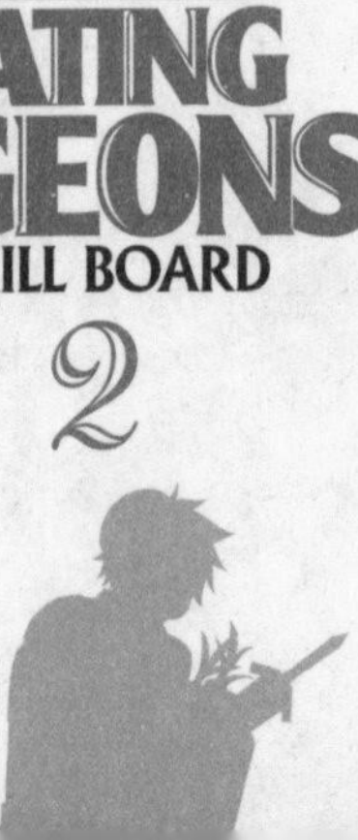

Chapter 7

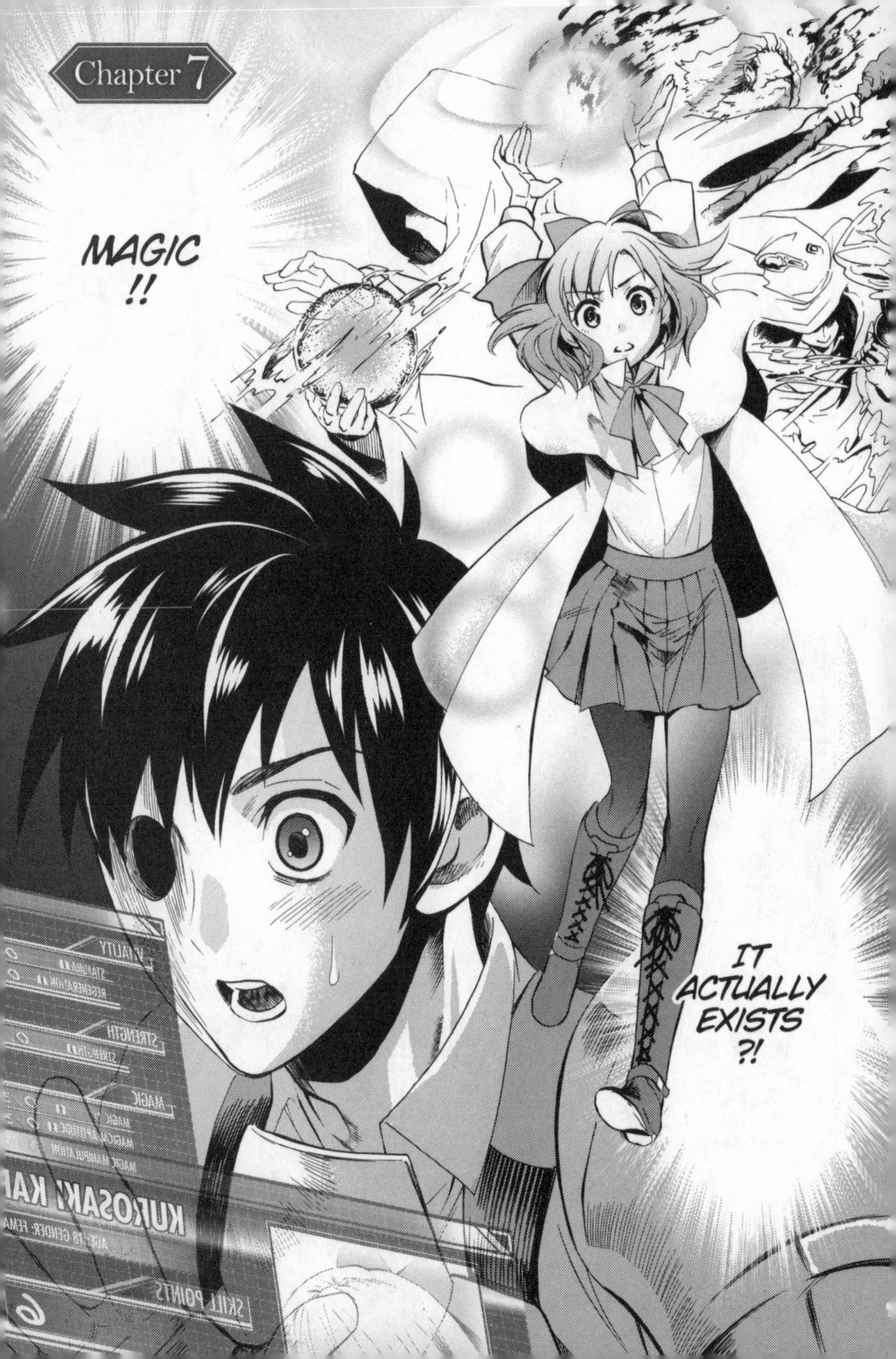
MAGIC !!
IT ACTUALLY EXISTS ?!

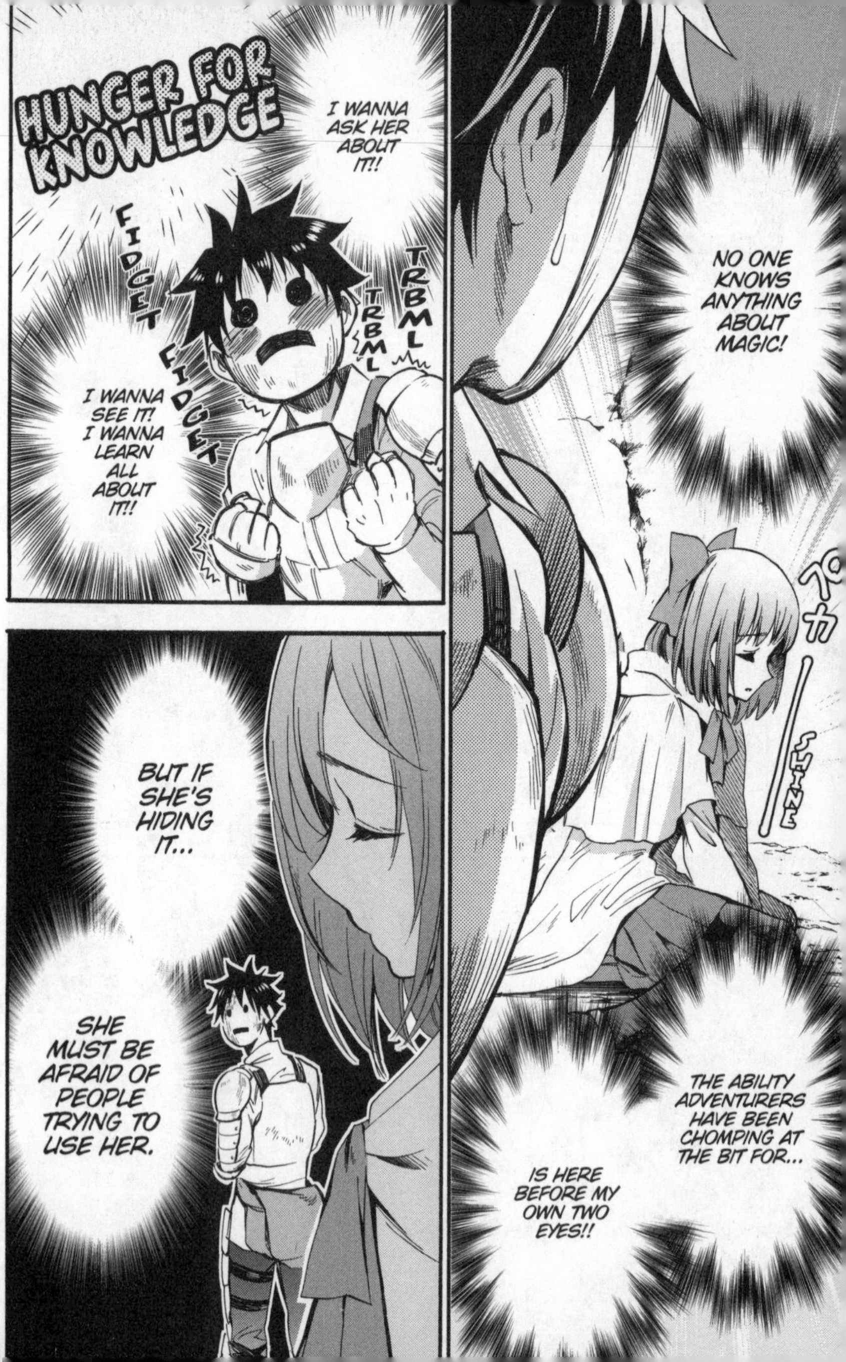
NO ONE KNOWS ANYTHING ABOUT MAGIC!
ペカー
SHINE
THE ABILITY ADVENTURERS HAVE BEEN CHOMPING AT THE BIT FOR...
IS HERE BEFORE MY OWN TWO EYES!!
HUNGER FOR KNOWLEDGE
I WANNA ASK HER ABOUT IT!!
TRBML
TRBML
FIDGET
FIDGET
I WANNA SEE IT! I WANNA LEARN ALL ABOUT IT!!
BUT IF SHE'S HIDING IT...
SHE MUST BE AFRAID OF PEOPLE TRYING TO USE HER.

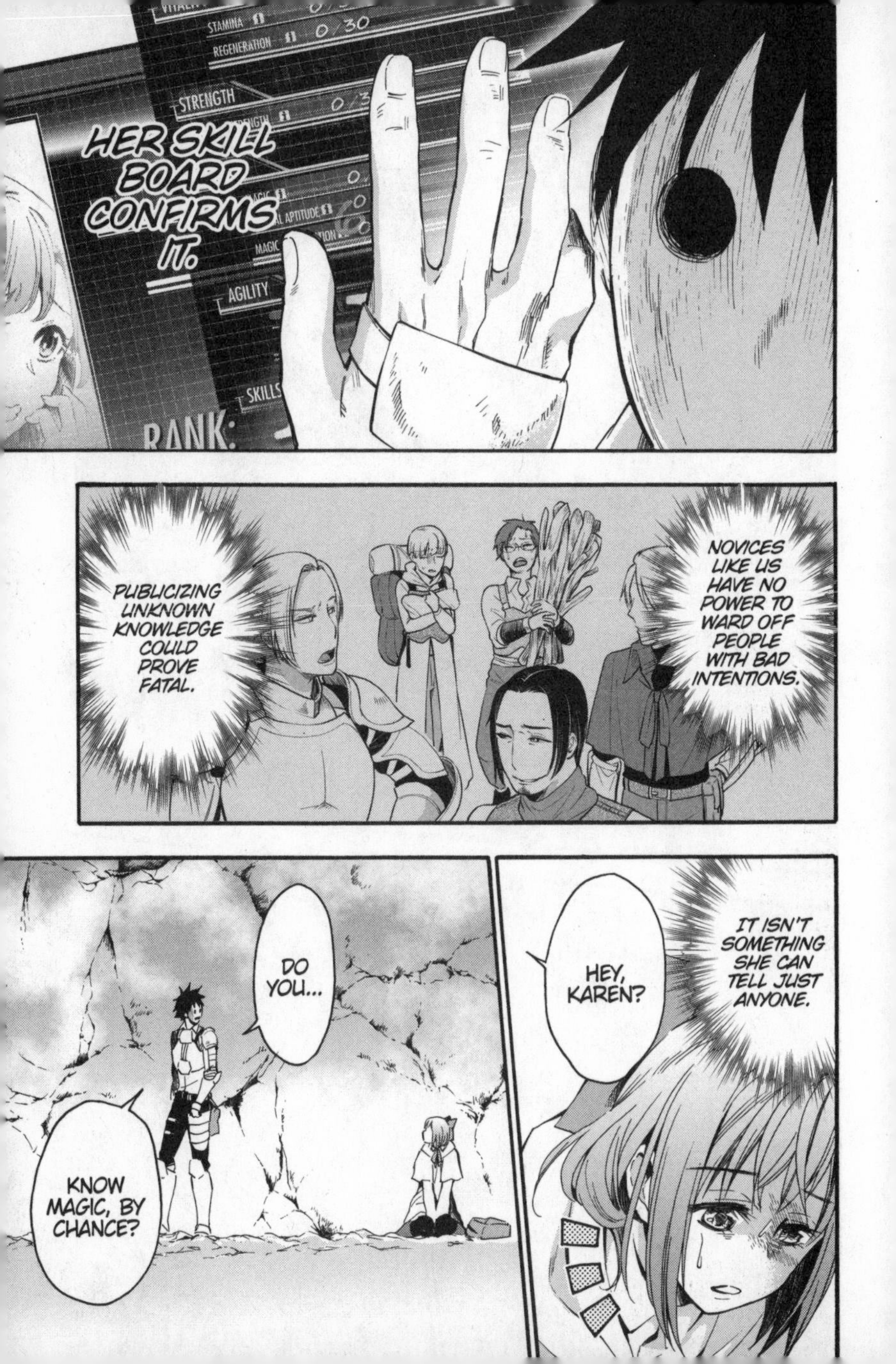
STAMINA
0/30
REGENERATION
STRENGTH
AGILITY
SKILLS
RANK:
HER SKILL BOARD CONFIRMS IT.
NOVICES LIKE US HAVE NO POWER TO WARD OFF PEOPLE WITH BAD INTENTIONS.
PUBLICIZING UNKNOWN KNOWLEDGE COULD PROVE FATAL.
IT ISN'T SOMETHING SHE CAN TELL JUST ANYONE.
HEY, KAREN?
DO YOU...
KNOW MAGIC, BY CHANCE?

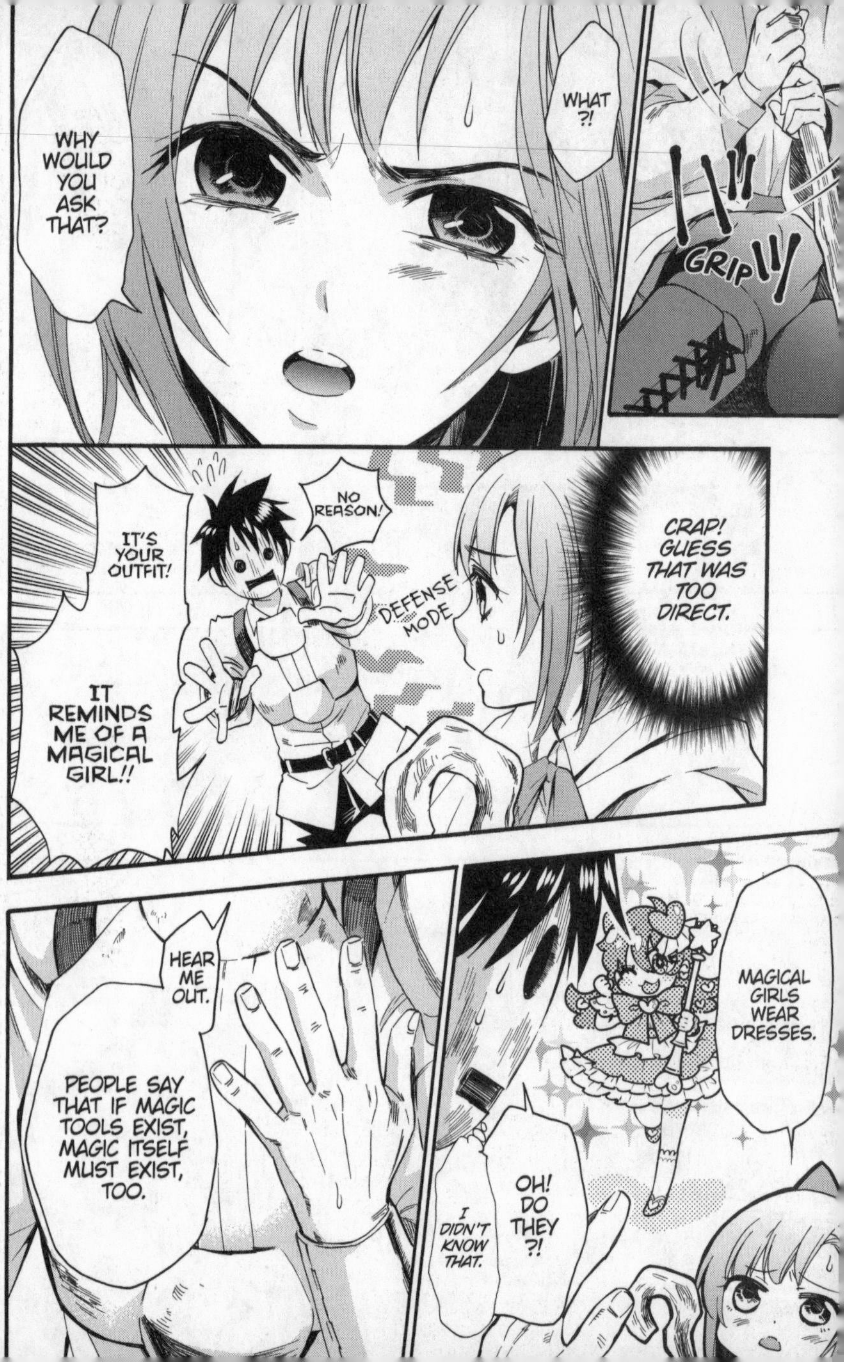
GRIP
WHAT ?!
WHY WOULD YOU ASK THAT?
CRAP! GUESS THAT WAS TOO DIRECT.
DEFENSE MODE
NO REASON!
IT'S YOUR OUTFIT!
IT REMINDS ME OF A MAGICAL GIRL!!
MAGICAL GIRLS WEAR DRESSES.
OH! DO THEY ?!
I DIDN'T KNOW THAT.
HEAR ME OUT.
PEOPLE SAY THAT IF MAGIC TOOLS EXIST, MAGIC ITSELF MUST EXIST, TOO.

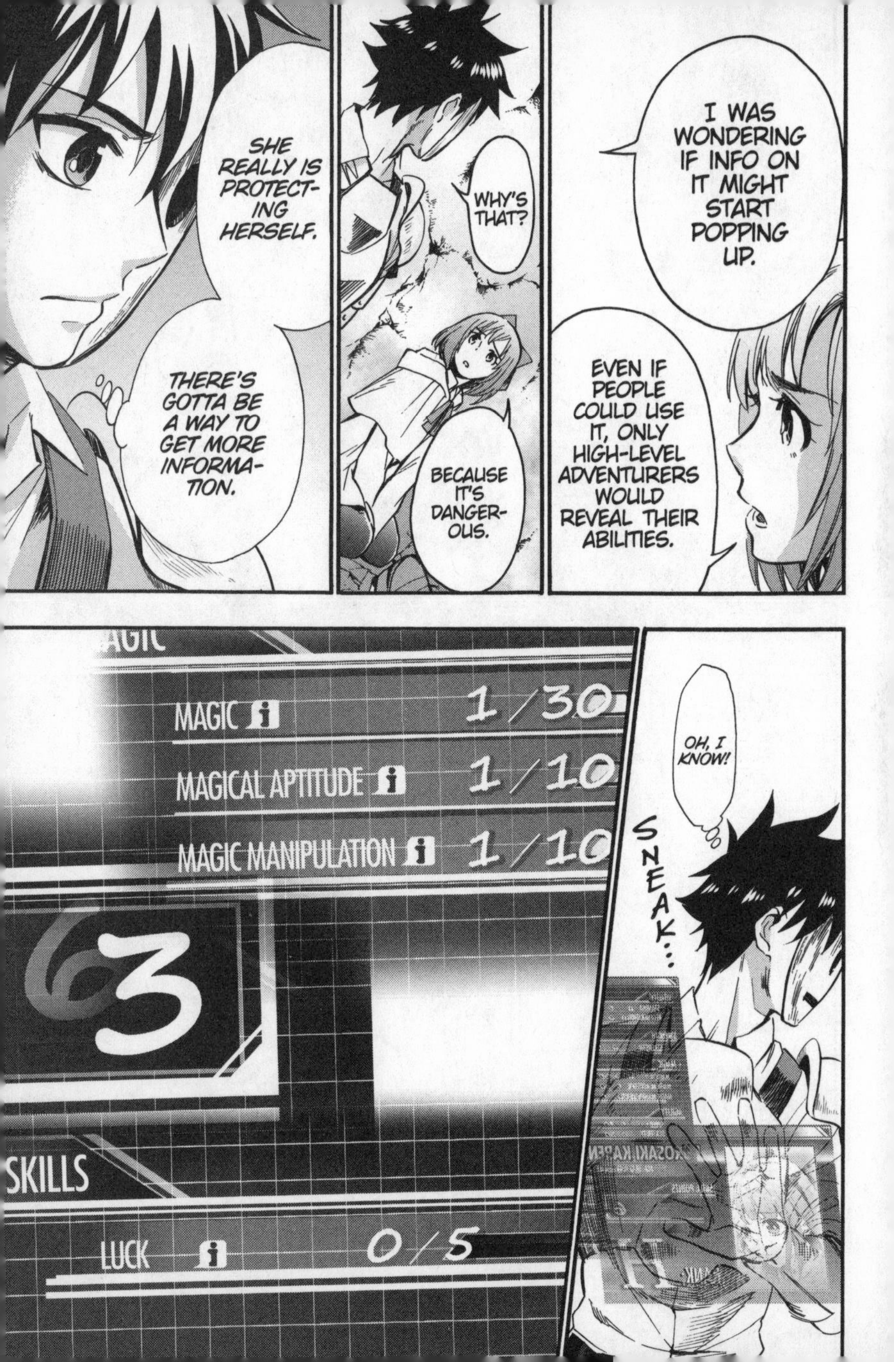
I WAS WONDERING IF INFO ON IT MIGHT START POPPING UP.
EVEN IF PEOPLE COULD USE IT, ONLY HIGH-LEVEL ADVENTURERS WOULD REVEAL THEIR ABILITIES.
WHY'S THAT?
BECAUSE IT'S DANGER-OUS.
SHE REALLY IS PROTECT-ING HERSELF.
THERE'S GOTTA BE A WAY TO GET MORE INFORMA-TION.
OH, I KNOW!
SNEAK...
MAGIC 1/30
MAGICAL APTITUDE 1/10
MAGIC MANIPULATION 1/10
3
SKILLS
LUCK 0/5

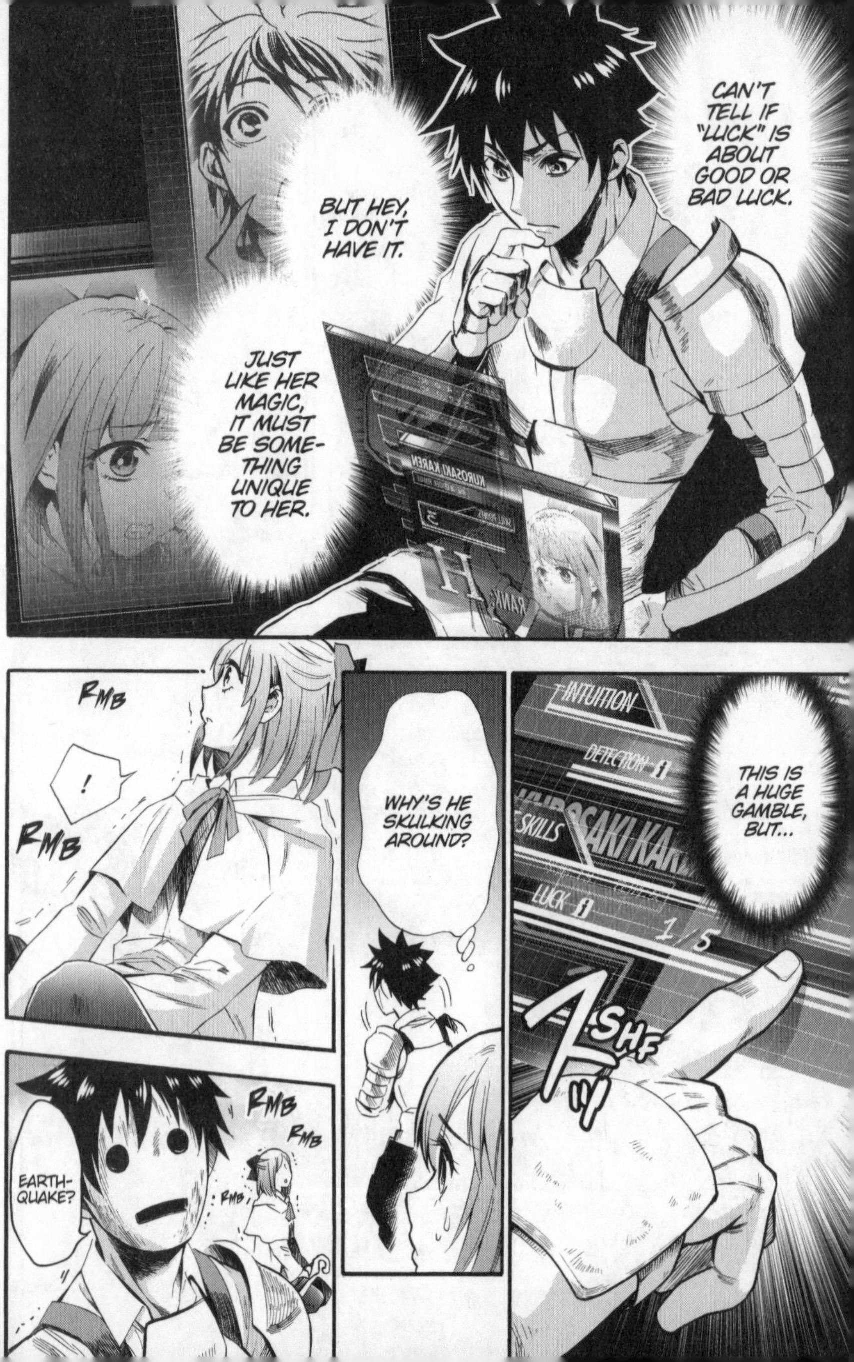
CAN'T TELL IF "LUCK" IS ABOUT GOOD OR BAD LUCK.
BUT HEY, I DON'T HAVE IT.
JUST LIKE HER MAGIC, IT MUST BE SOME-THING UNIQUE TO HER.
KUROSAKI KAREN
SKILL POINTS
3
RANK
H
INTUITION
DETECTION
SKILLS
LUCK
1/5
THIS IS A HUGE GAMBLE, BUT...
SHF
WHY'S HE SKULKING AROUND?
RMB
!
RMB
RMB
RMB
EARTH-QUAKE?
RMB

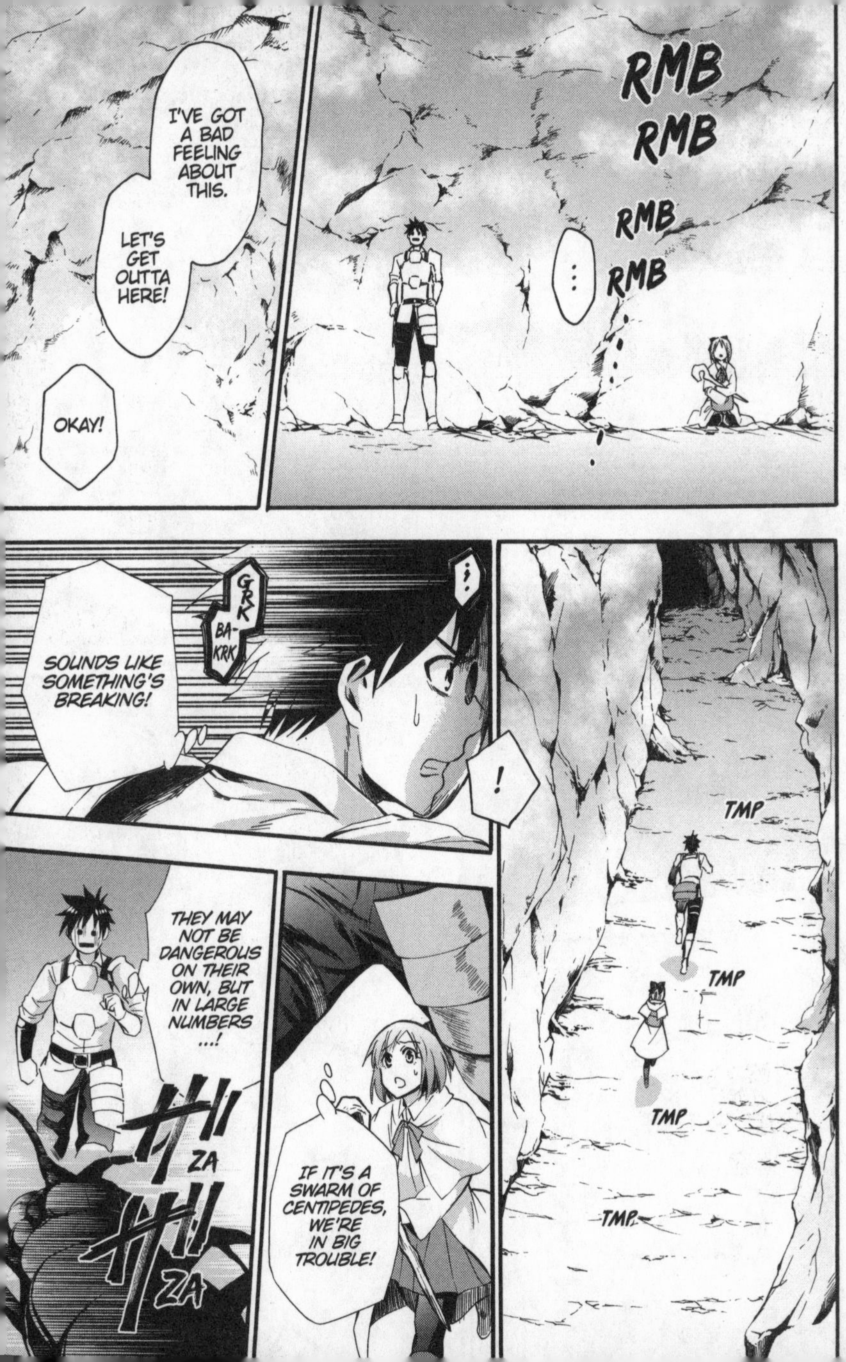
RMB
RMB
RMB
RMB
...
I'VE GOT A BAD FEELING ABOUT THIS.
LET'S GET OUTTA HERE!
OKAY!
TMP
TMP
TMP
TMP
?
GRK
BA-KRK
SOUNDS LIKE SOMETHING'S BREAKING!
!
IF IT'S A SWARM OF CENTIPEDES, WE'RE IN BIG TROUBLE!
THEY MAY NOT BE DANGEROUS ON THEIR OWN, BUT IN LARGE NUMBERS...!
ZA
ZA

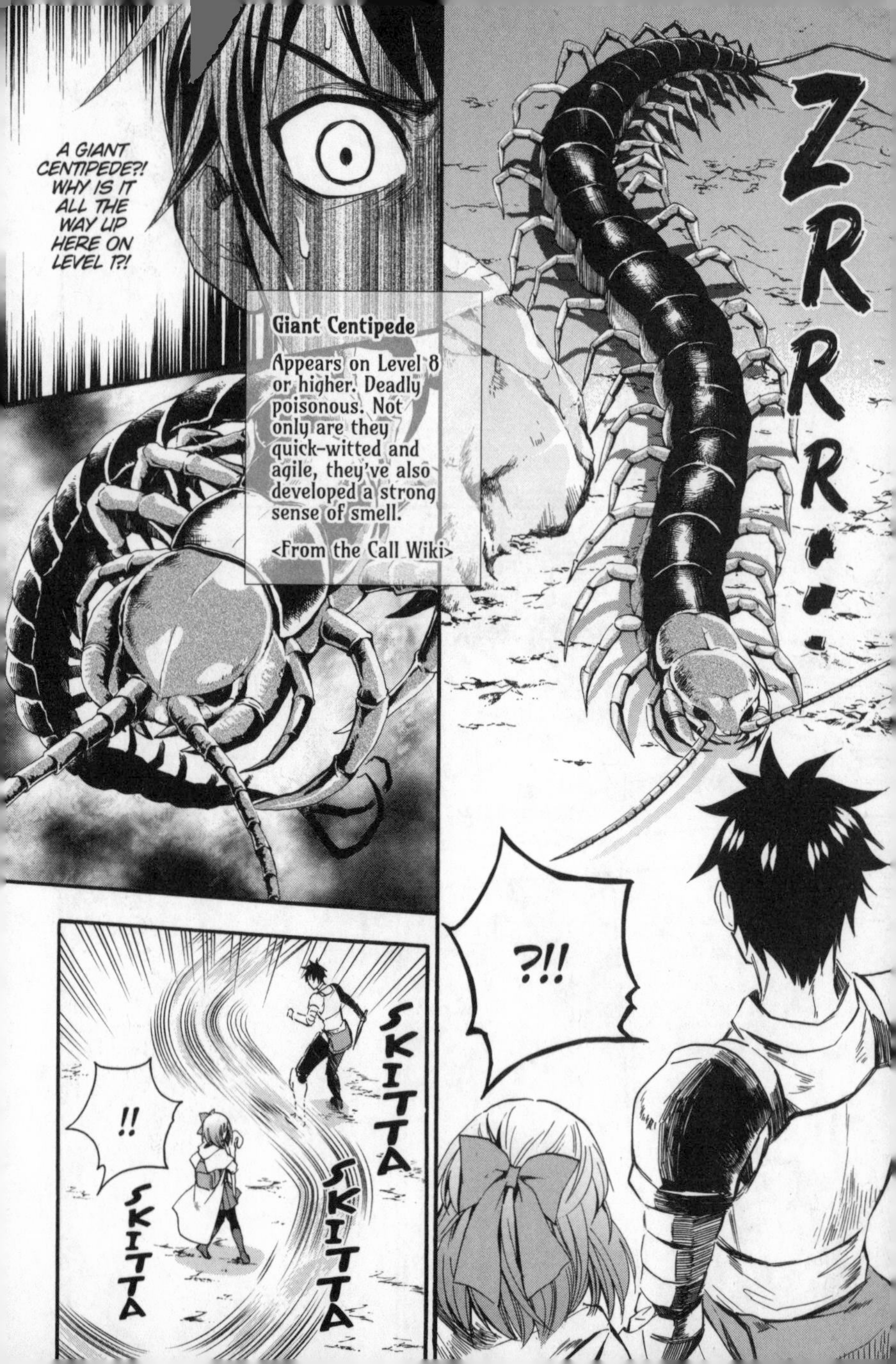
ZRRR...
?!!
A GIANT CENTIPEDE?! WHY IS IT ALL THE WAY UP HERE ON LEVEL 1?!
Giant Centipede
Appears on Level 8 or higher. Deadly poisonous. Not only are they quick-witted and agile, they've also developed a strong sense of smell.
<From the Call Wiki>
!!
SKITTA SKITTA
SKITTA SKITTA

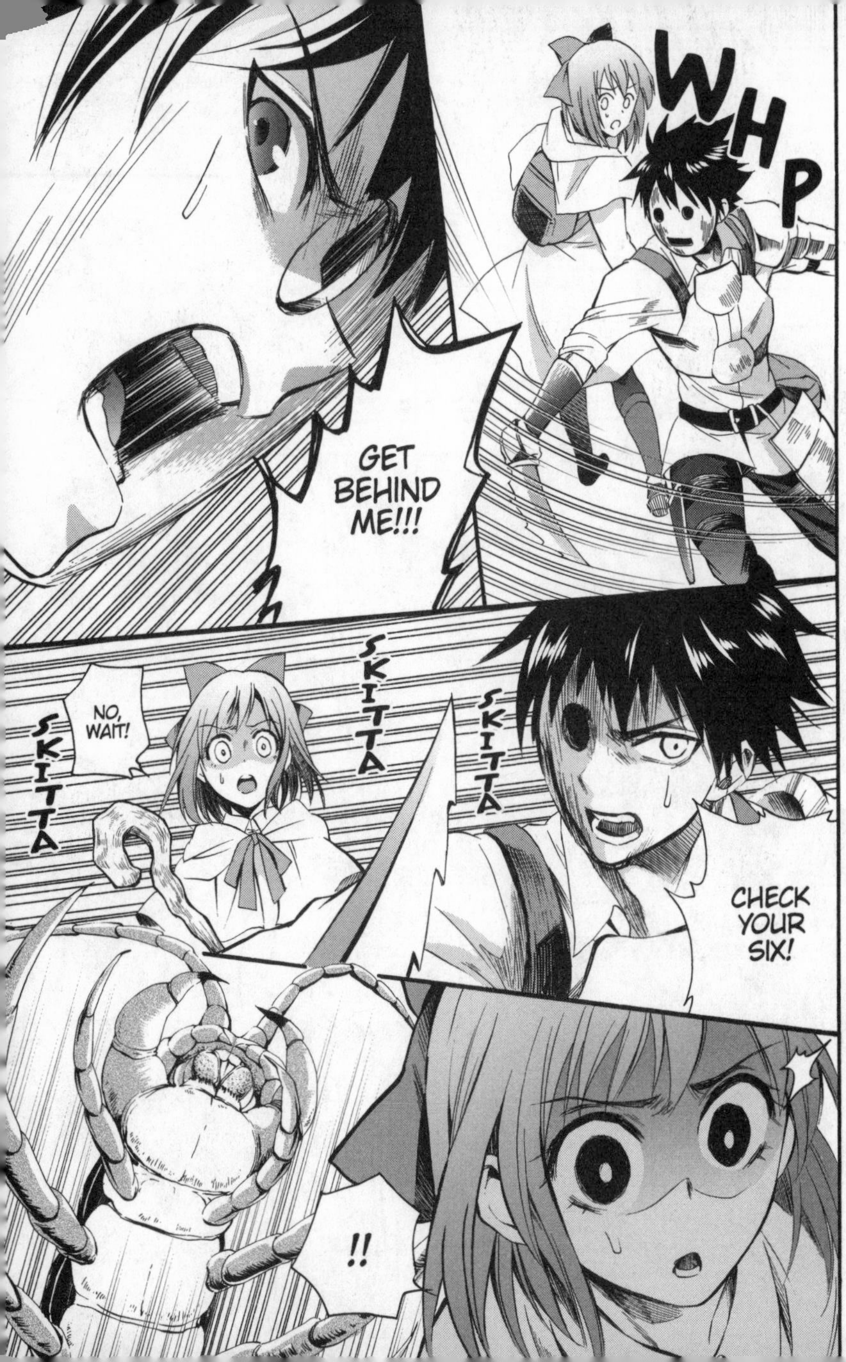
WHP
GET BEHIND ME!!!
CHECK YOUR SIX!
SKITTA
SKITTA
NO, WAIT!
SKITTA
!!

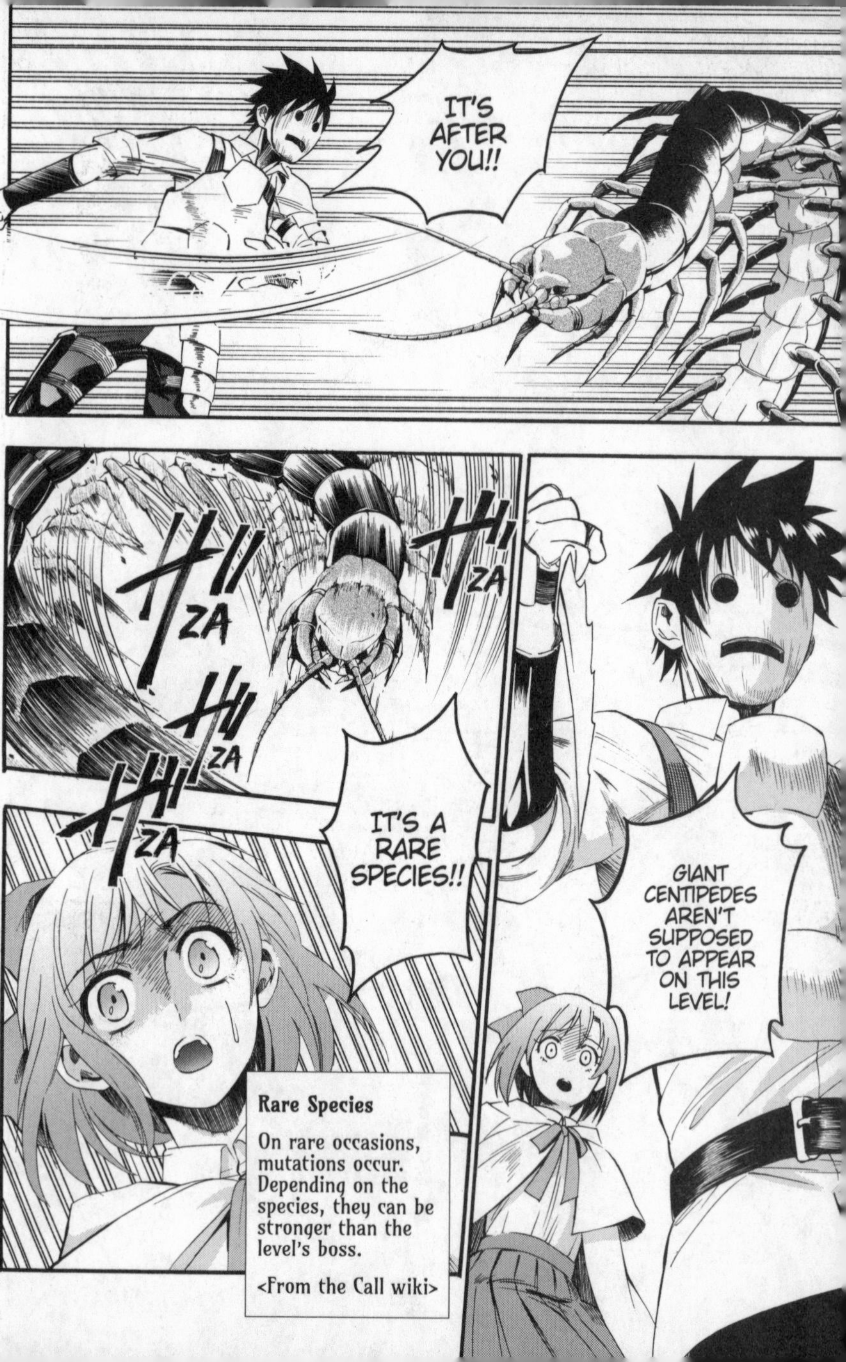
IT'S AFTER YOU!!
GIANT CENTIPEDES AREN'T SUPPOSED TO APPEAR ON THIS LEVEL!
ZA
ZA
ZA
ZA
IT'S A RARE SPECIES!!
Rare Species
On rare occasions, mutations occur. Depending on the species, they can be stronger than the level's boss.
<From the Call wiki>

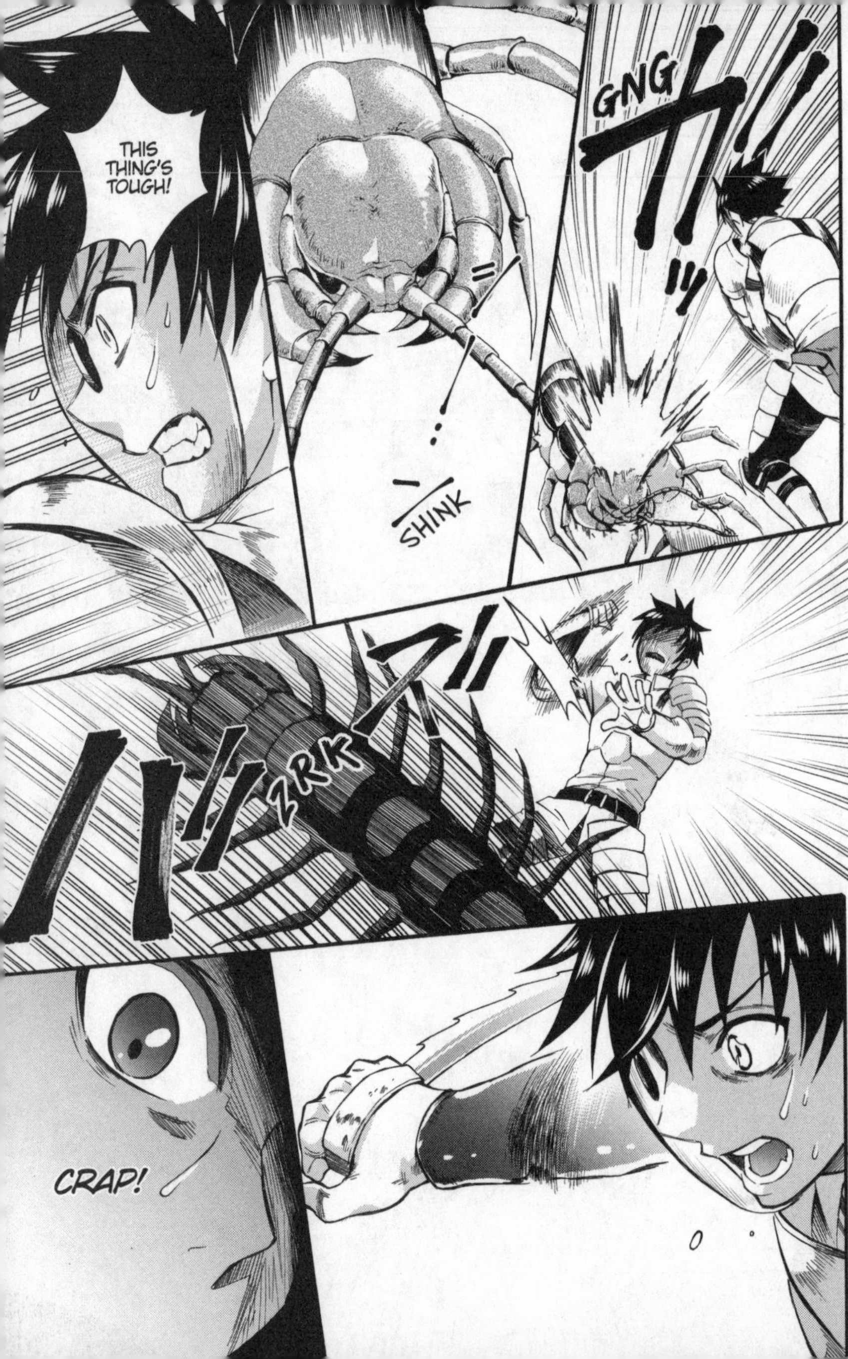
GNG
SHINK
THIS THING'S TOUGH!
ZRK
CRAP!

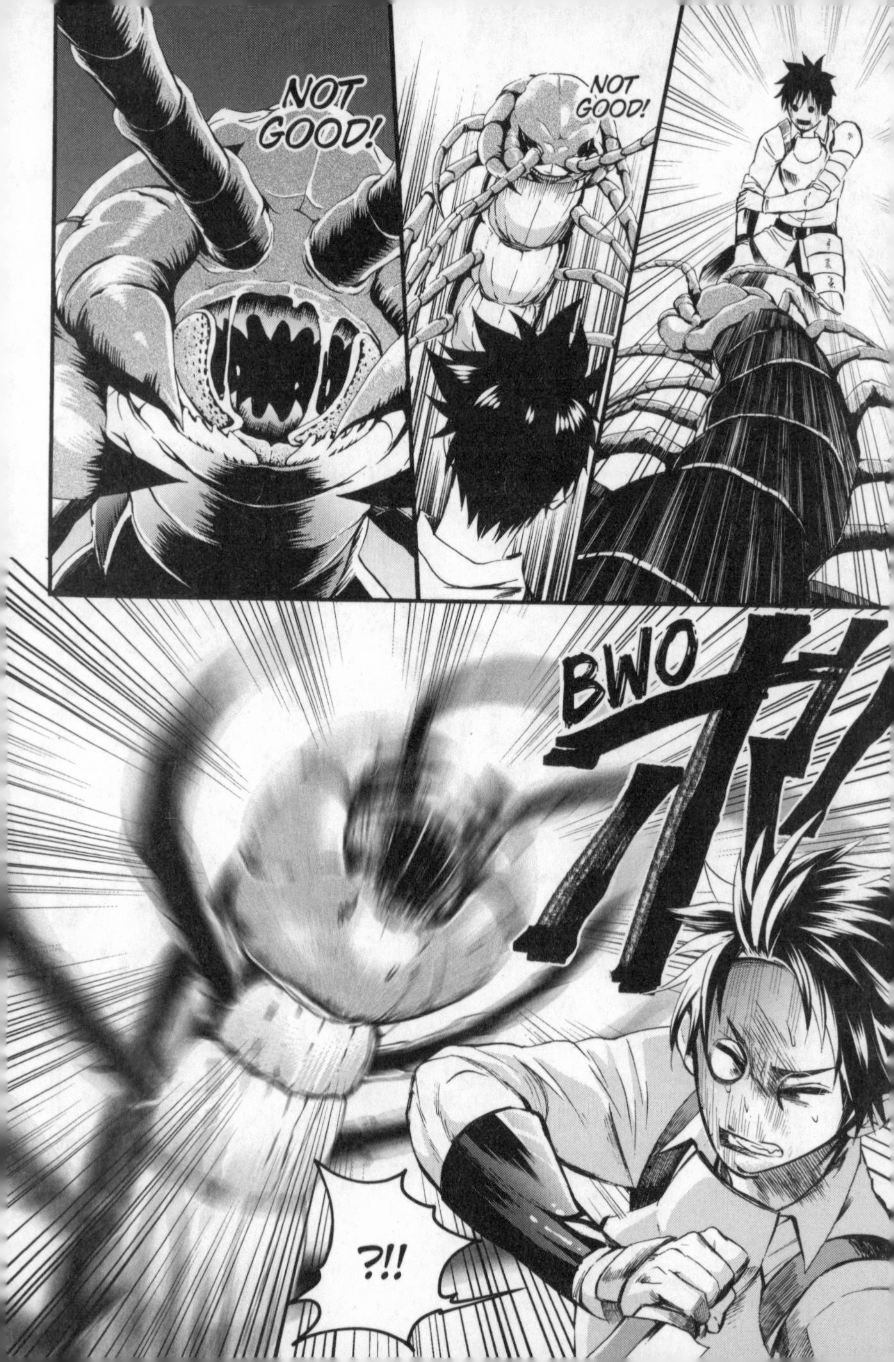
NOT GOOD!
NOT GOOD!
BWO
?!!

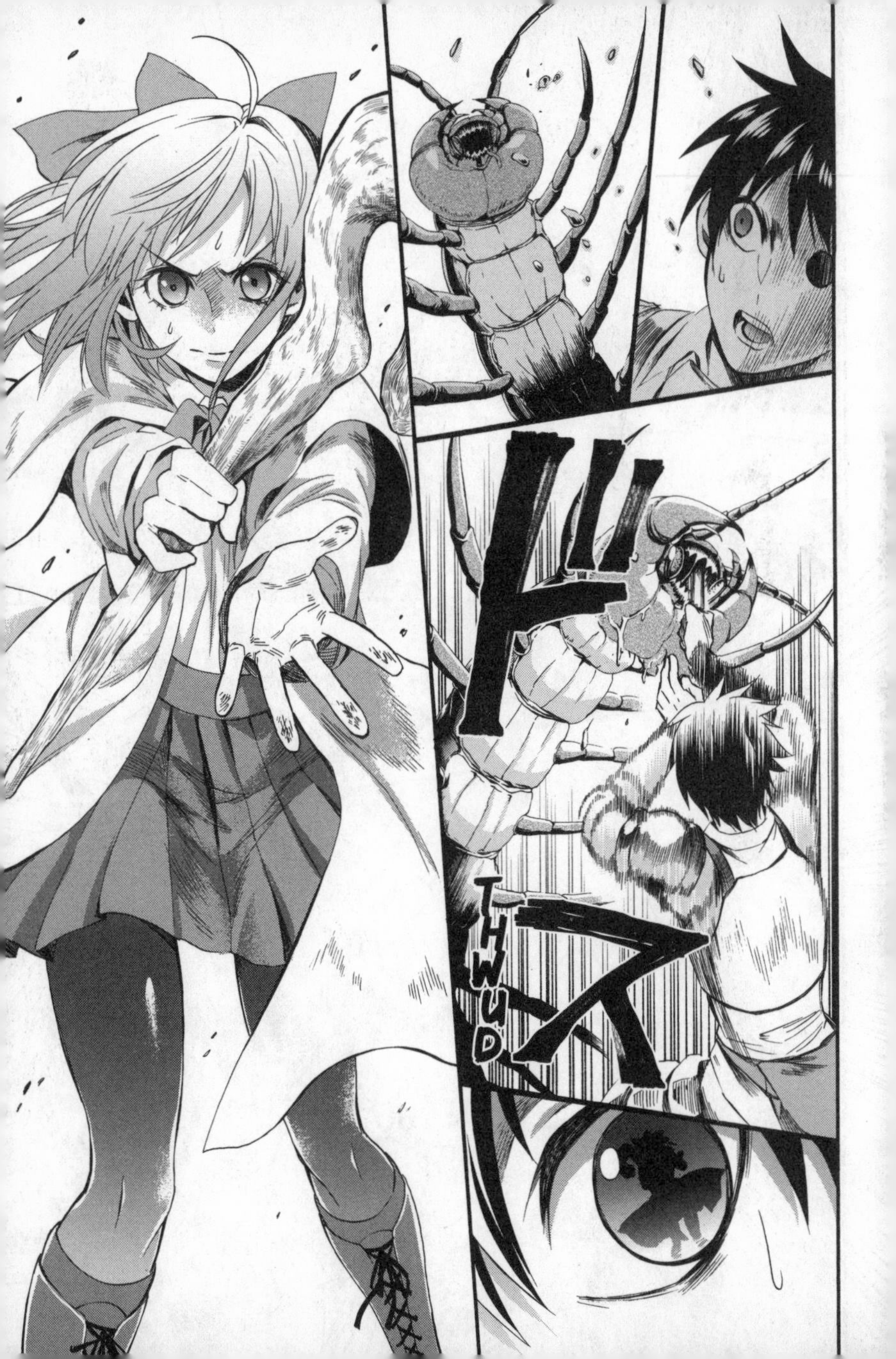
ドス
THWUD

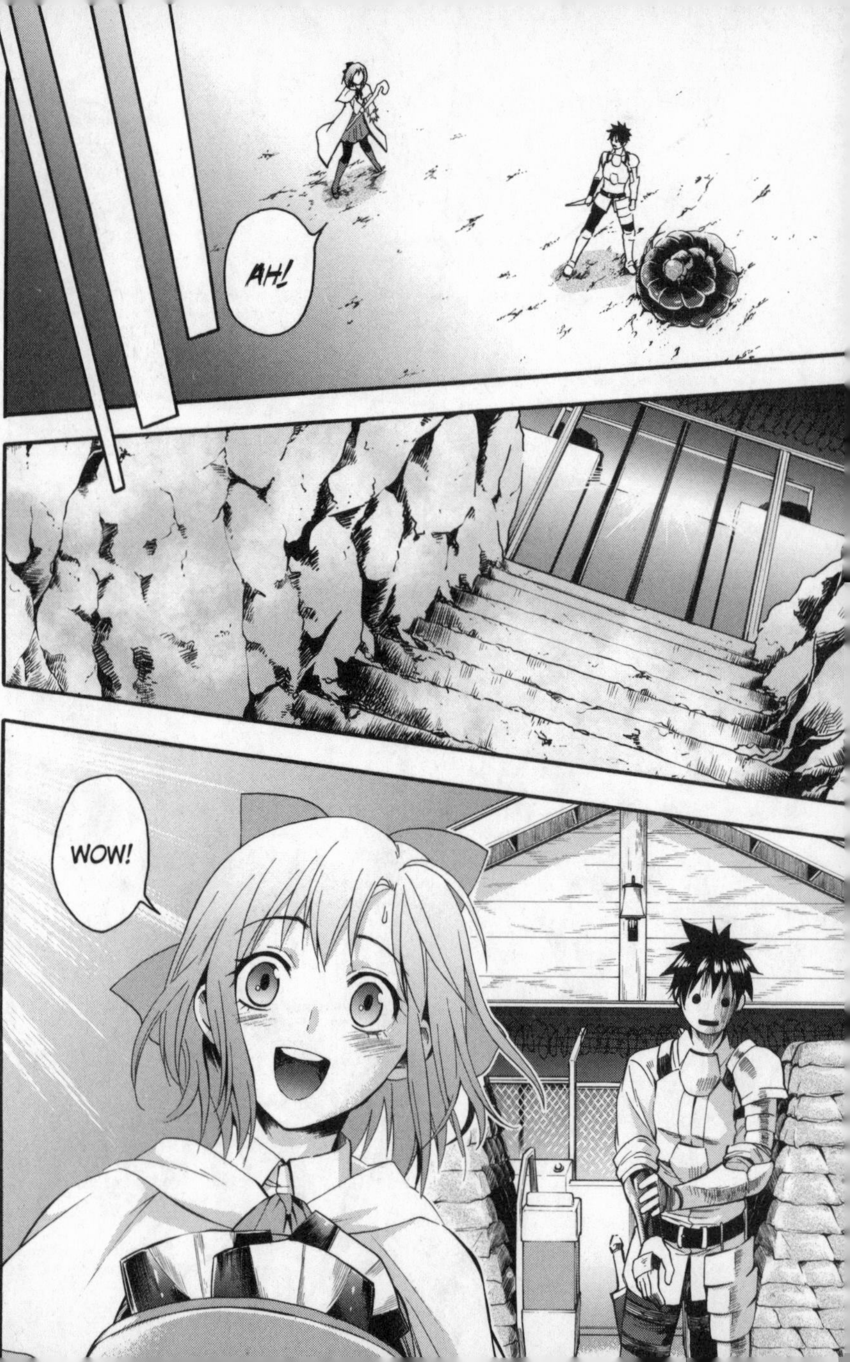
AH!
WOW!

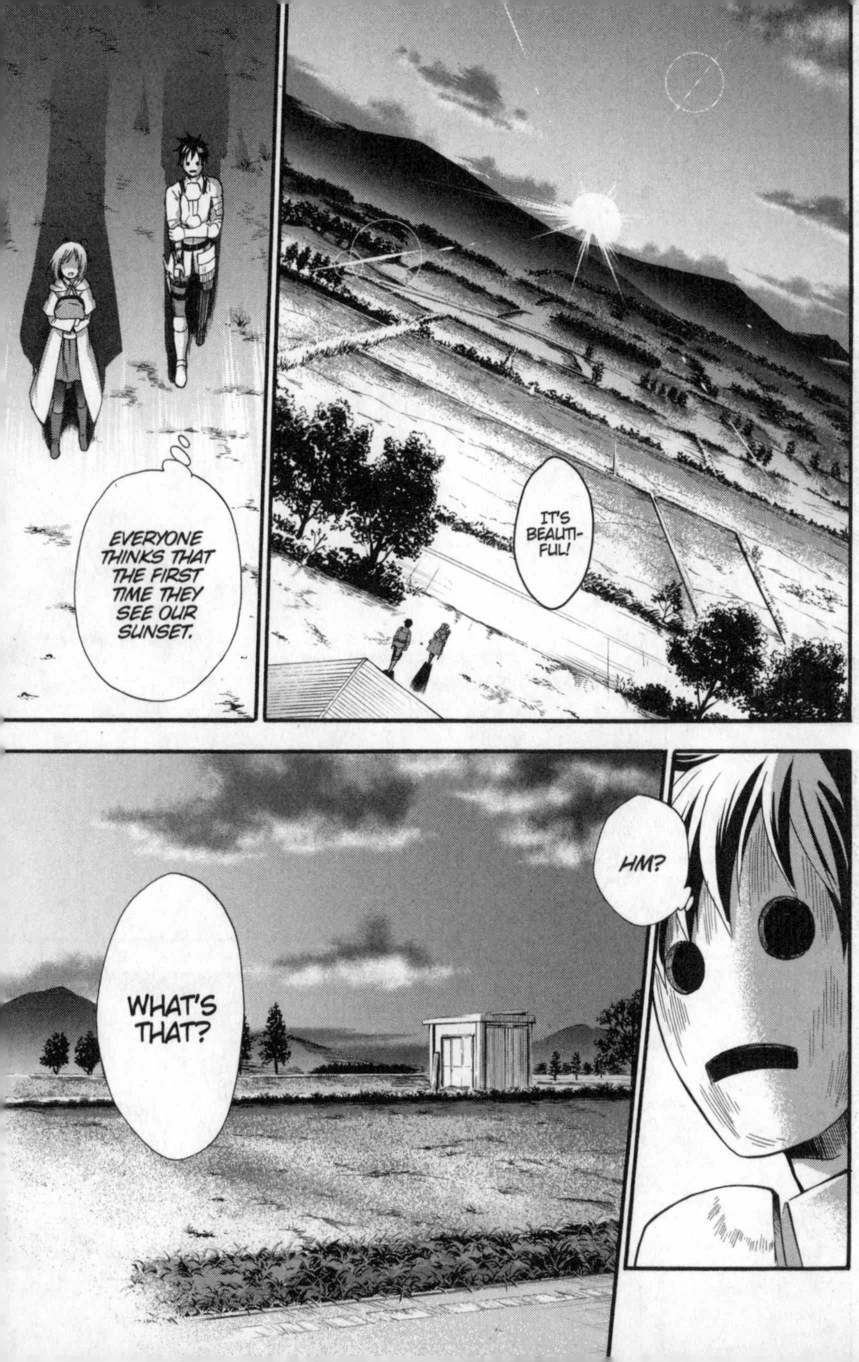
IT'S BEAUTIFUL!
EVERYONE THINKS THAT THE FIRST TIME THEY SEE OUR SUNSET.
HM?
WHAT'S THAT?

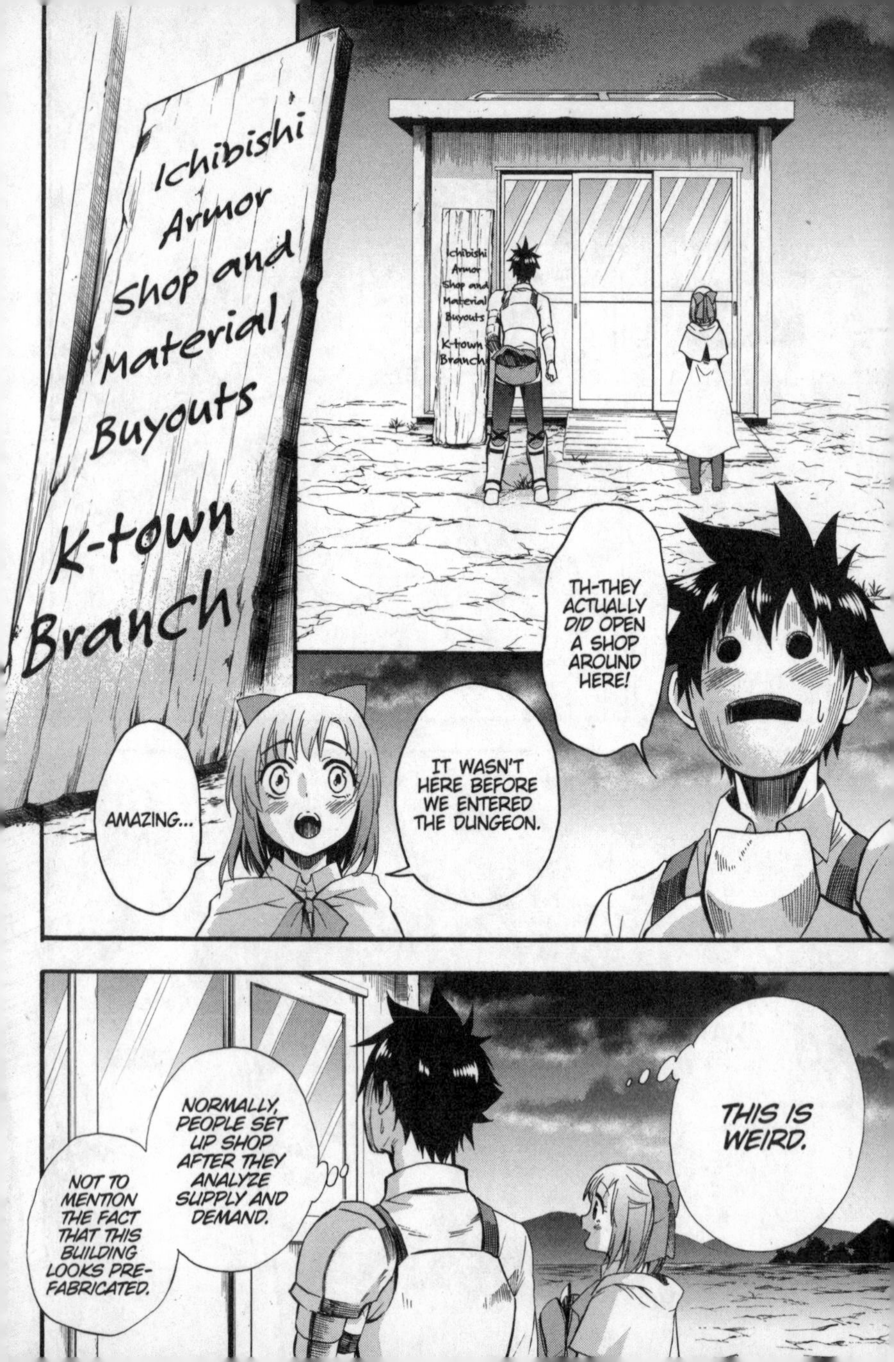
Ichibishi Armor Shop and Material Buyouts K-town Branch
TH-THEY ACTUALLY DID OPEN A SHOP AROUND HERE!
IT WASN'T HERE BEFORE WE ENTERED THE DUNGEON.
AMAZING...
Ichibishi Armor Shop and Material Buyouts
K-town Branch
THIS IS WEIRD.
NORMALLY, PEOPLE SET UP SHOP AFTER THEY ANALYZE SUPPLY AND DEMAND.
NOT TO MENTION THE FACT THAT THIS BUILDING LOOKS PRE-FABRICATED.

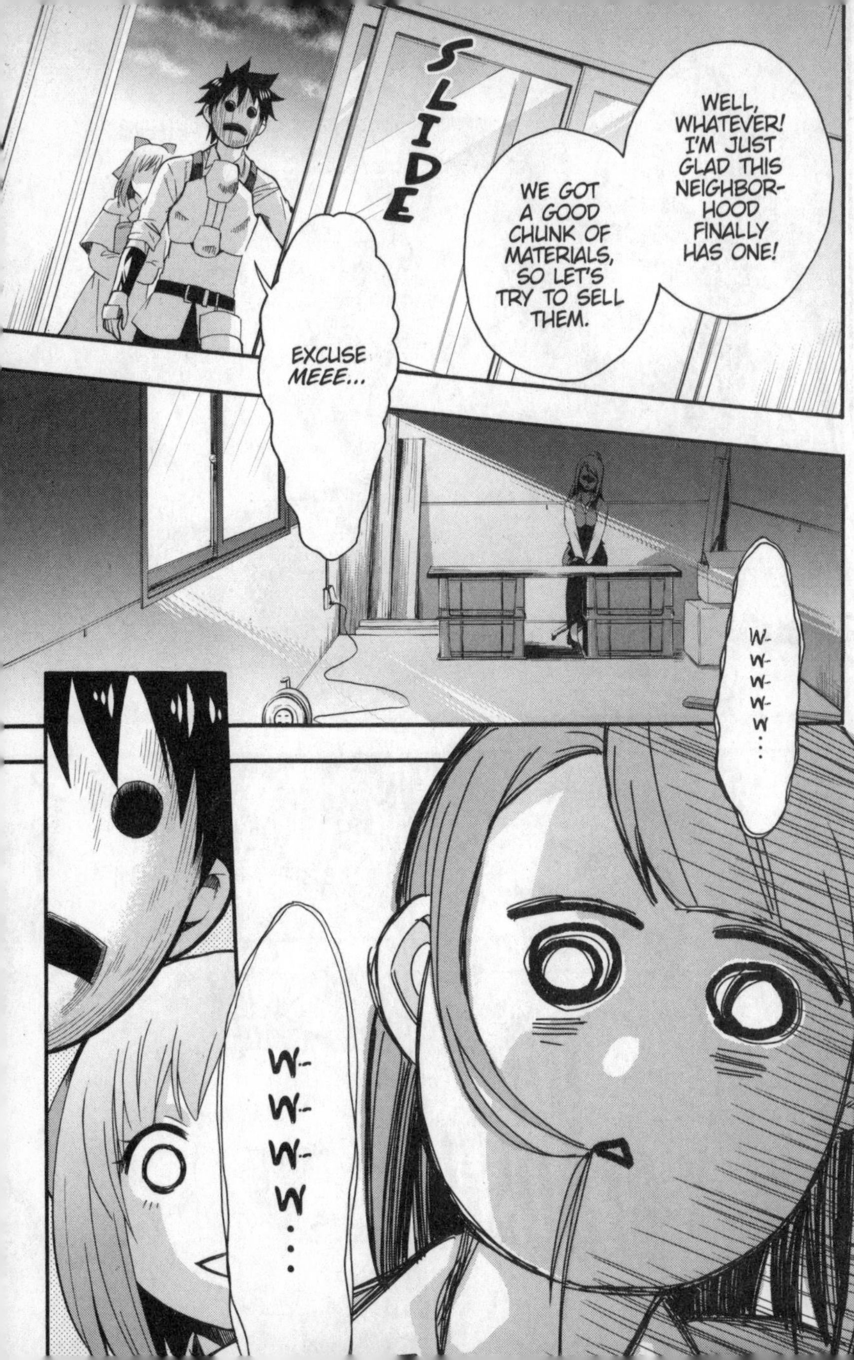
WELL, WHATEVER! I'M JUST GLAD THIS NEIGHBOR-HOOD FINALLY HAS ONE!
WE GOT A GOOD CHUNK OF MATERIALS, SO LET'S TRY TO SELL THEM.
SLIDE
EXCUSE MEEE...
W-W-W-W-W...
W-W-W-W...

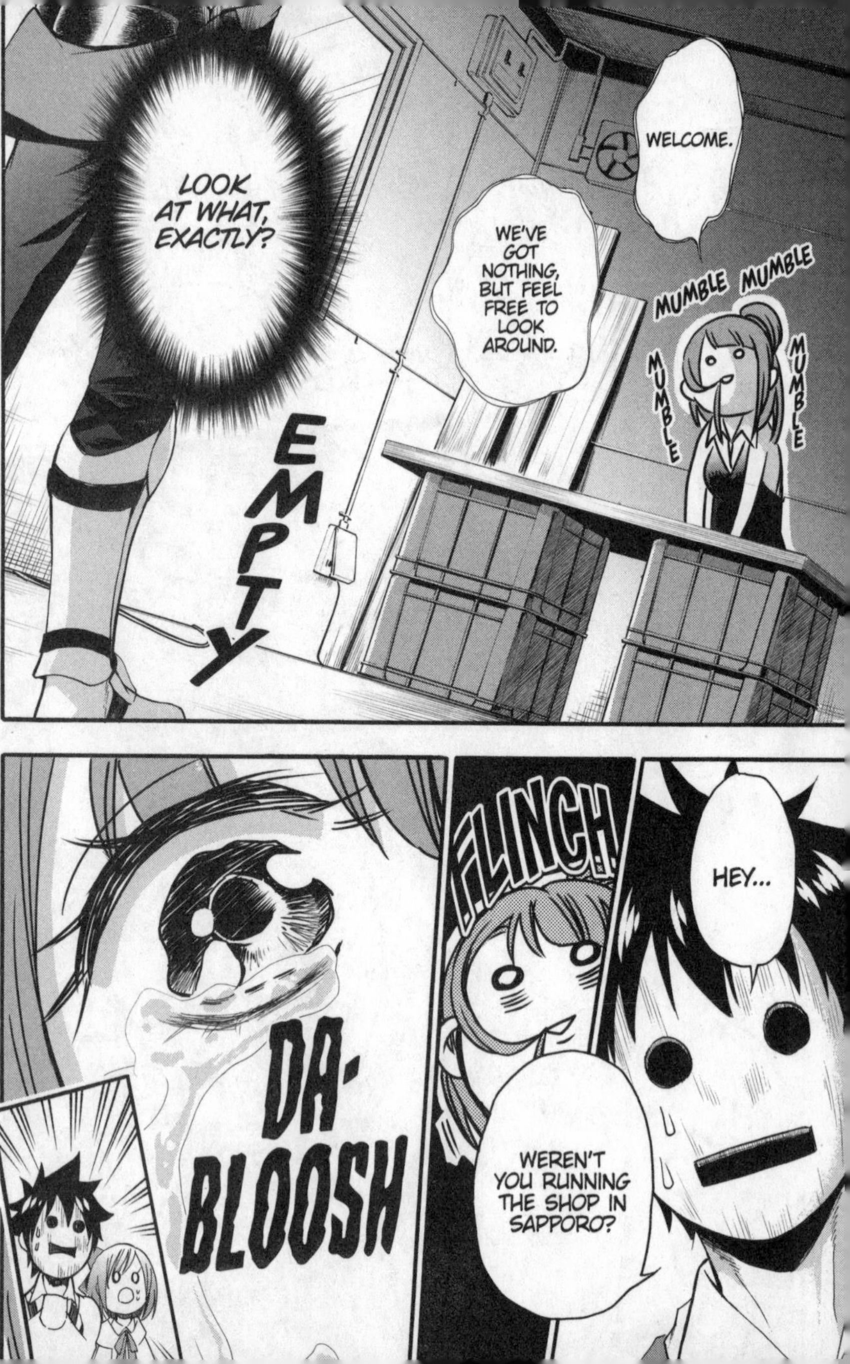
WELCOME.
MUMBLE MUMBLE
MUMBLE
WE'VE GOT NOTHING, BUT FEEL FREE TO LOOK AROUND.
MUMBLE
EMPTY
LOOK AT WHAT, EXACTLY?
HEY...
WEREN'T YOU RUNNING THE SHOP IN SAPPORO?
FLINCH!
DA-BLOOSH

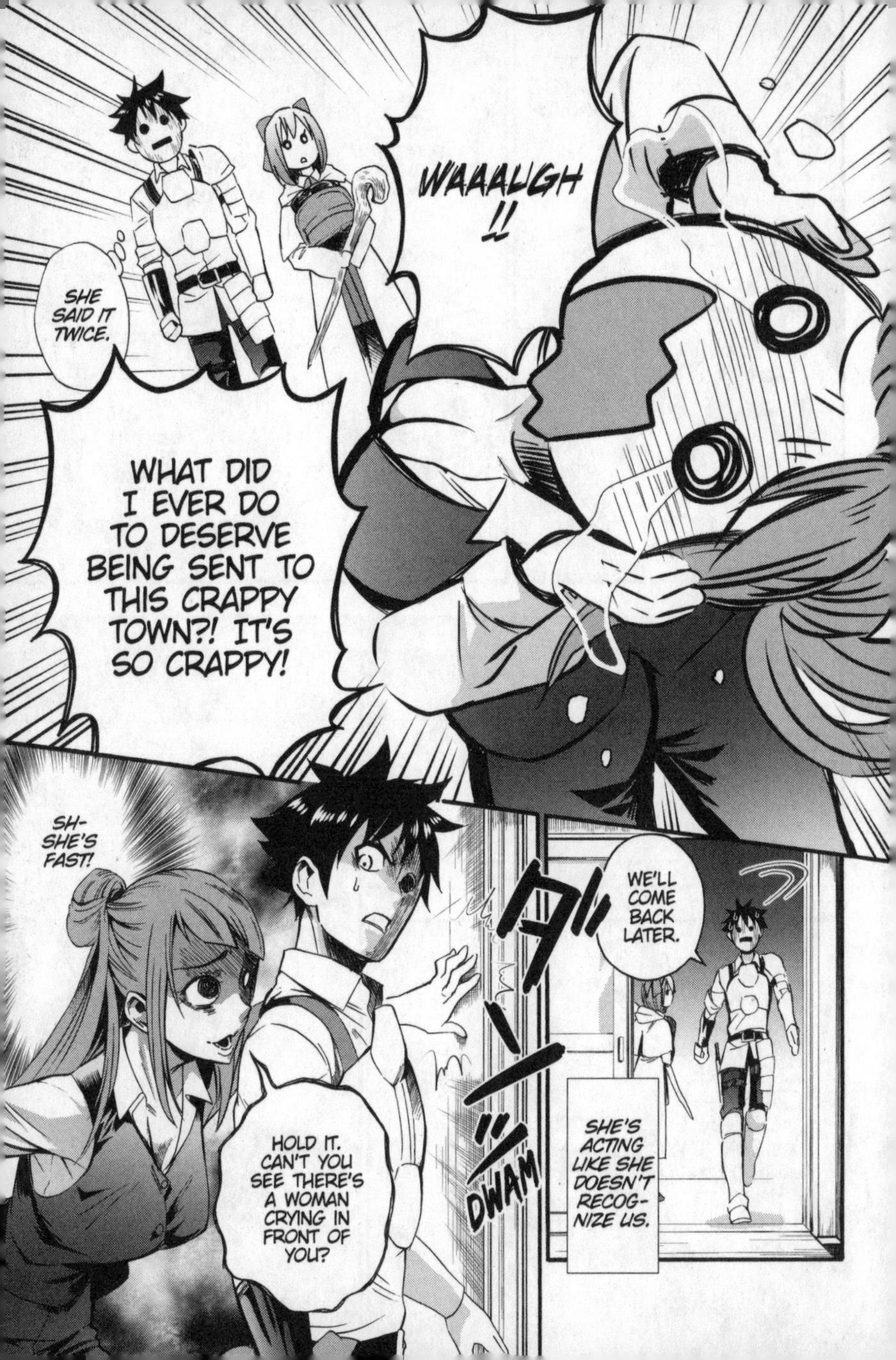
WAAAUGH !!
WHAT DID I EVER DO TO DESERVE BEING SENT TO THIS CRAPPY TOWN?! IT'S SO CRAPPY!
SHE SAID IT TWICE.
WE'LL COME BACK LATER.
SHE'S ACTING LIKE SHE DOESN'T RECOG-NIZE US.
DWAM
SH-SHE'S FAST!
HOLD IT. CAN'T YOU SEE THERE'S A WOMAN CRYING IN FRONT OF YOU?

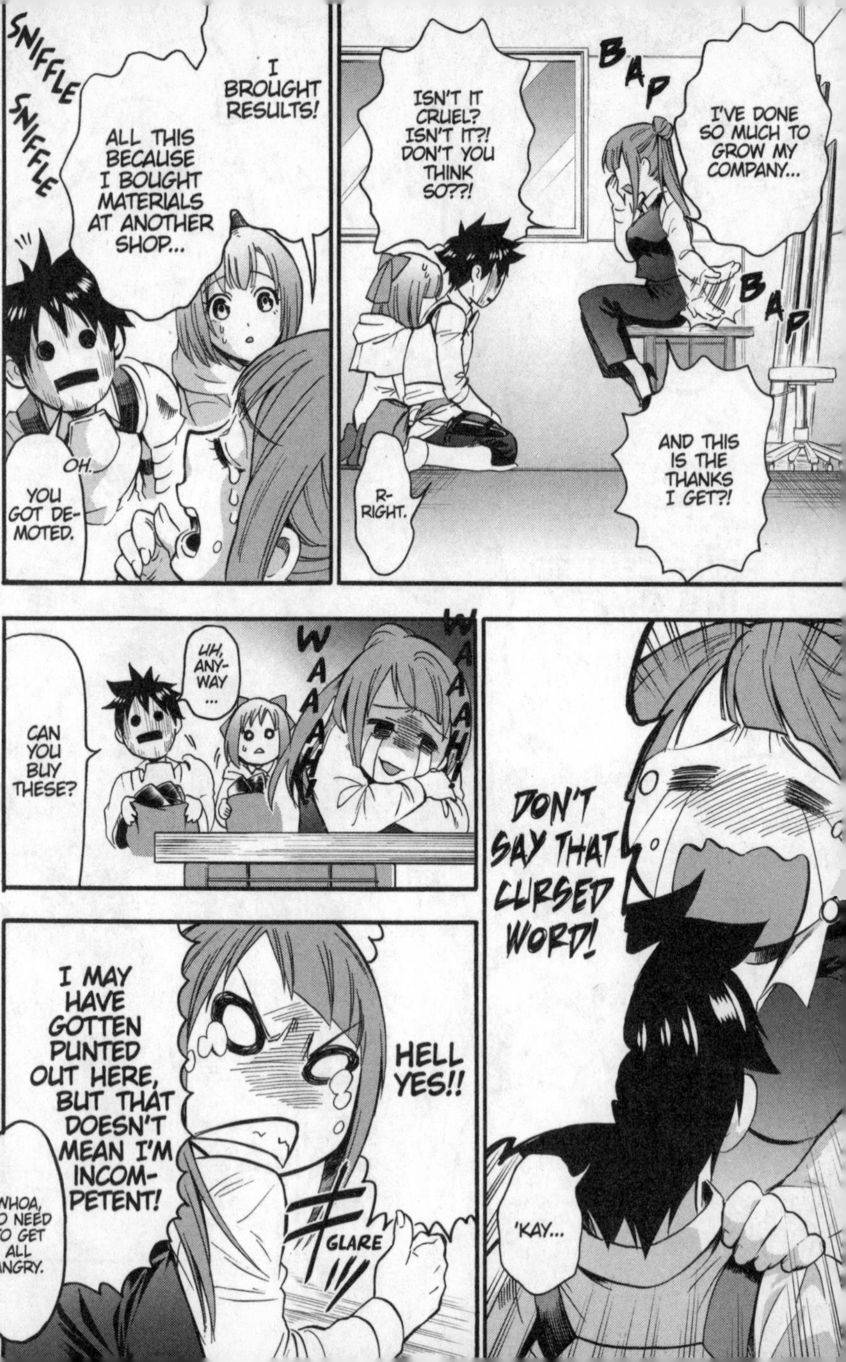

BAP
I'VE DONE SO MUCH TO GROW MY COMPANY...
ISN'T IT CRUEL? ISN'T IT?! DON'T YOU THINK SO??!
BAP
AND THIS IS THE THANKS I GET?!
R-RIGHT.
I BROUGHT RESULTS!
SNIFFLE SNIFFLE
ALL THIS BECAUSE I BOUGHT MATERIALS AT ANOTHER SHOP...
OH.
YOU GOT DE-MOTED.
DON'T SAY THAT CURSED WORD!
'KAY...
WAAAAAH
UH, ANY-WAY...
CAN YOU BUY THESE?
HELL YES!!
I MAY HAVE GOTTEN PUNTED OUT HERE, BUT THAT DOESN'T MEAN I'M INCOM-PETENT!
WHOA, NO NEED TO GET ALL ANGRY.
GLARE

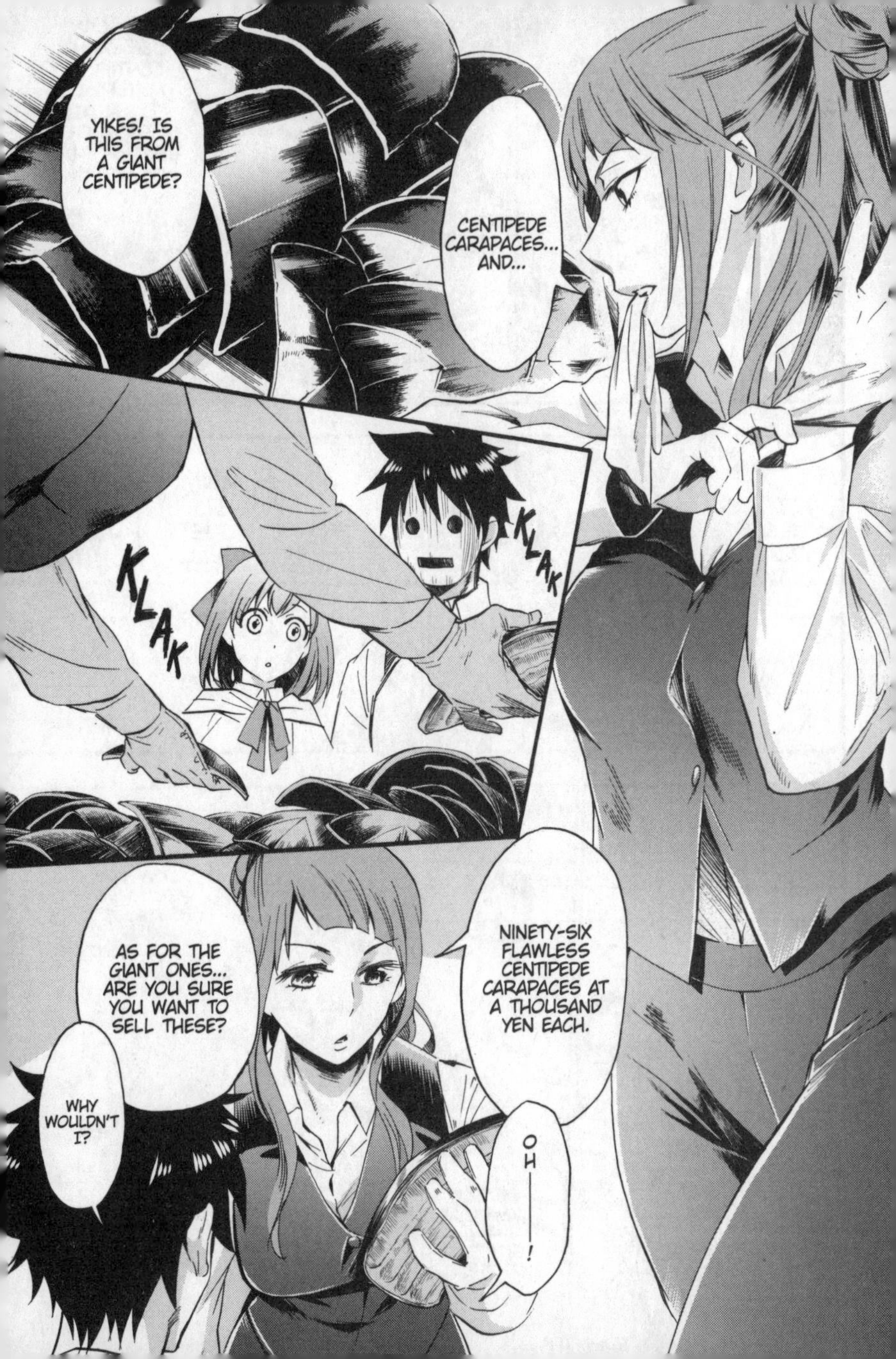
CENTIPEDE CARAPACES... AND...
YIKES! IS THIS FROM A GIANT CENTIPEDE?
KLAK
KLAK
NINETY-SIX FLAWLESS CENTIPEDE CARAPACES AT A THOUSAND YEN EACH.
AS FOR THE GIANT ONES... ARE YOU SURE YOU WANT TO SELL THESE?
WHY WOULDN'T I?
OH—!

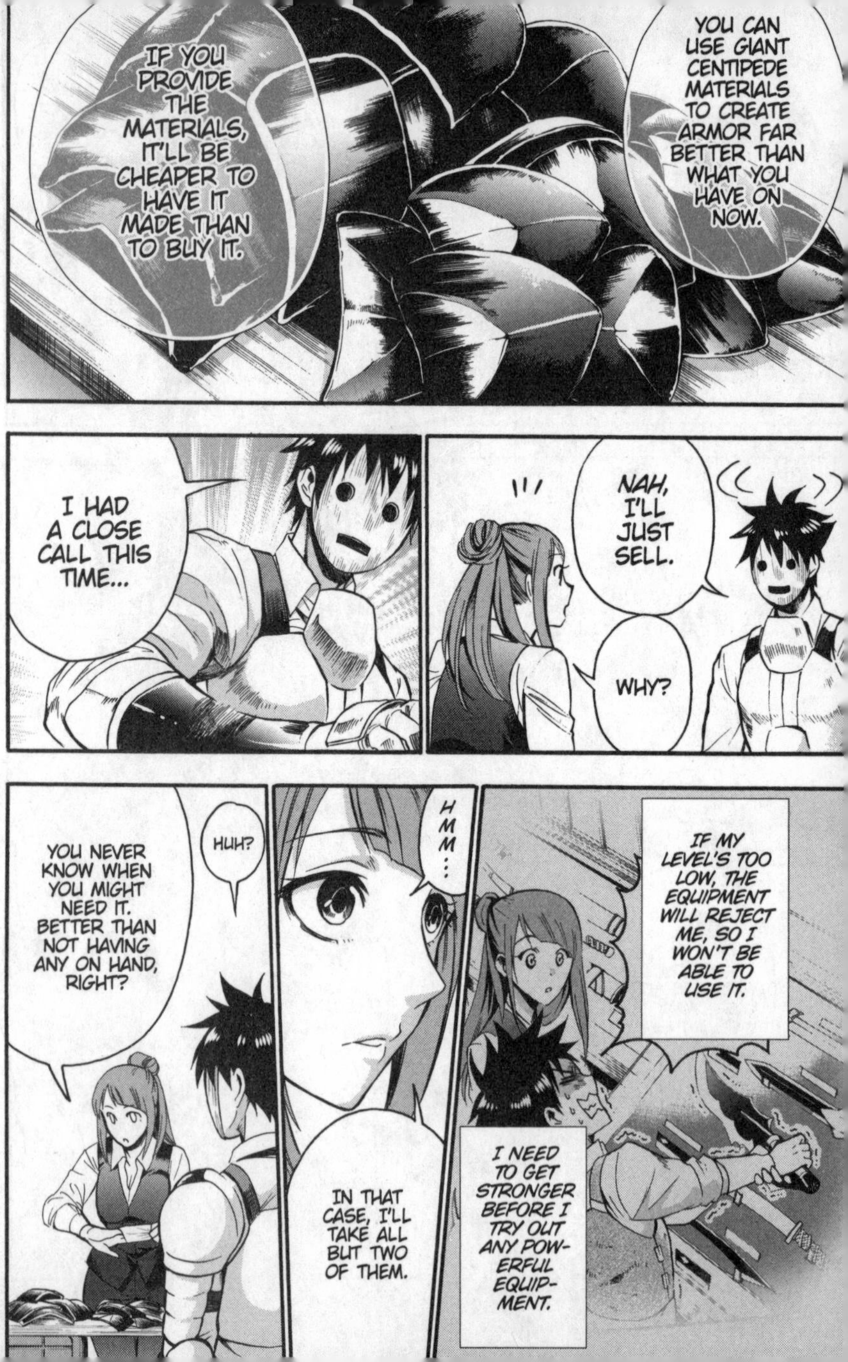
YOU CAN USE GIANT CENTIPEDE MATERIALS TO CREATE ARMOR FAR BETTER THAN WHAT YOU HAVE ON NOW.
IF YOU PROVIDE THE MATERIALS, IT'LL BE CHEAPER TO HAVE IT MADE THAN TO BUY IT.
NAH, I'LL JUST SELL.
WHY?
I HAD A CLOSE CALL THIS TIME...
IF MY LEVEL'S TOO LOW, THE EQUIPMENT WILL REJECT ME, SO I WON'T BE ABLE TO USE IT.
I NEED TO GET STRONGER BEFORE I TRY OUT ANY POW-ERFUL EQUIP-MENT.
HMM...
IN THAT CASE, I'LL TAKE ALL BUT TWO OF THEM.
HUH?
YOU NEVER KNOW WHEN YOU MIGHT NEED IT. BETTER THAN NOT HAVING ANY ON HAND, RIGHT?

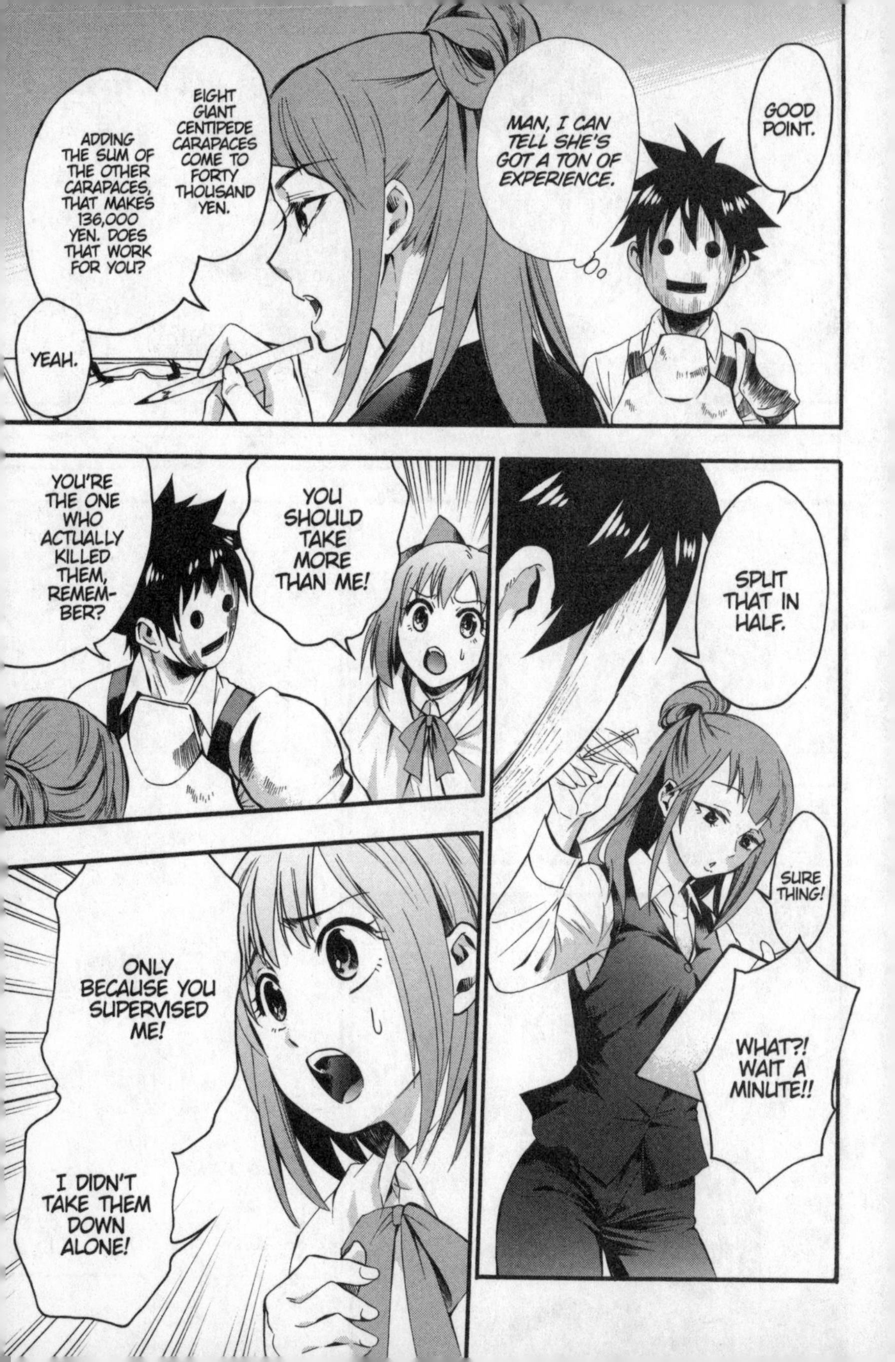
GOOD POINT.
MAN, I CAN TELL SHE'S GOT A TON OF EXPERIENCE.
EIGHT GIANT CENTIPEDE CARAPACES COME TO FORTY THOUSAND YEN.
ADDING THE SUM OF THE OTHER CARAPACES, THAT MAKES 136,000 YEN. DOES THAT WORK FOR YOU?
YEAH.
SPLIT THAT IN HALF.
SURE THING!
WHAT?! WAIT A MINUTE!!
YOU SHOULD TAKE MORE THAN ME!
YOU'RE THE ONE WHO ACTUALLY KILLED THEM, REMEMBER-BER?
ONLY BECAUSE YOU SUPERVISED ME!
I DIDN'T TAKE THEM DOWN ALONE!

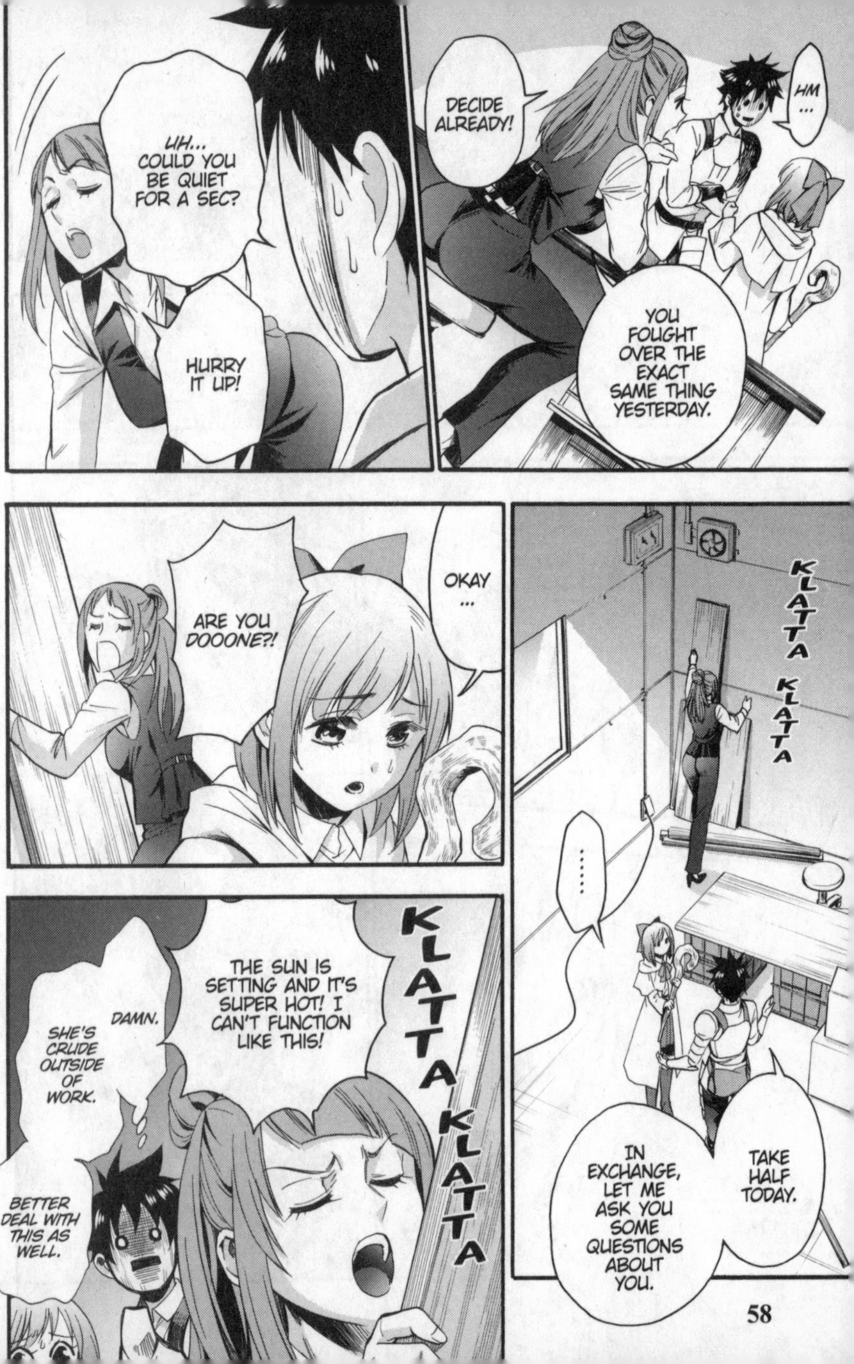
HM ...
DECIDE ALREADY!
YOU FOUGHT OVER THE EXACT SAME THING YESTERDAY.
UH... COULD YOU BE QUIET FOR A SEC?
HURRY IT UP!
KLATTA KLATTA KLATTA
......
TAKE HALF TODAY.
IN EXCHANGE, LET ME ASK YOU SOME QUESTIONS ABOUT YOU.
OKAY ...
ARE YOU DOOONE?!
KLATTA KLATTA
THE SUN IS SETTING AND IT'S SUPER HOT! I CAN'T FUNCTION LIKE THIS!
DAMN.
SHE'S CRUDE OUTSIDE OF WORK.
BETTER DEAL WITH THIS AS WELL.

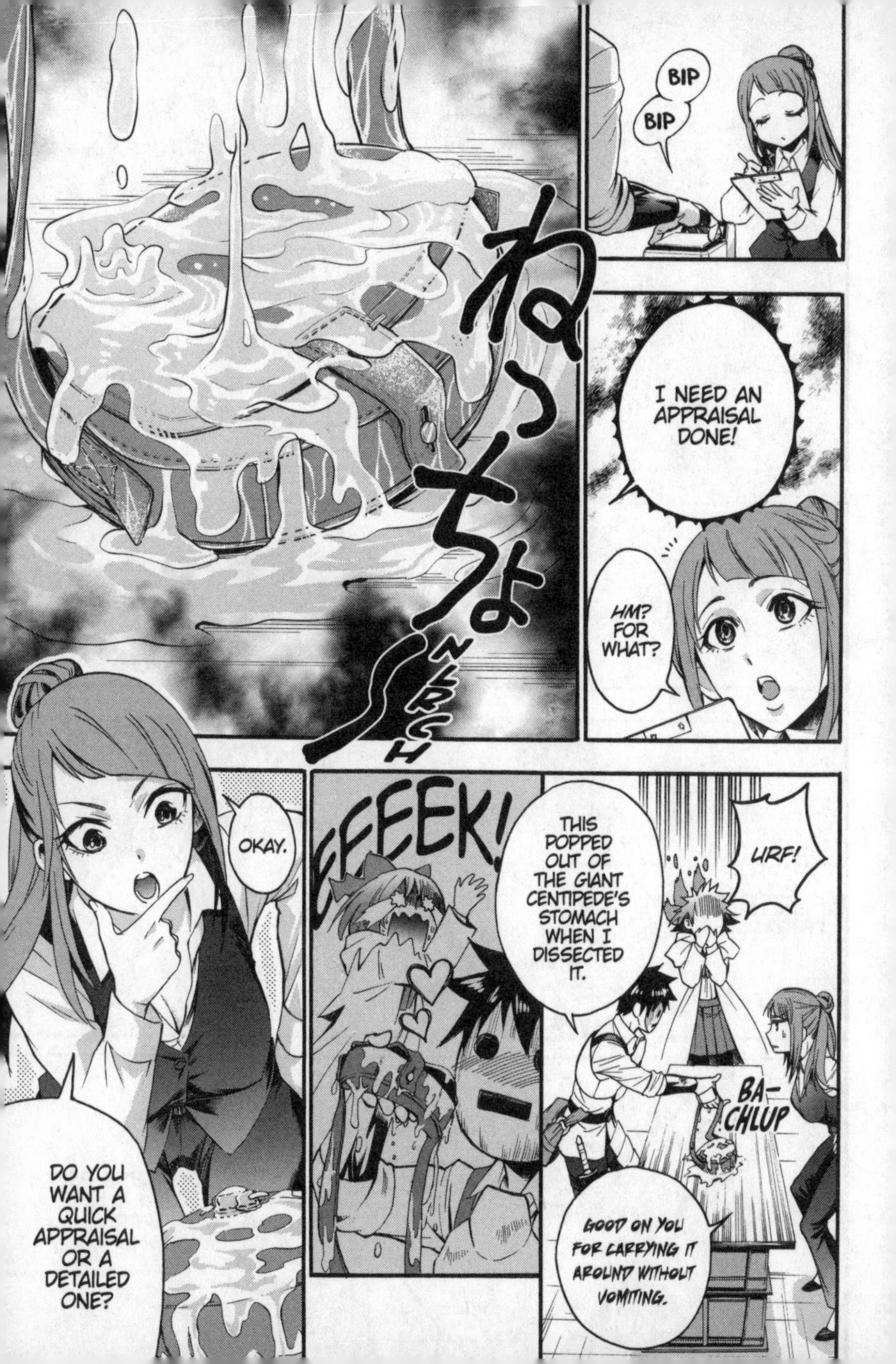
BIP
BIP
I NEED AN APPRAISAL DONE!
HM? FOR WHAT?
ねっちょ
NTRCH
URF!
THIS POPPED OUT OF THE GIANT CENTIPEDE'S STOMACH WHEN I DISSECTED IT.
BA-CHLUP
GOOD ON YOU FOR CARRYING IT AROUND WITHOUT VOMITING.
EEEEK!
OKAY.
DO YOU WANT A QUICK APPRAISAL OR A DETAILED ONE?

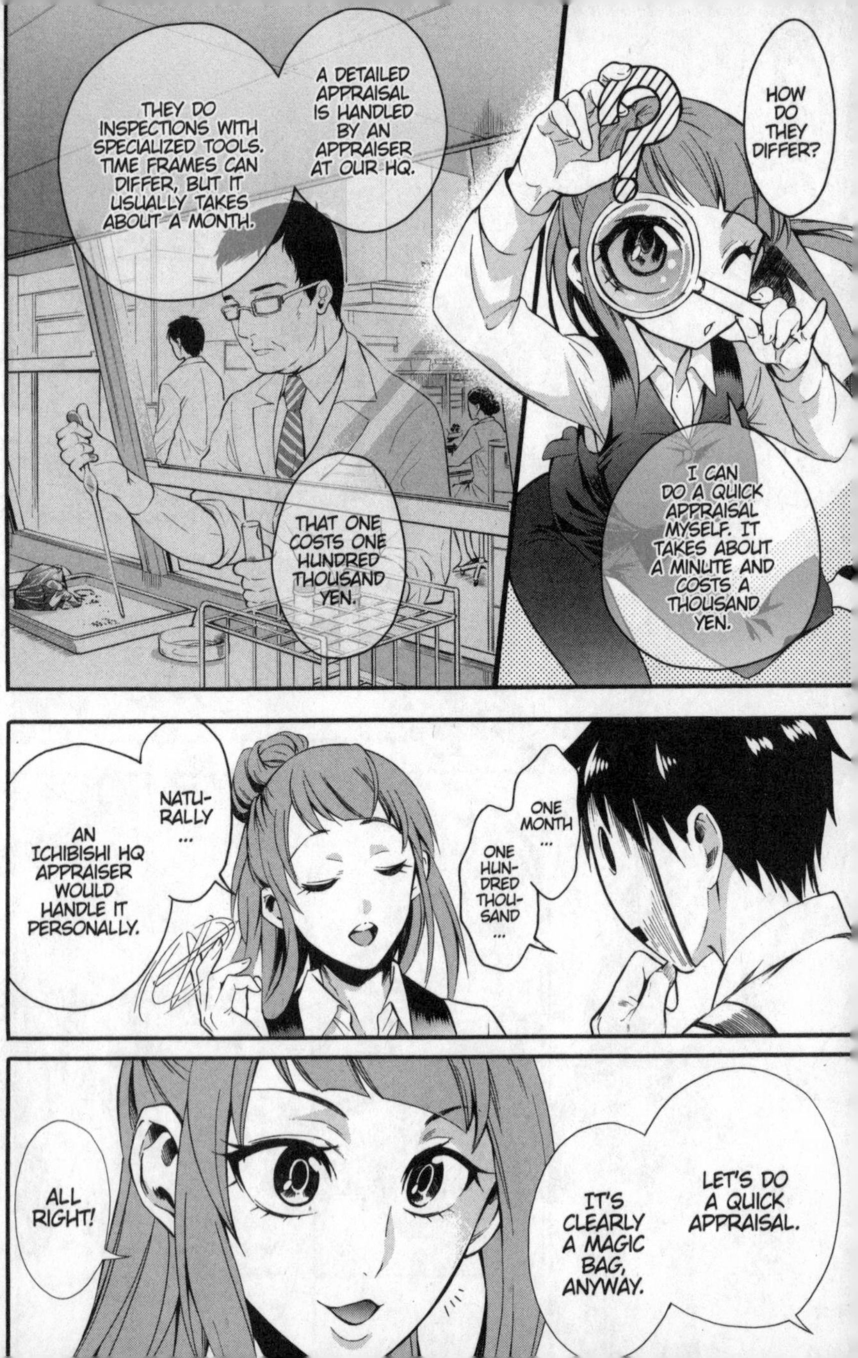
HOW DO THEY DIFFER?
I CAN DO A QUICK APPRAISAL MYSELF. IT TAKES ABOUT A MINUTE AND COSTS A THOUSAND YEN.
A DETAILED APPRAISAL IS HANDLED BY AN APPRAISER AT OUR HQ.
THEY DO INSPECTIONS WITH SPECIALIZED TOOLS. TIME FRAMES CAN DIFFER, BUT IT USUALLY TAKES ABOUT A MONTH.
THAT ONE COSTS ONE HUNDRED THOUSAND YEN.
ONE MONTH ...
ONE HUNDRED THOUSAND ...
NATURALLY ...
AN ICHIBISHI HQ APPRAISER WOULD HANDLE IT PERSONALLY.
LET'S DO A QUICK APPRAISAL.
IT'S CLEARLY A MAGIC BAG, ANYWAY.
ALL RIGHT!

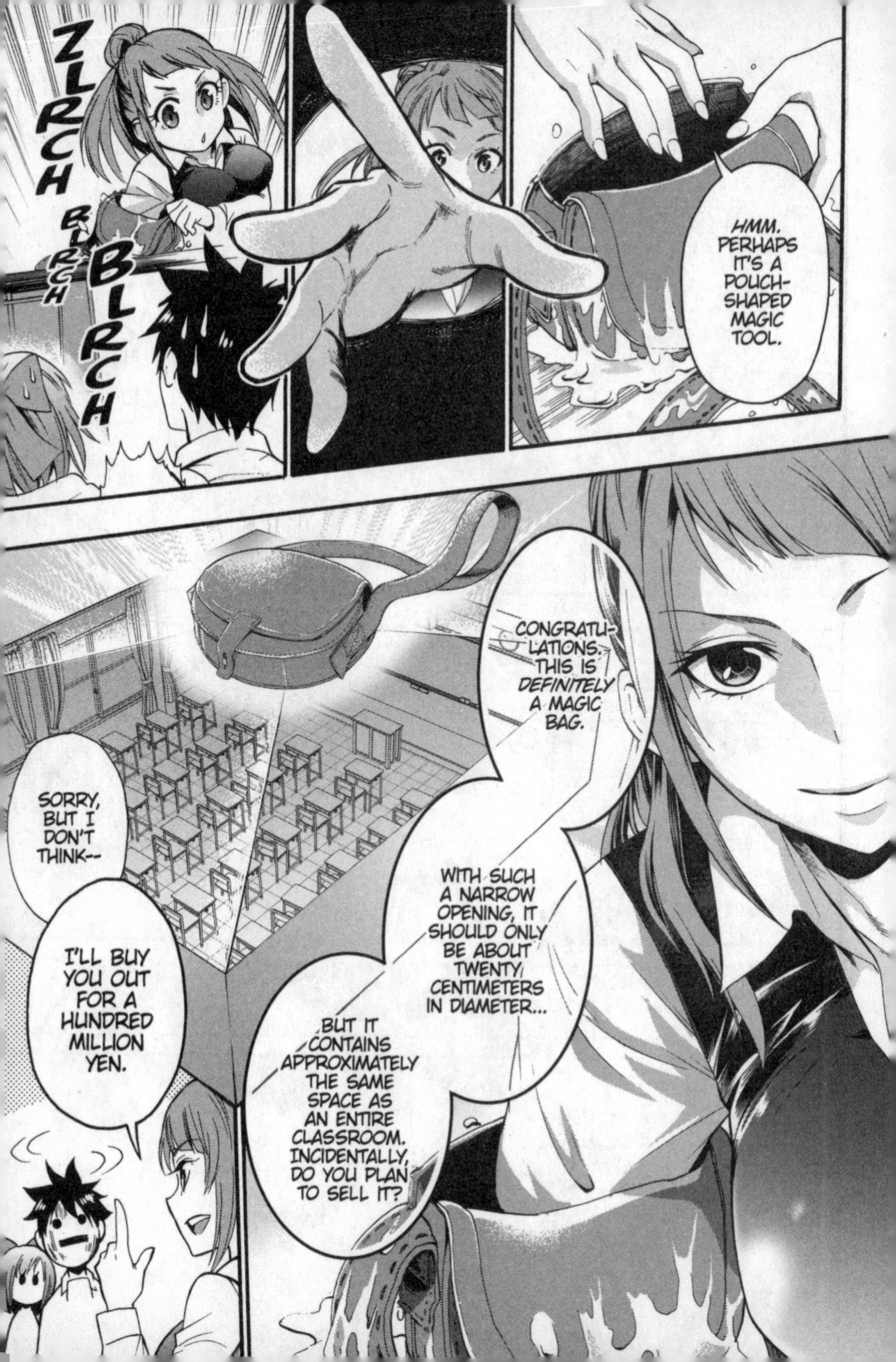
HMM. PERHAPS IT'S A POUCH-SHAPED MAGIC TOOL.
ZLRCH
BLRCH
BLRCH
CONGRATULATIONS. THIS IS DEFINITELY A MAGIC BAG.
WITH SUCH A NARROW OPENING, IT SHOULD ONLY BE ABOUT TWENTY CENTIMETERS IN DIAMETER...
...BUT IT CONTAINS APPROXIMATELY THE SAME SPACE AS AN ENTIRE CLASSROOM. INCIDENTALLY, DO YOU PLAN TO SELL IT?
SORRY, BUT I DON'T THINK--
I'LL BUY YOU OUT FOR A HUNDRED MILLION YEN.

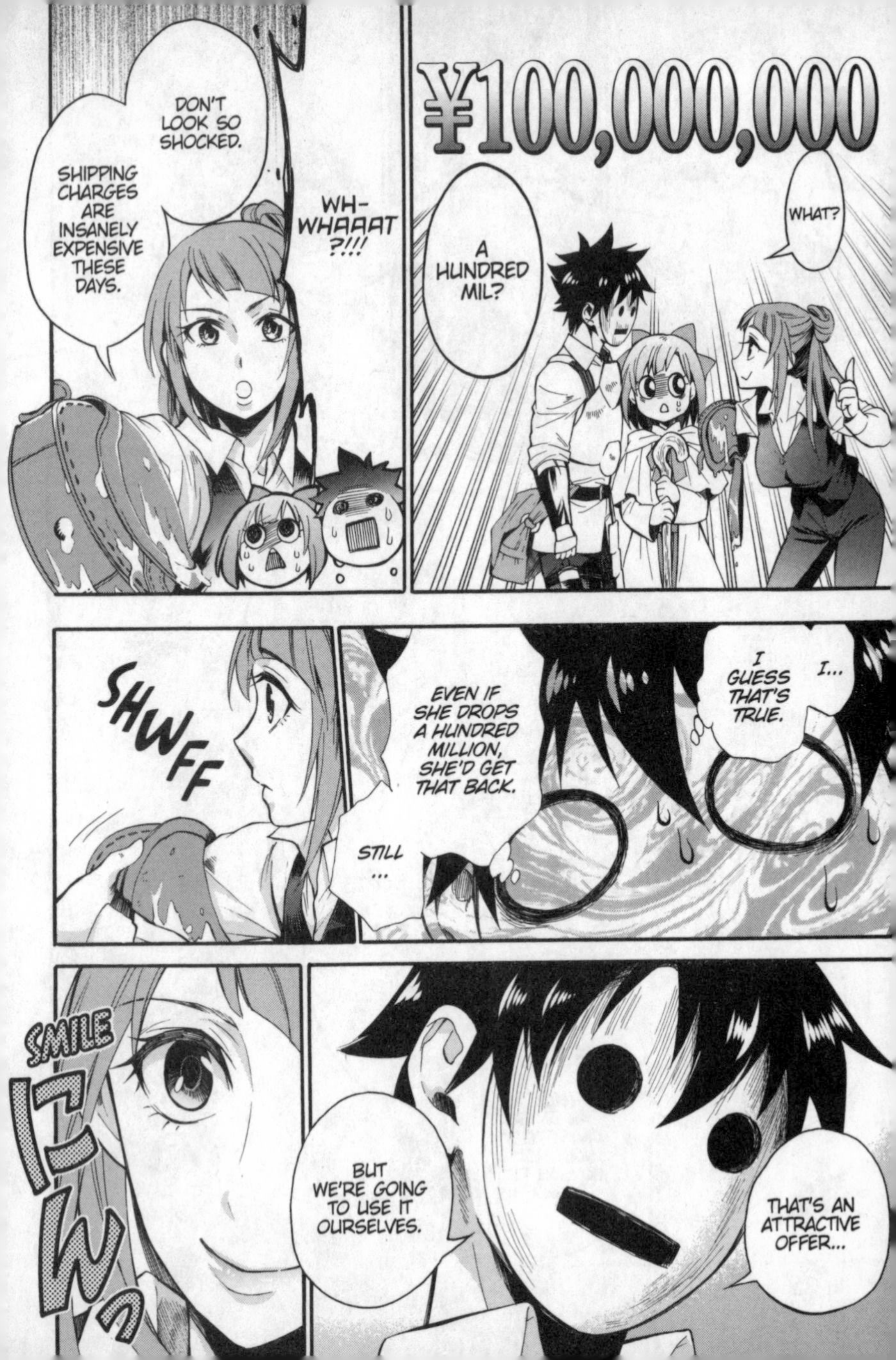
¥100,000,000
WHAT?
A HUNDRED MIL?
WH-WHAAAT?!!!
DON'T LOOK SO SHOCKED.
SHIPPING CHARGES ARE INSANELY EXPENSIVE THESE DAYS.
I...
I GUESS THAT'S TRUE.
EVEN IF SHE DROPS A HUNDRED MILLION, SHE'D GET THAT BACK.
STILL...
SHWFF
THAT'S AN ATTRACTIVE OFFER...
BUT WE'RE GOING TO USE IT OURSELVES.
SMILE

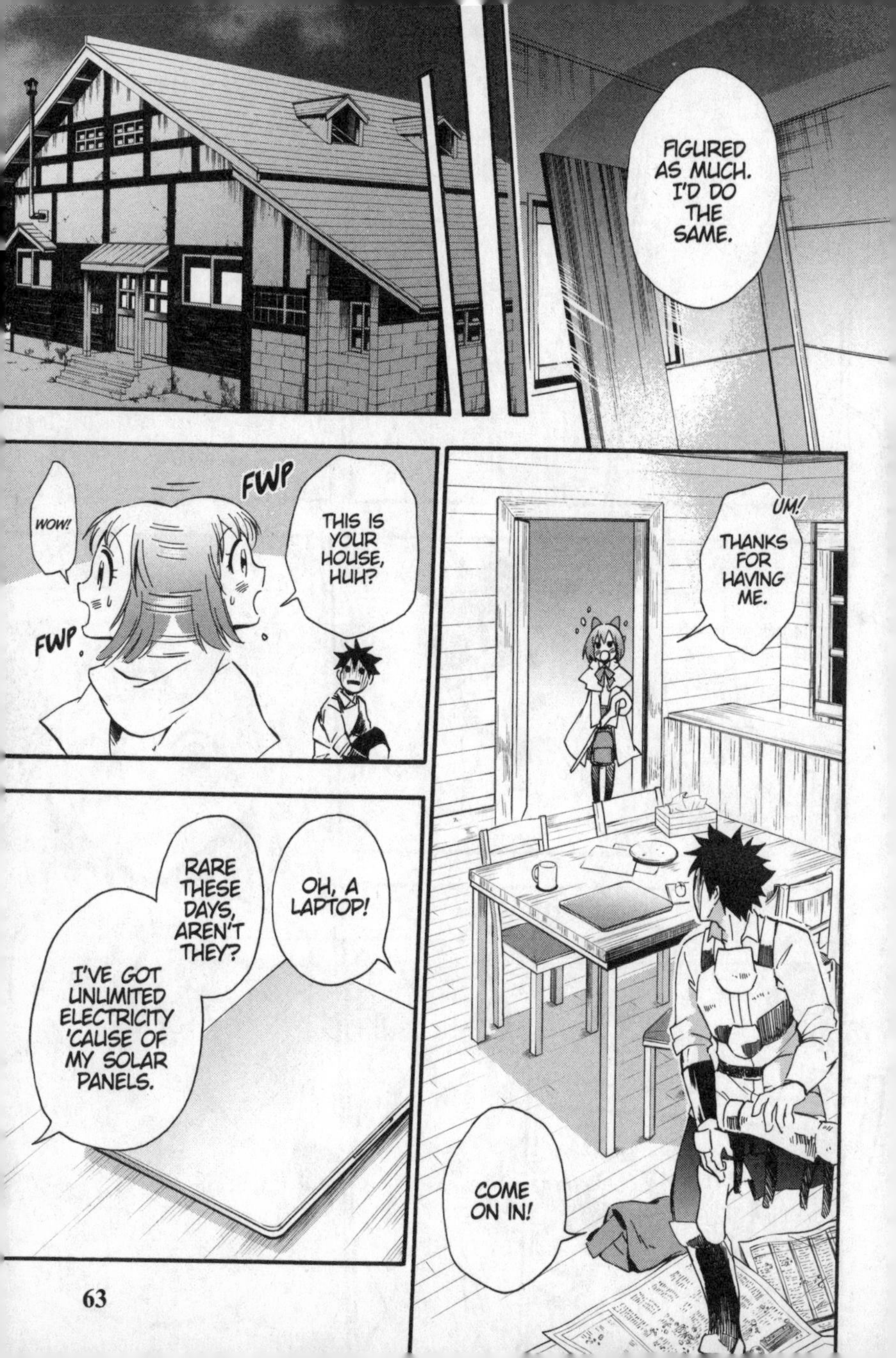
FIGURED AS MUCH. I'D DO THE SAME.
UM!
THANKS FOR HAVING ME.
COME ON IN!
FWP
THIS IS YOUR HOUSE, HUH?
WOW!
FWP
OH, A LAPTOP!
RARE THESE DAYS, AREN'T THEY?
I'VE GOT UNLIMITED ELECTRICITY 'CAUSE OF MY SOLAR PANELS.

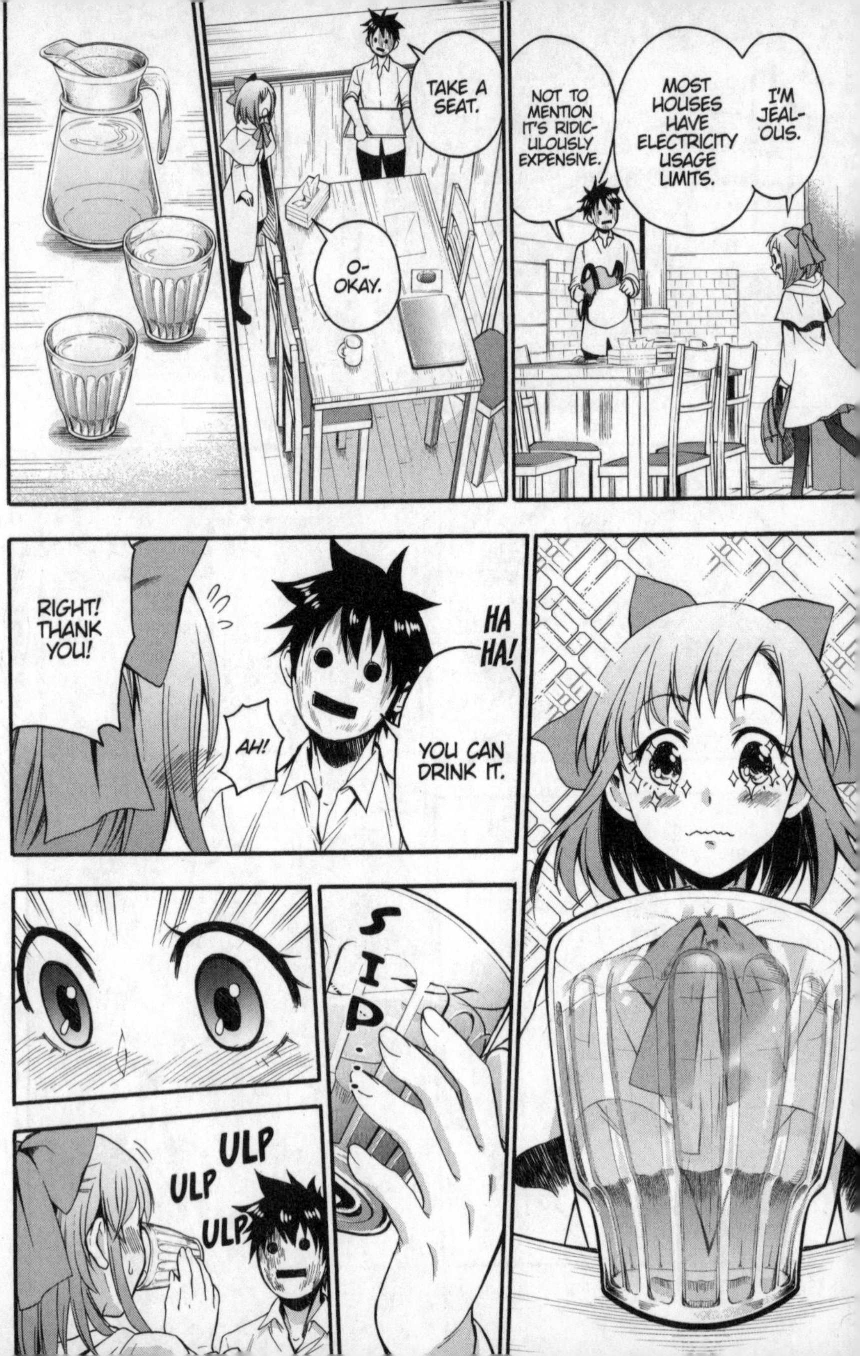
I'M JEAL-OUS.
MOST HOUSES HAVE ELECTRICITY USAGE LIMITS.
NOT TO MENTION IT'S RIDIC-ULOUSLY EXPENSIVE.
TAKE A SEAT.
O-OKAY.
HA HA!
YOU CAN DRINK IT.
AH!
RIGHT! THANK YOU!
SIP...
ULP
ULP
ULP

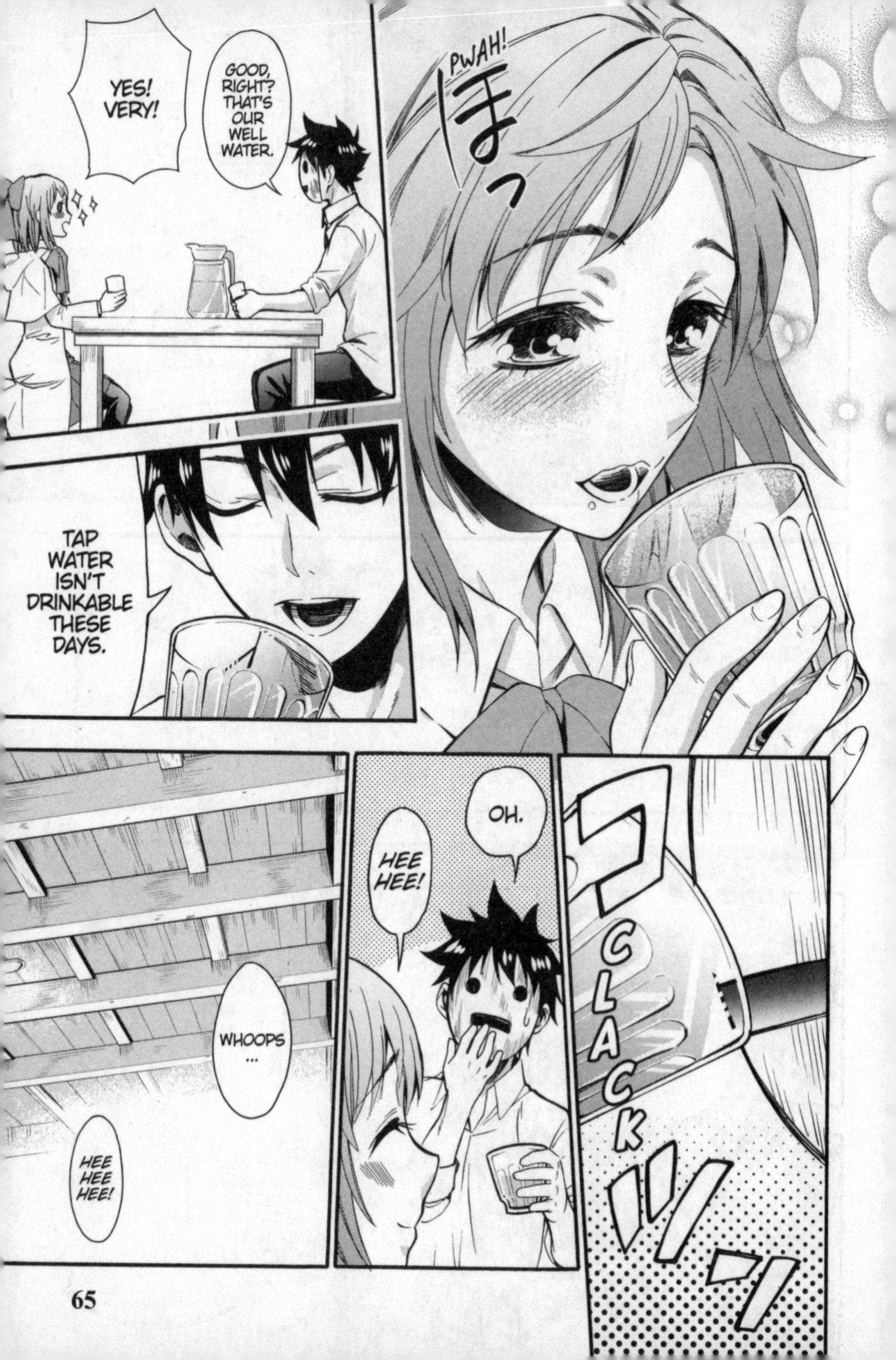
PWAH!
ほっ
GOOD, RIGHT? THAT'S OUR WELL WATER.
YES! VERY!
TAP WATER ISN'T DRINKABLE THESE DAYS.
CLACK
OH.
HEE HEE!
WHOOPS ...
HEE HEE HEE!

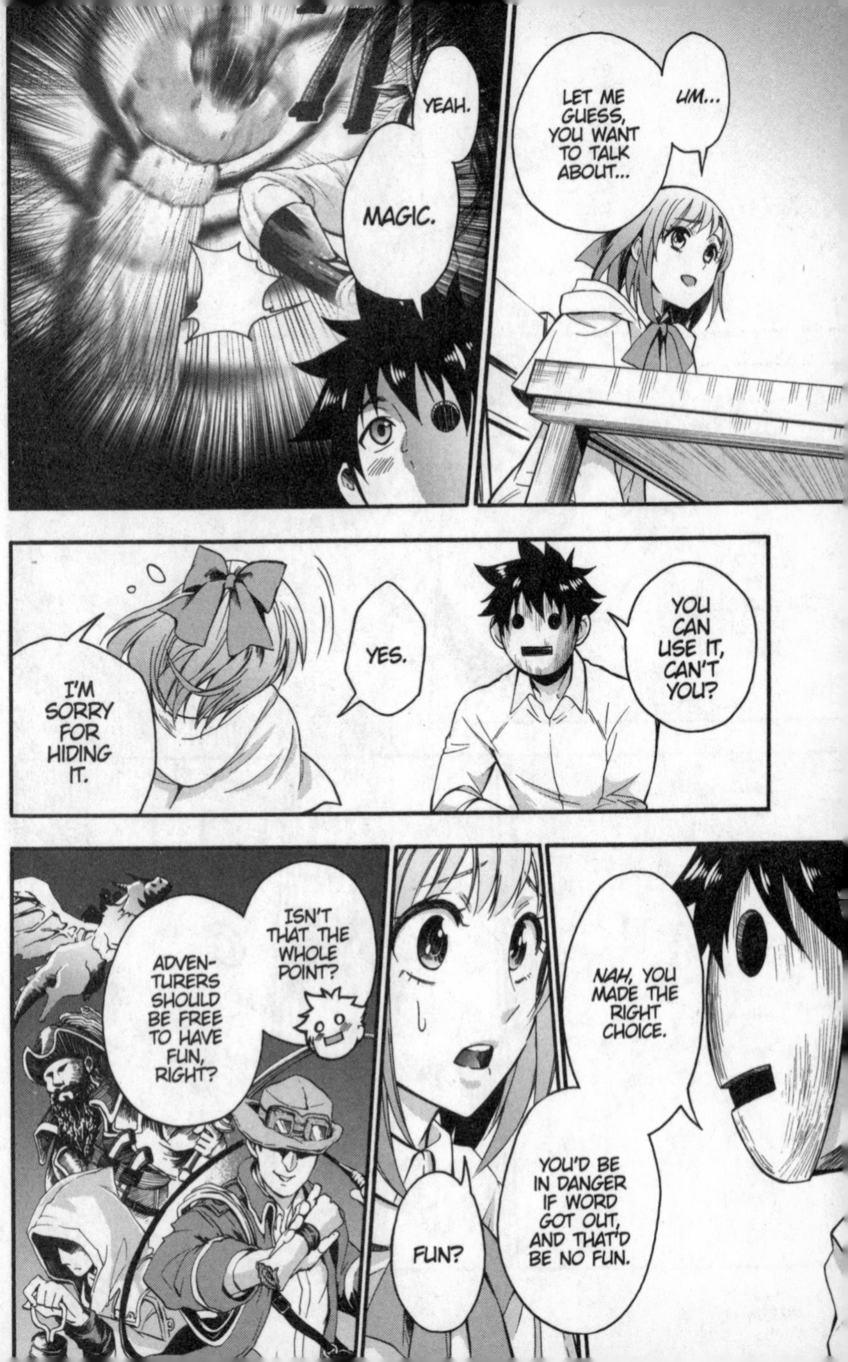
UM...
LET ME GUESS, YOU WANT TO TALK ABOUT...
YEAH.
MAGIC.
YOU CAN USE IT, CAN'T YOU?
YES.
I'M SORRY FOR HIDING IT.
NAH, YOU MADE THE RIGHT CHOICE.
YOU'D BE IN DANGER IF WORD GOT OUT, AND THAT'D BE NO FUN.
FUN?
ISN'T THAT THE WHOLE POINT?
ADVEN-TURERS SHOULD BE FREE TO HAVE FUN, RIGHT?

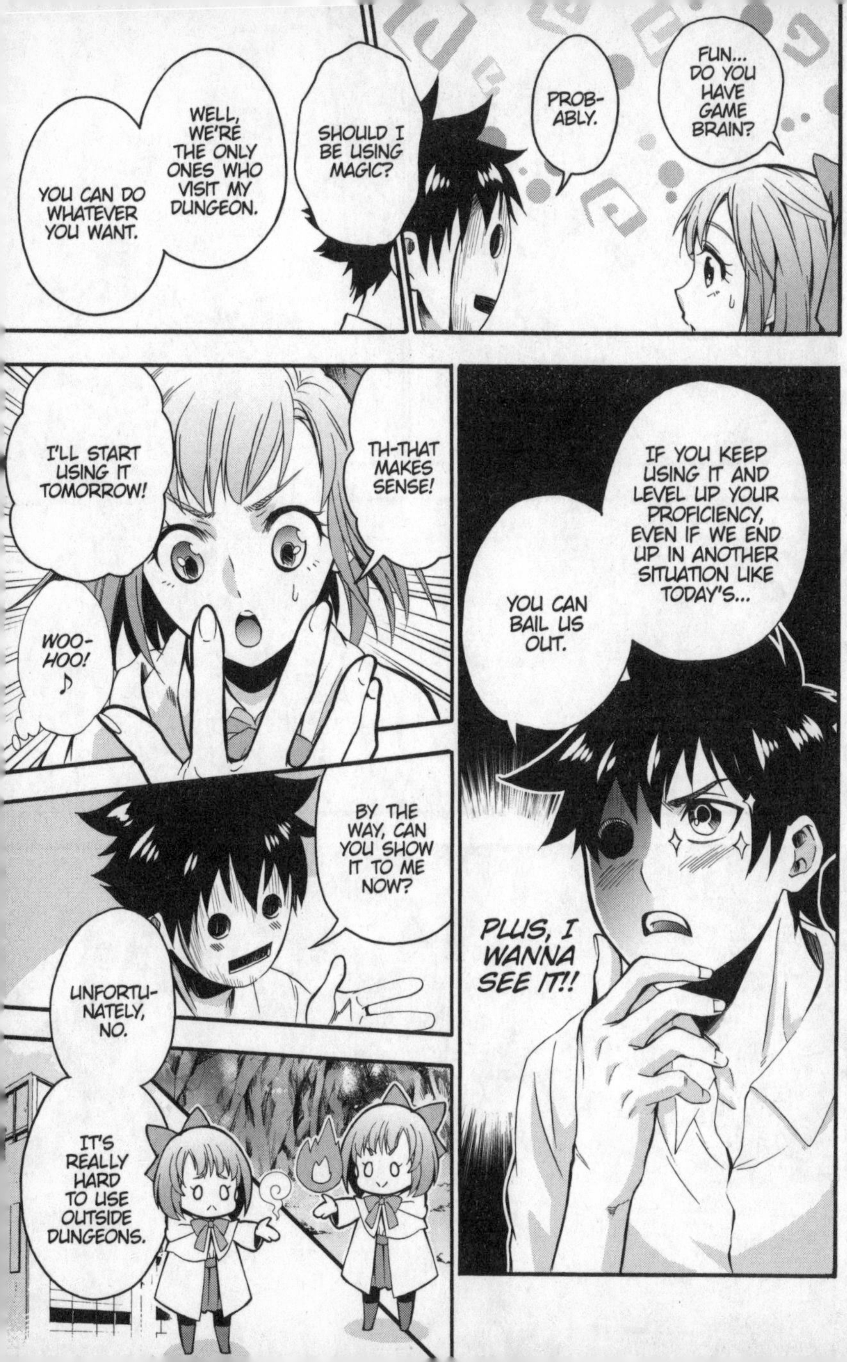
FUN... DO YOU HAVE GAME BRAIN?
PROB-ABLY.
SHOULD I BE USING MAGIC?
WELL, WE'RE THE ONLY ONES WHO VISIT MY DUNGEON.
YOU CAN DO WHATEVER YOU WANT.
IF YOU KEEP USING IT AND LEVEL UP YOUR PROFICIENCY, EVEN IF WE END UP IN ANOTHER SITUATION LIKE TODAY'S...
YOU CAN BAIL US OUT.
PLUS, I WANNA SEE IT!!
TH-THAT MAKES SENSE!
I'LL START USING IT TOMORROW!
WOO-HOO! ♪
BY THE WAY, CAN YOU SHOW IT TO ME NOW?
UNFORTU-NATELY, NO.
IT'S REALLY HARD TO USE OUTSIDE DUNGEONS.

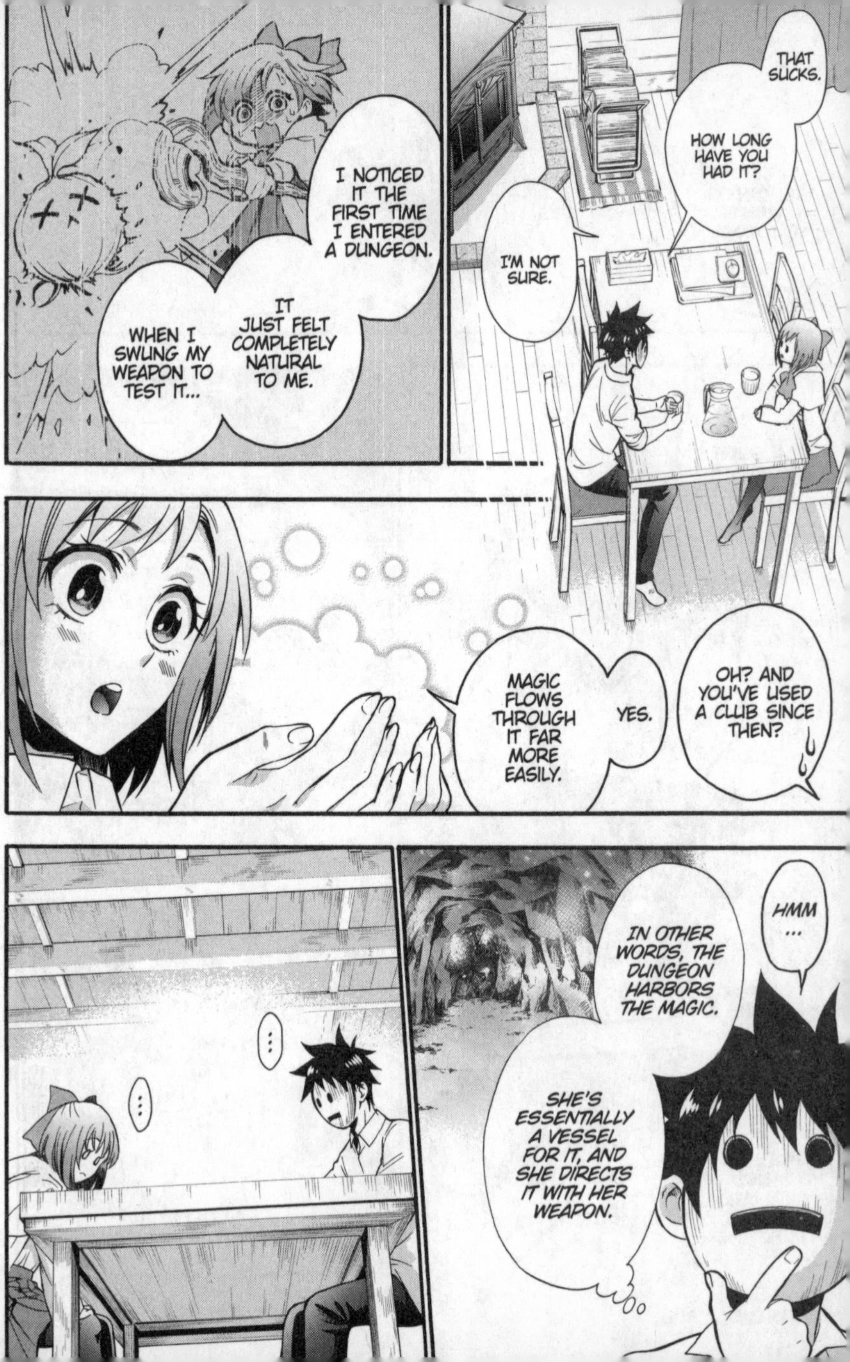
THAT SUCKS.
HOW LONG HAVE YOU HAD IT?
I'M NOT SURE.
I NOTICED IT THE FIRST TIME I ENTERED A DUNGEON.
IT JUST FELT COMPLETELY NATURAL TO ME.
WHEN I SWUNG MY WEAPON TO TEST IT...
OH? AND YOU'VE USED A CLUB SINCE THEN?
YES.
MAGIC FLOWS THROUGH IT FAR MORE EASILY.
HMM...
IN OTHER WORDS, THE DUNGEON HARBORS THE MAGIC.
SHE'S ESSENTIALLY A VESSEL FOR IT, AND SHE DIRECTS IT WITH HER WEAPON.
...
...

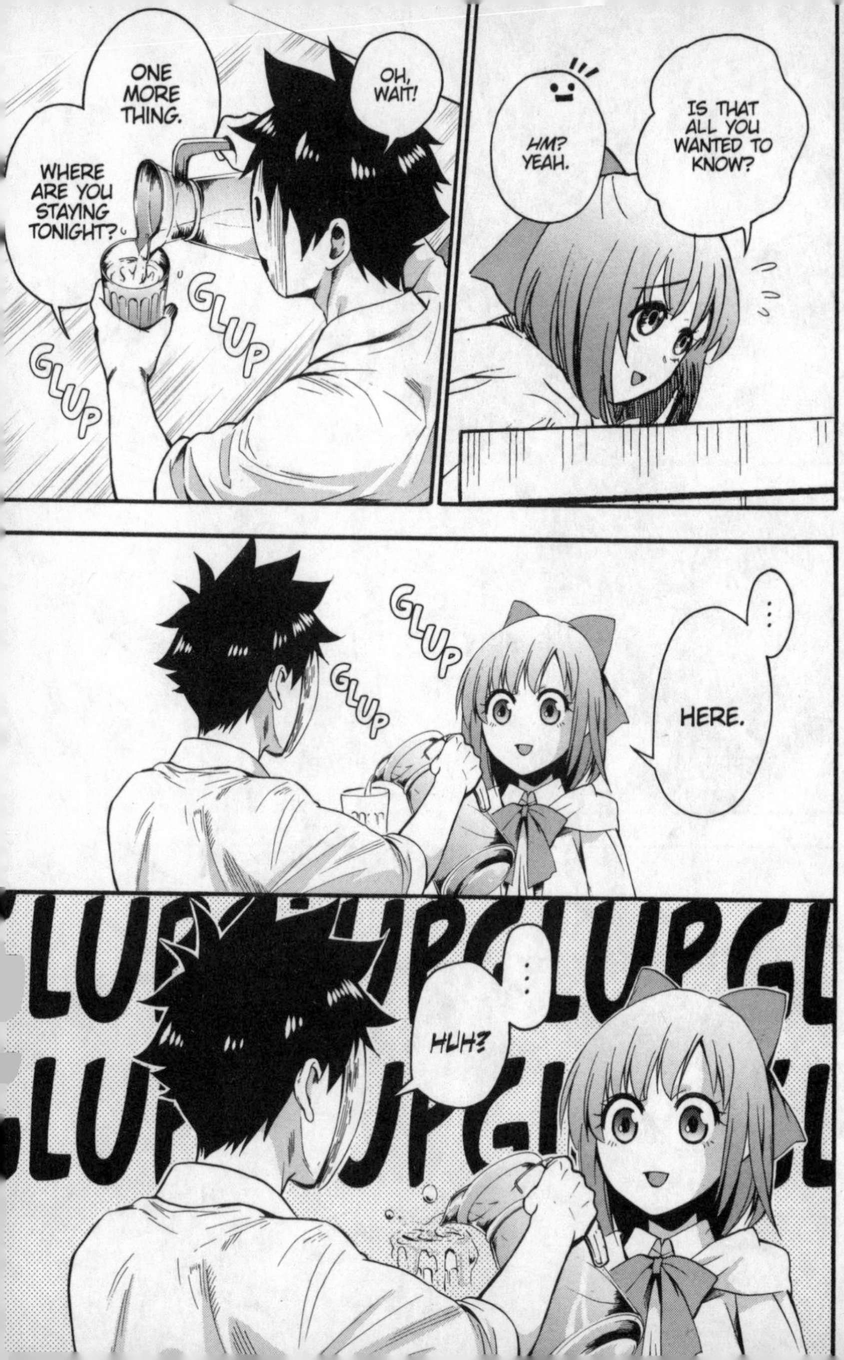
IS THAT ALL YOU WANTED TO KNOW?
HM? YEAH.
OH, WAIT!
ONE MORE THING.
WHERE ARE YOU STAYING TONIGHT?
GLUP
GLUP
... HERE.
GLUP
GLUP
... HUH?

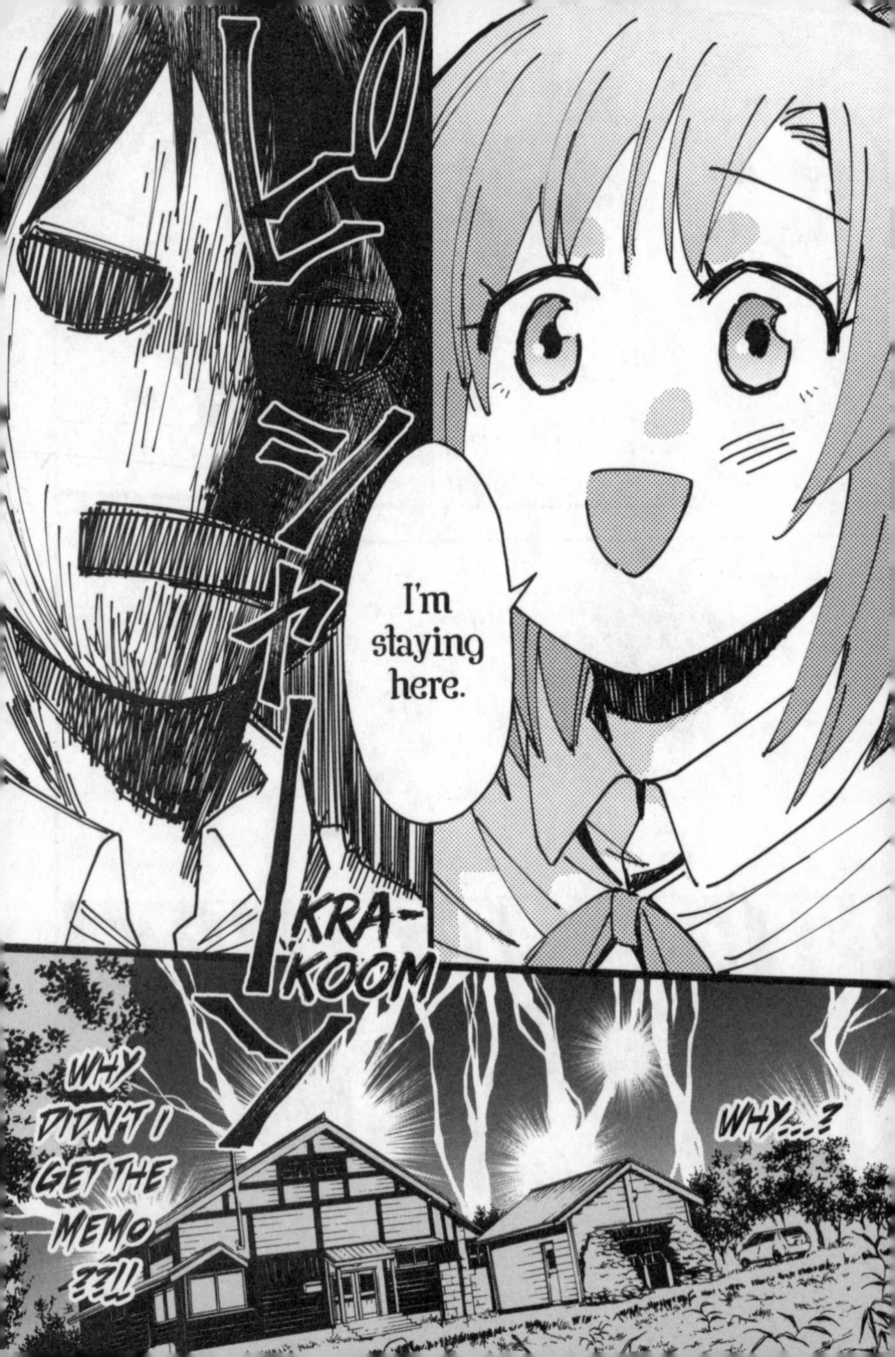
I'm staying here.
KRA-KOOM
WHY...?
WHY DIDN'T I GET THE MEMO ?!!

CALL TO ADVENTURE!

DEFEATING DUNGEONS WITH A SKILL BOARD

2

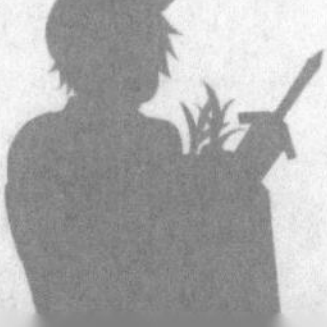

[Hard-core] Conquer all dungeons! Thread #132 [Latest info]

that's wild lol

128: Name: Anonymous front liner
Was Chikaho bright?

129 Name: Anonymous front liner
What's going on? a festival?

130 Name: Anonymous front liner
Did they take down the first boss?

131 Name: Anonymous front liner
Pretty sure Masatsugu-san is campaigning there.

132 Name: Anonymous front liner
Figures.
Bro's a freak

133 Name: Anonymous front liner
Didn't he get to Hokkaido by rowboat?

134 Name: Anonymous front liner

137 Name: Masatsugu★
Hey. Been a while.

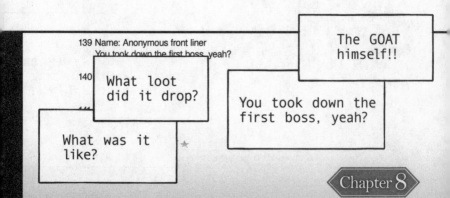

139 Name: Anonymous front liner
You took down the first boss, yeah?

140

The GOAT himself!!

You took down the first boss, yeah?

What loot did it drop?

What was it like?

★

Chapter 8

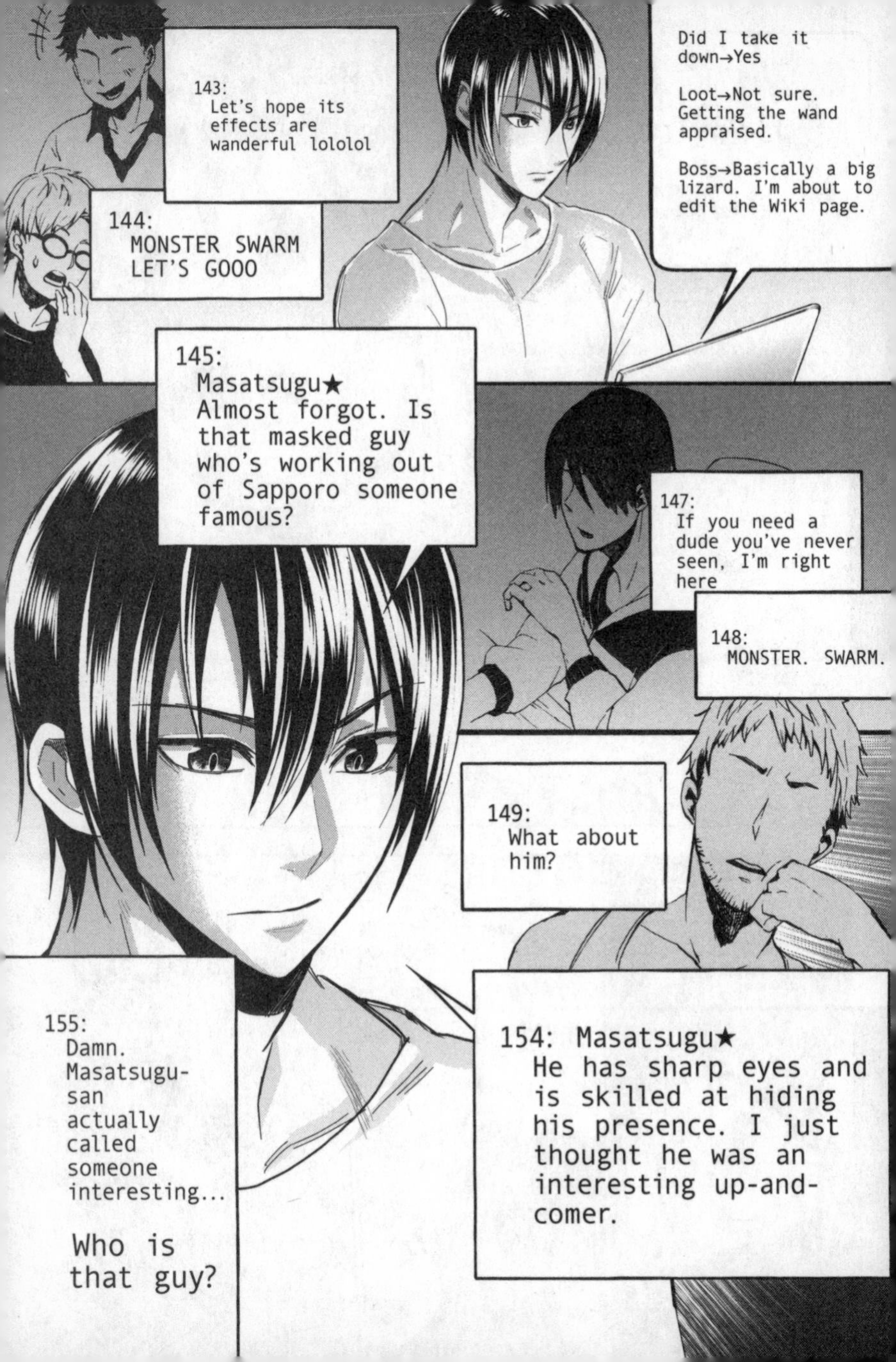

Did I take it down→Yes
Loot→Not sure. Getting the wand appraised.
Boss→Basically a big lizard. I'm about to edit the Wiki page.
143: Let's hope its effects are wanderful lololol
144: MONSTER SWARM LET'S GOOO
145: Masatsugu★ Almost forgot. Is that masked guy who's working out of Sapporo someone famous?
147: If you need a dude you've never seen, I'm right here
148: MONSTER. SWARM.
149: What about him?
154: Masatsugu★ He has sharp eyes and is skilled at hiding his presence. I just thought he was an interesting up-and-comer.
155: Damn. Masatsugu-san actually called someone interesting...
Who is that guy?

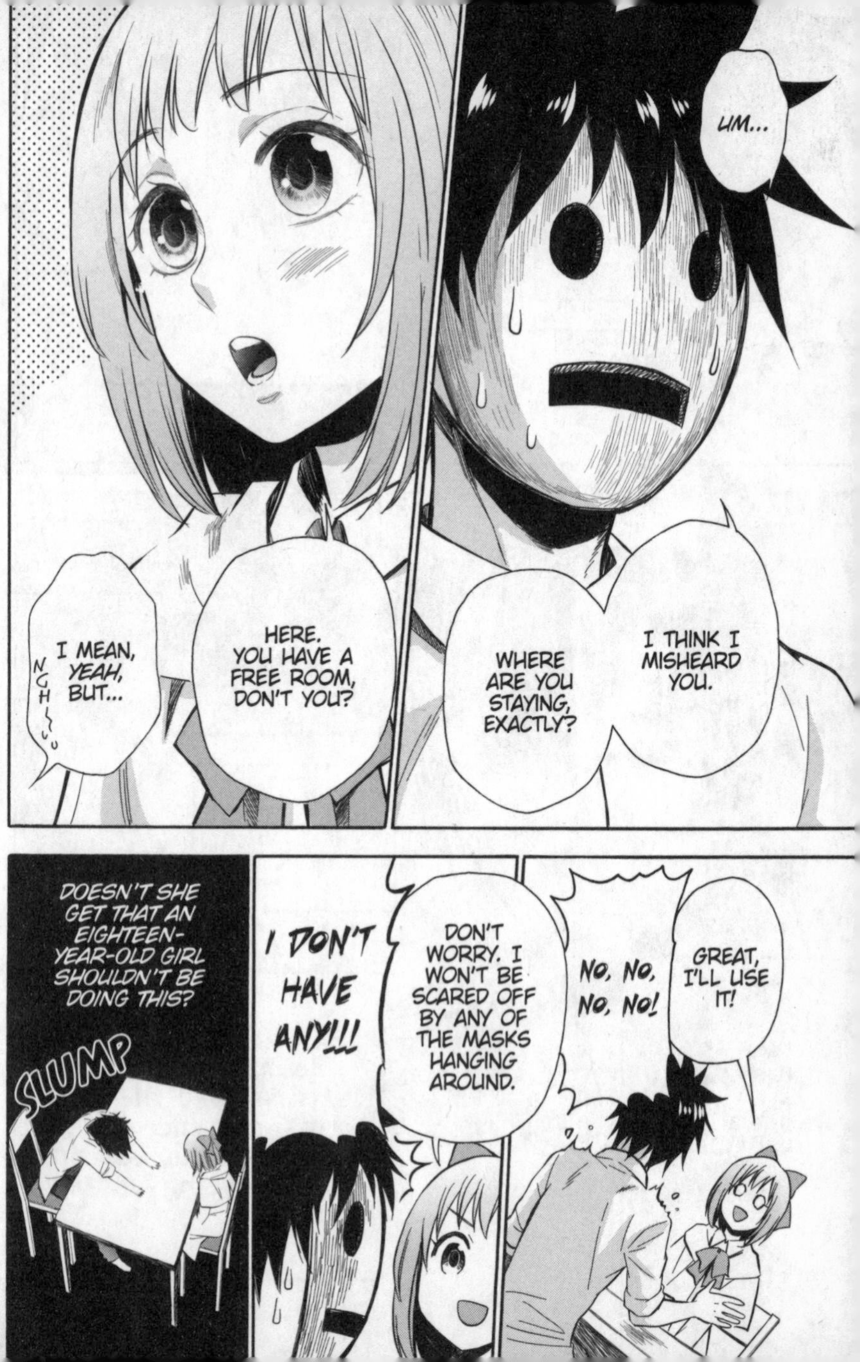
UM...
I THINK I MISHEARD YOU.
WHERE ARE YOU STAYING, EXACTLY?
HERE. YOU HAVE A FREE ROOM, DON'T YOU?
I MEAN, YEAH, BUT...
NGH
GREAT, I'LL USE IT!
NO, NO, NO, NO!
DON'T WORRY. I WON'T BE SCARED OFF BY ANY OF THE MASKS HANGING AROUND.
I DON'T HAVE ANY!!!
DOESN'T SHE GET THAT AN EIGHTEEN-YEAR-OLD GIRL SHOULDN'T BE DOING THIS?
SLUMP

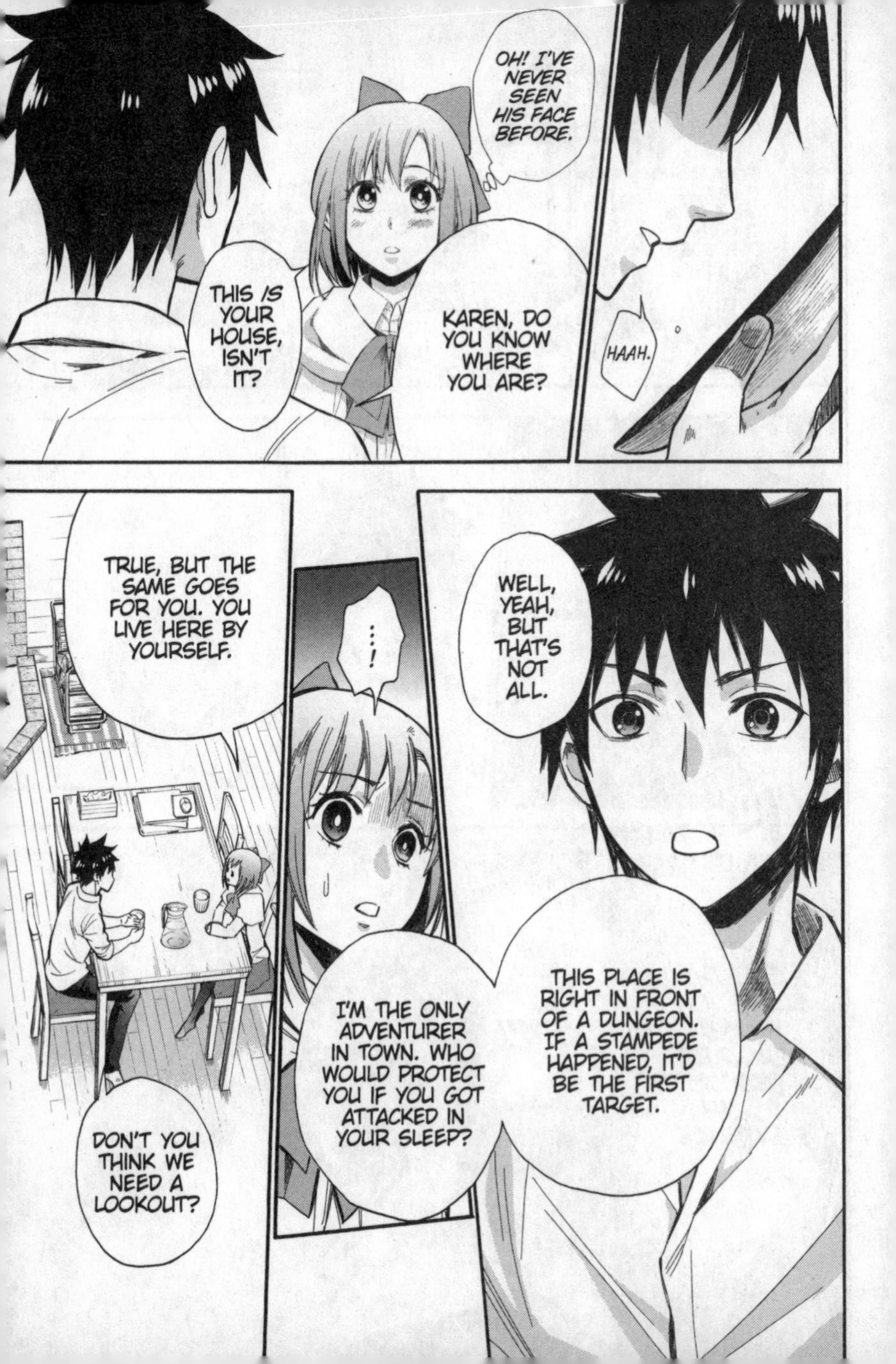
HAAH.
OH! I'VE NEVER SEEN HIS FACE BEFORE.
KAREN, DO YOU KNOW WHERE YOU ARE?
THIS IS YOUR HOUSE, ISN'T IT?
WELL, YEAH, BUT THAT'S NOT ALL.
THIS PLACE IS RIGHT IN FRONT OF A DUNGEON. IF A STAMPEDE HAPPENED, IT'D BE THE FIRST TARGET.
...!
I'M THE ONLY ADVENTURER IN TOWN. WHO WOULD PROTECT YOU IF YOU GOT ATTACKED IN YOUR SLEEP?
TRUE, BUT THE SAME GOES FOR YOU. YOU LIVE HERE BY YOURSELF.
DON'T YOU THINK WE NEED A LOOKOUT?

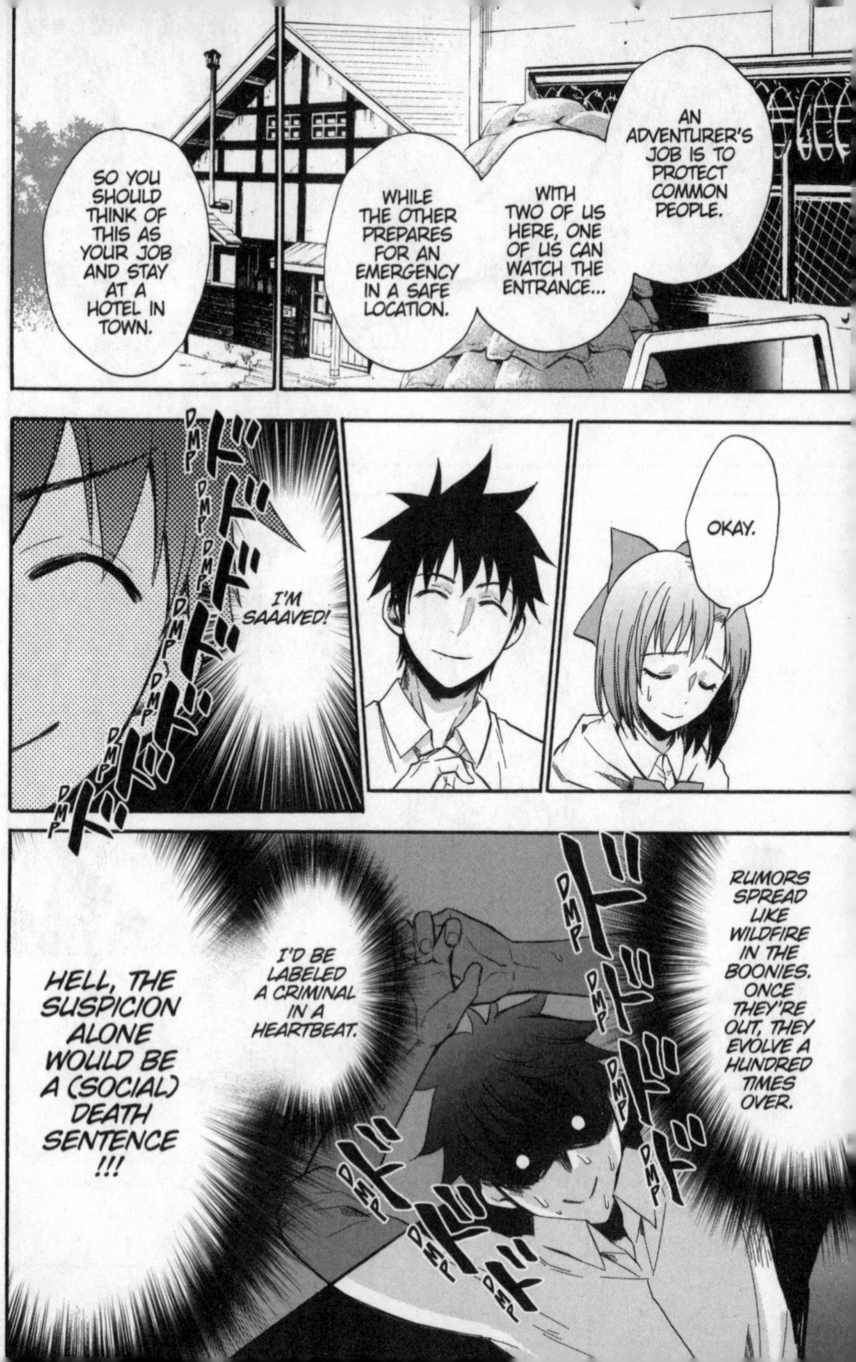
AN ADVENTURER'S JOB IS TO PROTECT COMMON PEOPLE.
WITH TWO OF US HERE, ONE OF US CAN WATCH THE ENTRANCE...
WHILE THE OTHER PREPARES FOR AN EMERGENCY IN A SAFE LOCATION.
SO YOU SHOULD THINK OF THIS AS YOUR JOB AND STAY AT A HOTEL IN TOWN.
OKAY.
I'M SAAAVED!
DMP DMP DMP DMP DMP DMP DMP
RUMORS SPREAD LIKE WILDFIRE IN THE BOONIES. ONCE THEY'RE OUT, THEY EVOLVE A HUNDRED TIMES OVER.
I'D BE LABELED A CRIMINAL IN A HEARTBEAT.
HELL, THE SUSPICION ALONE WOULD BE A (SOCIAL) DEATH SENTENCE!!!
DMP DMP DMP DMP DMP DMP DMP

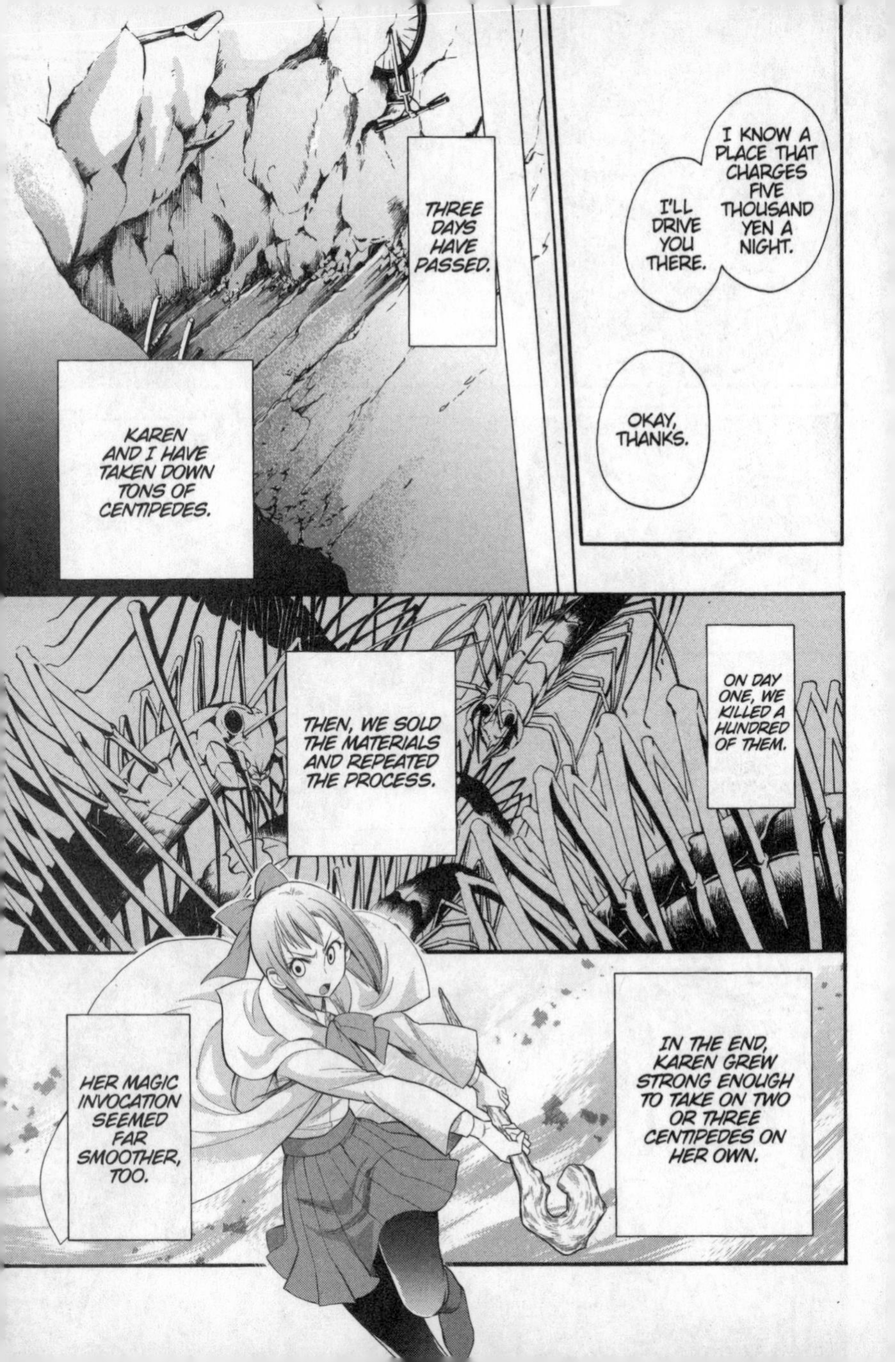
I KNOW A PLACE THAT CHARGES FIVE THOUSAND YEN A NIGHT.
I'LL DRIVE YOU THERE.
OKAY, THANKS.
THREE DAYS HAVE PASSED.
KAREN AND I HAVE TAKEN DOWN TONS OF CENTIPEDES.
ON DAY ONE, WE KILLED A HUNDRED OF THEM.
THEN, WE SOLD THE MATERIALS AND REPEATED THE PROCESS.
IN THE END, KAREN GREW STRONG ENOUGH TO TAKE ON TWO OR THREE CENTIPEDES ON HER OWN.
HER MAGIC INVOCATION SEEMED FAR SMOOTHER, TOO.

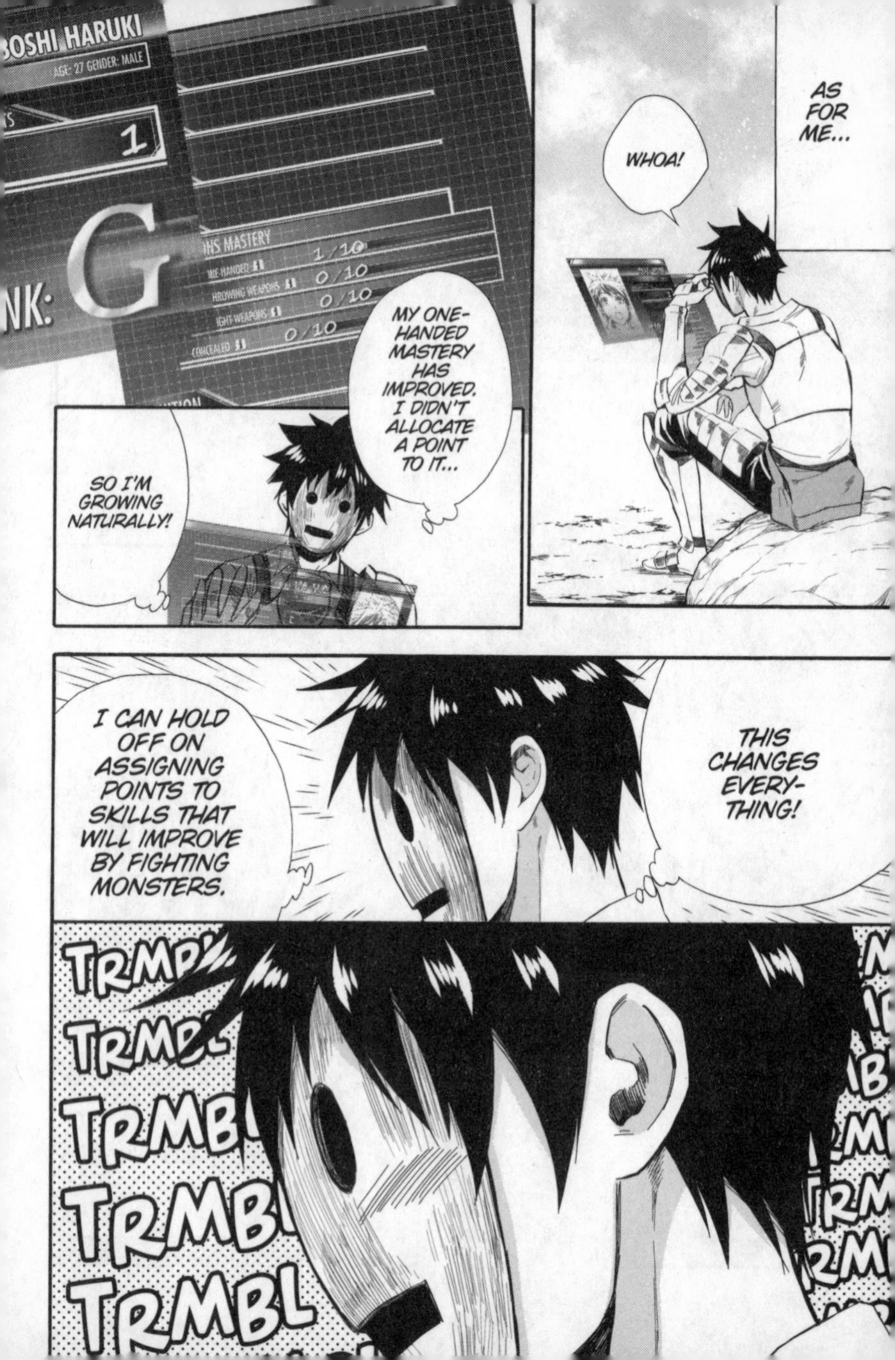

AS FOR ME...
WHOA!
BOSHI HARUKI
AGE: 27 GENDER: MALE
1
NK: G
ONS MASTERY
1/10
0/10
0/10
0/10
CONCEALED
MY ONE-HANDED MASTERY HAS IMPROVED. I DIDN'T ALLOCATE A POINT TO IT...
SO I'M GROWING NATURALLY!
THIS CHANGES EVERYTHING!
I CAN HOLD OFF ON ASSIGNING POINTS TO SKILLS THAT WILL IMPROVE BY FIGHTING MONSTERS.
TRMBL
TRMBL
TRMBL
TRMBL
TRMBL

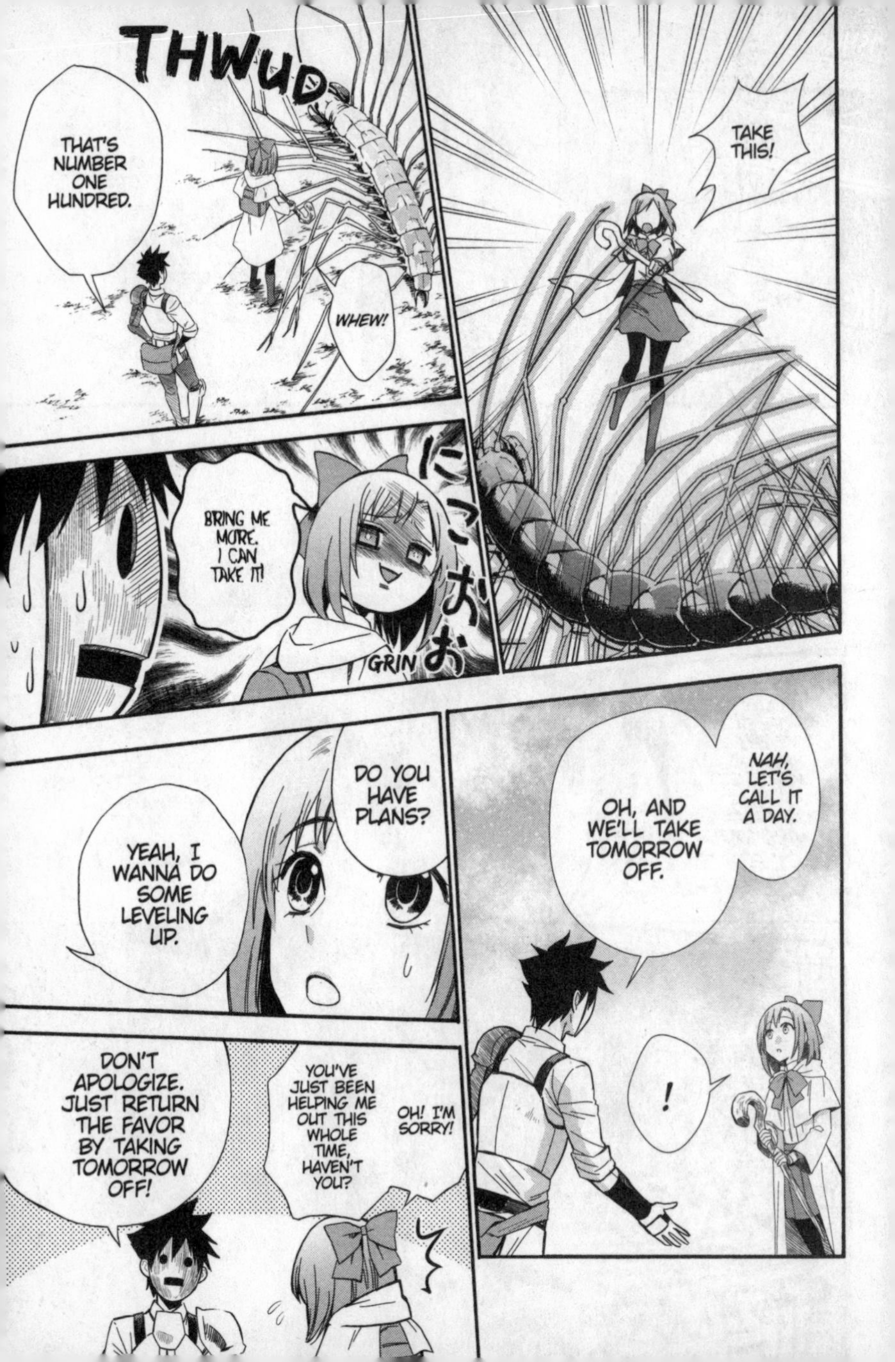
TAKE THIS!
THWUD
WHEW!
THAT'S NUMBER ONE HUNDRED.
にこぉぉ
GRIN
BRING ME MORE. I CAN TAKE IT!
NAH, LET'S CALL IT A DAY.
OH, AND WE'LL TAKE TOMORROW OFF.
!
DO YOU HAVE PLANS?
YEAH, I WANNA DO SOME LEVELING UP.
OH! I'M SORRY!
YOU'VE JUST BEEN HELPING ME OUT THIS WHOLE TIME, HAVEN'T YOU?
DON'T APOLOGIZE. JUST RETURN THE FAVOR BY TAKING TOMORROW OFF!

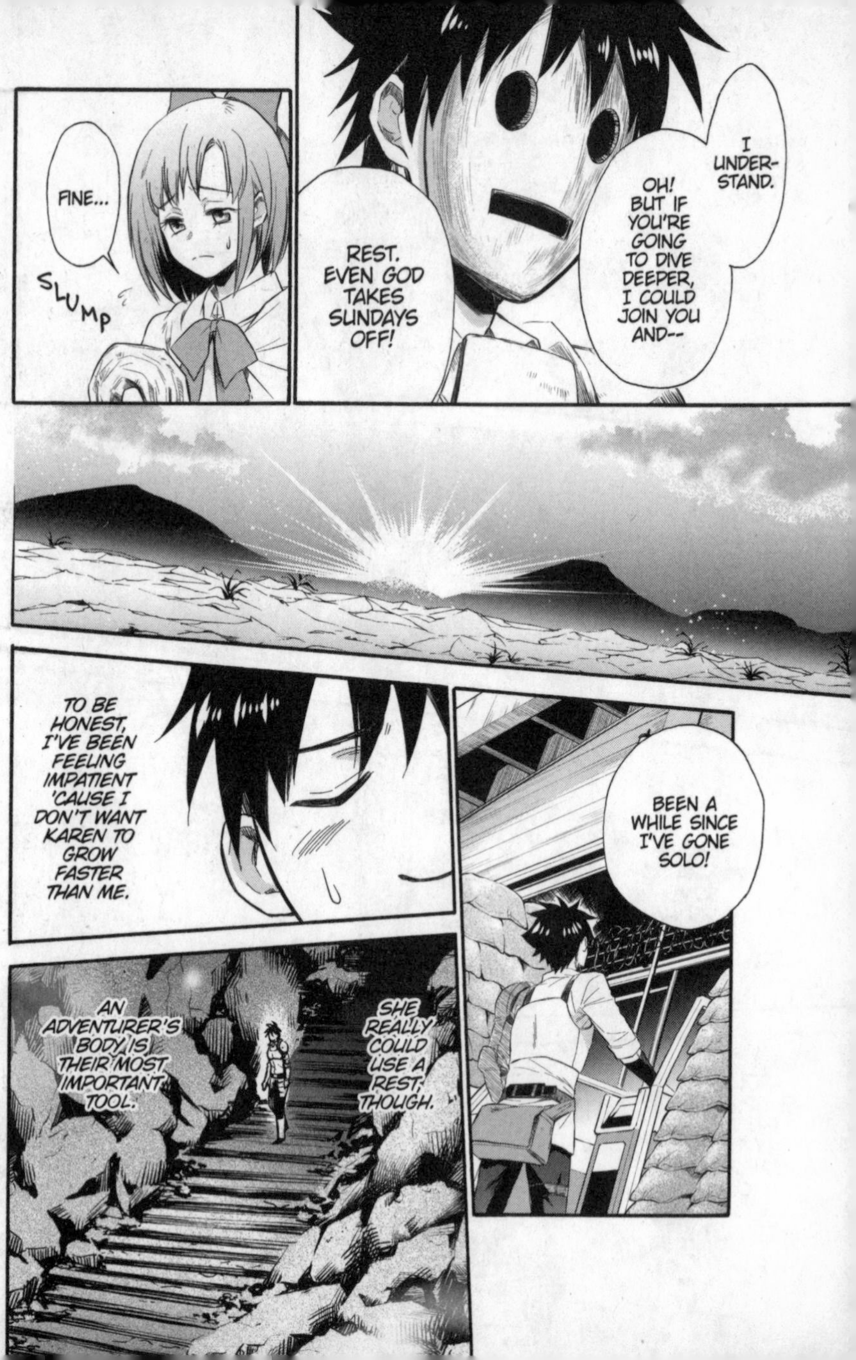
I UNDERSTAND.
OH! BUT IF YOU'RE GOING TO DIVE DEEPER, I COULD JOIN YOU AND--
REST. EVEN GOD TAKES SUNDAYS OFF!
FINE...
SLUMP
BEEN A WHILE SINCE I'VE GONE SOLO!
TO BE HONEST, I'VE BEEN FEELING IMPATIENT 'CAUSE I DON'T WANT KAREN TO GROW FASTER THAN ME.
SHE REALLY COULD USE A REST, THOUGH.
AN ADVENTURER'S BODY IS THEIR MOST IMPORTANT TOOL.

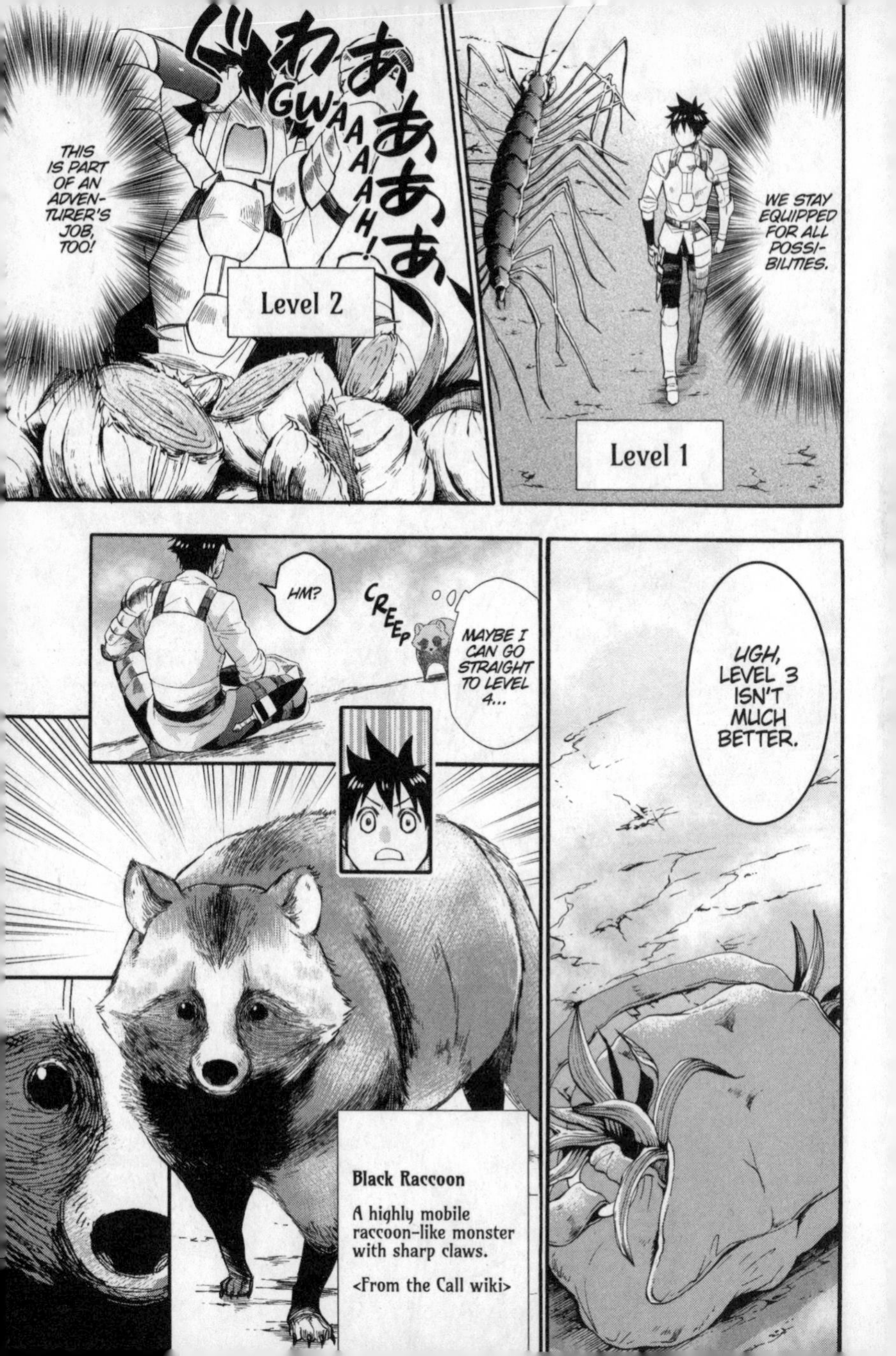
WE STAY EQUIPPED FOR ALL POSSI-BILITIES.
Level 1
ぐわああああ
GWAAAAAH!
Level 2
THIS IS PART OF AN ADVEN-TURER'S JOB, TOO!
UGH, LEVEL 3 ISN'T MUCH BETTER.
MAYBE I CAN GO STRAIGHT TO LEVEL 4...
CREEP
HM?
Black Raccoon
A highly mobile raccoon-like monster with sharp claws.
<From the Call wiki>

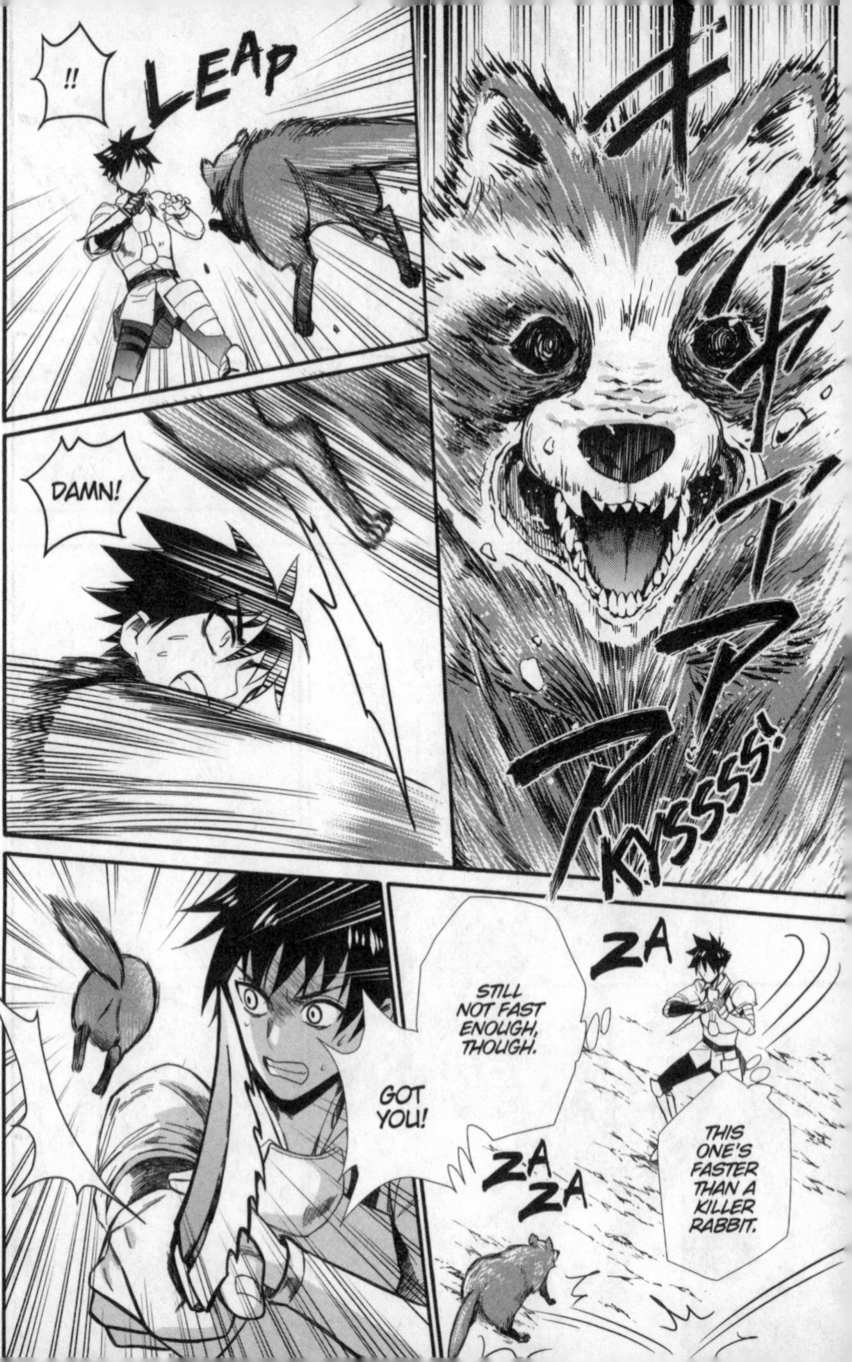
KYSSSSS!
!!
LEAP
DAMN!
ZA
STILL NOT FAST ENOUGH, THOUGH.
THIS ONE'S FASTER THAN A KILLER RABBIT.
ZA ZA
GOT YOU!

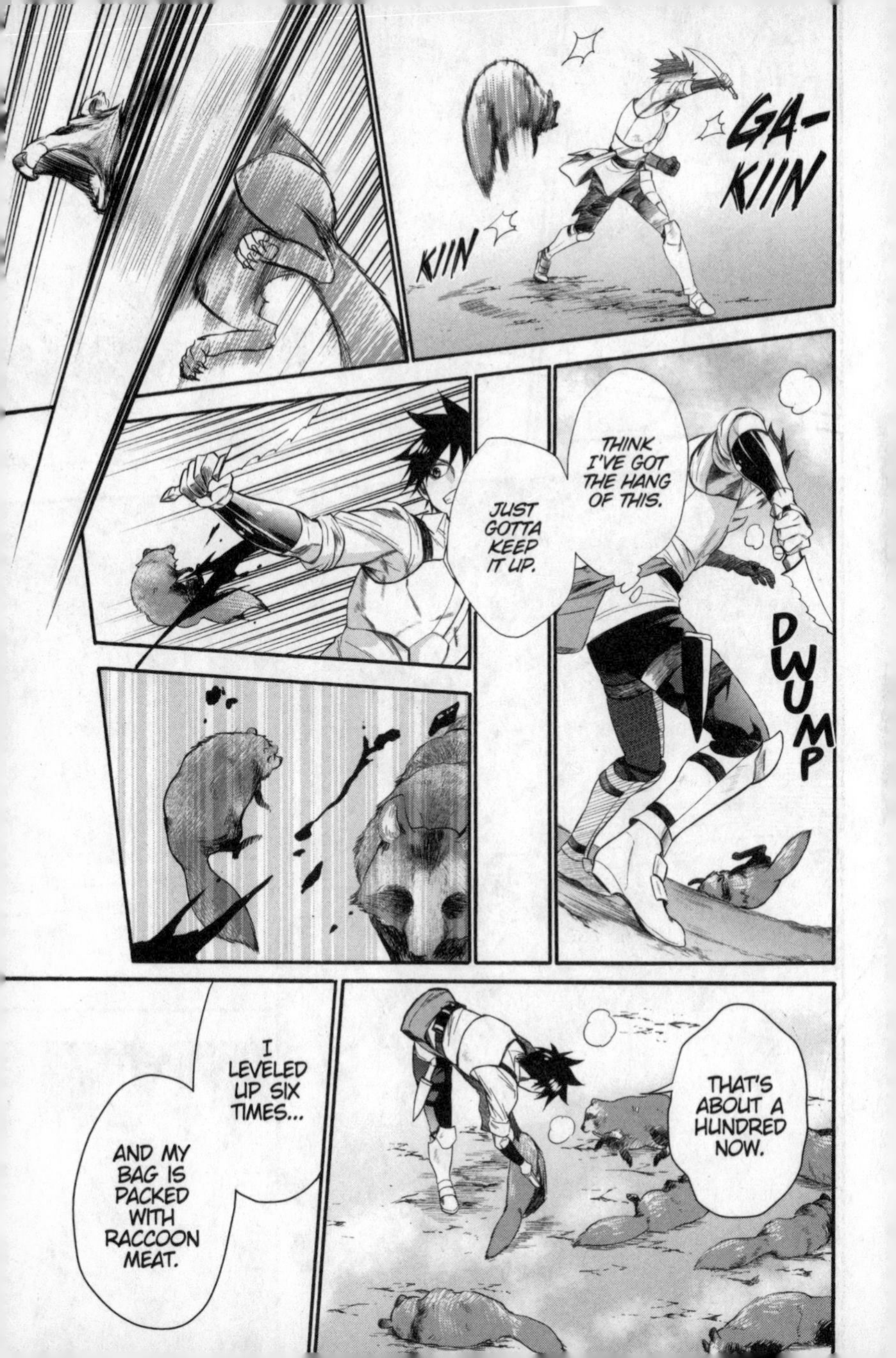
GA-KIIN
KIIN
THINK I'VE GOT THE HANG OF THIS.
JUST GOTTA KEEP IT UP.
DWUMP
THAT'S ABOUT A HUNDRED NOW.
I LEVELED UP SIX TIMES...
AND MY BAG IS PACKED WITH RACCOON MEAT.

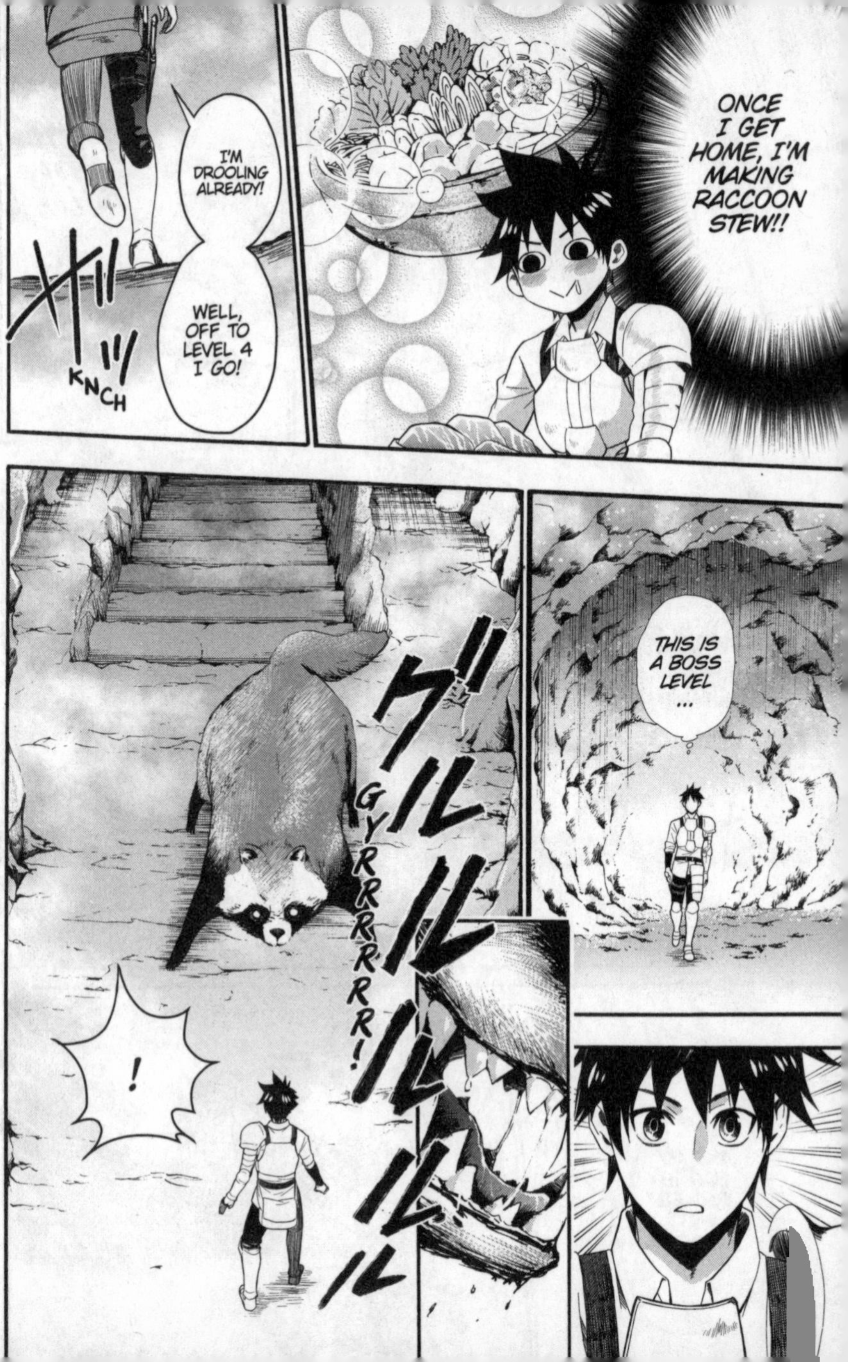
ONCE I GET HOME, I'M MAKING RACCOON STEW!!
I'M DROOLING ALREADY!
WELL, OFF TO LEVEL 4 I GO!
KNCH
THIS IS A BOSS LEVEL ...
GYRRRRRRRR!
!

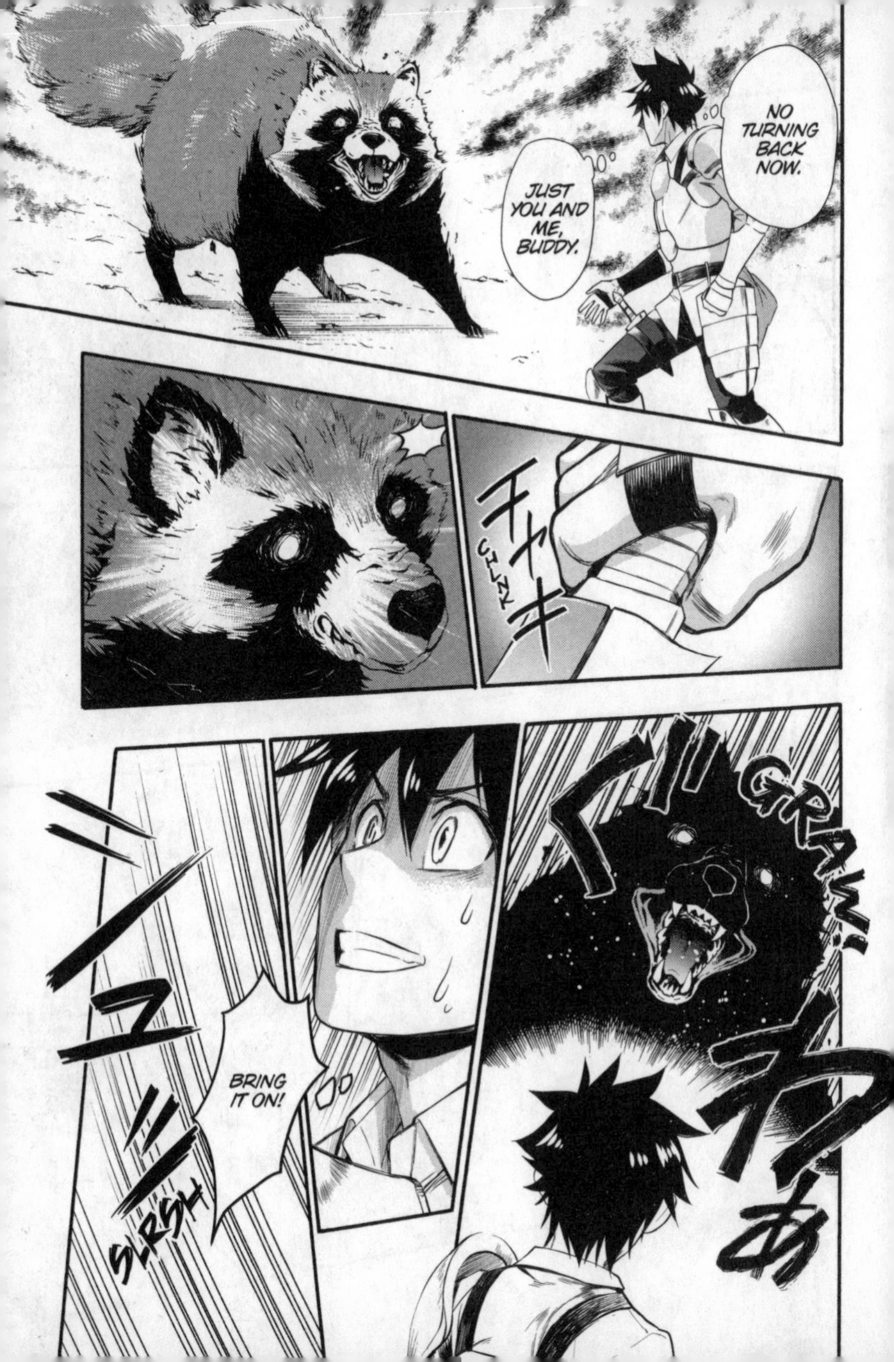
NO TURNING BACK NOW.
JUST YOU AND ME, BUDDY.
CHLNK
GRAW!
BRING IT ON!
SLRSH

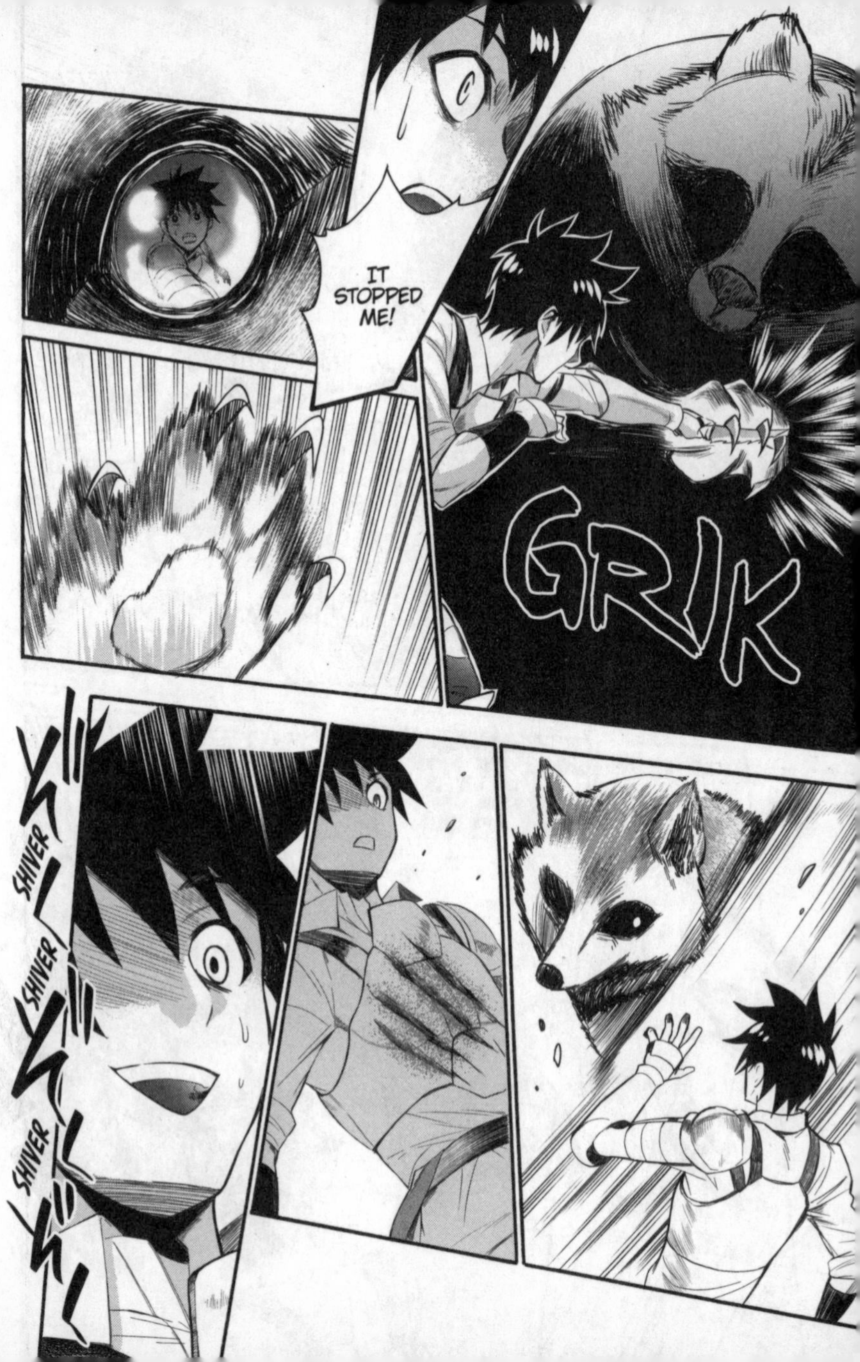
IT STOPPED ME!
GRIK
SHIVER
SHIVER
SHIVER

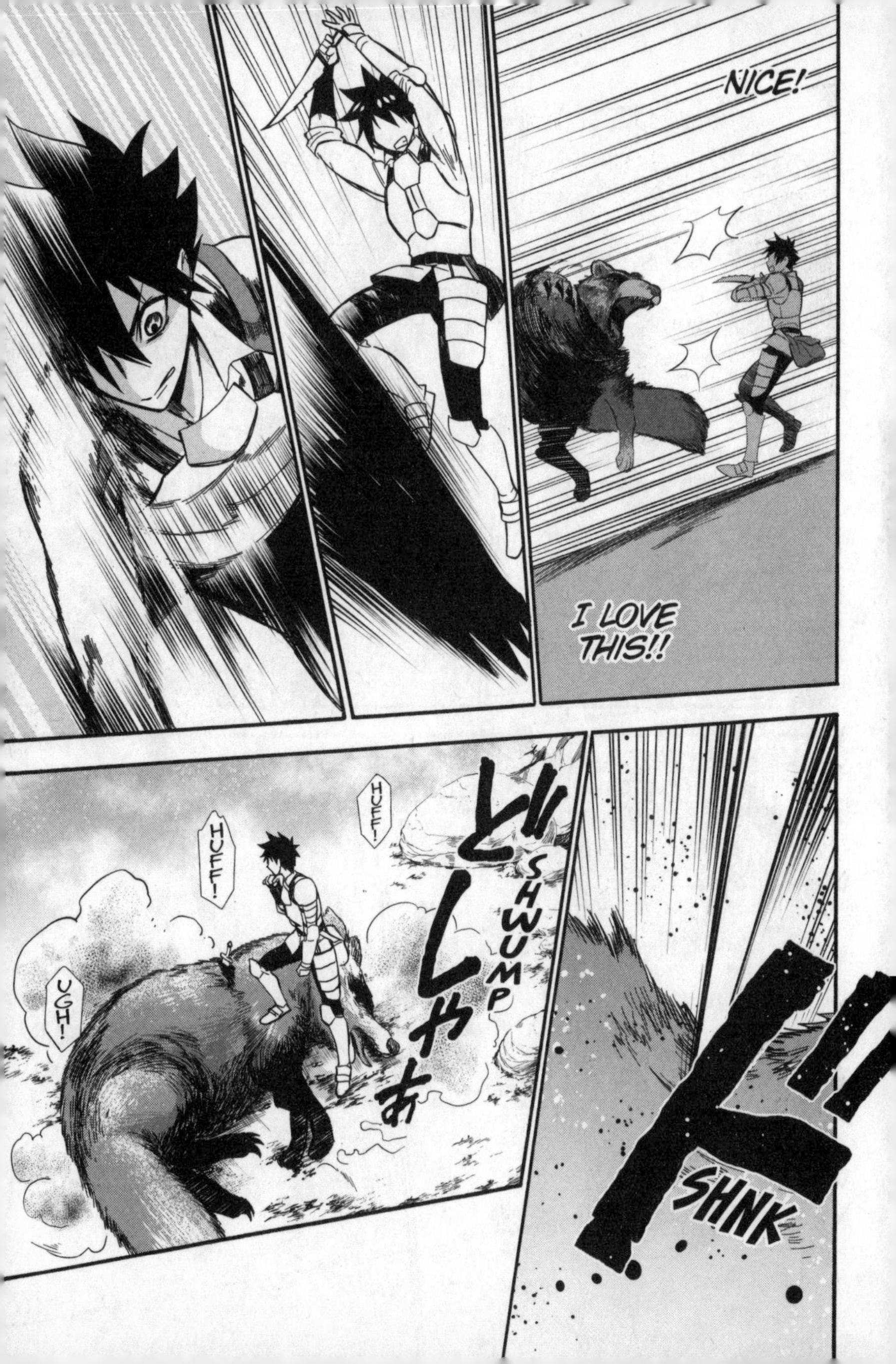
NICE!
I LOVE THIS!!
SHNK
どしゃあ
SHWUMP
HUFF!
HUFF!
UGH!

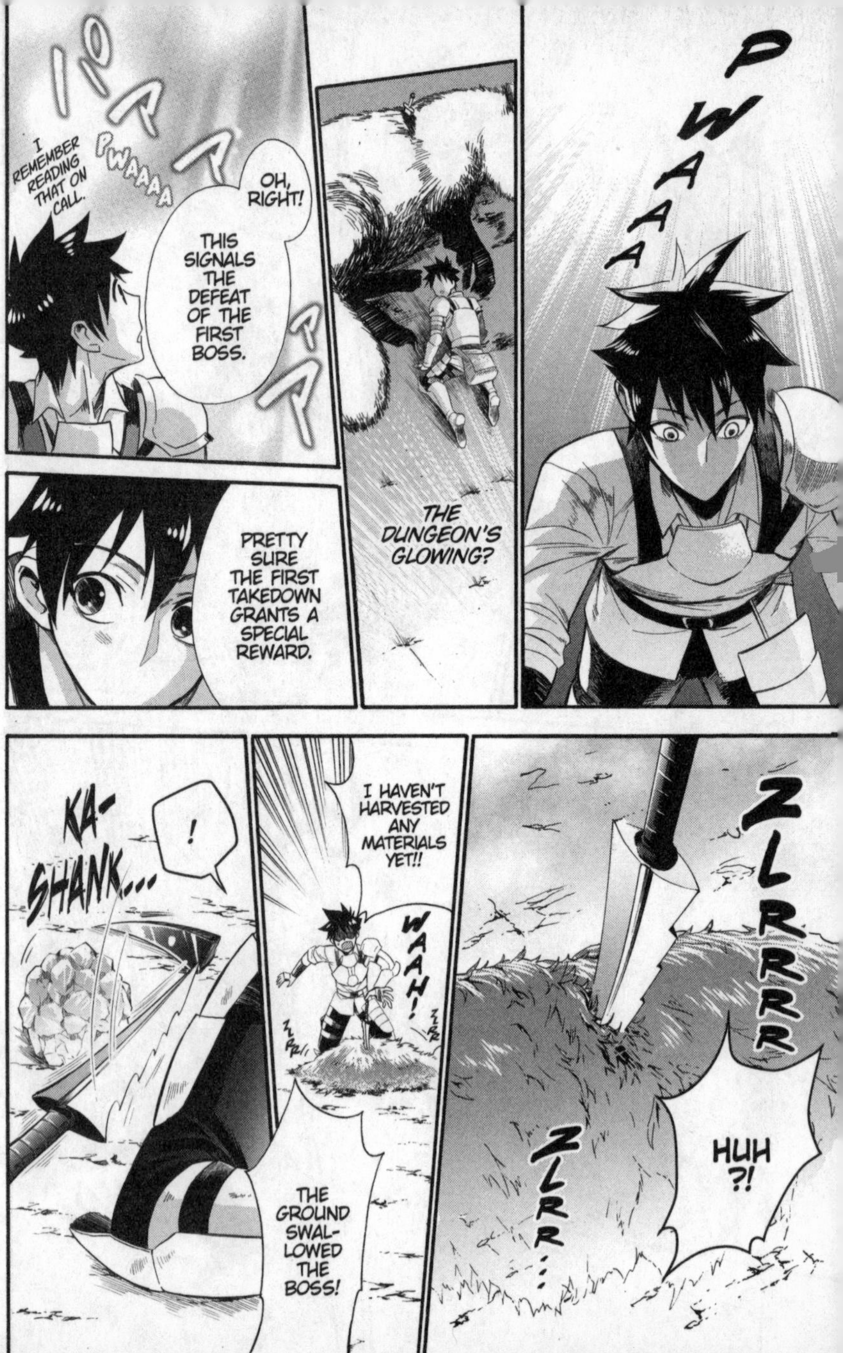
PWAAAA
THE DUNGEON'S GLOWING?
パァァァァ
PWAAAA
OH, RIGHT!
THIS SIGNALS THE DEFEAT OF THE FIRST BOSS.
I REMEMBER READING THAT ON CALL.
PRETTY SURE THE FIRST TAKEDOWN GRANTS A SPECIAL REWARD.
ZLRRRR
HUH ?!
ZLRR...
I HAVEN'T HARVESTED ANY MATERIALS YET!!
WAAAH!
!
KA-SHANK...
THE GROUND SWAL-LOWED THE BOSS!

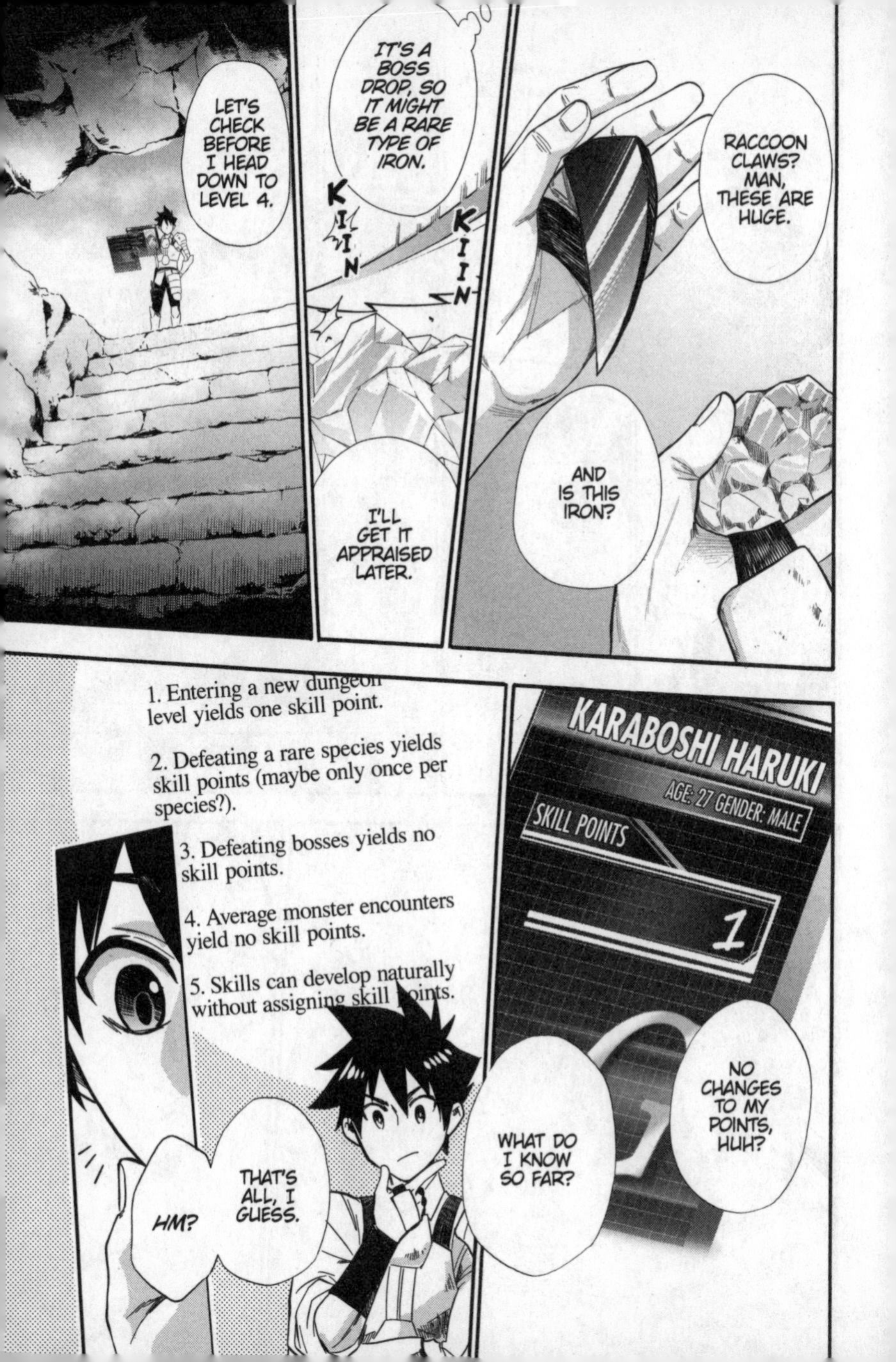
RACCOON CLAWS? MAN, THESE ARE HUGE.
AND IS THIS IRON?
IT'S A BOSS DROP, SO IT MIGHT BE A RARE TYPE OF IRON.
KIIN
KIIN
I'LL GET IT APPRAISED LATER.
LET'S CHECK BEFORE I HEAD DOWN TO LEVEL 4.
KARABOSHI HARUKI
AGE: 27 GENDER: MALE
SKILL POINTS
1
NO CHANGES TO MY POINTS, HUH?
WHAT DO I KNOW SO FAR?
1. Entering a new dungeon level yields one skill point.
2. Defeating a rare species yields skill points (maybe only once per species?).
3. Defeating bosses yields no skill points.
4. Average monster encounters yield no skill points.
5. Skills can develop naturally without assigning skill points.
THAT'S ALL, I GUESS.
HM?

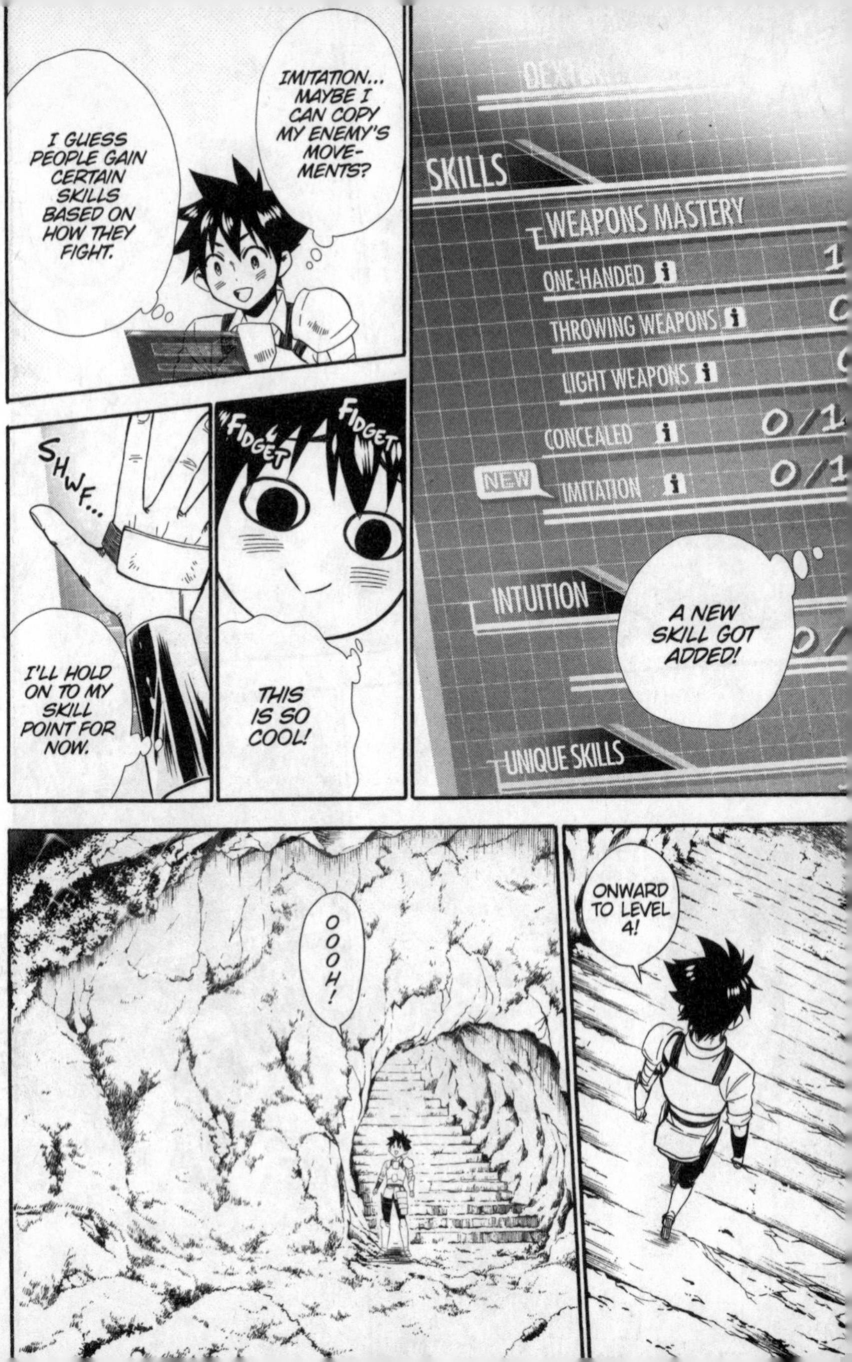
SKILLS
WEAPONS MASTERY
ONE-HANDED
THROWING WEAPONS
LIGHT WEAPONS
CONCEALED 0/1
NEW
IMITATION 0/1
INTUITION
UNIQUE SKILLS
A NEW SKILL GOT ADDED!
IMITATION... MAYBE I CAN COPY MY ENEMY'S MOVE-MENTS?
I GUESS PEOPLE GAIN CERTAIN SKILLS BASED ON HOW THEY FIGHT.
FIDGET
FIDGET
THIS IS SO COOL!
SHWF...
I'LL HOLD ON TO MY SKILL POINT FOR NOW.
ONWARD TO LEVEL 4!
OOOOH!

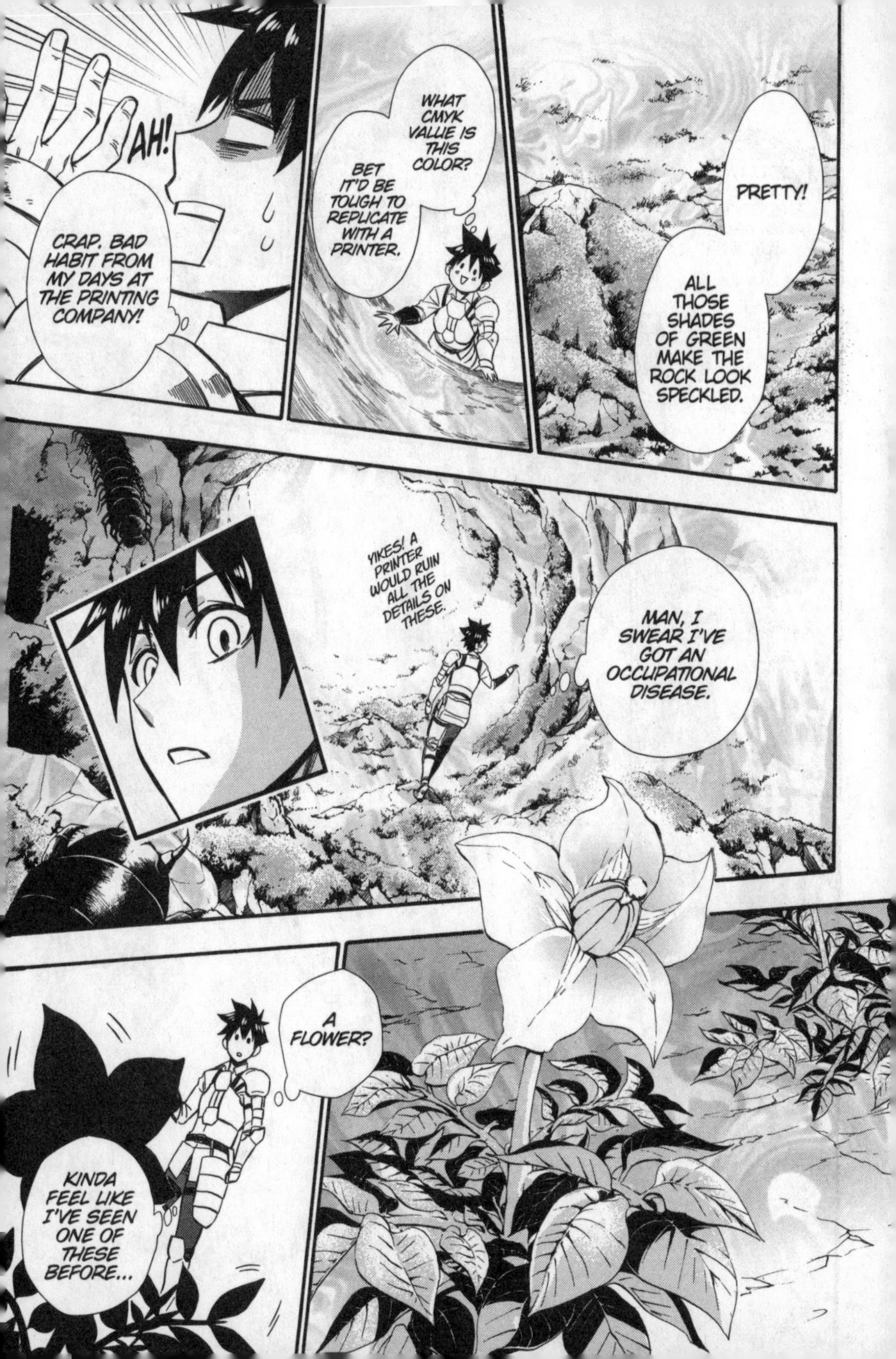
PRETTY!
ALL THOSE SHADES OF GREEN MAKE THE ROCK LOOK SPECKLED.
WHAT CMYK VALUE IS THIS COLOR?
BET IT'D BE TOUGH TO REPLICATE WITH A PRINTER.
AH!
CRAP. BAD HABIT FROM MY DAYS AT THE PRINTING COMPANY!
MAN, I SWEAR I'VE GOT AN OCCUPATIONAL DISEASE.
YIKES! A PRINTER WOULD RUIN ALL THE DETAILS ON THESE.
A FLOWER?
KINDA FEEL LIKE I'VE SEEN ONE OF THESE BEFORE...

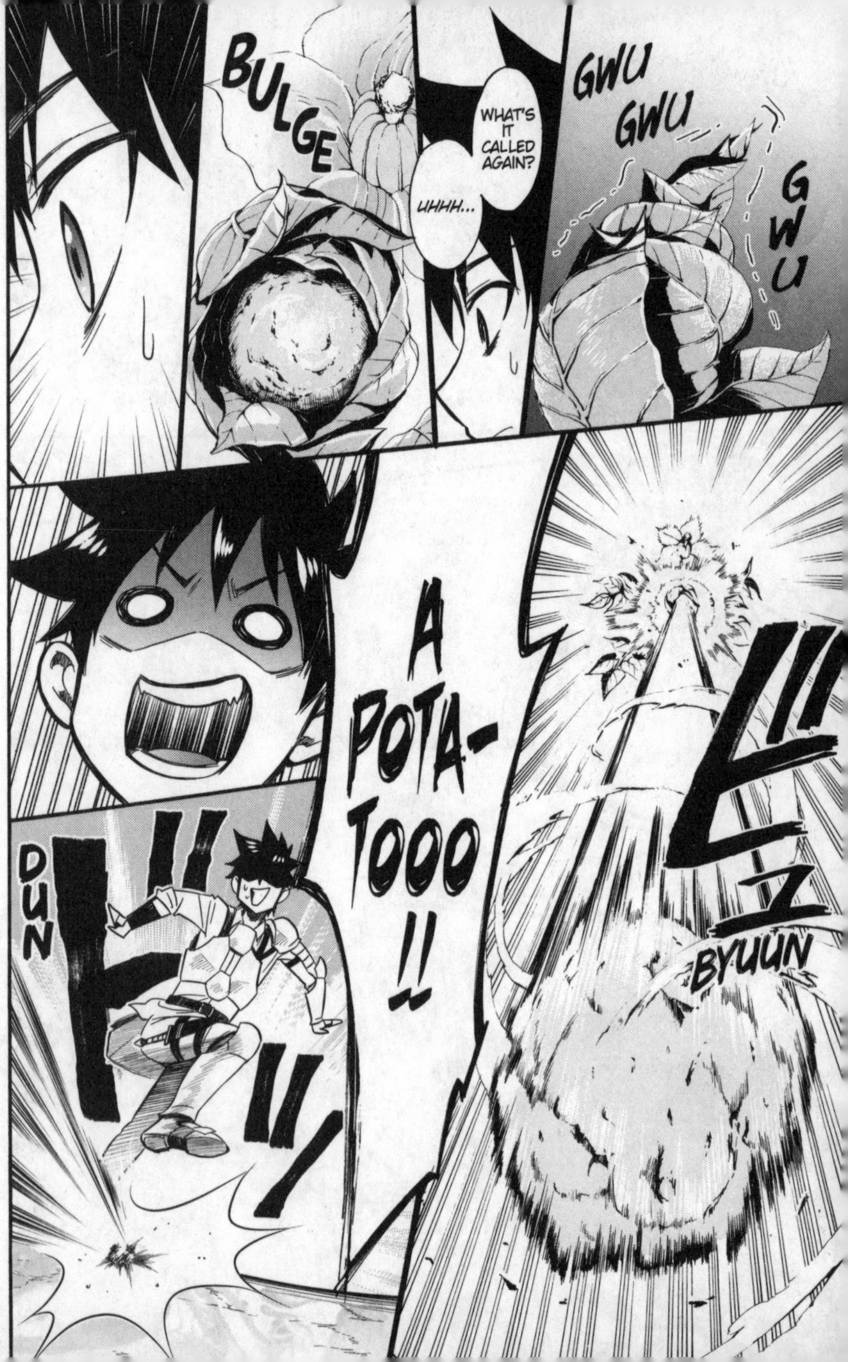
GWU GWU
GWU GWU
WHAT'S IT CALLED AGAIN?
UHHH...
BULGE
BYUUN
A POTA-TOOO!!
DUN

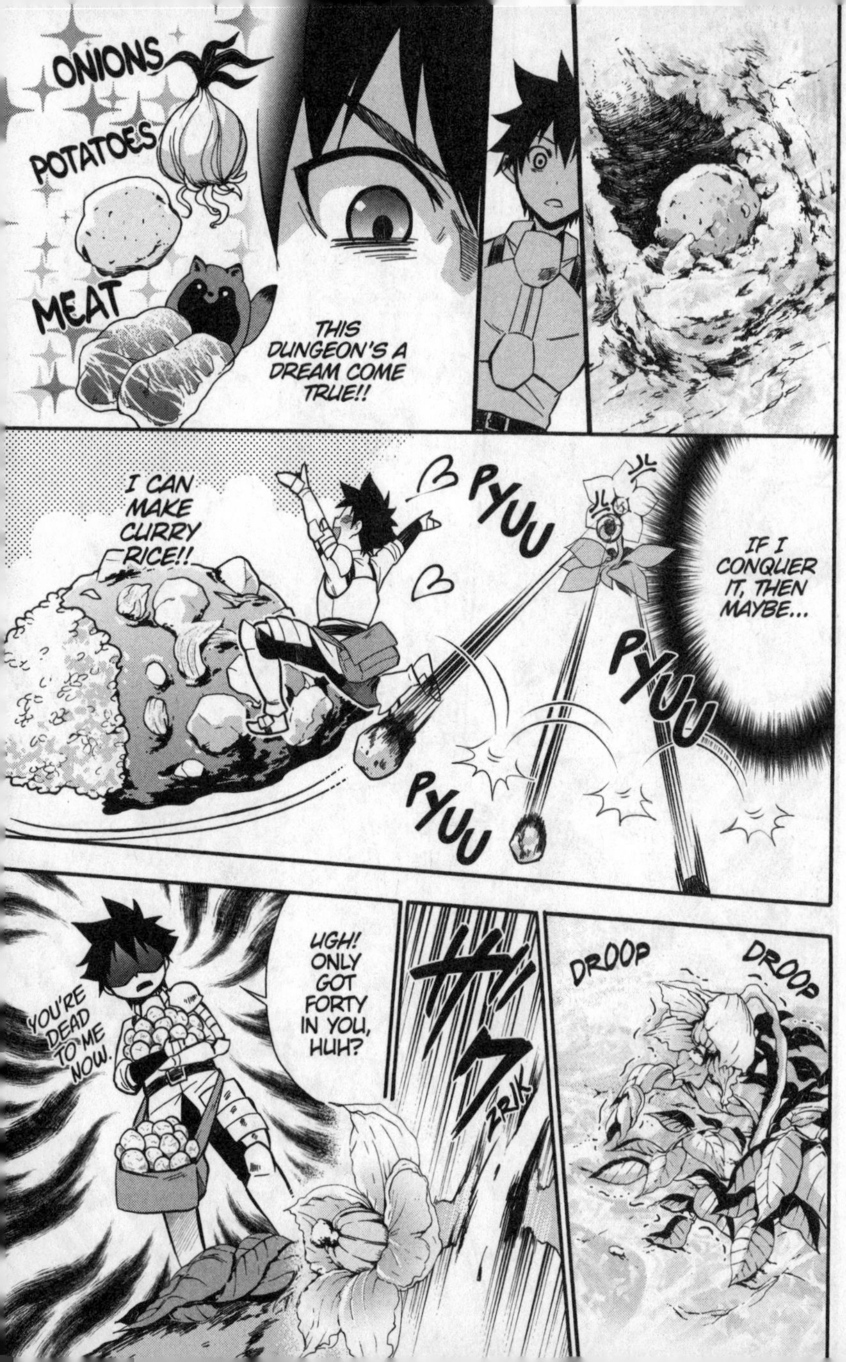
THIS DUNGEON'S A DREAM COME TRUE!!
ONIONS
POTATOES
MEAT
IF I CONQUER IT, THEN MAYBE...
PYUU
PYUU
PYUU
I CAN MAKE CURRY RICE!!
DROOP
DROOP
ZRIK
UGH! ONLY GOT FORTY IN YOU, HUH?
YOU'RE DEAD TO ME NOW.

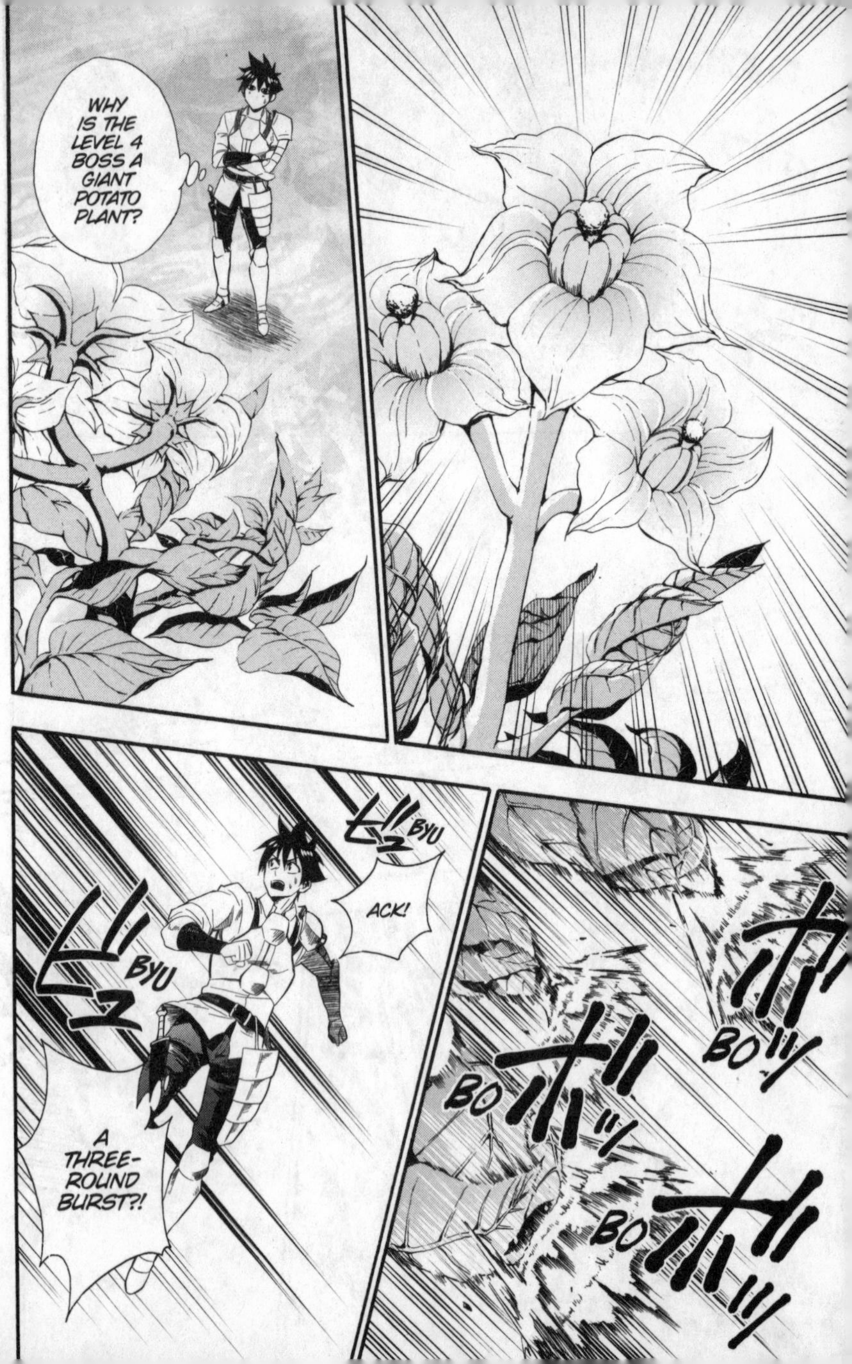
WHY IS THE LEVEL 4 BOSS A GIANT POTATO PLANT?
BO
BO
BO
BYU
ACK!
BYU
A THREE-ROUND BURST?!

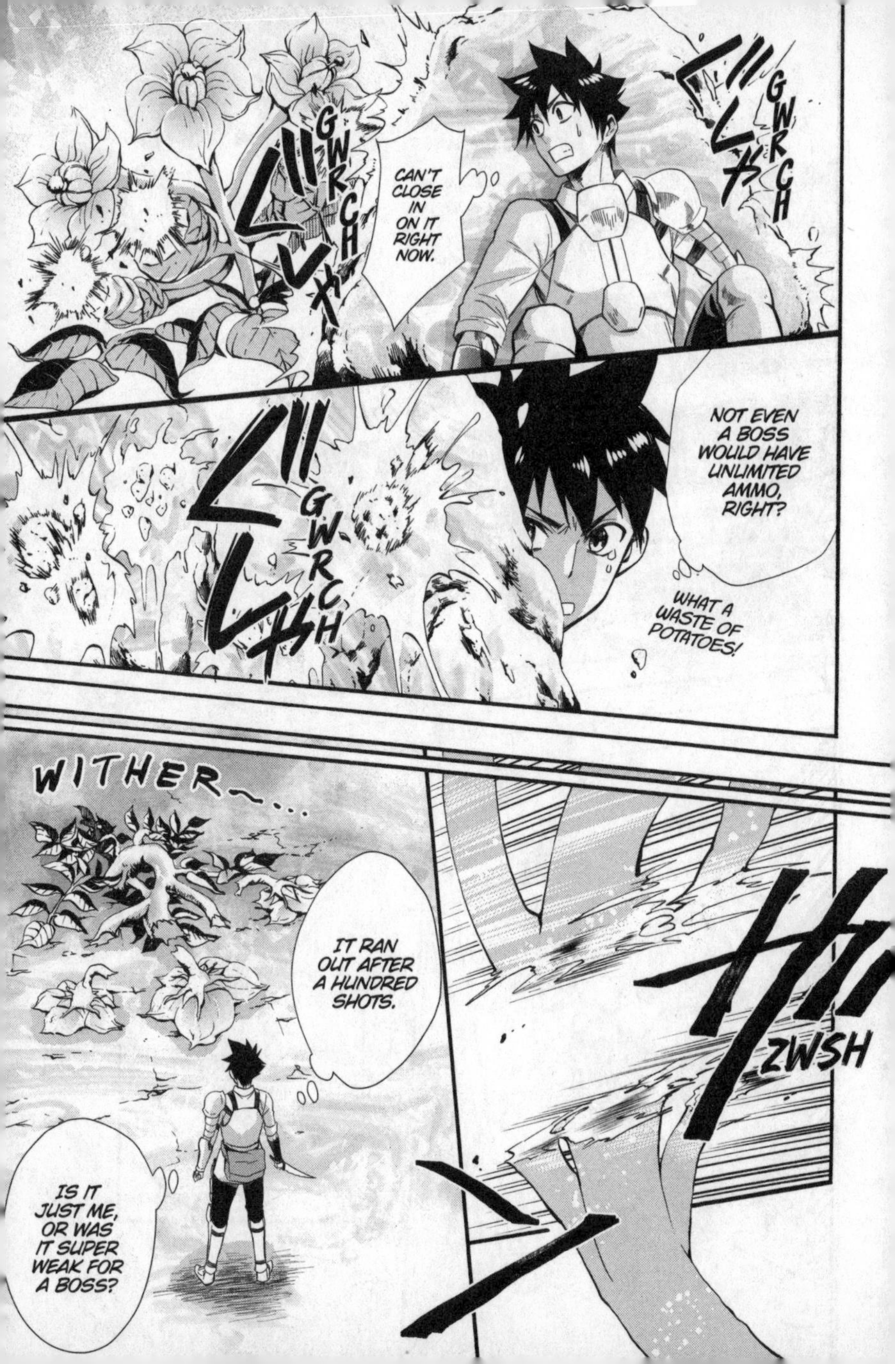
GWRCH
CAN'T CLOSE IN ON IT RIGHT NOW.
GWRCH
NOT EVEN A BOSS WOULD HAVE UNLIMITED AMMO, RIGHT?
WHAT A WASTE OF POTATOES!
GWRCH
ZWSH
WITHER~...
IT RAN OUT AFTER A HUNDRED SHOTS.
IS IT JUST ME, OR WAS IT SUPER WEAK FOR A BOSS?

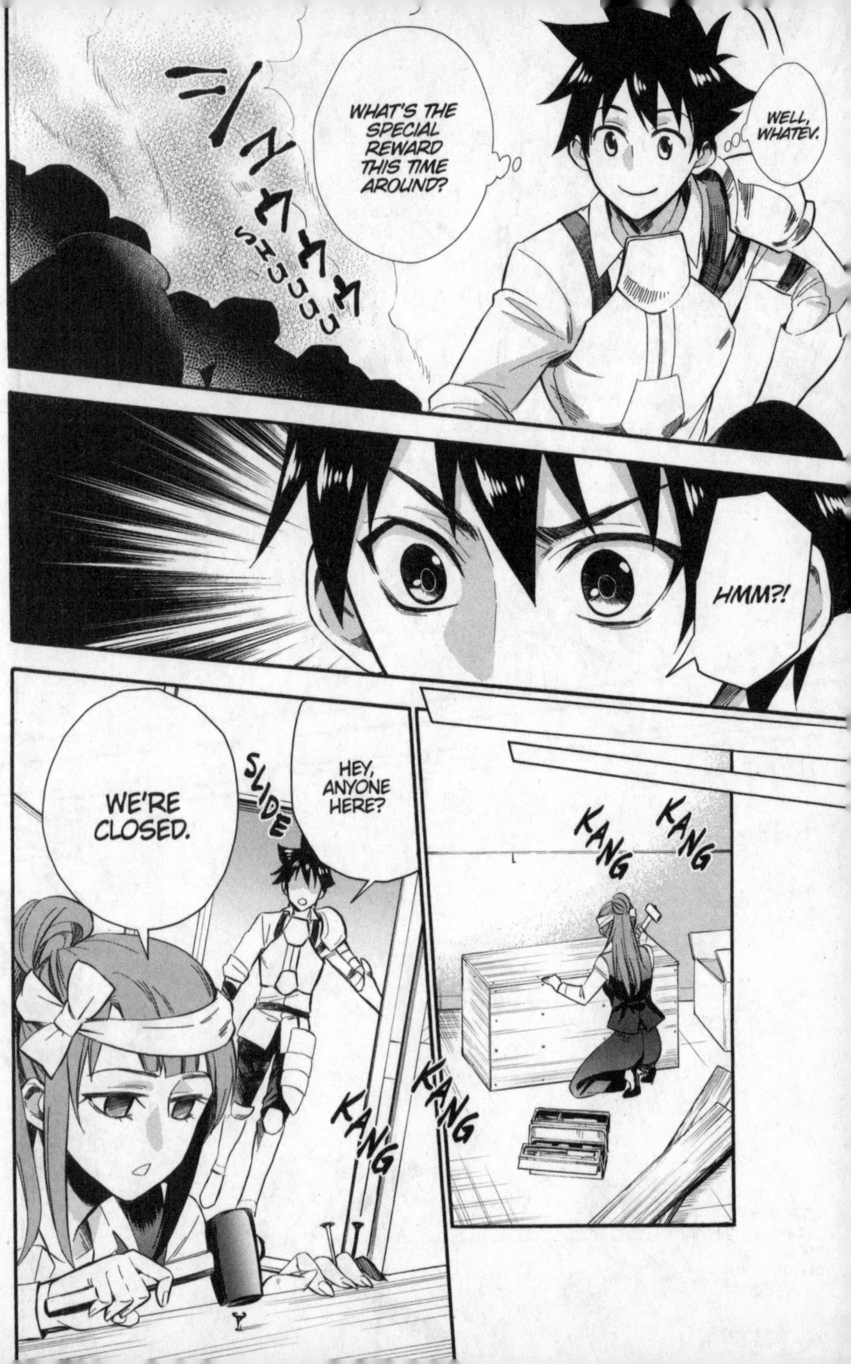
WELL, WHATEV.
WHAT'S THE SPECIAL REWARD THIS TIME AROUND?
SHUUUUU
HMM?!
KANG KANG
HEY, ANYONE HERE?
SLIDE
WE'RE CLOSED.
KANG KANG

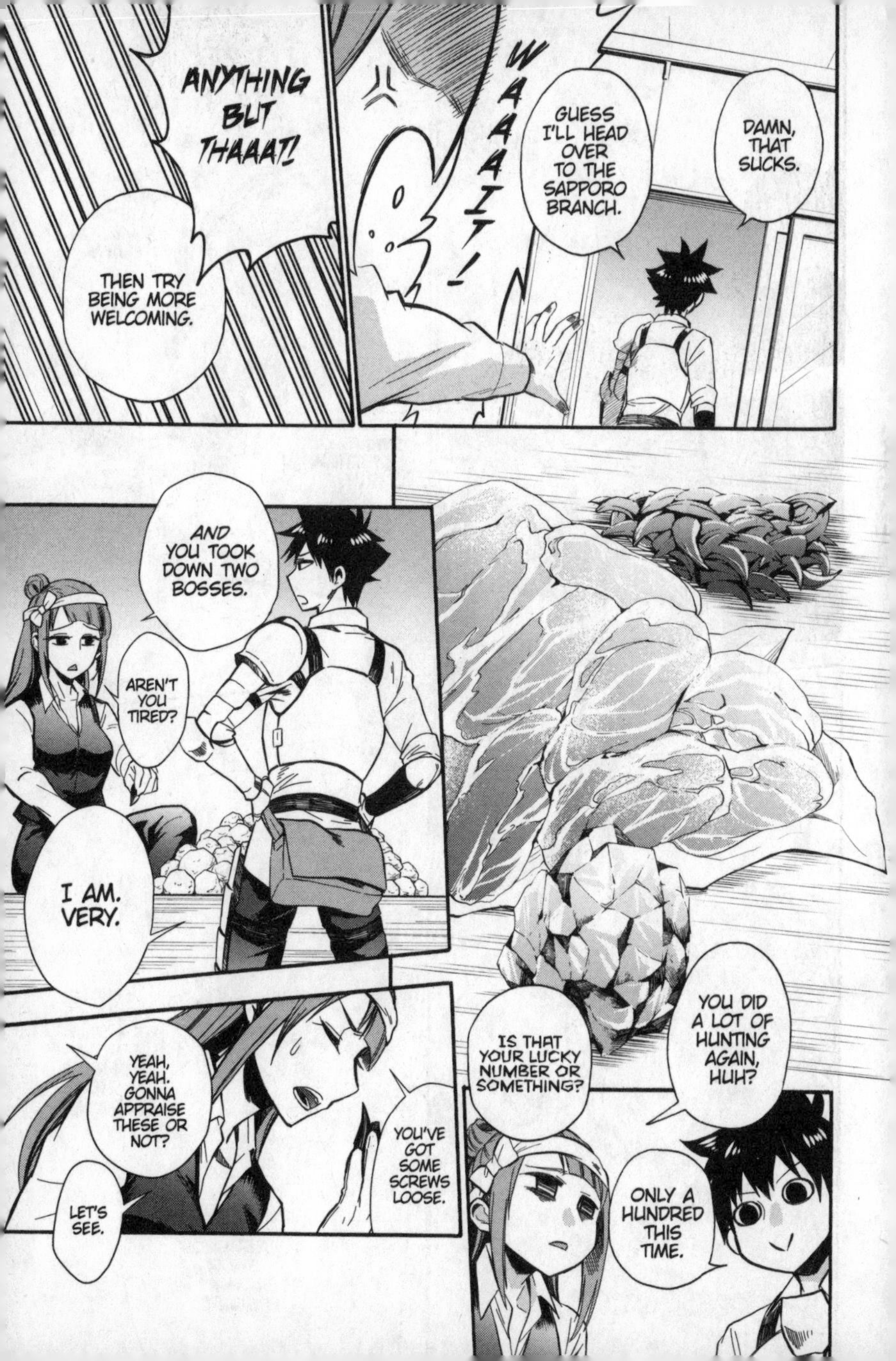
DAMN, THAT SUCKS.
GUESS I'LL HEAD OVER TO THE SAPPORO BRANCH.
WAAAAIT!
ANYTHING BUT THAAAT!
THEN TRY BEING MORE WELCOMING.
YOU DID A LOT OF HUNTING AGAIN, HUH?
ONLY A HUNDRED THIS TIME.
IS THAT YOUR LUCKY NUMBER OR SOMETHING?
AND YOU TOOK DOWN TWO BOSSES.
AREN'T YOU TIRED?
I AM. VERY.
YOU'VE GOT SOME SCREWS LOOSE.
YEAH, YEAH. GONNA APPRAISE THESE OR NOT?
LET'S SEE.

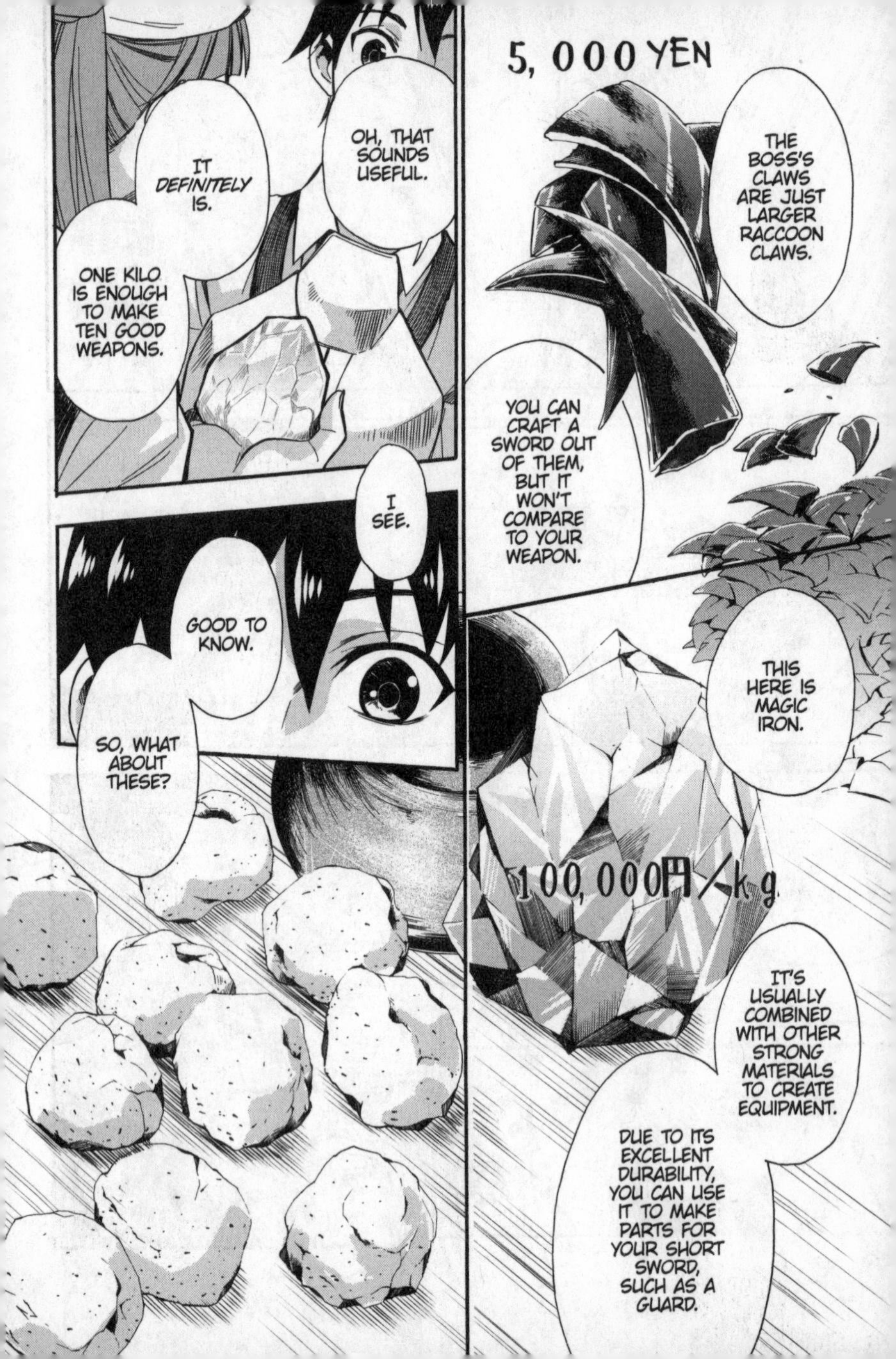
5,000 YEN
THE BOSS'S CLAWS ARE JUST LARGER RACCOON CLAWS.
YOU CAN CRAFT A SWORD OUT OF THEM, BUT IT WON'T COMPARE TO YOUR WEAPON.
THIS HERE IS MAGIC IRON.
100,000円/kg
IT'S USUALLY COMBINED WITH OTHER STRONG MATERIALS TO CREATE EQUIPMENT.
DUE TO ITS EXCELLENT DURABILITY, YOU CAN USE IT TO MAKE PARTS FOR YOUR SHORT SWORD, SUCH AS A GUARD.
OH, THAT SOUNDS USEFUL.
IT DEFINITELY IS.
ONE KILO IS ENOUGH TO MAKE TEN GOOD WEAPONS.
I SEE.
GOOD TO KNOW.
SO, WHAT ABOUT THESE?

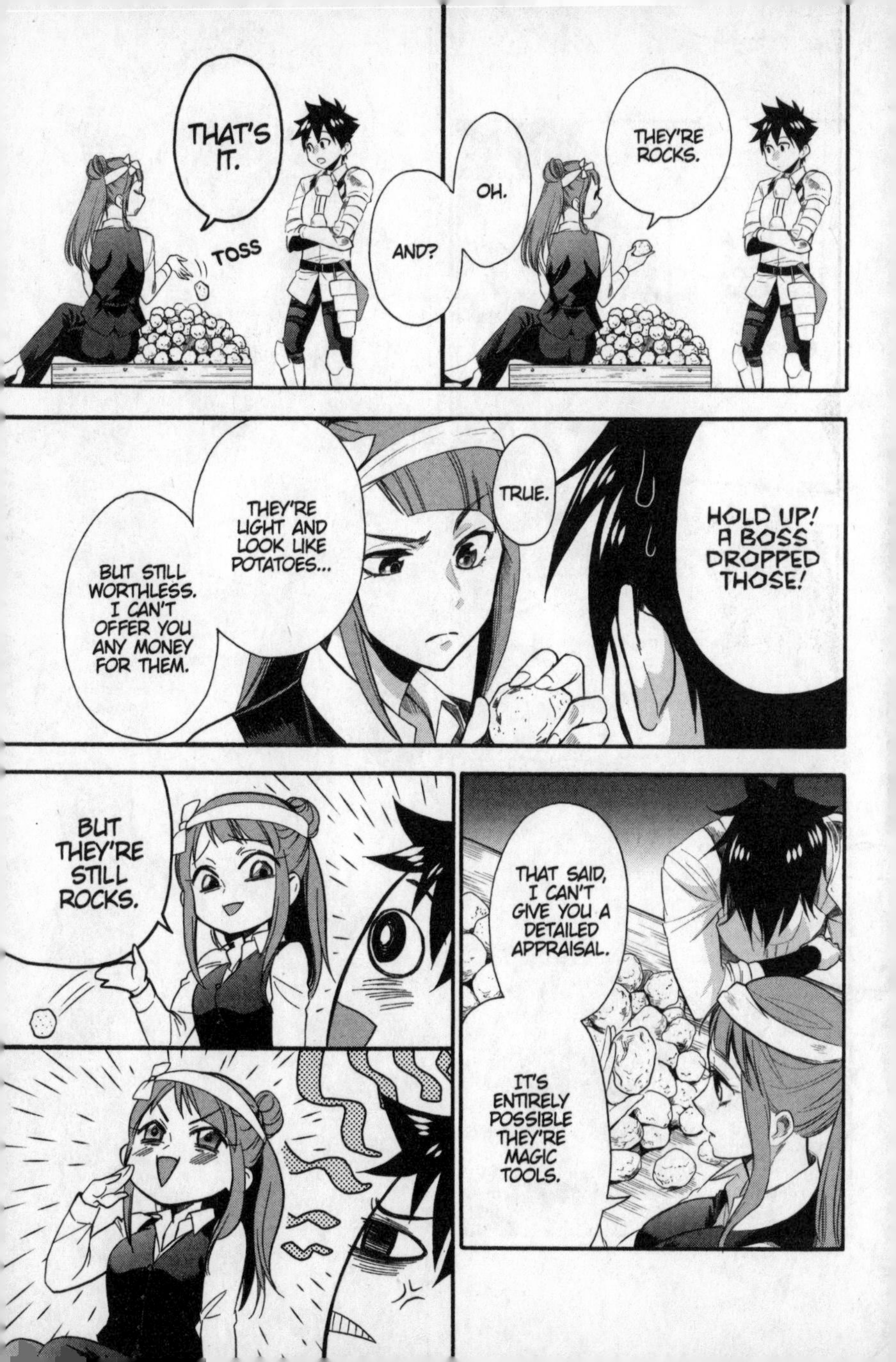
THEY'RE ROCKS.
OH.
AND?
THAT'S IT.
TOSS
HOLD UP! A BOSS DROPPED THOSE!
TRUE.
THEY'RE LIGHT AND LOOK LIKE POTATOES...
BUT STILL WORTHLESS. I CAN'T OFFER YOU ANY MONEY FOR THEM.
THAT SAID, I CAN'T GIVE YOU A DETAILED APPRAISAL.
IT'S ENTIRELY POSSIBLE THEY'RE MAGIC TOOLS.
BUT THEY'RE STILL ROCKS.

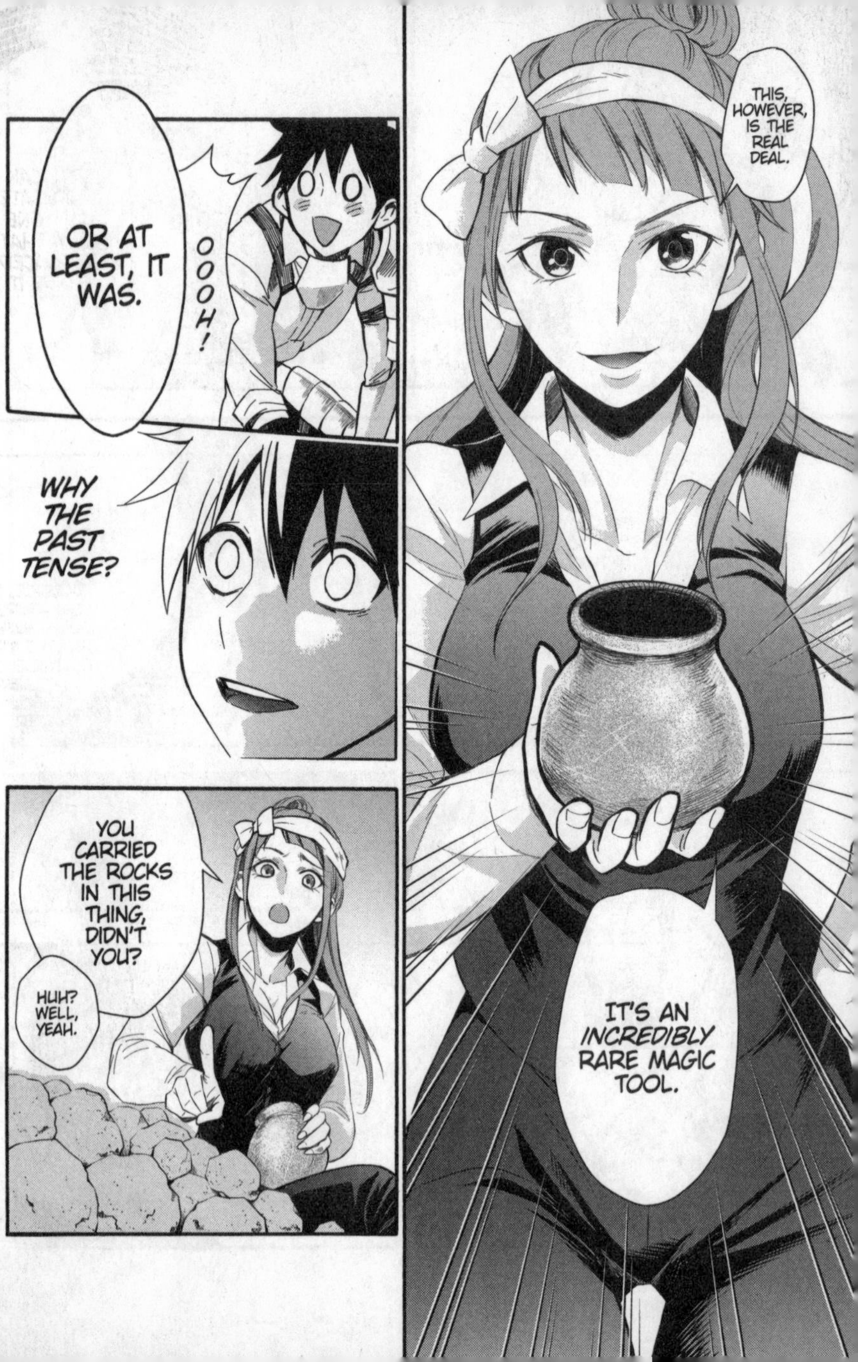
THIS, HOWEVER, IS THE REAL DEAL.
IT'S AN *INCREDIBLY* RARE MAGIC TOOL.
OOOOH!
OR AT LEAST, IT WAS.
WHY THE PAST TENSE?
YOU CARRIED THE ROCKS IN THIS THING, DIDN'T YOU?
HUH? WELL, YEAH.

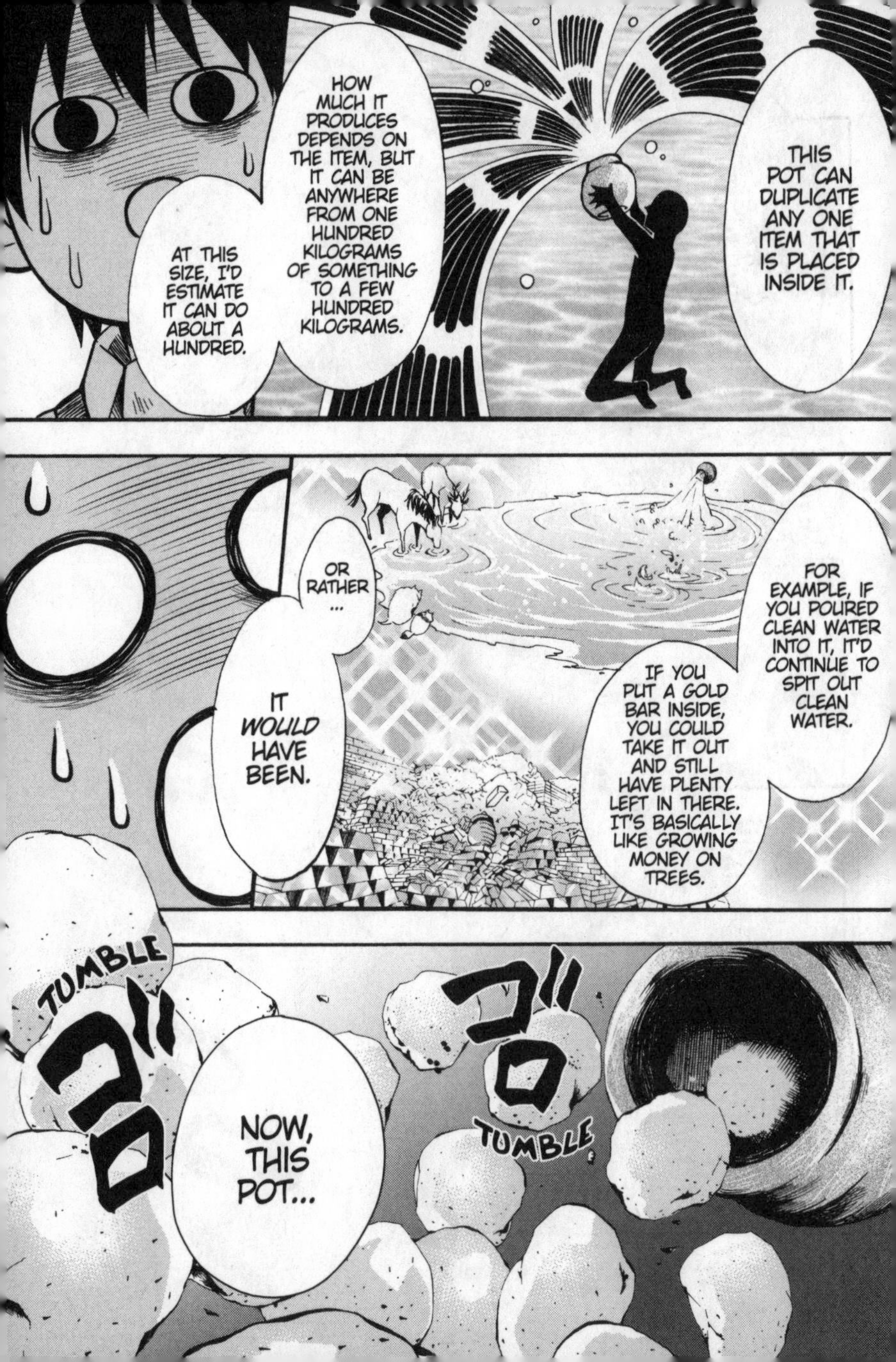
THIS POT CAN DUPLICATE ANY ONE ITEM THAT IS PLACED INSIDE IT.
HOW MUCH IT PRODUCES DEPENDS ON THE ITEM, BUT IT CAN BE ANYWHERE FROM ONE HUNDRED KILOGRAMS OF SOMETHING TO A FEW HUNDRED KILOGRAMS.
AT THIS SIZE, I'D ESTIMATE IT CAN DO ABOUT A HUNDRED.
FOR EXAMPLE, IF YOU POURED CLEAN WATER INTO IT, IT'D CONTINUE TO SPIT OUT CLEAN WATER.
IF YOU PUT A GOLD BAR INSIDE, YOU COULD TAKE IT OUT AND STILL HAVE PLENTY LEFT IN THERE. IT'S BASICALLY LIKE GROWING MONEY ON TREES.
OR RATHER...
IT *WOULD* HAVE BEEN.
ゴロ
TUMBLE
NOW, THIS POT...
ゴロ
TUMBLE

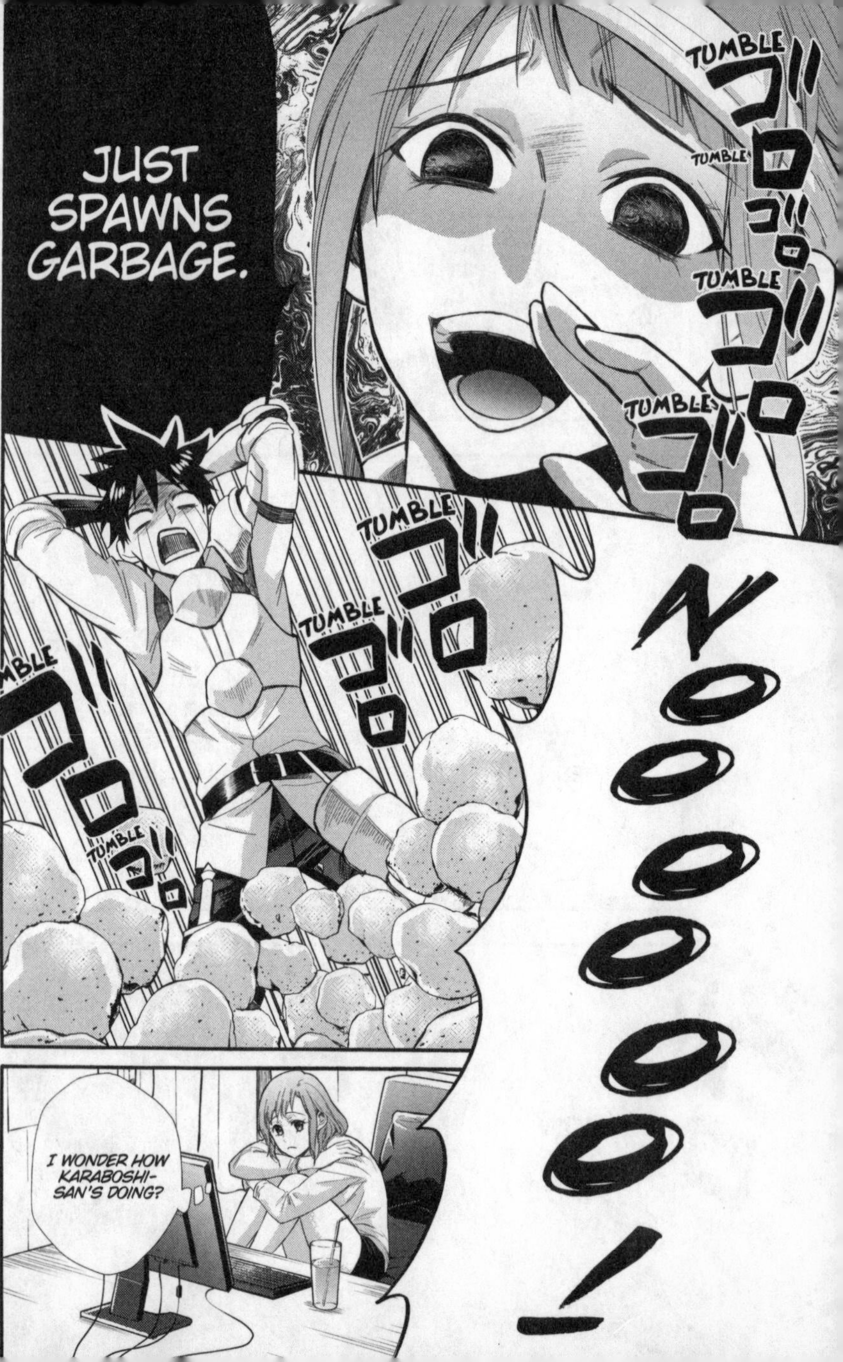
TUMBLE
TUMBLE
TUMBLE
TUMBLE
JUST SPAWNS GARBAGE.
NOOOOOOOOOO!
TUMBLE
TUMBLE
TUMBLE
TUMBLE
I WONDER HOW KARABOSHI-SAN'S DOING?

CALL TO ADVENTURE!

DEFEATING DUNGEONS
WITH A SKILL BOARD

2

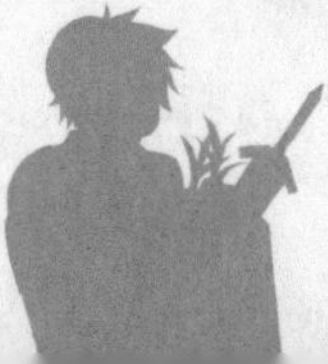

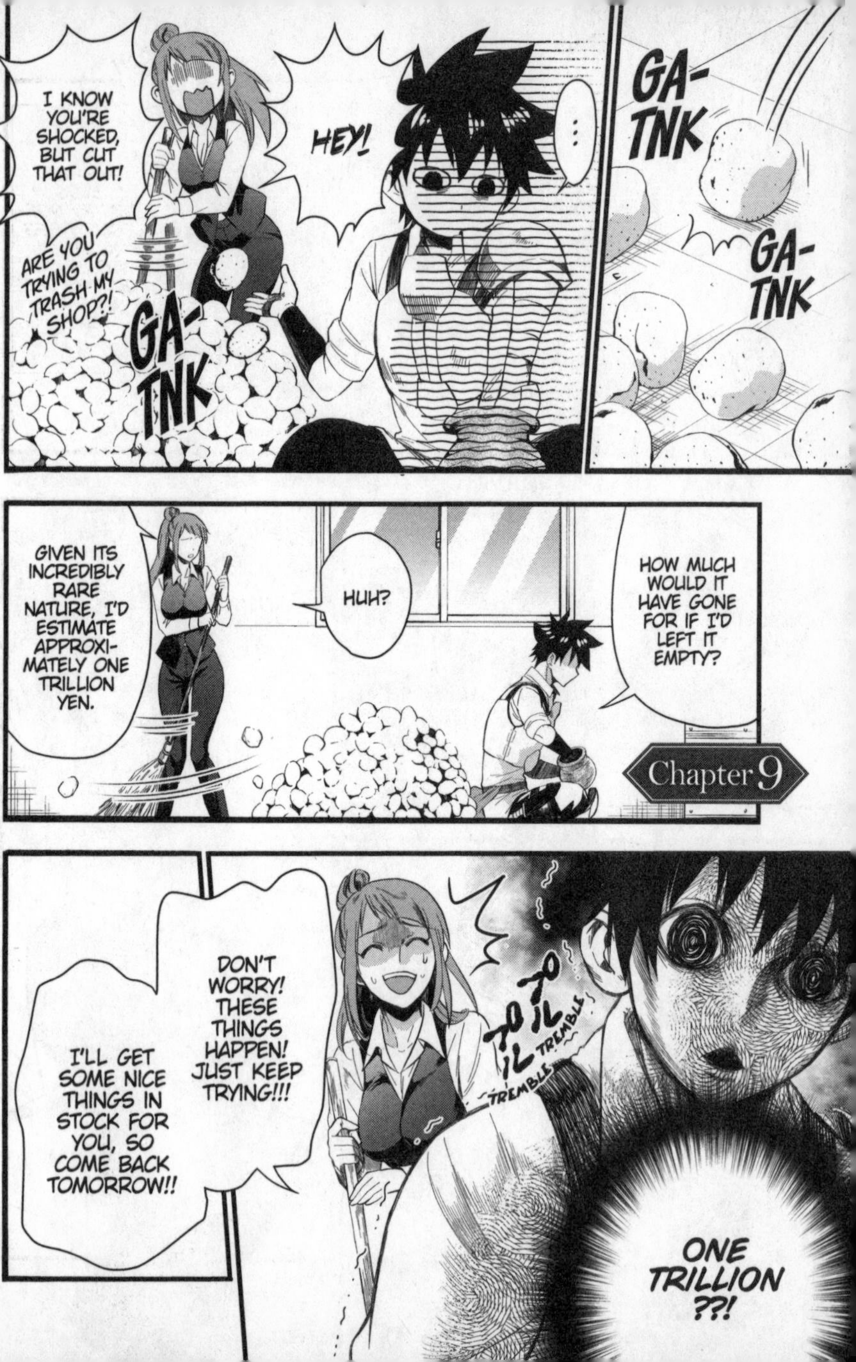
GA-TNK
GA-TNK
...
HEY!
I KNOW YOU'RE SHOCKED, BUT CUT THAT OUT!
ARE YOU TRYING TO TRASH MY SHOP?!
GA-TNK
HOW MUCH WOULD IT HAVE GONE FOR IF I'D LEFT IT EMPTY?
HUH?
GIVEN ITS INCREDIBLY RARE NATURE, I'D ESTIMATE APPROXIMATELY ONE TRILLION YEN.
Chapter 9
ONE TRILLION ??!
プル プル
TREMBLE TREMBLE
DON'T WORRY! THESE THINGS HAPPEN! JUST KEEP TRYING!!!
I'LL GET SOME NICE THINGS IN STOCK FOR YOU, SO COME BACK TOMORROW!!

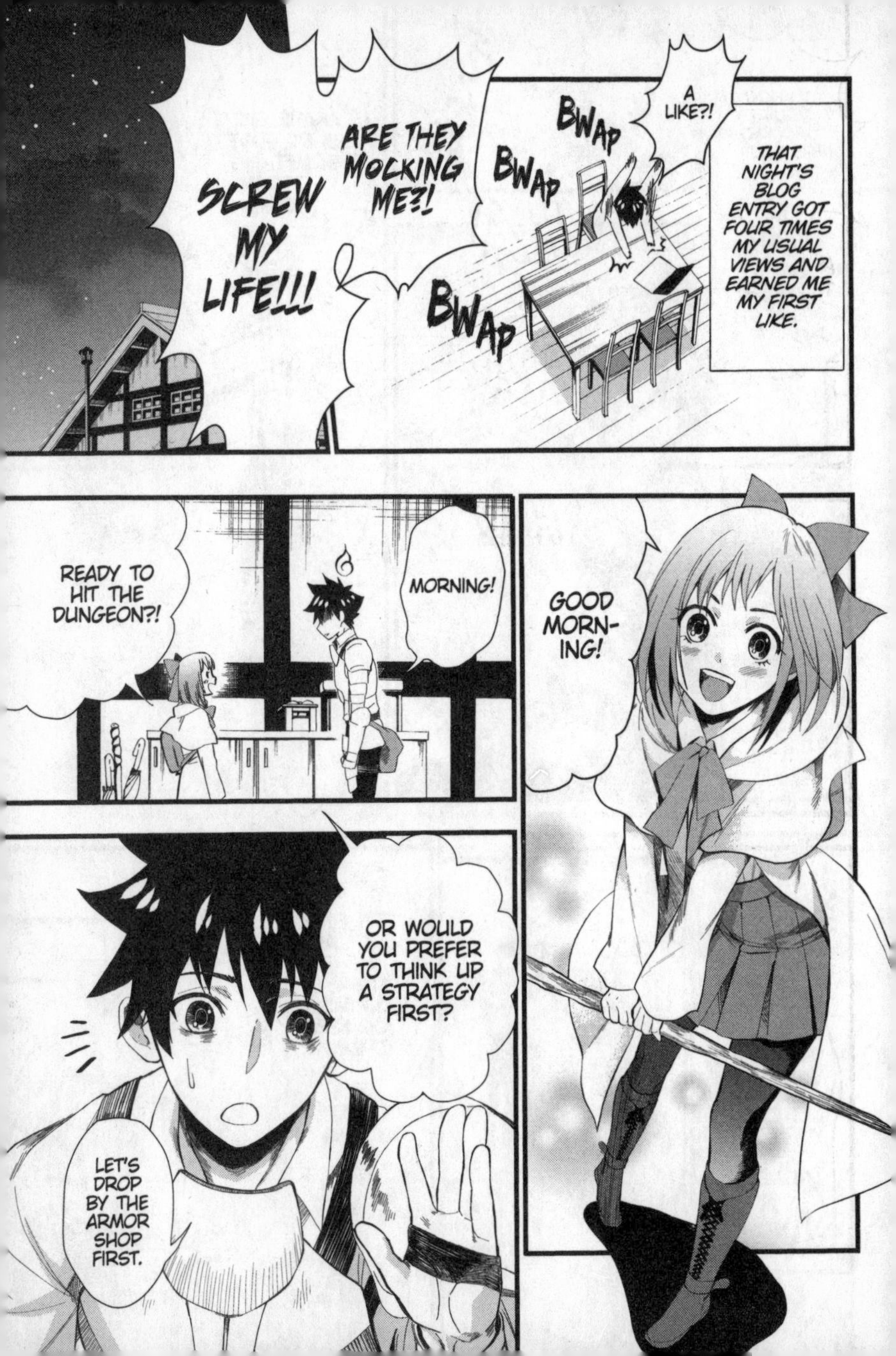
THAT NIGHT'S BLOG ENTRY GOT FOUR TIMES MY USUAL VIEWS AND EARNED ME MY FIRST LIKE.
A LIKE?!
BWAP
BWAP
BWAP
ARE THEY MOCKING ME?!
SCREW MY LIFE!!!
GOOD MORN-ING!
MORNING!
READY TO HIT THE DUNGEON?!
OR WOULD YOU PREFER TO THINK UP A STRATEGY FIRST?
LET'S DROP BY THE ARMOR SHOP FIRST.

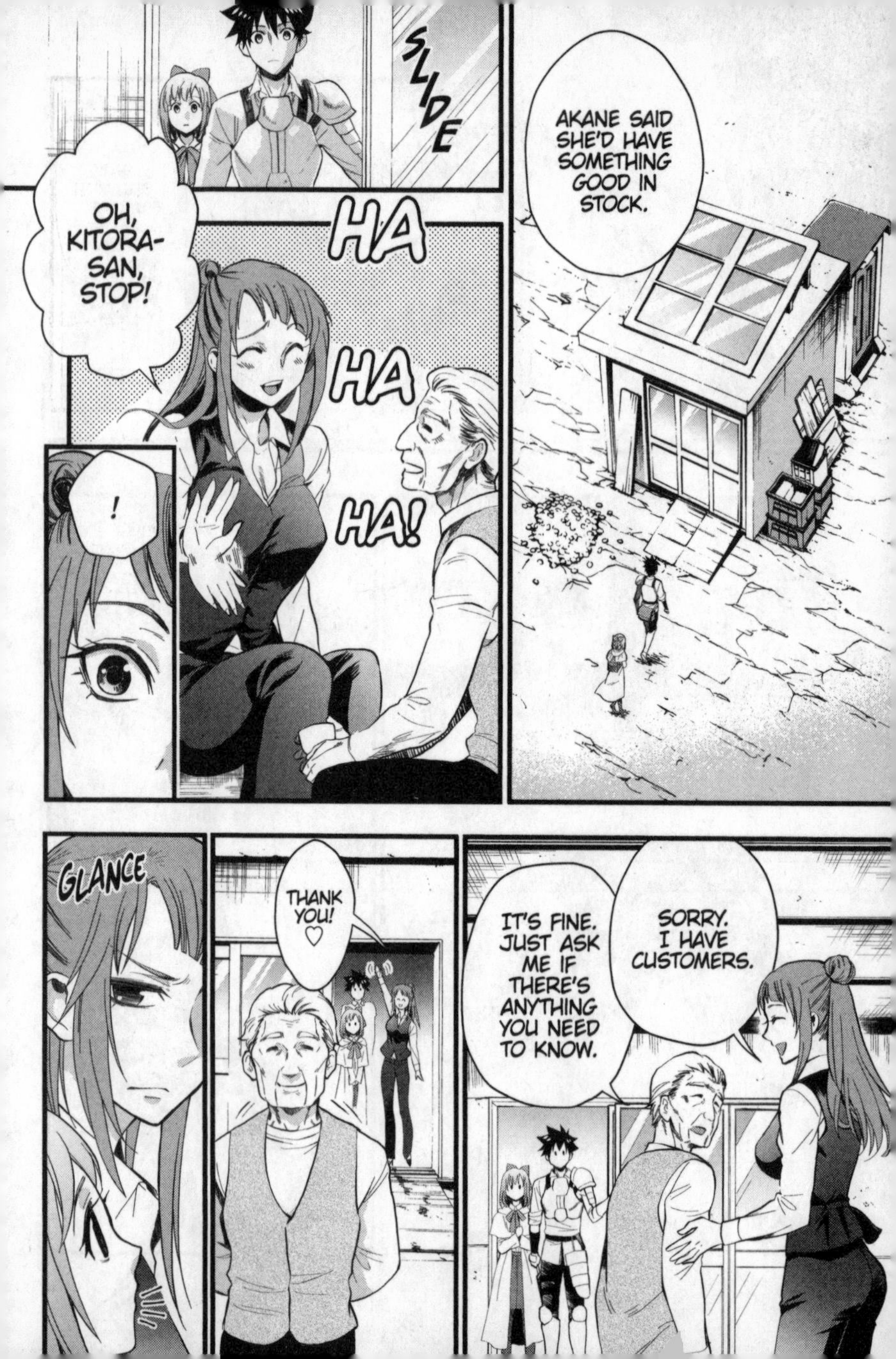
AKANE SAID SHE'D HAVE SOMETHING GOOD IN STOCK.
SLIDE
OH, KITORA-SAN, STOP!
HA
HA
HA!
!
SORRY. I HAVE CUSTOMERS.
IT'S FINE. JUST ASK ME IF THERE'S ANYTHING YOU NEED TO KNOW.
THANK YOU! ♡
GLANCE

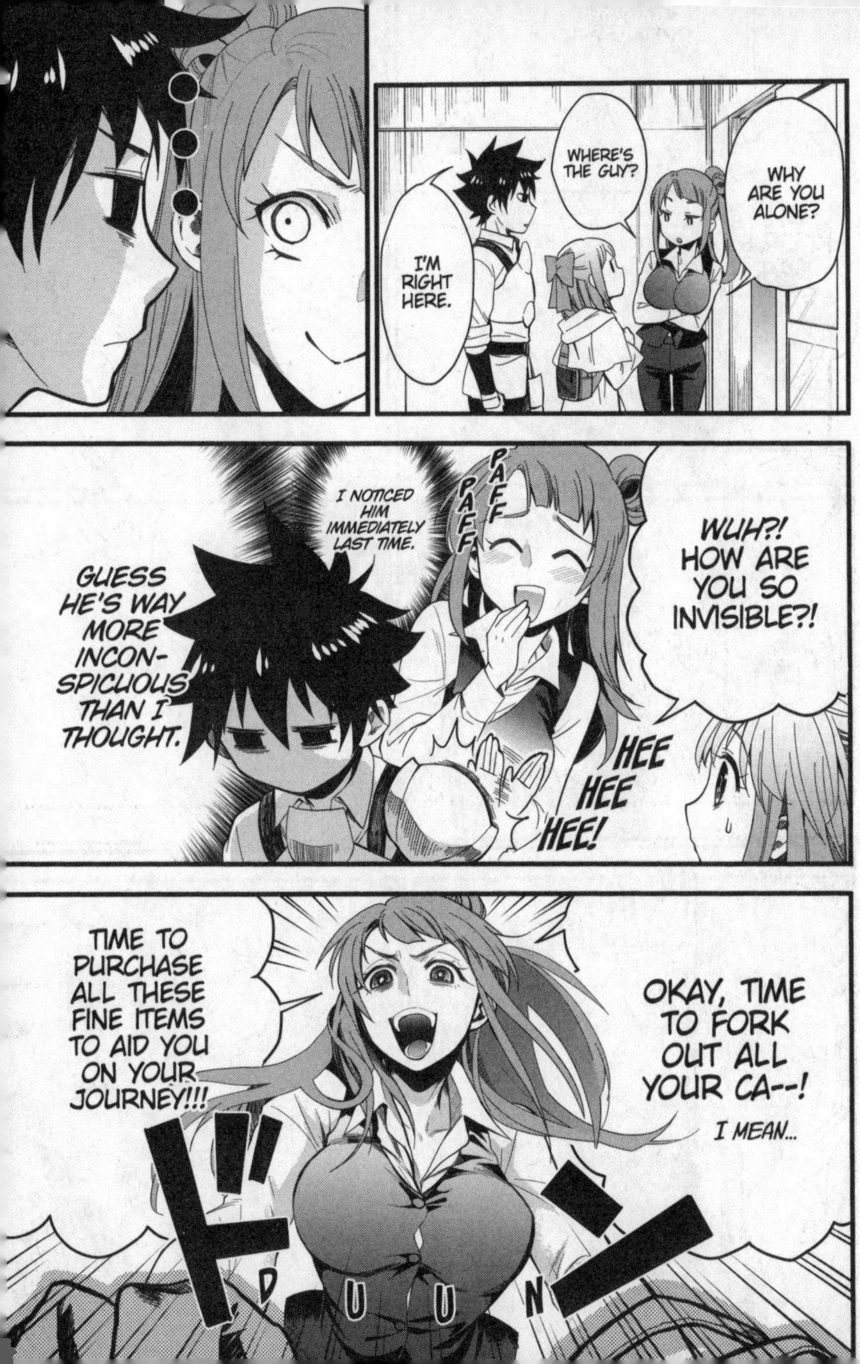
WHY ARE YOU ALONE?
WHERE'S THE GUY?
I'M RIGHT HERE.
WUH?! HOW ARE YOU SO INVISIBLE?!
PAFF PAFF PAFF
I NOTICED HIM IMMEDIATELY LAST TIME.
HEE HEE HEE!
GUESS HE'S WAY MORE INCON-SPICUOUS THAN I THOUGHT.
OKAY, TIME TO FORK OUT ALL YOUR CA--!
I MEAN...
TIME TO PURCHASE ALL THESE FINE ITEMS TO AID YOU ON YOUR JOURNEY!!!
DUUUN

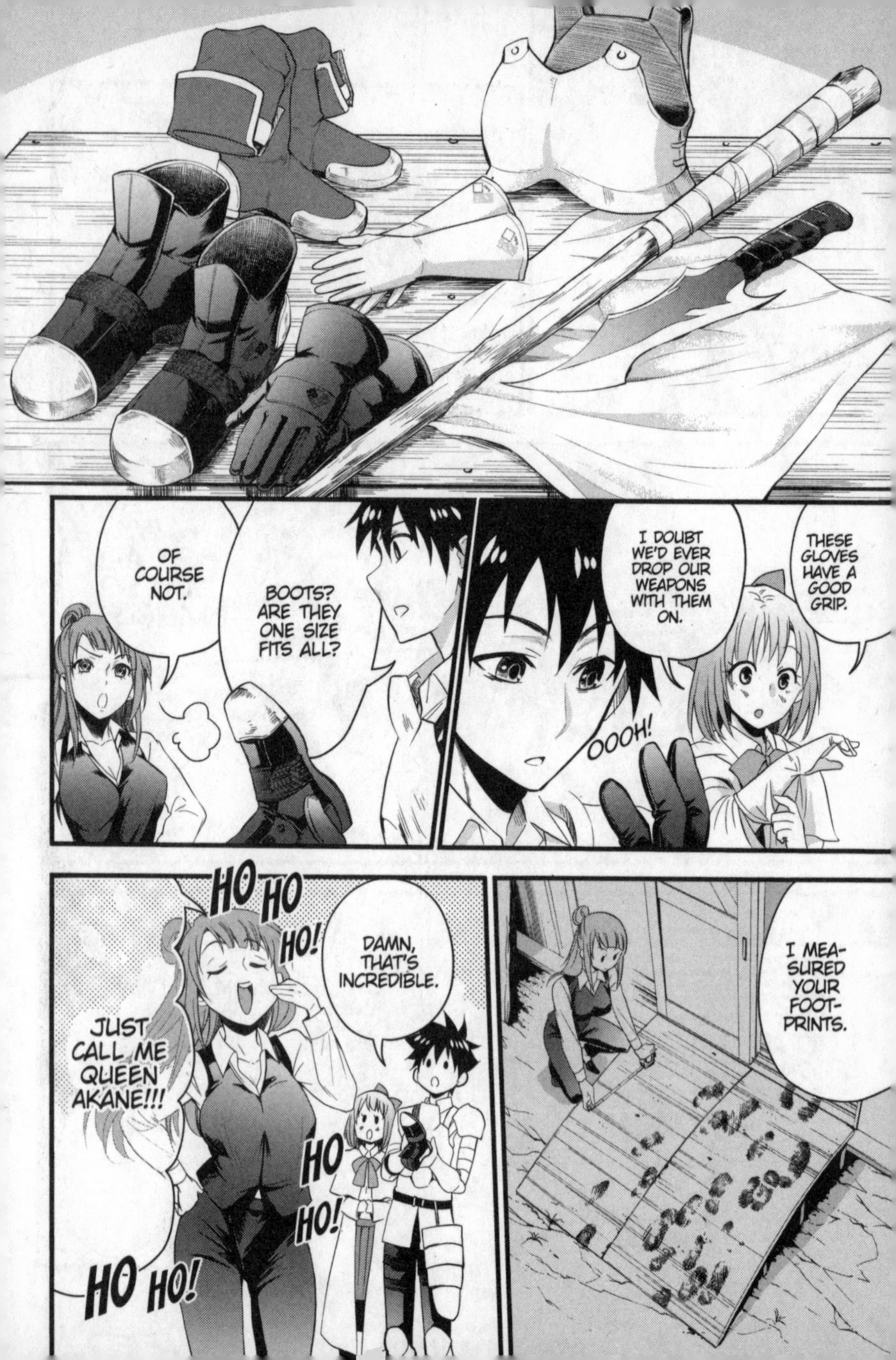
THESE GLOVES HAVE A GOOD GRIP.
I DOUBT WE'D EVER DROP OUR WEAPONS WITH THEM ON.
OOOH!
BOOTS? ARE THEY ONE SIZE FITS ALL?
OF COURSE NOT.
I MEA-SURED YOUR FOOT-PRINTS.
HO HO HO!
DAMN, THAT'S INCREDIBLE.
JUST CALL ME QUEEN AKANE!!!
HO HO!
HO HO!

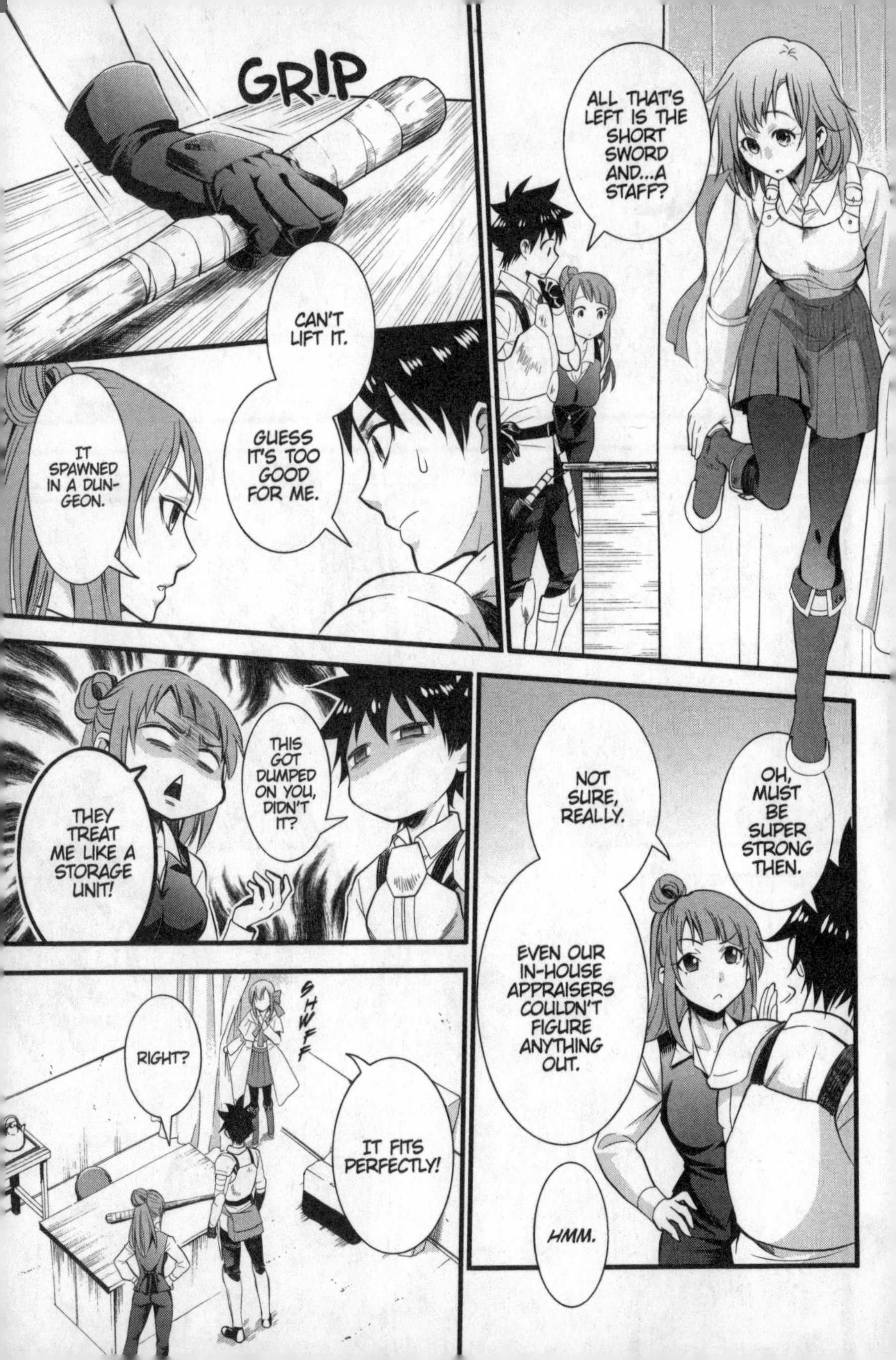

ALL THAT'S LEFT IS THE SHORT SWORD AND...A STAFF?
GRIP
CAN'T LIFT IT.
GUESS IT'S TOO GOOD FOR ME.
IT SPAWNED IN A DUNGEON.
OH, MUST BE SUPER STRONG THEN.
NOT SURE, REALLY.
EVEN OUR IN-HOUSE APPRAISERS COULDN'T FIGURE ANYTHING OUT.
HMM.
THIS GOT DUMPED ON YOU, DIDN'T IT?
THEY TREAT ME LIKE A STORAGE UNIT!
SHWFF
IT FITS PERFECTLY!
RIGHT?

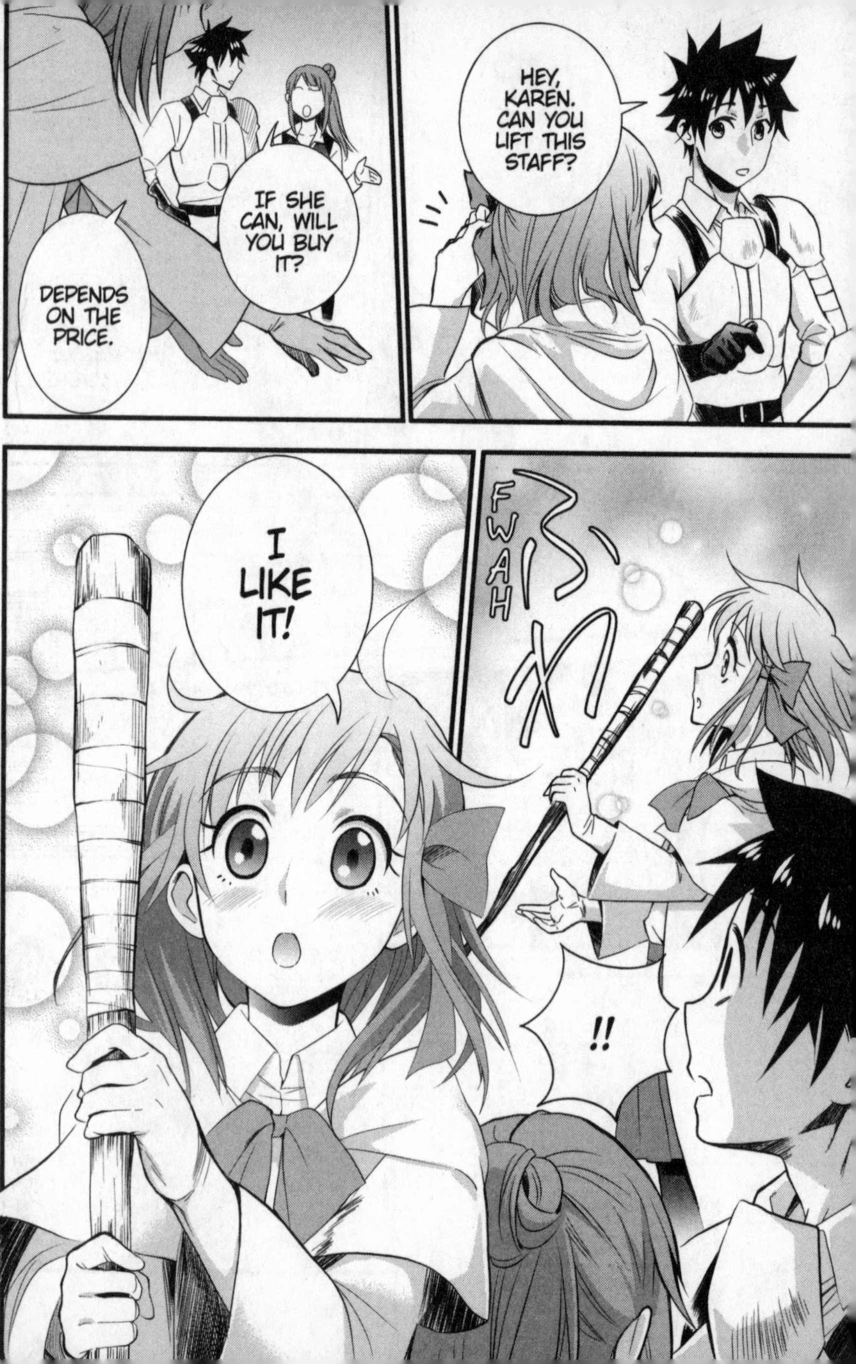
HEY, KAREN. CAN YOU LIFT THIS STAFF?
IF SHE CAN, WILL YOU BUY IT?
DEPENDS ON THE PRICE.
FWAH
!!
I LIKE IT!

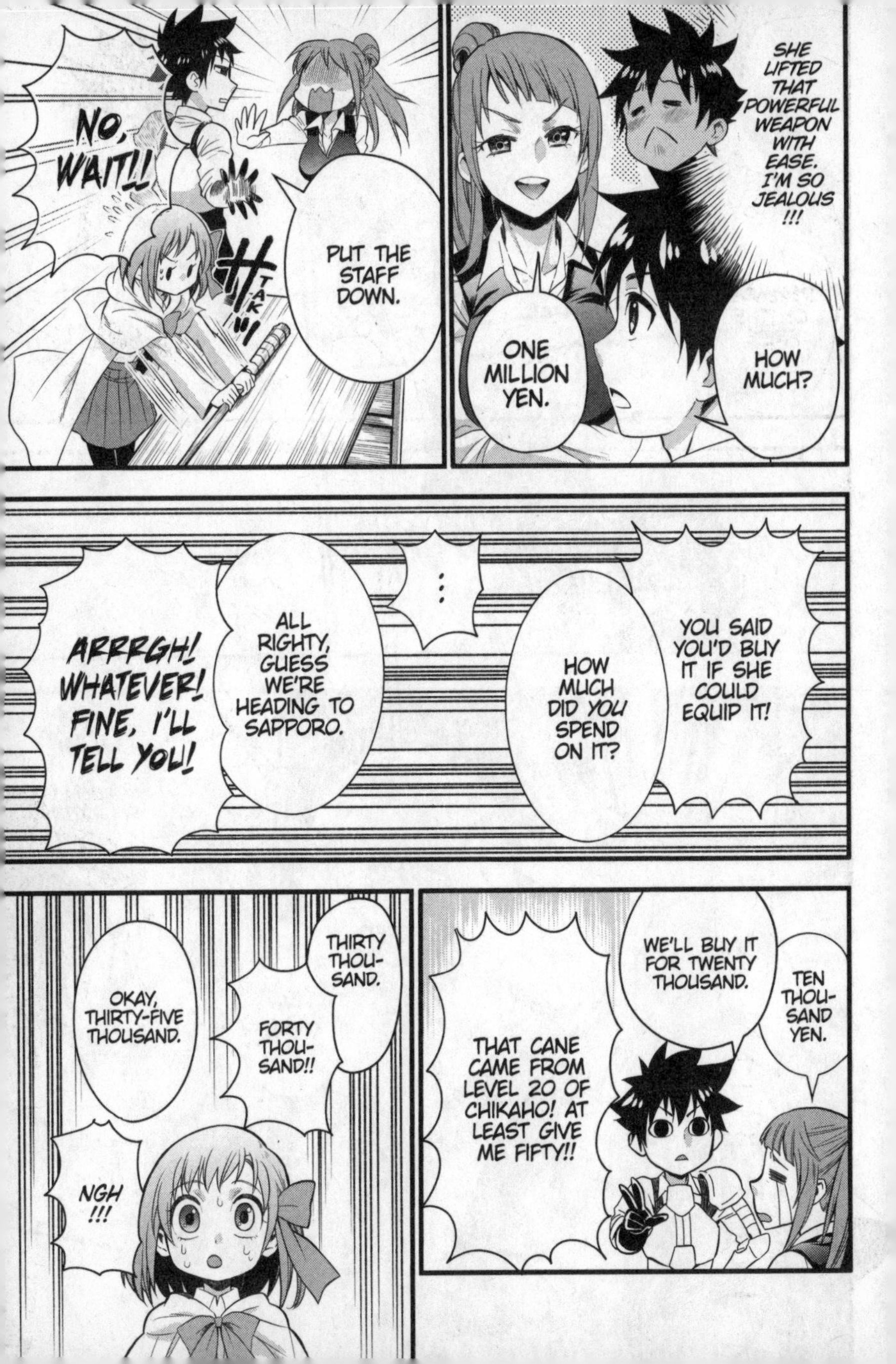
SHE LIFTED THAT POWERFUL WEAPON WITH EASE. I'M SO JEALOUS!!!
HOW MUCH?
ONE MILLION YEN.
PUT THE STAFF DOWN.
TAK
NO, WAIT!!
YOU SAID YOU'D BUY IT IF SHE COULD EQUIP IT!
HOW MUCH DID YOU SPEND ON IT?
...
ALL RIGHTY, GUESS WE'RE HEADING TO SAPPORO.
ARRRGH! WHATEVER! FINE, I'LL TELL YOU!
TEN THOUSAND YEN.
WE'LL BUY IT FOR TWENTY THOUSAND.
THAT CANE CAME FROM LEVEL 20 OF CHIKAHO! AT LEAST GIVE ME FIFTY!!
THIRTY THOUSAND.
OKAY, THIRTY-FIVE THOUSAND.
FORTY THOUSAND!!
NGH!!!

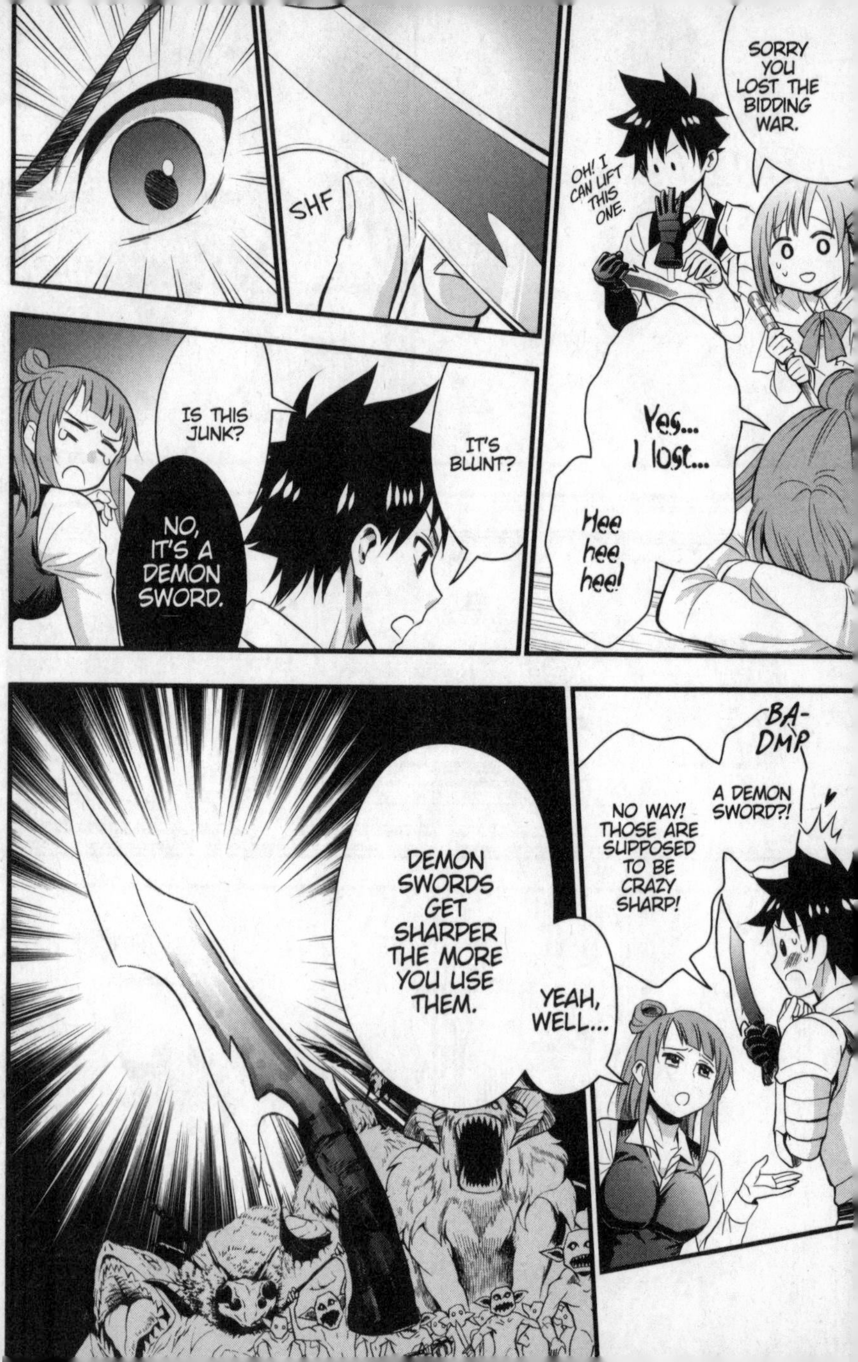
SORRY YOU LOST THE BIDDING WAR.
OH! I CAN LIFT THIS ONE.
Yes... I lost...
Hee hee hee!
SHF
IT'S BLUNT?
IS THIS JUNK?
NO, IT'S A DEMON SWORD.
BA-DMP
A DEMON SWORD?!
NO WAY! THOSE ARE SUPPOSED TO BE CRAZY SHARP!
YEAH, WELL...
DEMON SWORDS GET SHARPER THE MORE YOU USE THEM.

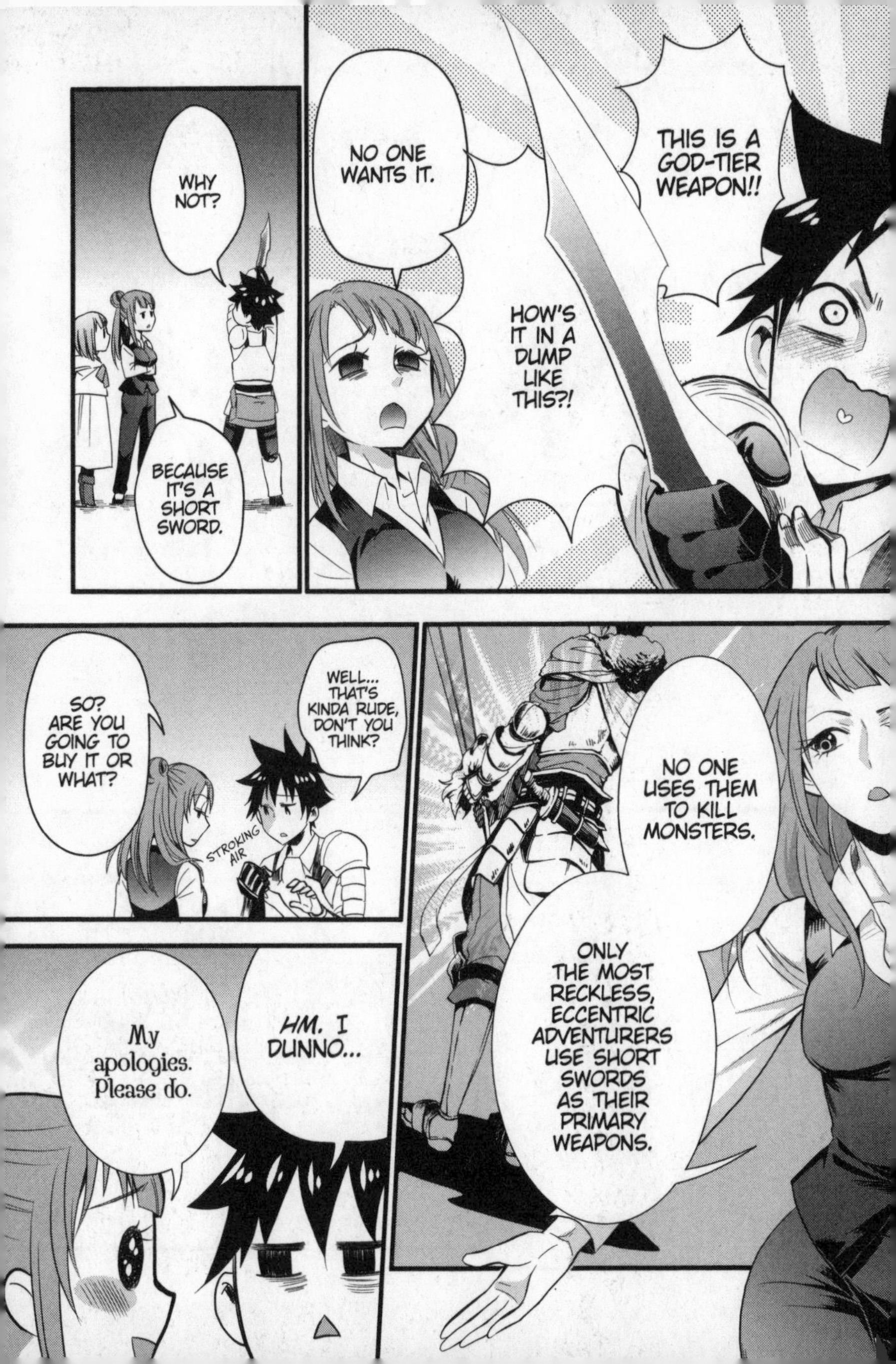
THIS IS A GOD-TIER WEAPON!!
HOW'S IT IN A DUMP LIKE THIS?!
NO ONE WANTS IT.
WHY NOT?
BECAUSE IT'S A SHORT SWORD.
NO ONE USES THEM TO KILL MONSTERS.
ONLY THE MOST RECKLESS, ECCENTRIC ADVENTURERS USE SHORT SWORDS AS THEIR PRIMARY WEAPONS.
WELL... THAT'S KINDA RUDE, DON'T YOU THINK?
STROKING AIR
SO? ARE YOU GOING TO BUY IT OR WHAT?
HM. I DUNNO...
My apologies. Please do.

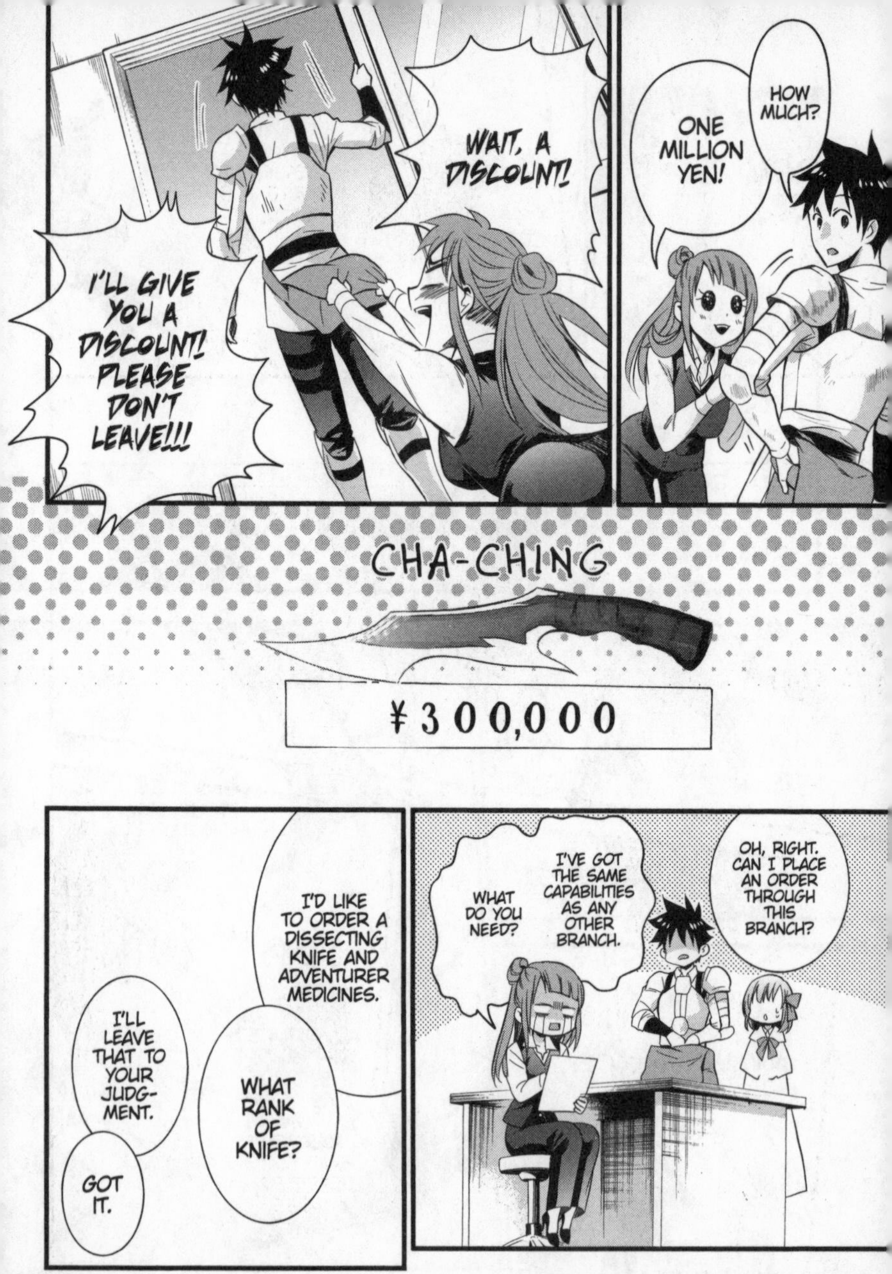
HOW MUCH?
ONE MILLION YEN!
WAIT, A DISCOUNT!
I'LL GIVE YOU A DISCOUNT! PLEASE DON'T LEAVE!!!
CHA-CHING
¥300,000
OH, RIGHT. CAN I PLACE AN ORDER THROUGH THIS BRANCH?
I'VE GOT THE SAME CAPABILITIES AS ANY OTHER BRANCH.
WHAT DO YOU NEED?
I'D LIKE TO ORDER A DISSECTING KNIFE AND ADVENTURER MEDICINES.
WHAT RANK OF KNIFE?
I'LL LEAVE THAT TO YOUR JUDGMENT.
GOT IT.

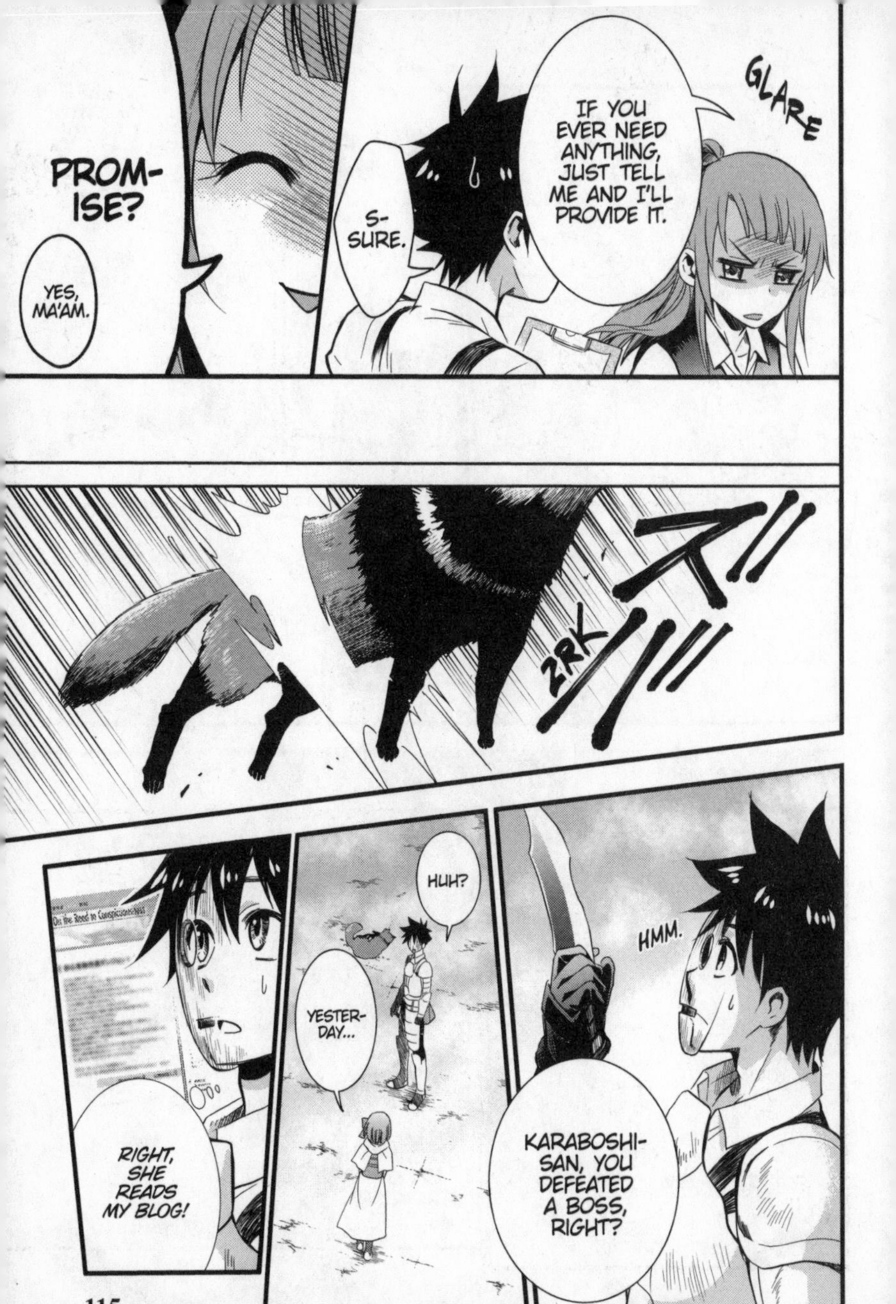
GLARE
IF YOU EVER NEED ANYTHING, JUST TELL ME AND I'LL PROVIDE IT.
S-SURE.
PROMISE?
YES, MA'AM.
ZRK
HMM.
KARABOSHI-SAN, YOU DEFEATED A BOSS, RIGHT?
HUH?
YESTERDAY...
RIGHT, SHE READS MY BLOG!

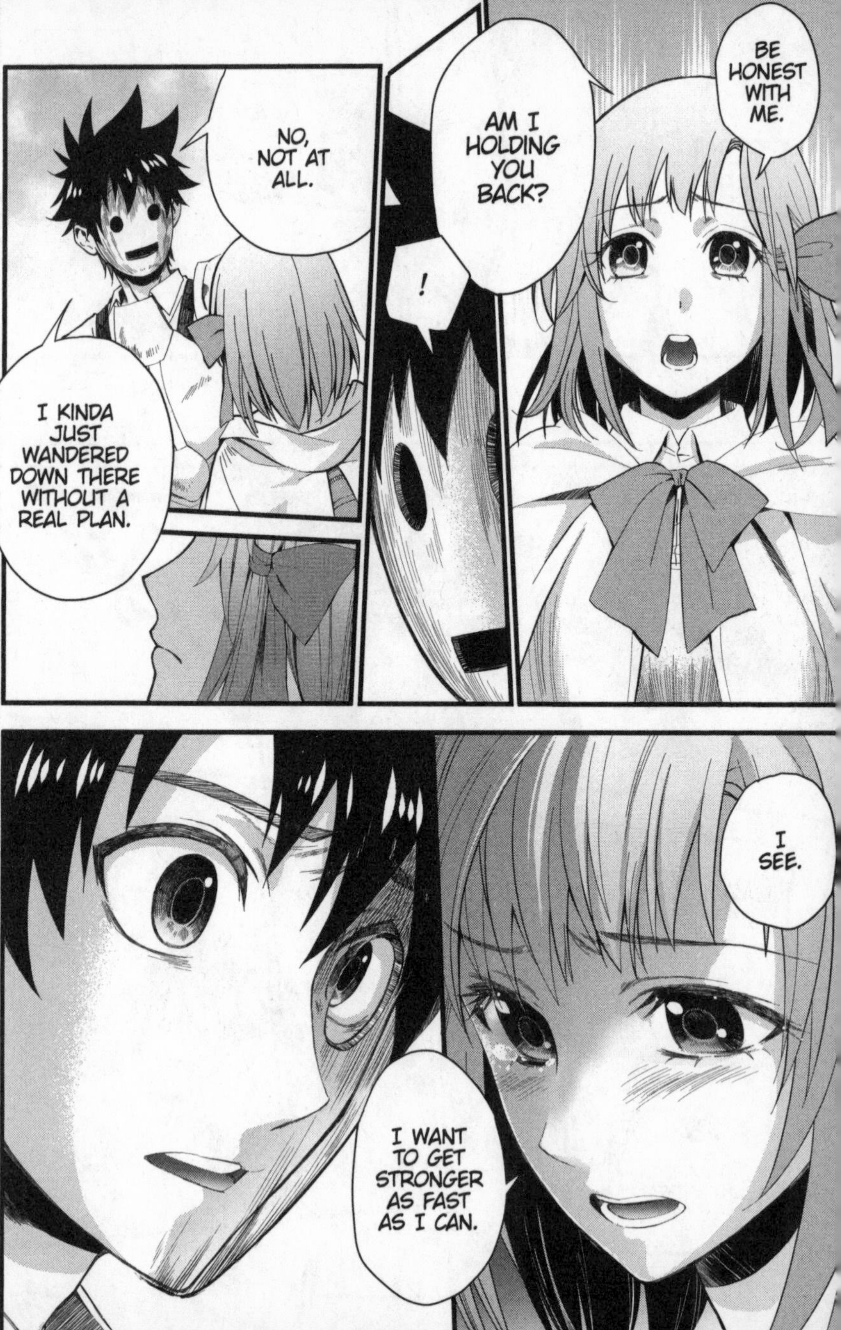
BE HONEST WITH ME.
AM I HOLDING YOU BACK?
!
NO, NOT AT ALL.
I KINDA JUST WANDERED DOWN THERE WITHOUT A REAL PLAN.
I SEE.
I WANT TO GET STRONGER AS FAST AS I CAN.

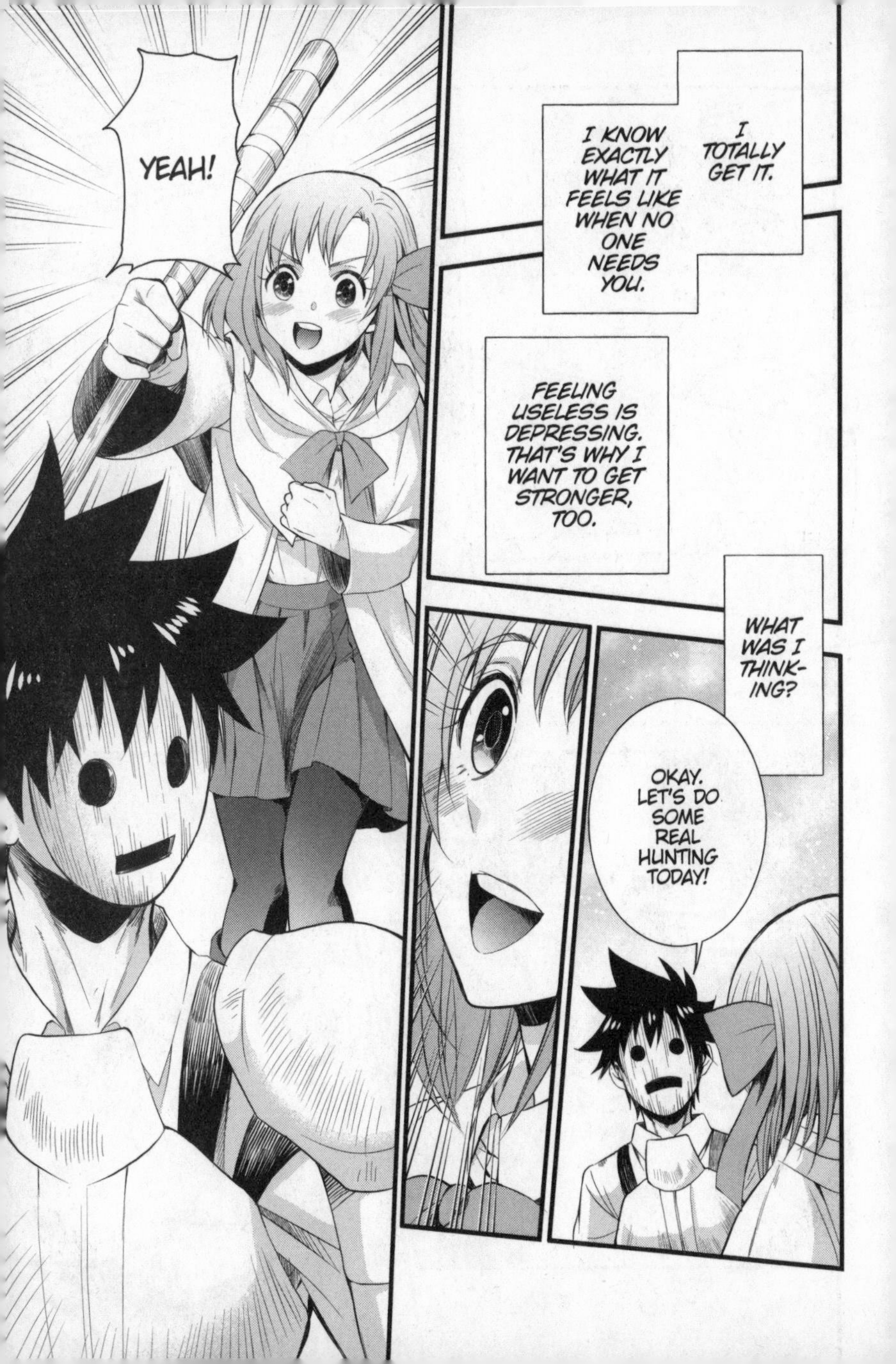
I TOTALLY GET IT.
I KNOW EXACTLY WHAT IT FEELS LIKE WHEN NO ONE NEEDS YOU.
FEELING USELESS IS DEPRESSING. THAT'S WHY I WANT TO GET STRONGER, TOO.
WHAT WAS I THINKING?
OKAY. LET'S DO SOME REAL HUNTING TODAY!
YEAH!

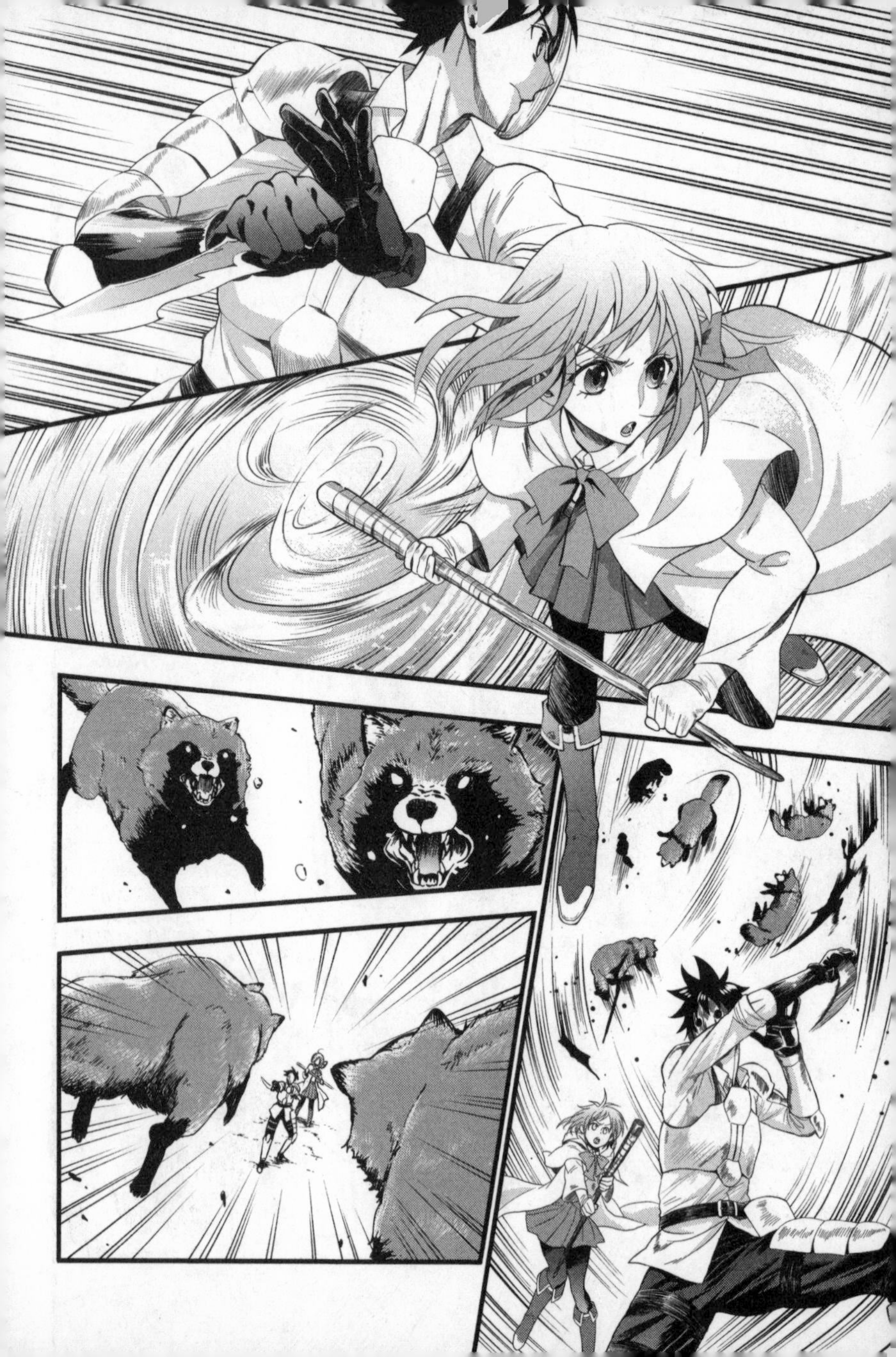

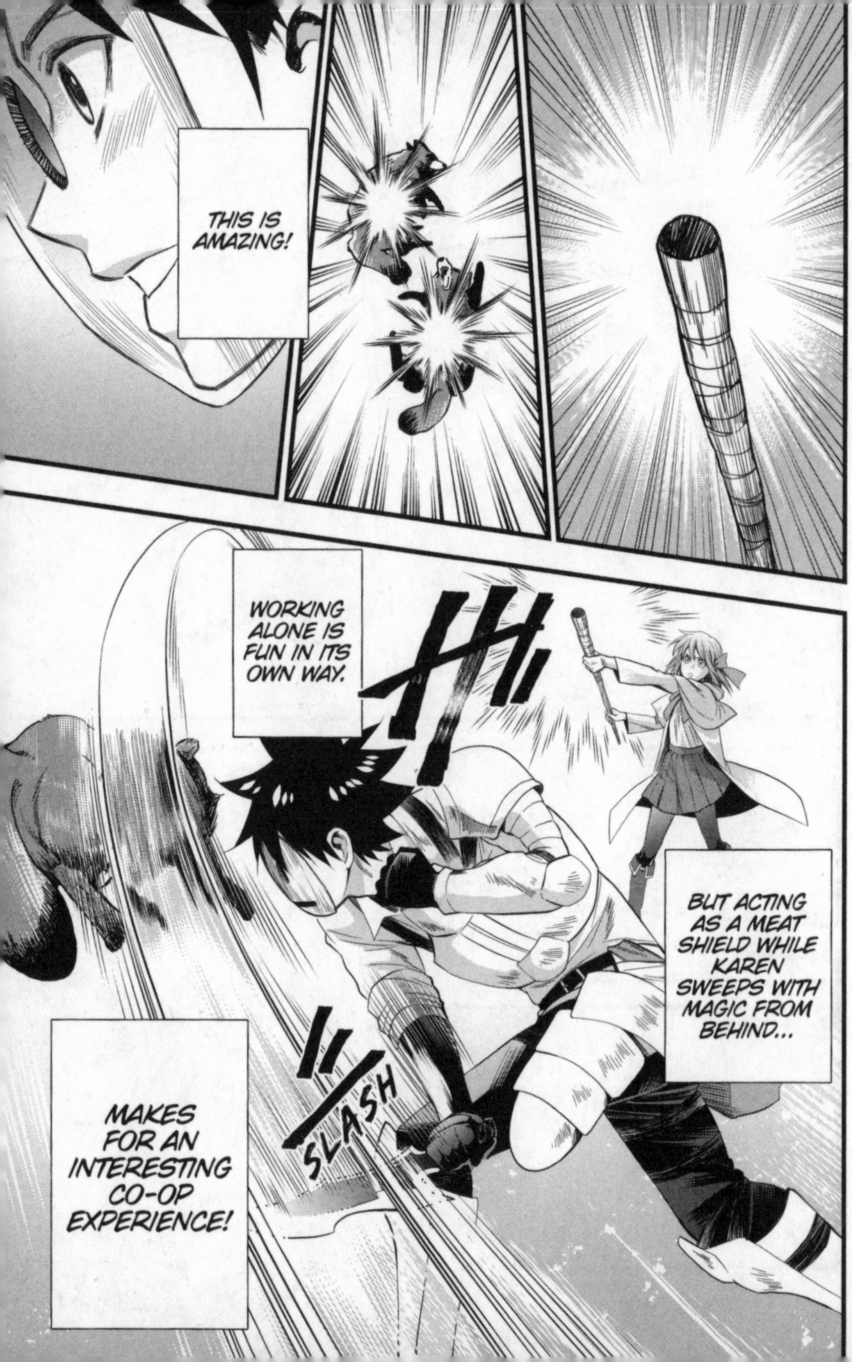
THIS IS AMAZING!
WORKING ALONE IS FUN IN ITS OWN WAY.
BUT ACTING AS A MEAT SHIELD WHILE KAREN SWEEPS WITH MAGIC FROM BEHIND...
SLASH
MAKES FOR AN INTERESTING CO-OP EXPERIENCE!

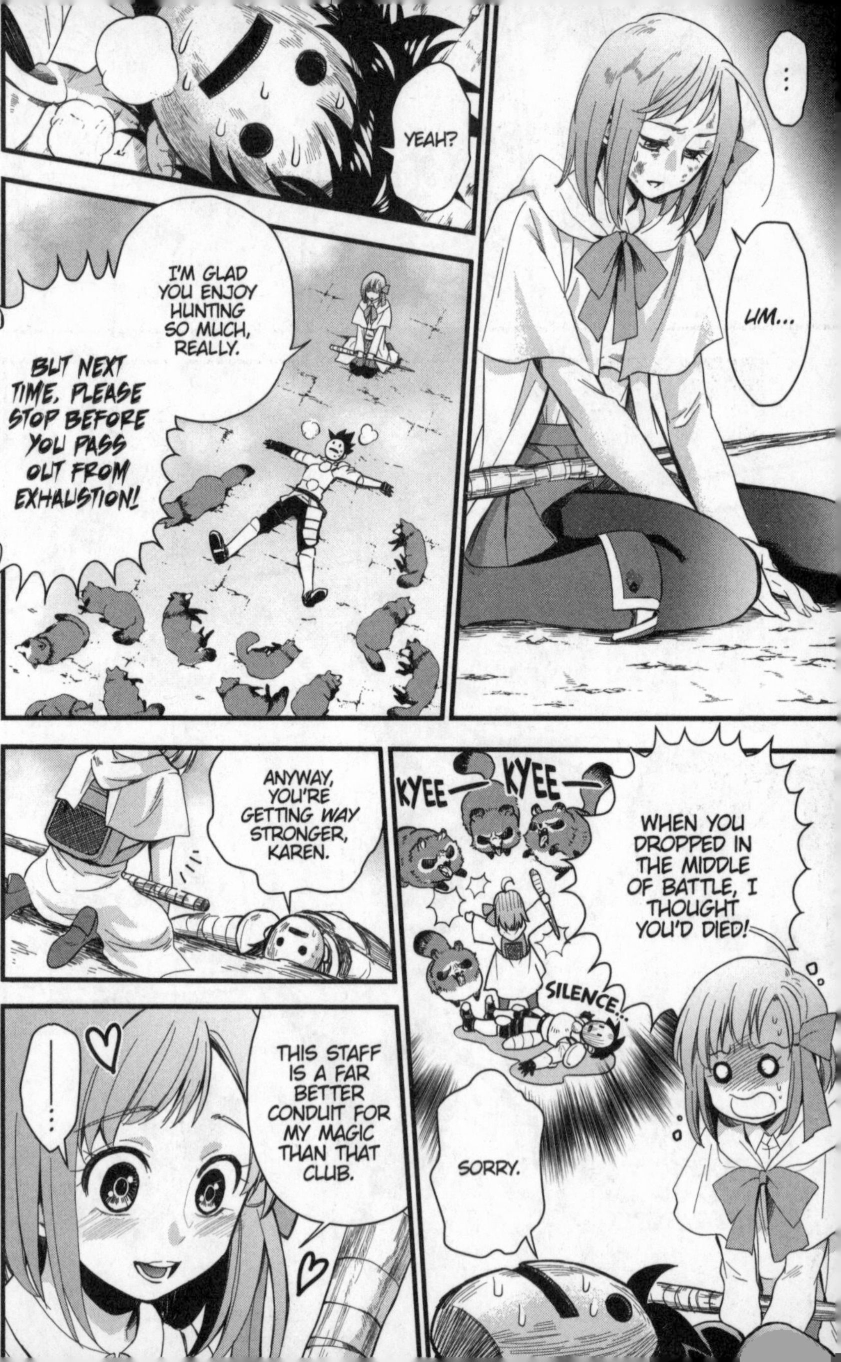
...
UM...
YEAH?
I'M GLAD YOU ENJOY HUNTING SO MUCH, REALLY.
BUT NEXT TIME, PLEASE STOP BEFORE YOU PASS OUT FROM EXHAUSTION!
WHEN YOU DROPPED IN THE MIDDLE OF BATTLE, I THOUGHT YOU'D DIED!
KYEE— KYEE—
SILENCE...
SORRY.
ANYWAY, YOU'RE GETTING WAY STRONGER, KAREN.
THIS STAFF IS A FAR BETTER CONDUIT FOR MY MAGIC THAN THAT CLUB.
!...

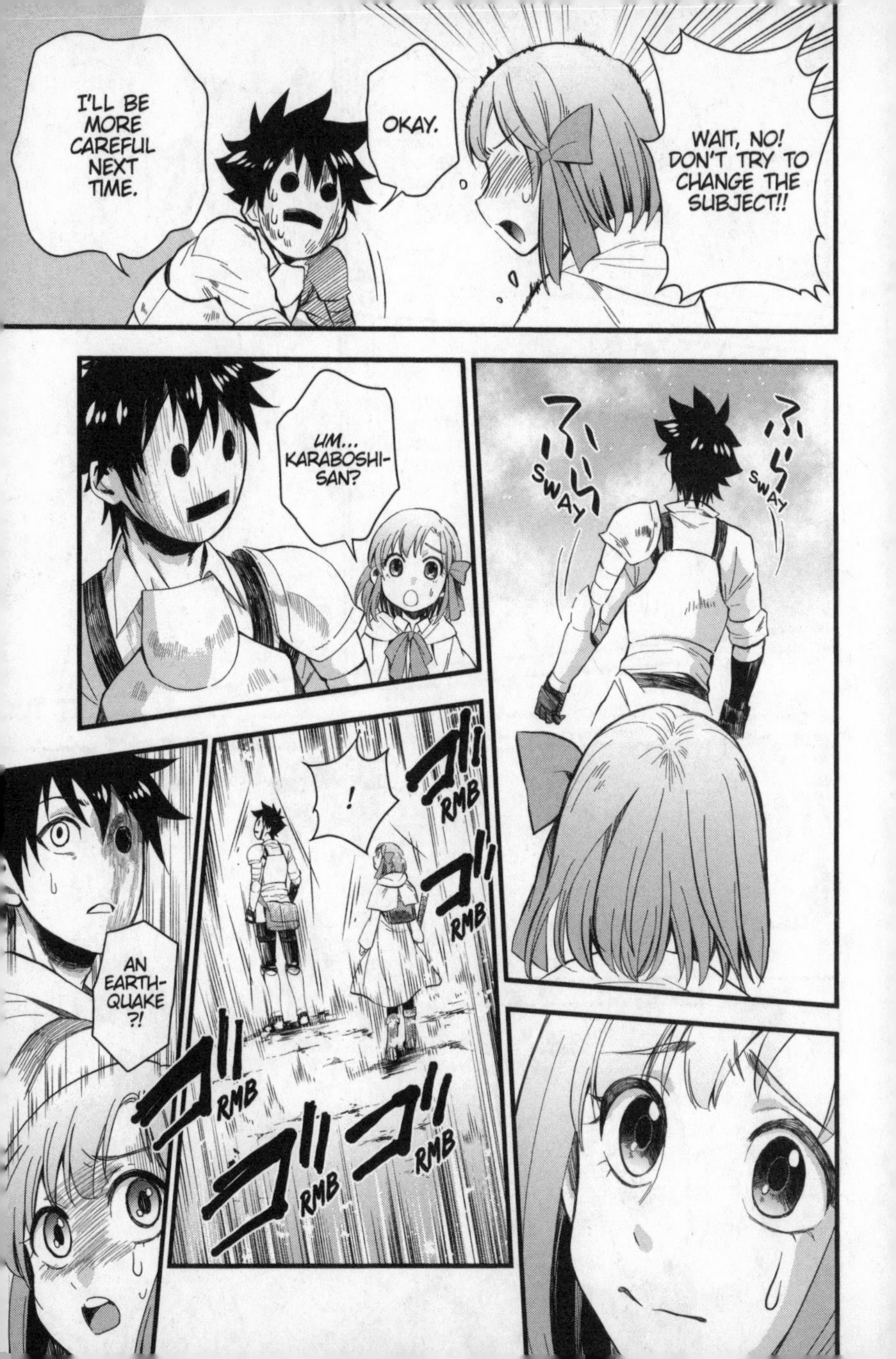
WAIT, NO! DON'T TRY TO CHANGE THE SUBJECT!!
OKAY.
I'LL BE MORE CAREFUL NEXT TIME.
ふらふら
SWAY SWAY
UM... KARABOSHI-SAN?
ゴゴゴ
RMB RMB
!
AN EARTH-QUAKE?!
ゴゴゴ
RMB RMB RMB

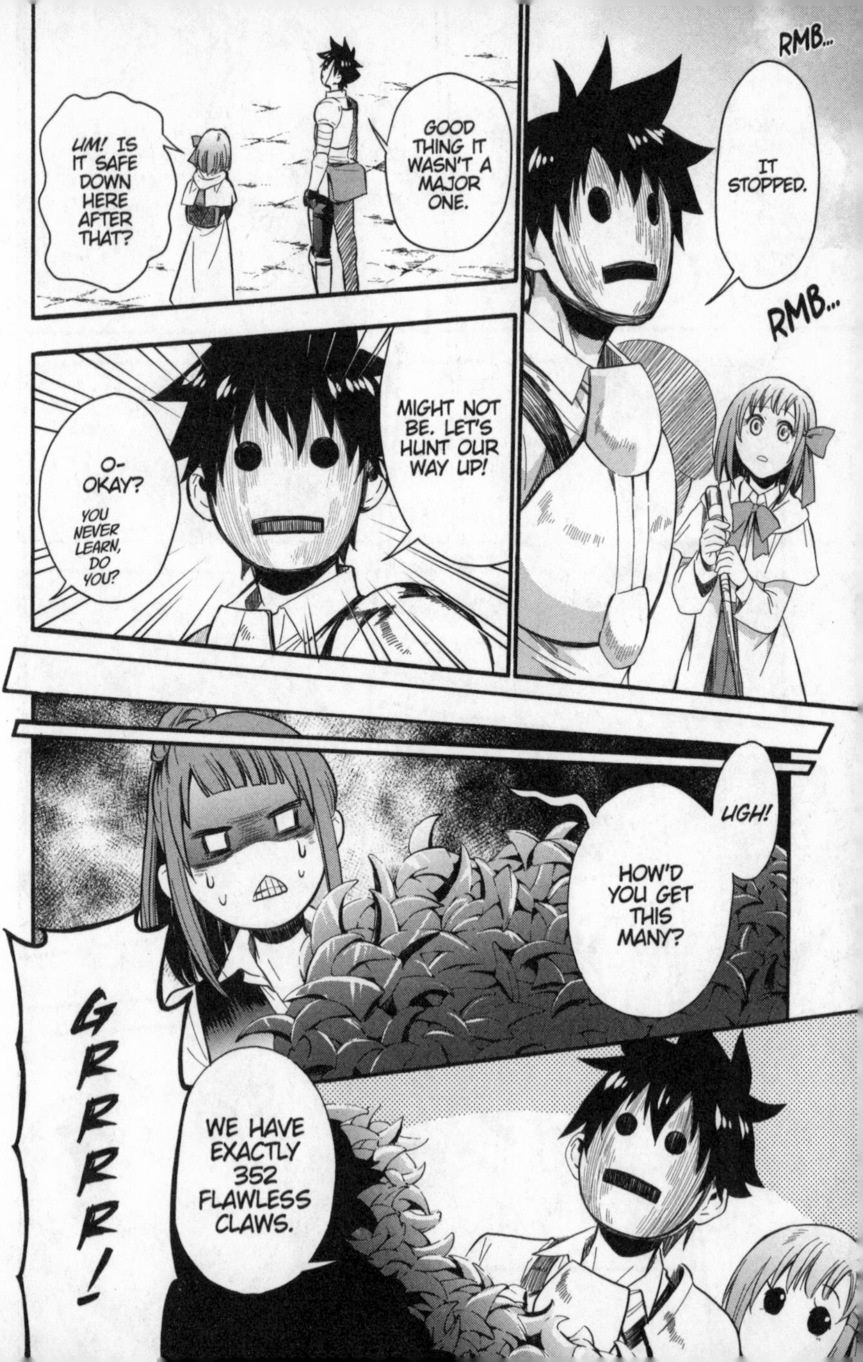
RMB...
IT STOPPED.
RMB...
GOOD THING IT WASN'T A MAJOR ONE.
UM! IS IT SAFE DOWN HERE AFTER THAT?
MIGHT NOT BE. LET'S HUNT OUR WAY UP!
O-OKAY?
YOU NEVER LEARN, DO YOU?
UGH!
HOW'D YOU GET THIS MANY?
GRRRR!
WE HAVE EXACTLY 352 FLAWLESS CLAWS.

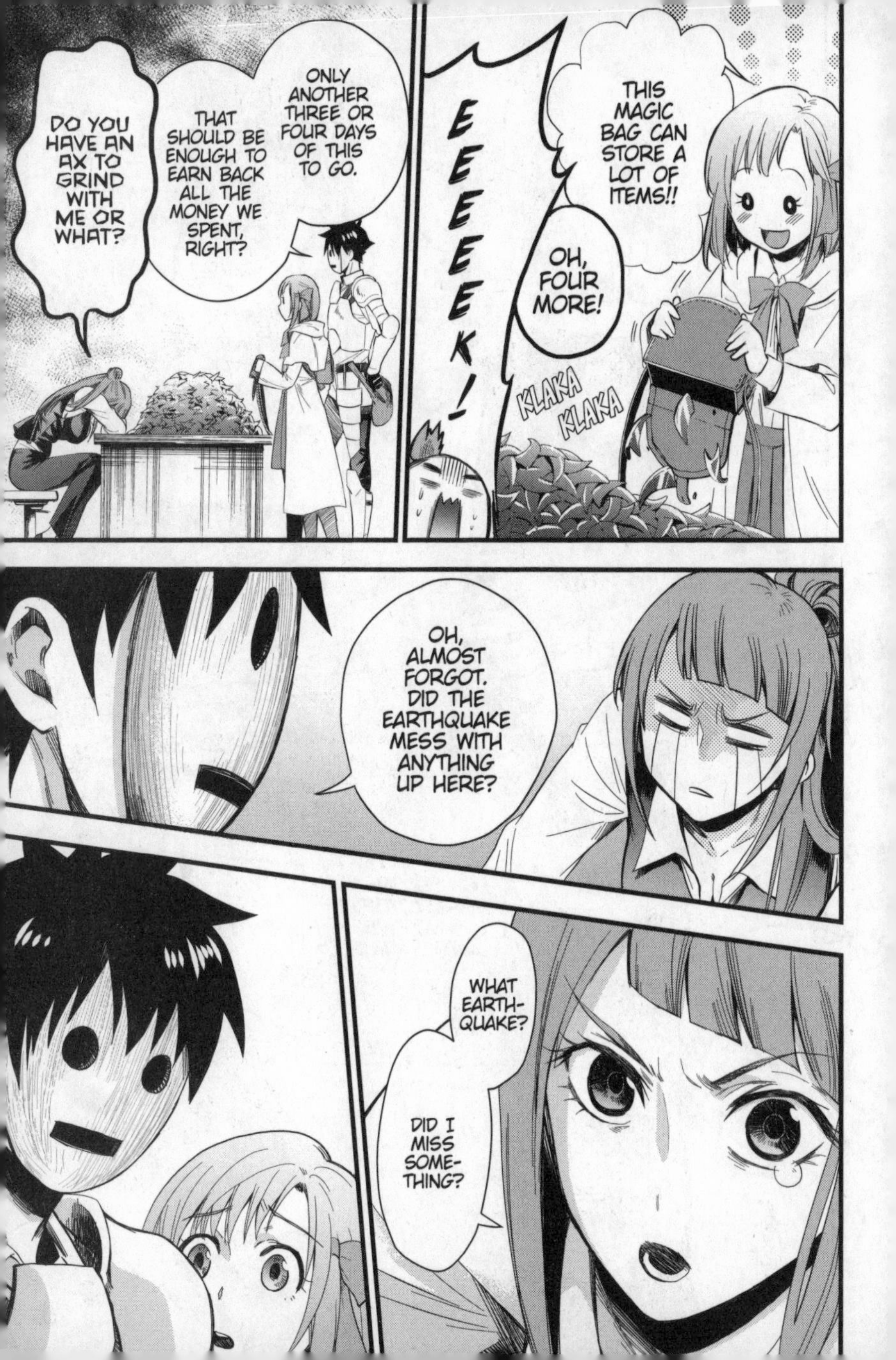
THIS MAGIC BAG CAN STORE A LOT OF ITEMS!!
OH, FOUR MORE!
KLAKA KLAKA
EEEEEK!
ONLY ANOTHER THREE OR FOUR DAYS OF THIS TO GO.
THAT SHOULD BE ENOUGH TO EARN BACK ALL THE MONEY WE SPENT, RIGHT?
DO YOU HAVE AN AX TO GRIND WITH ME OR WHAT?
OH, ALMOST FORGOT. DID THE EARTHQUAKE MESS WITH ANYTHING UP HERE?
WHAT EARTH-QUAKE?
DID I MISS SOME-THING?

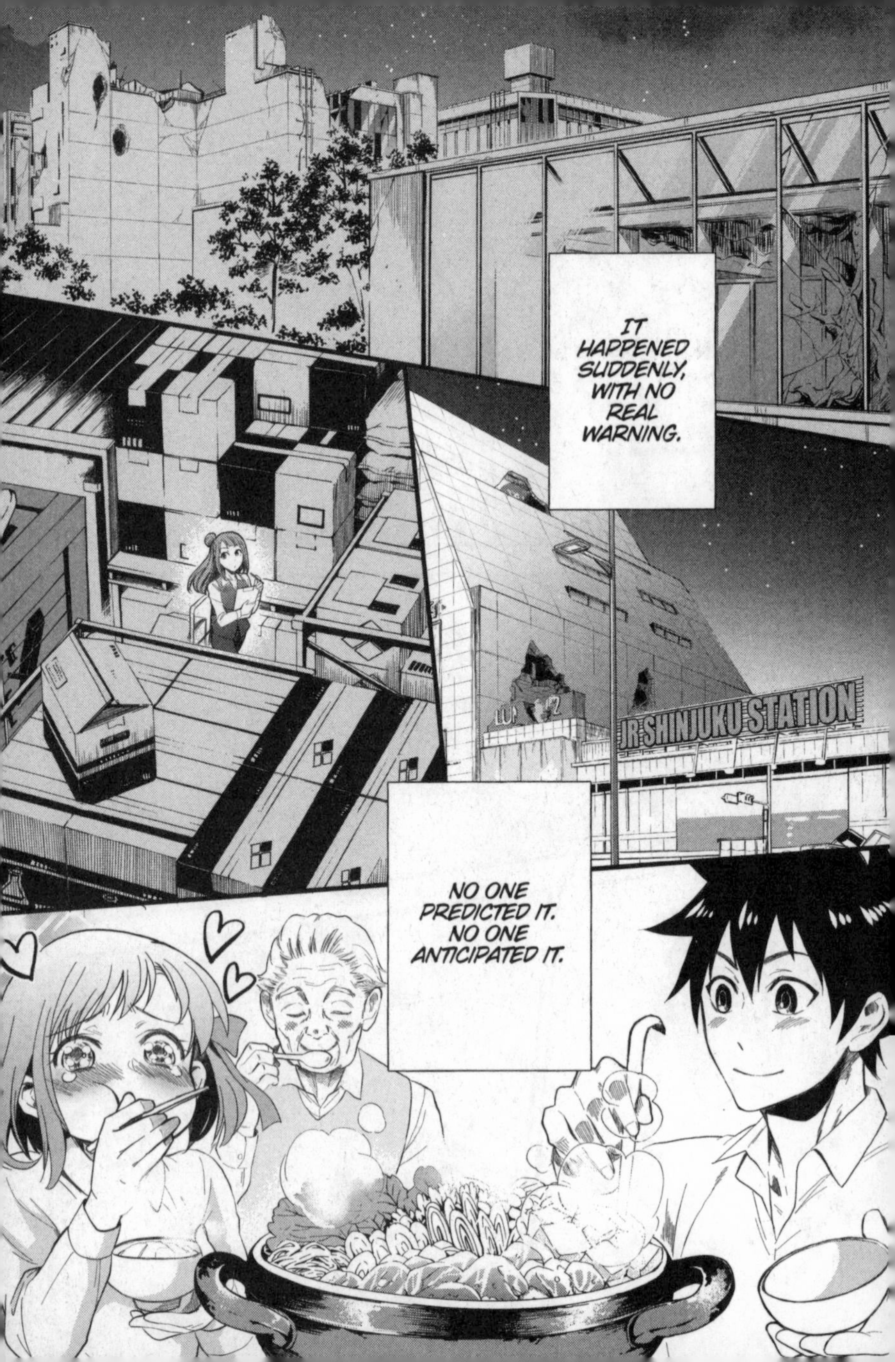
IT HAPPENED SUDDENLY, WITH NO REAL WARNING.
JR SHINJUKU STATION
NO ONE PREDICTED IT. NO ONE ANTICIPATED IT.

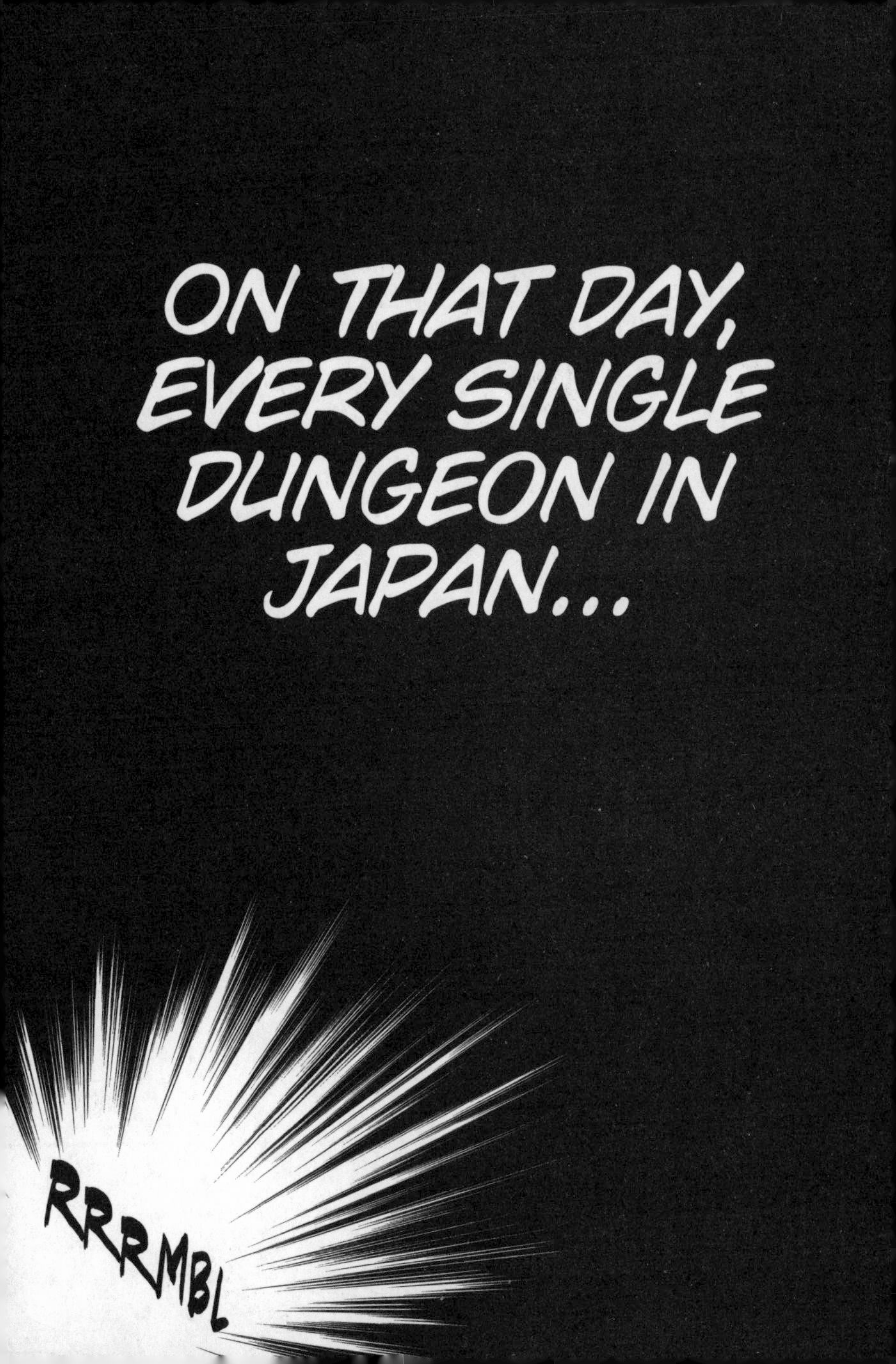
ON THAT DAY, EVERY SINGLE DUNGEON IN JAPAN...
RRRMBL

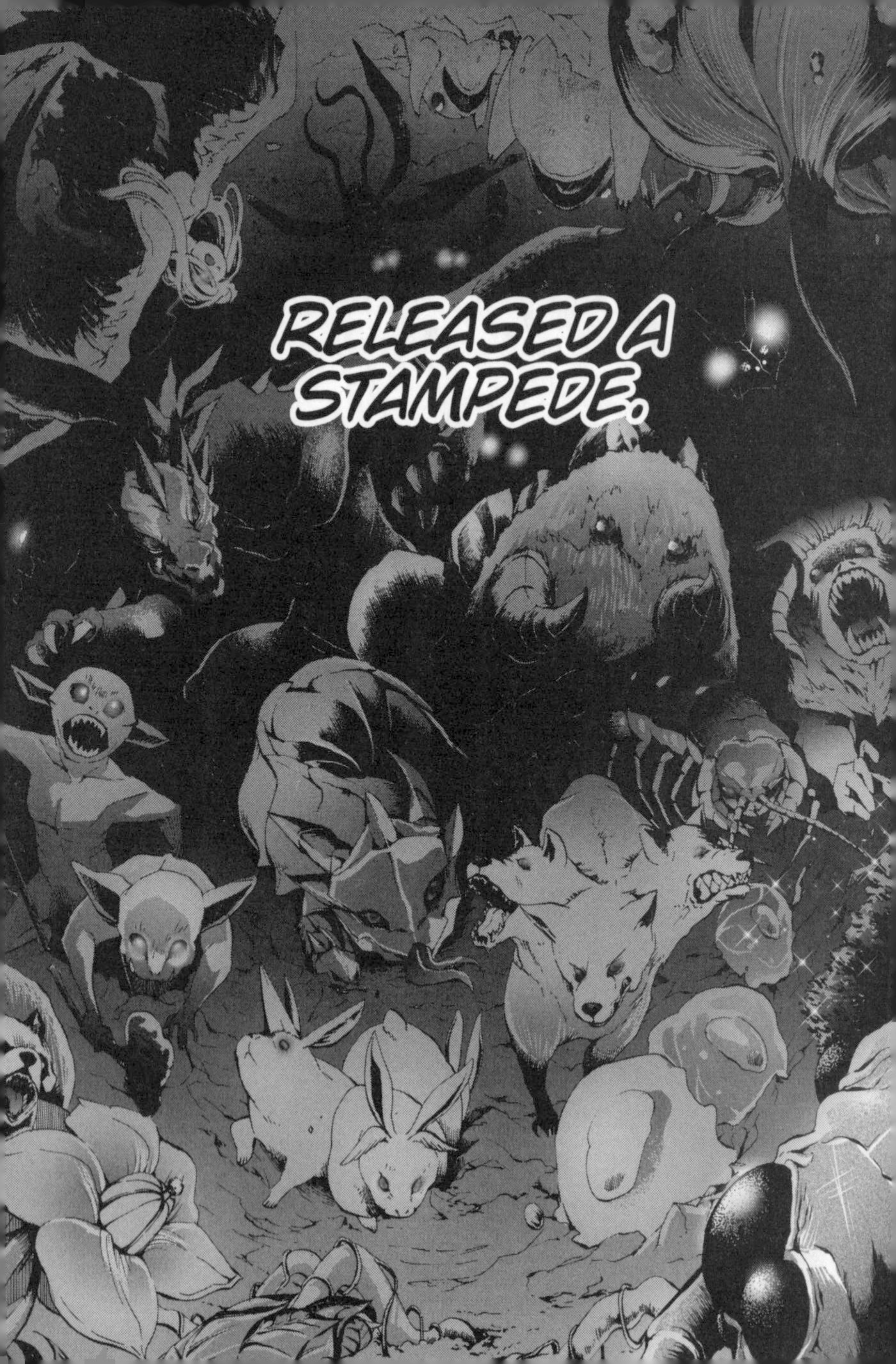
RELEASED A STAMPEDE.

CALL TO ADVENTURE!

DEFEATING DUNGEONS WITH A SKILL BOARD

2

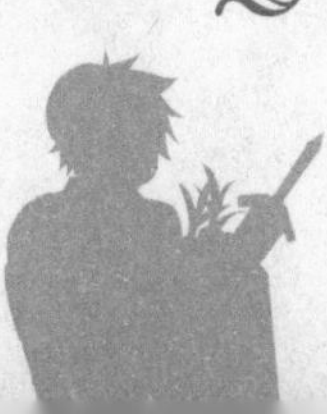

Chapter 10

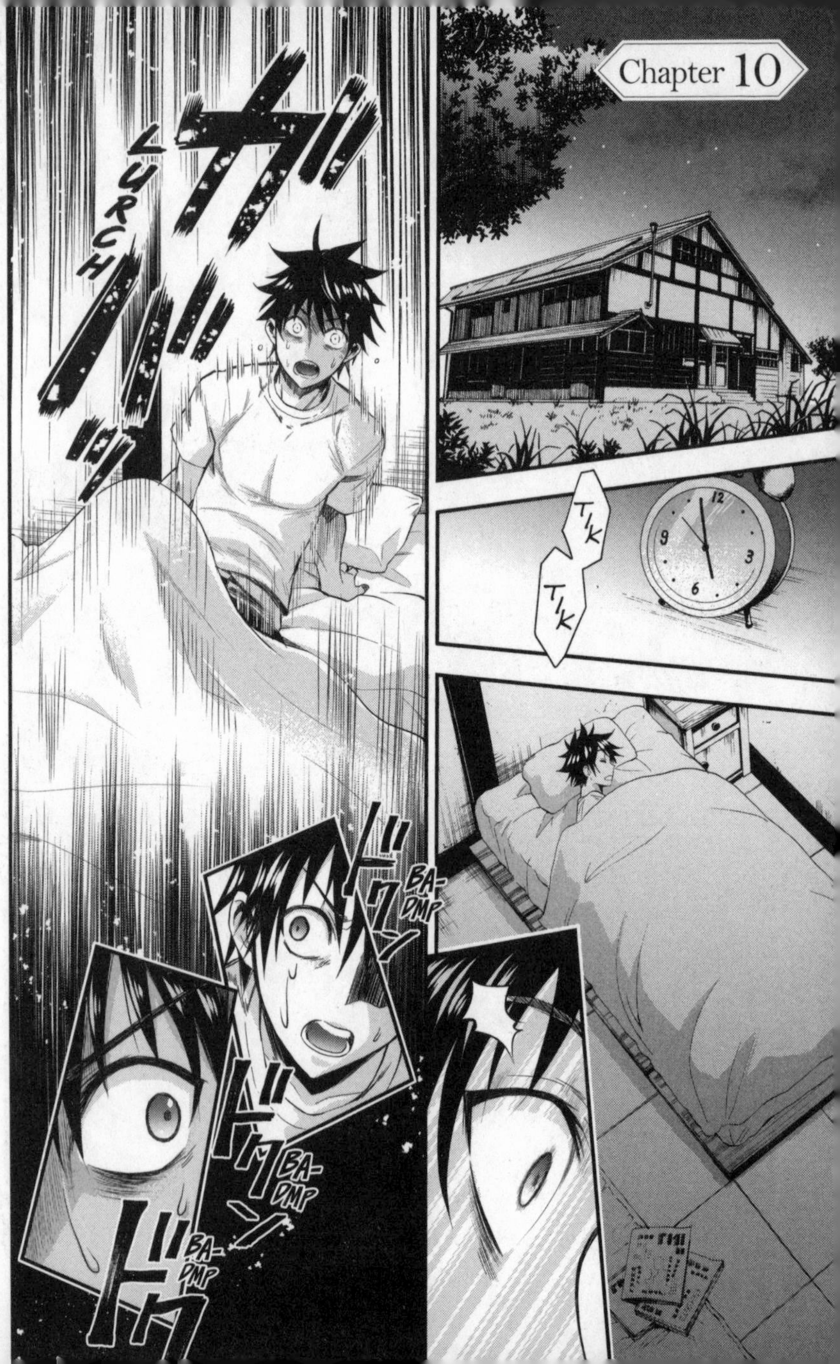
TIK
TIK
LURCH
BA-DMP
BA-DMP
BA-DMP

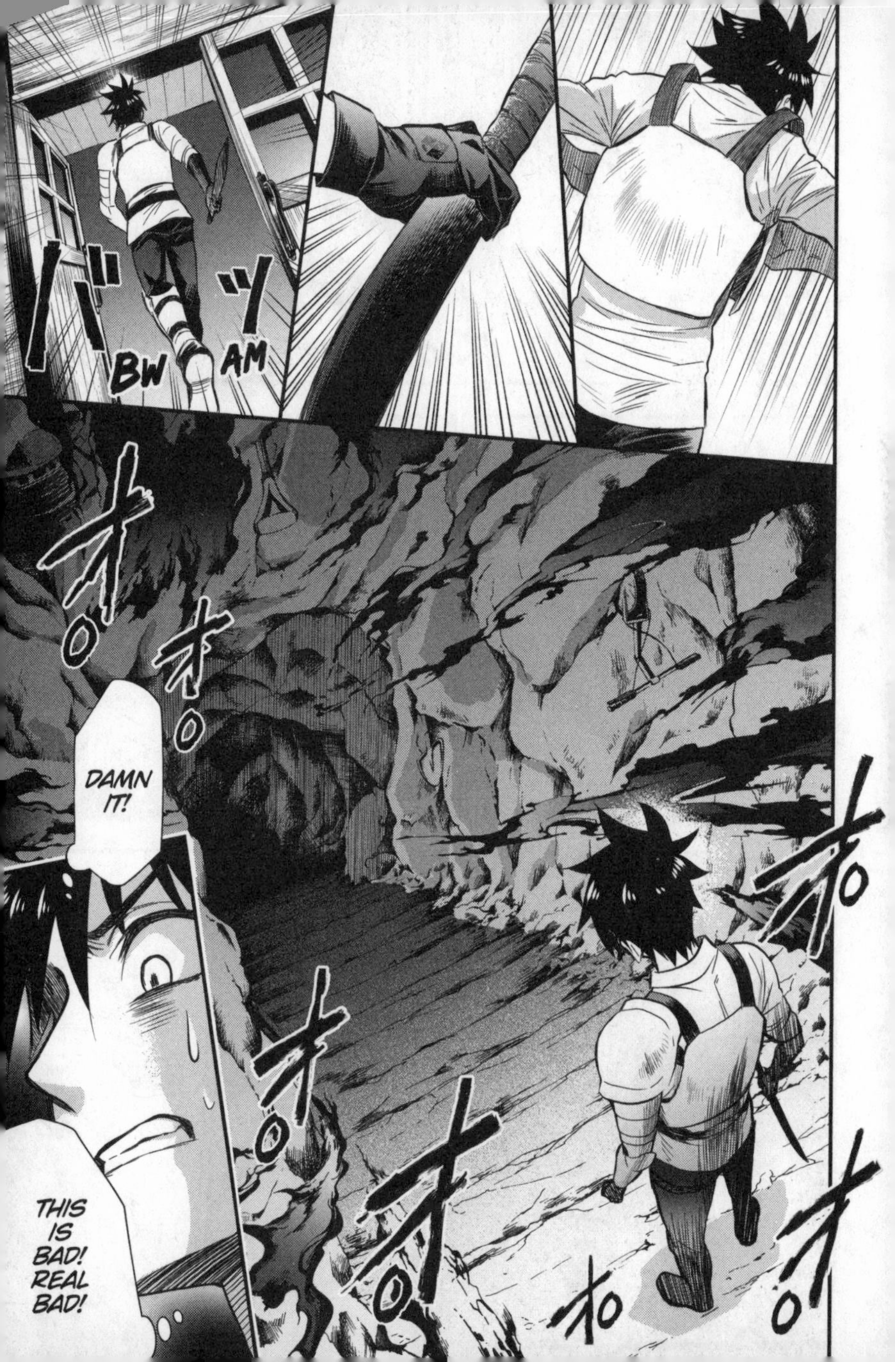
BW AM
DAMN IT!
THIS IS BAD! REAL BAD!

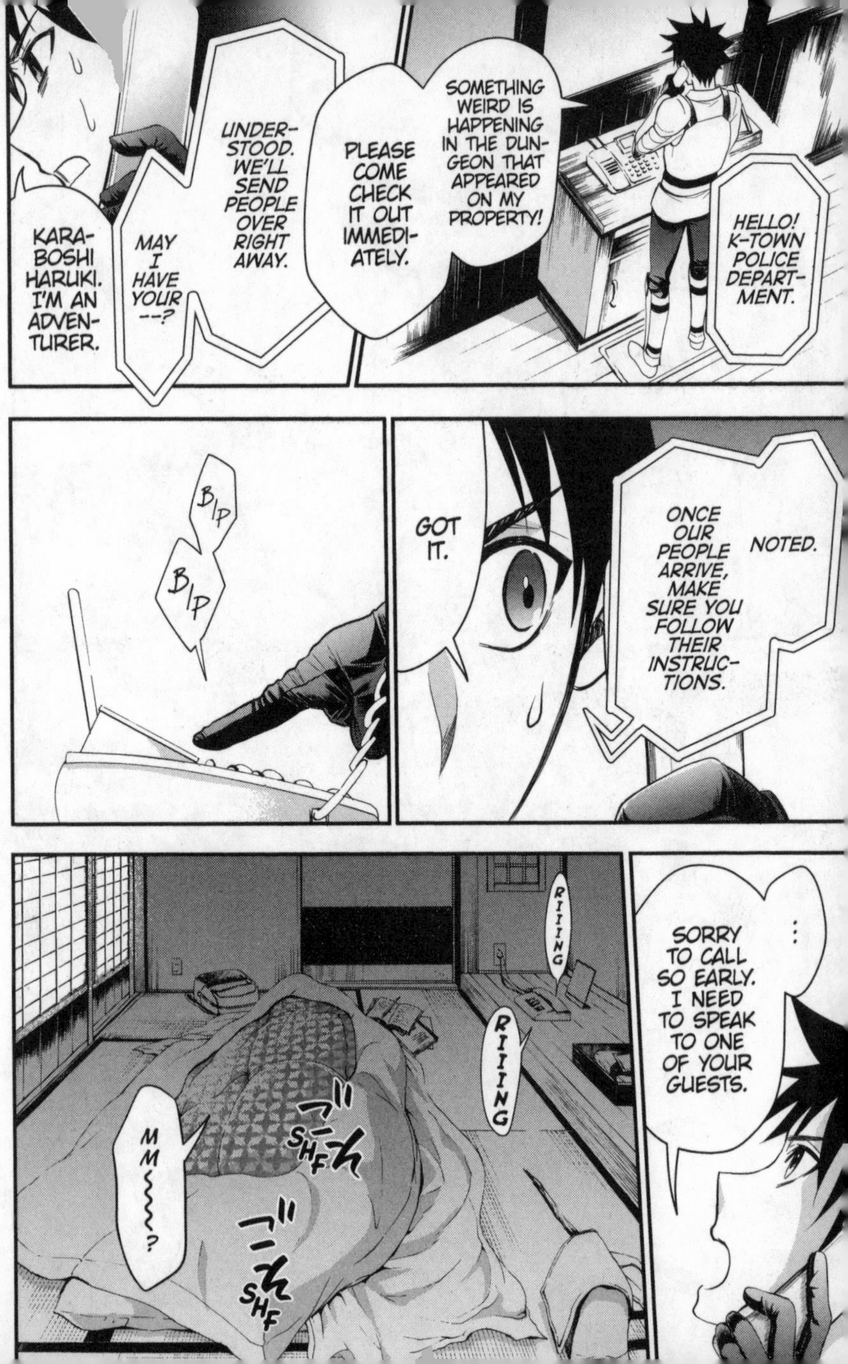
HELLO! K-TOWN POLICE DEPARTMENT.
SOMETHING WEIRD IS HAPPENING IN THE DUNGEON THAT APPEARED ON MY PROPERTY!
PLEASE COME CHECK IT OUT IMMEDIATELY.
UNDERSTOOD. WE'LL SEND PEOPLE OVER RIGHT AWAY.
MAY I HAVE YOUR--?
KARABOSHI HARUKI. I'M AN ADVENTURER.
NOTED.
ONCE OUR PEOPLE ARRIVE, MAKE SURE YOU FOLLOW THEIR INSTRUCTIONS.
GOT IT.
BIP
BIP
...
SORRY TO CALL SO EARLY. I NEED TO SPEAK TO ONE OF YOUR GUESTS.
RIIING
RIIING
SHF
MM~~~?
SHF

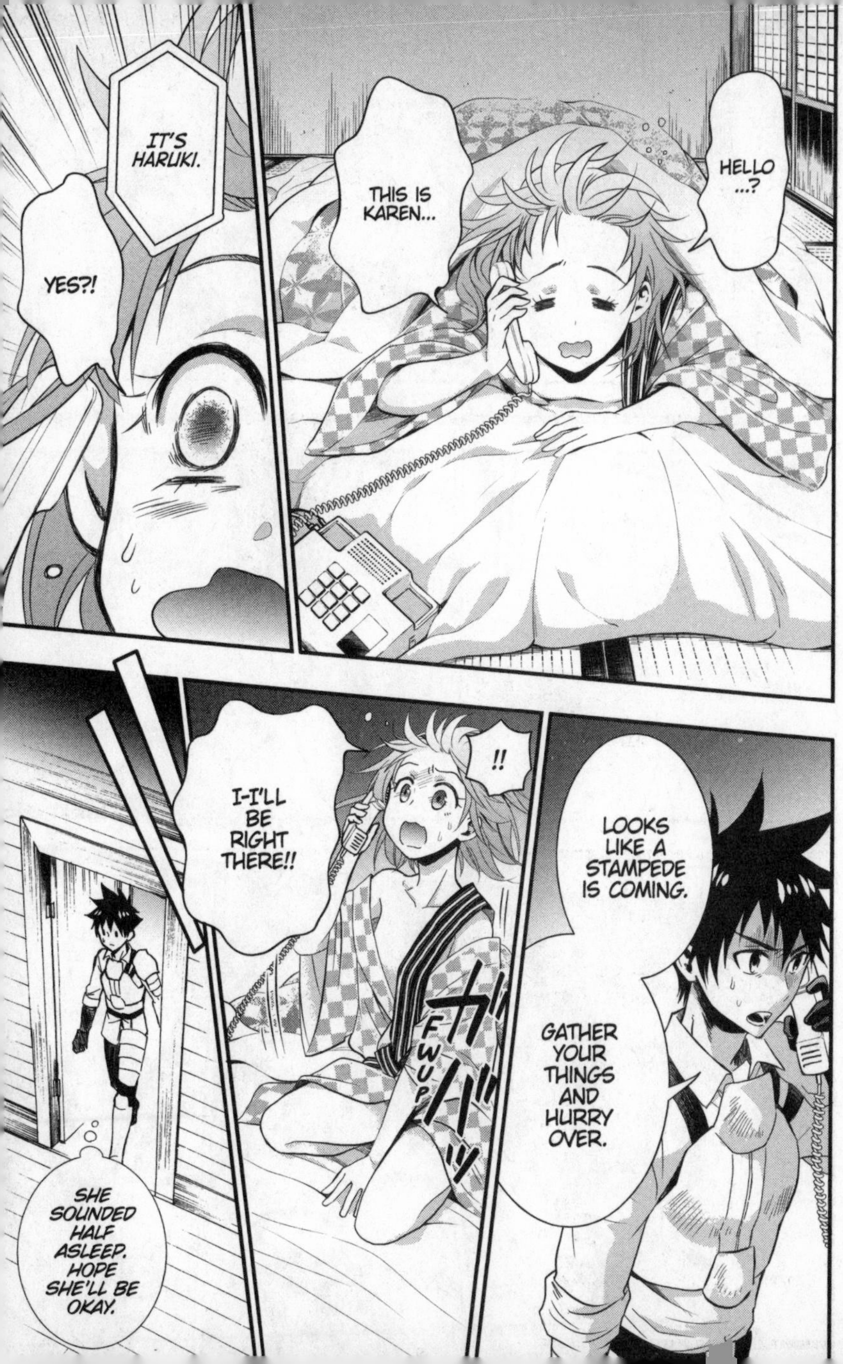
HELLO ...?
THIS IS KAREN...
IT'S HARUKI.
YES?!
LOOKS LIKE A STAMPEDE IS COMING.
GATHER YOUR THINGS AND HURRY OVER.
!!
I-I'LL BE RIGHT THERE!!
FWUP
SHE SOUNDED HALF ASLEEP. HOPE SHE'LL BE OKAY.

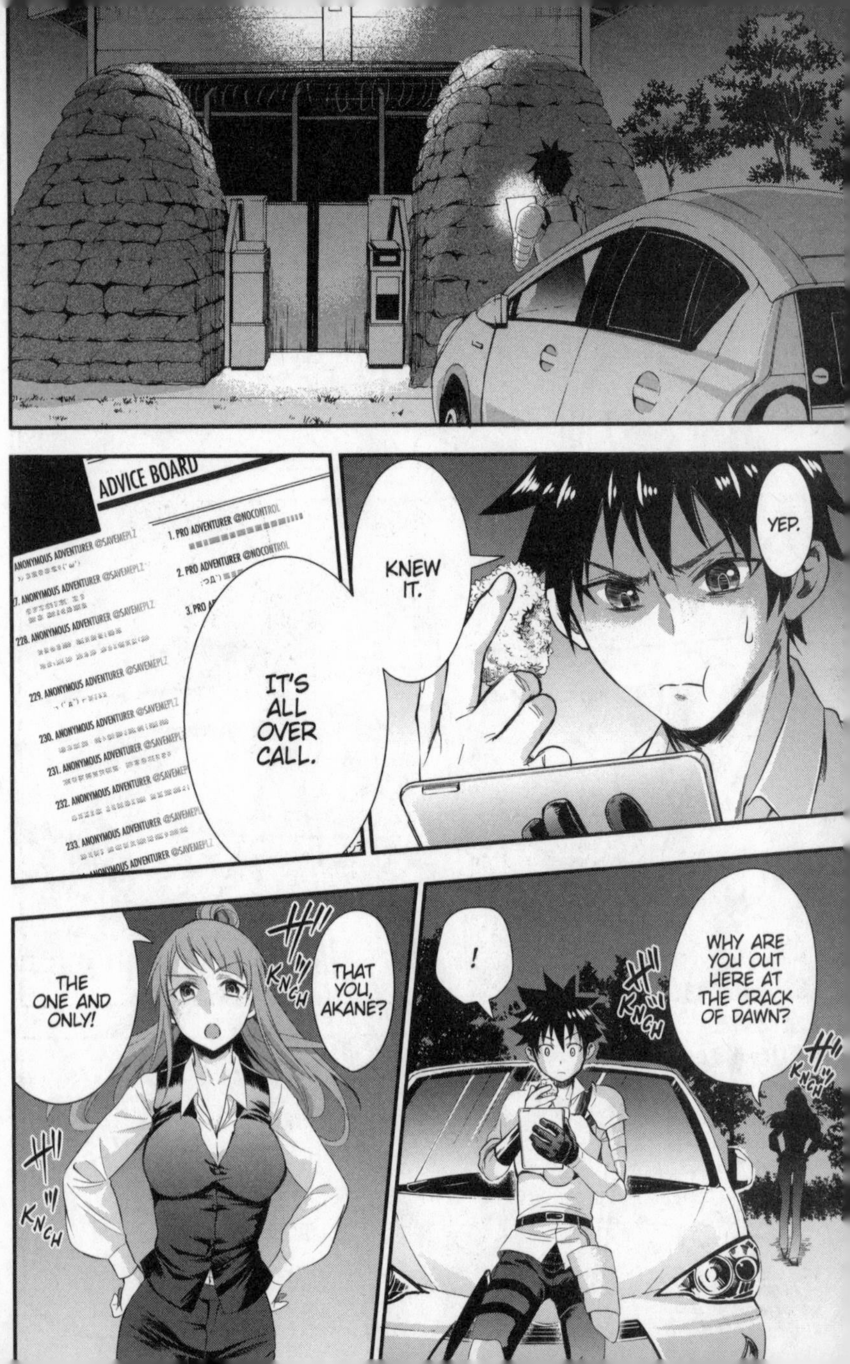
YEP.
KNEW IT.
IT'S ALL OVER CALL.
ADVICE BOARD
1. PRO ADVENTURER @NOCONTROL
2. PRO ADVENTURER @NOCONTROL
ANONYMOUS ADVENTURER @SAVEMEPLZ
227. ANONYMOUS ADVENTURER @SAVEMEPLZ
228. ANONYMOUS ADVENTURER @SAVEMEPLZ
229. ANONYMOUS ADVENTURER @SAVEMEPLZ
230. ANONYMOUS ADVENTURER @SAVEMEPLZ
231. ANONYMOUS ADVENTURER @SAVEMEPLZ
232. ANONYMOUS ADVENTURER
233. ANONYMOUS ADVENTURER @SAVEMEPLZ
WHY ARE YOU OUT HERE AT THE CRACK OF DAWN?
KNCH
KNCH
!
THAT YOU, AKANE?
KNCH
THE ONE AND ONLY!
KNCH

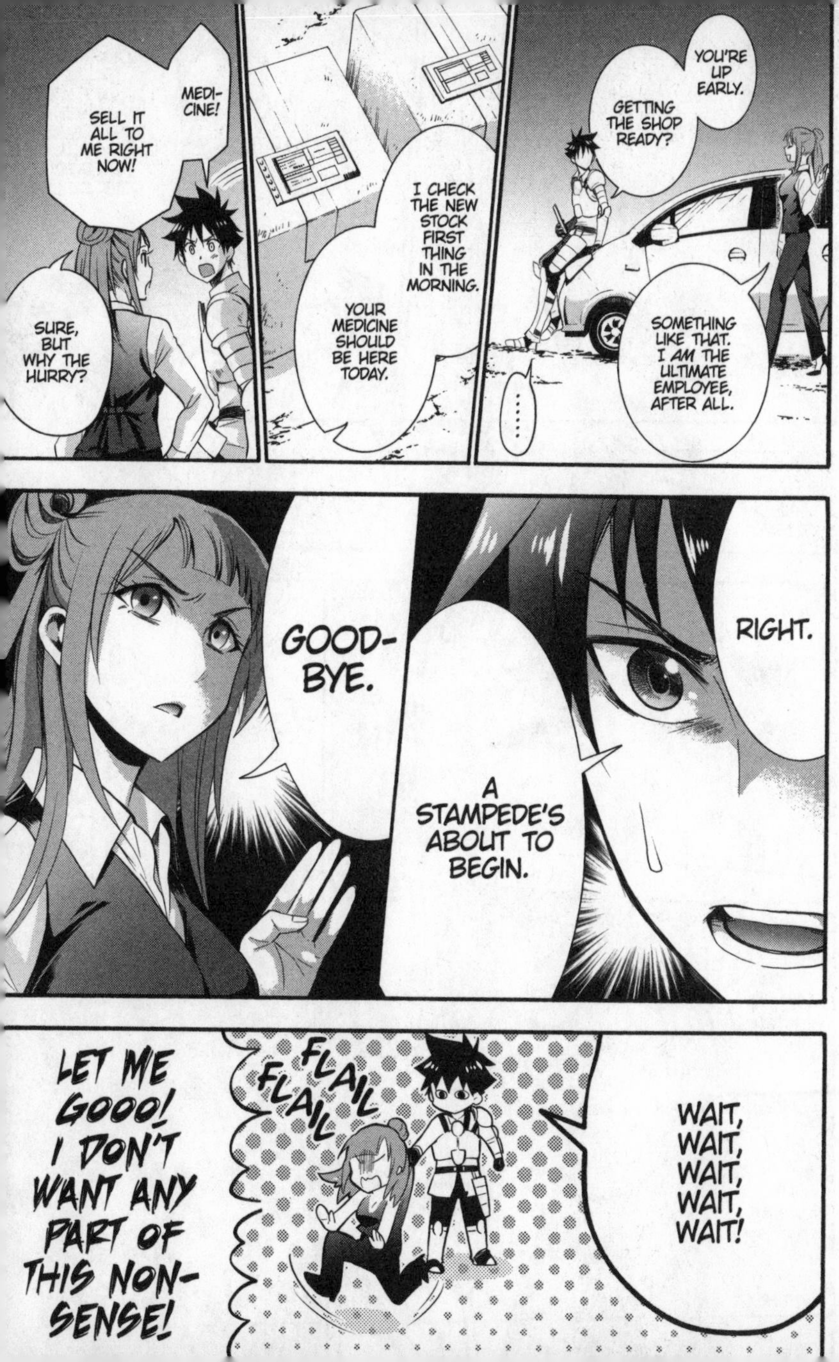
YOU'RE UP EARLY.
GETTING THE SHOP READY?
SOMETHING LIKE THAT. I *AM* THE ULTIMATE EMPLOYEE, AFTER ALL.
......
I CHECK THE NEW STOCK FIRST THING IN THE MORNING.
YOUR MEDICINE SHOULD BE HERE TODAY.
MEDI-CINE!
SELL IT ALL TO ME RIGHT NOW!
SURE, BUT WHY THE HURRY?
RIGHT.
A STAMPEDE'S ABOUT TO BEGIN.
GOOD-BYE.
WAIT, WAIT, WAIT, WAIT, WAIT!
FLAIL FLAIL
LET ME GOOO! I DON'T WANT ANY PART OF THIS NON-SENSE!

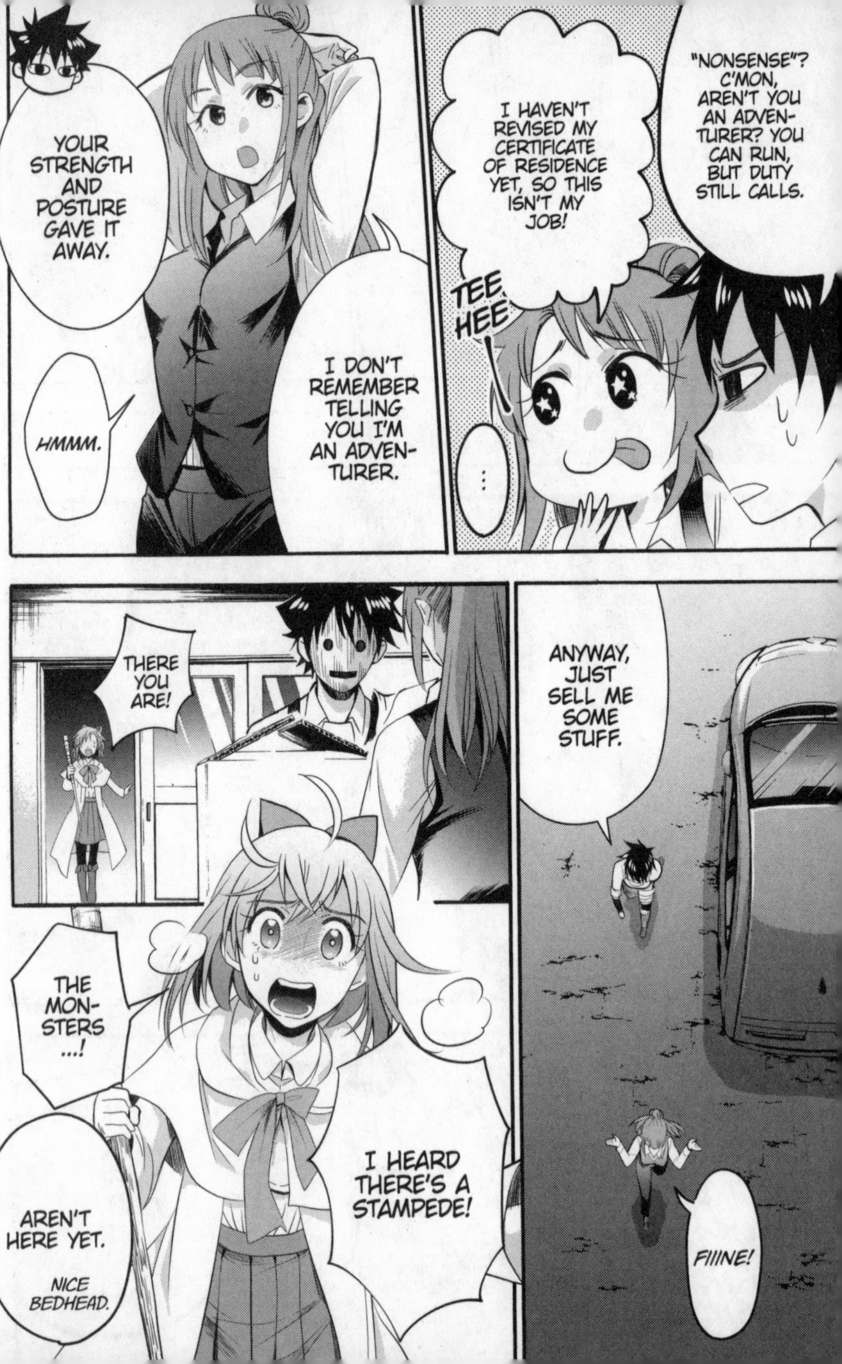
"NONSENSE"? C'MON, AREN'T YOU AN ADVENTURER? YOU CAN RUN, BUT DUTY STILL CALLS.
I HAVEN'T REVISED MY CERTIFICATE OF RESIDENCE YET, SO THIS ISN'T MY JOB!
TEE HEE
...
I DON'T REMEMBER TELLING YOU I'M AN ADVENTURER.
YOUR STRENGTH AND POSTURE GAVE IT AWAY.
HMMM.
ANYWAY, JUST SELL ME SOME STUFF.
FIIINE!
THERE YOU ARE!
I HEARD THERE'S A STAMPEDE!
THE MONSTERS ...!
AREN'T HERE YET.
NICE BEDHEAD.

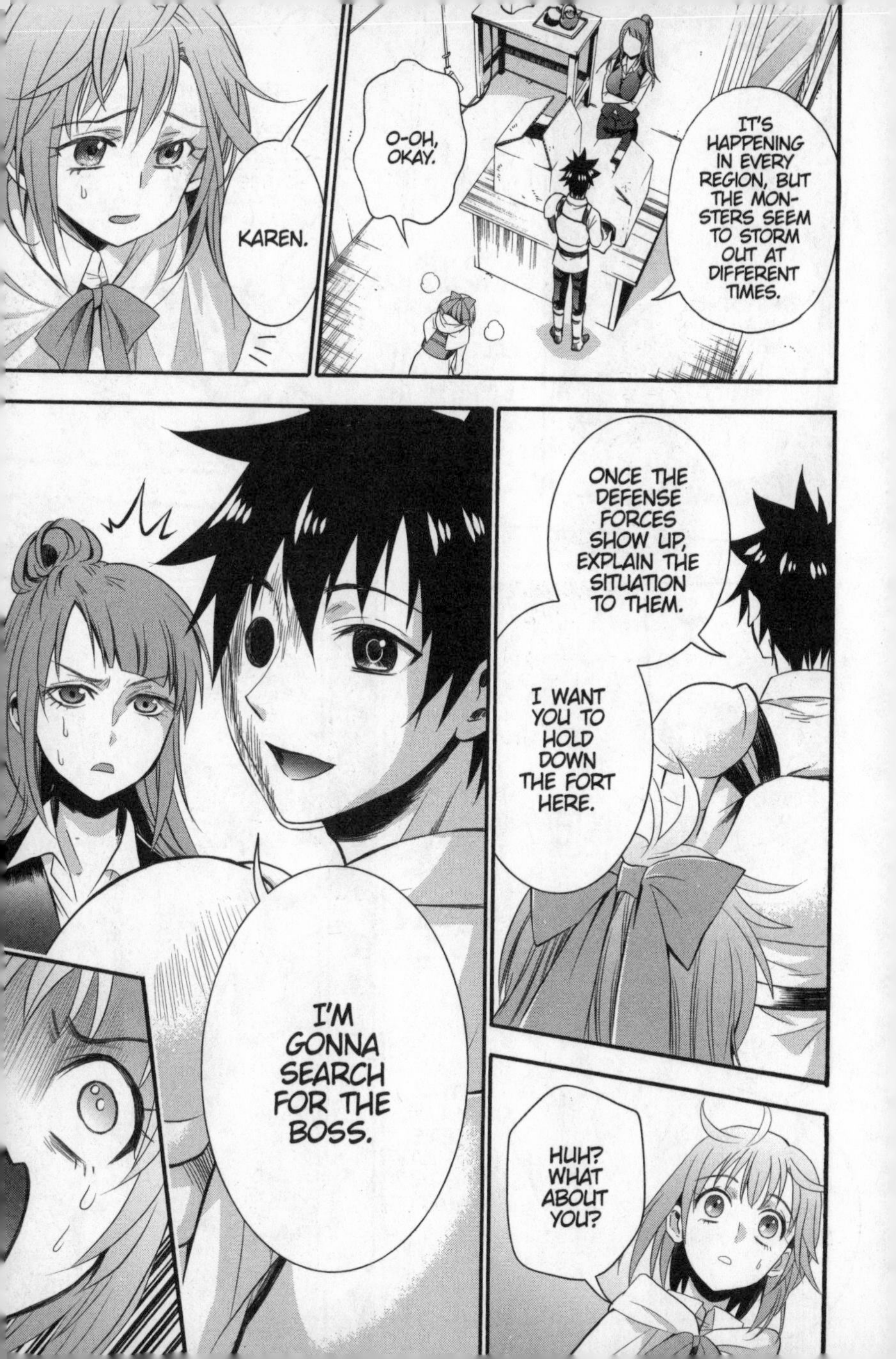
IT'S HAPPENING IN EVERY REGION, BUT THE MON-STERS SEEM TO STORM OUT AT DIFFERENT TIMES.
O-OH, OKAY.
KAREN.
ONCE THE DEFENSE FORCES SHOW UP, EXPLAIN THE SITUATION TO THEM.
I WANT YOU TO HOLD DOWN THE FORT HERE.
HUH? WHAT ABOUT YOU?
I'M GONNA SEARCH FOR THE BOSS.

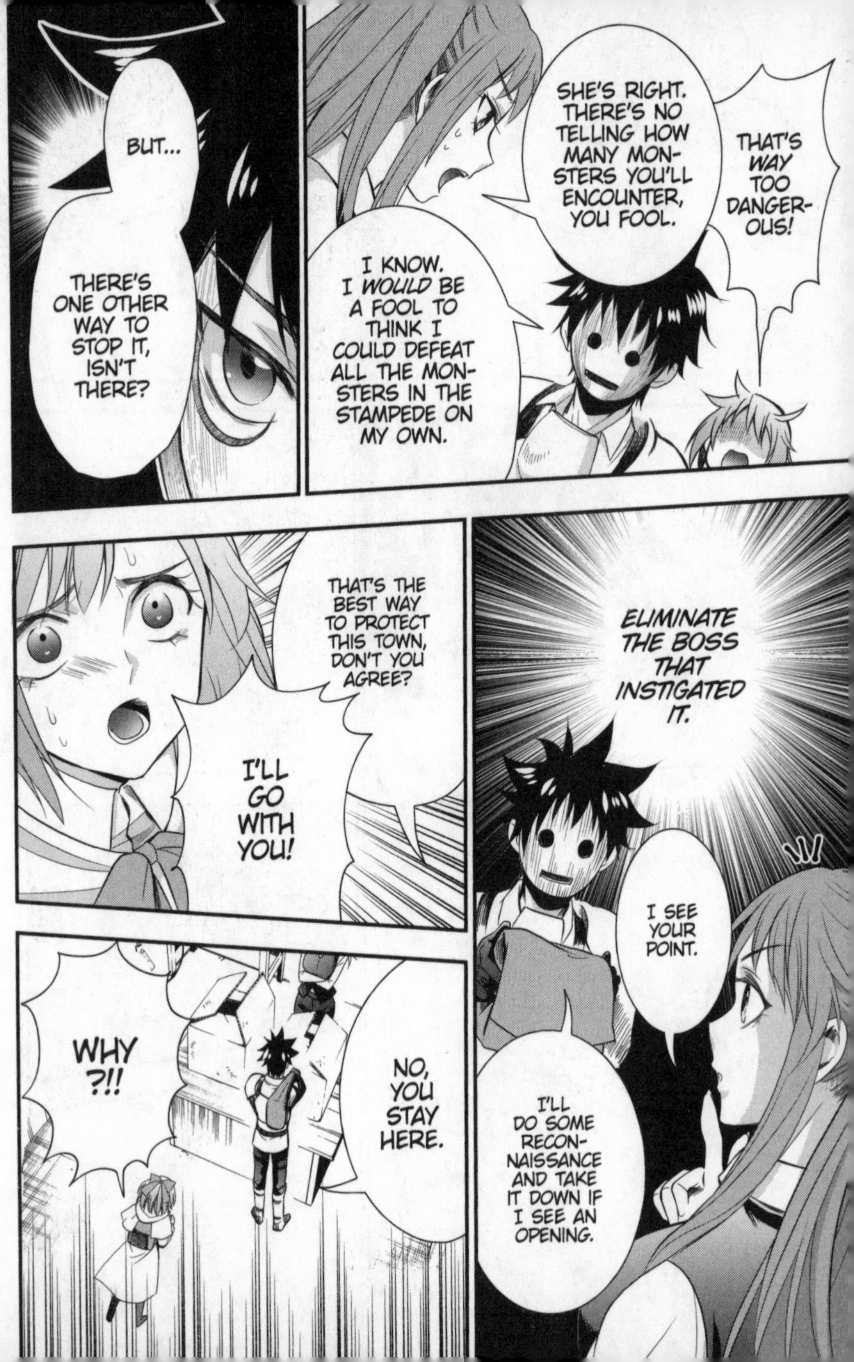
THAT'S *WAY* TOO DANGER-OUS!
SHE'S RIGHT. THERE'S NO TELLING HOW MANY MON-STERS YOU'LL ENCOUNTER, YOU FOOL.
I KNOW. I *WOULD* BE A FOOL TO THINK I COULD DEFEAT ALL THE MON-STERS IN THE STAMPEDE ON MY OWN.
BUT...
THERE'S ONE OTHER WAY TO STOP IT, ISN'T THERE?
ELIMINATE THE BOSS THAT INSTIGATED IT.
I SEE YOUR POINT.
I'LL DO SOME RECON-NAISSANCE AND TAKE IT DOWN IF I SEE AN OPENING.
THAT'S THE BEST WAY TO PROTECT THIS TOWN, DON'T YOU AGREE?
I'LL GO WITH YOU!
NO, YOU STAY HERE.
WHY?!!

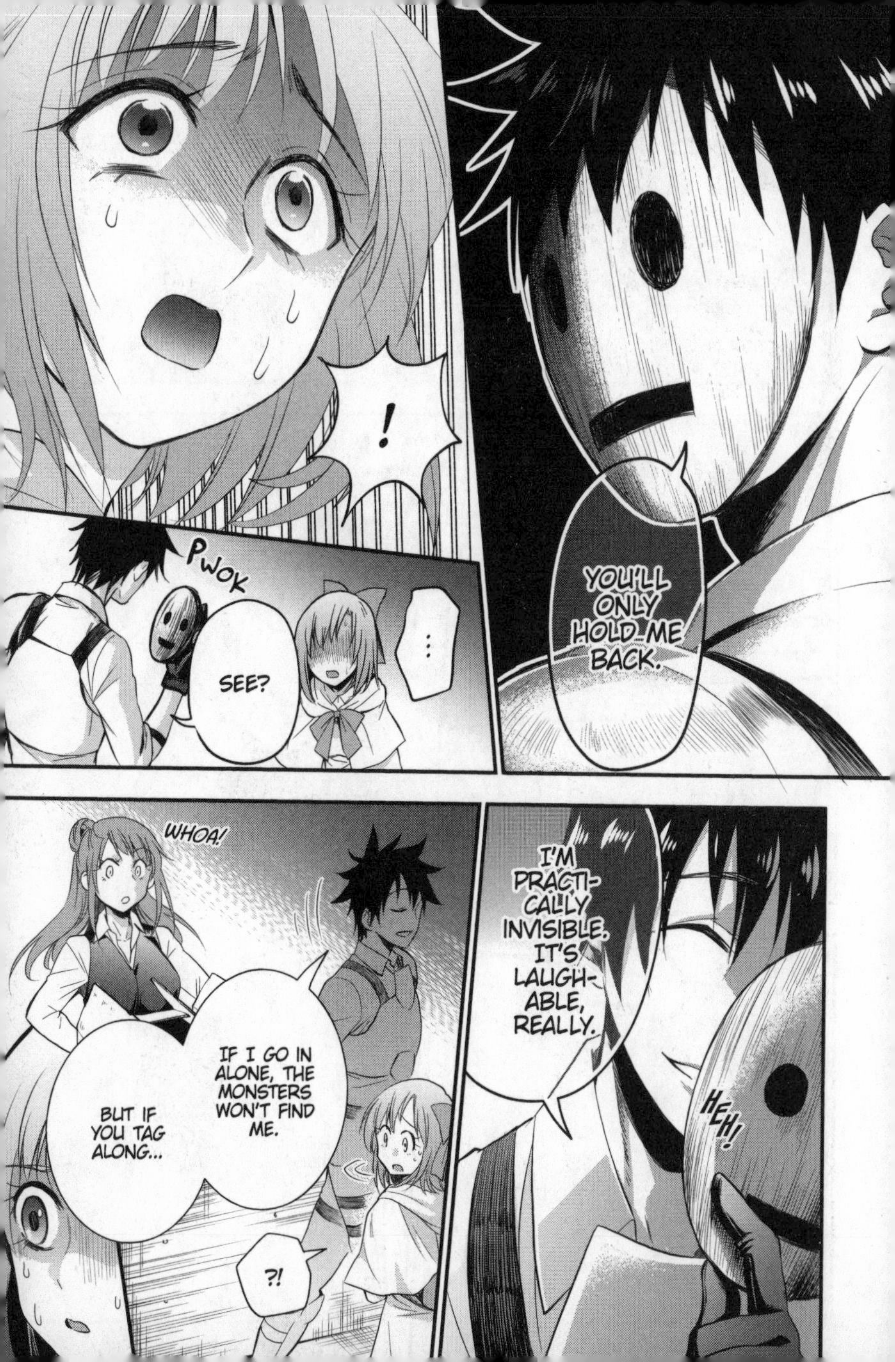
YOU'LL ONLY HOLD ME BACK.
!
PWOK
SEE?
...
I'M PRACTI-CALLY INVISIBLE. IT'S LAUGH-ABLE, REALLY.
HEH!
WHOA!
IF I GO IN ALONE, THE MONSTERS WON'T FIND ME.
BUT IF YOU TAG ALONG...
?!

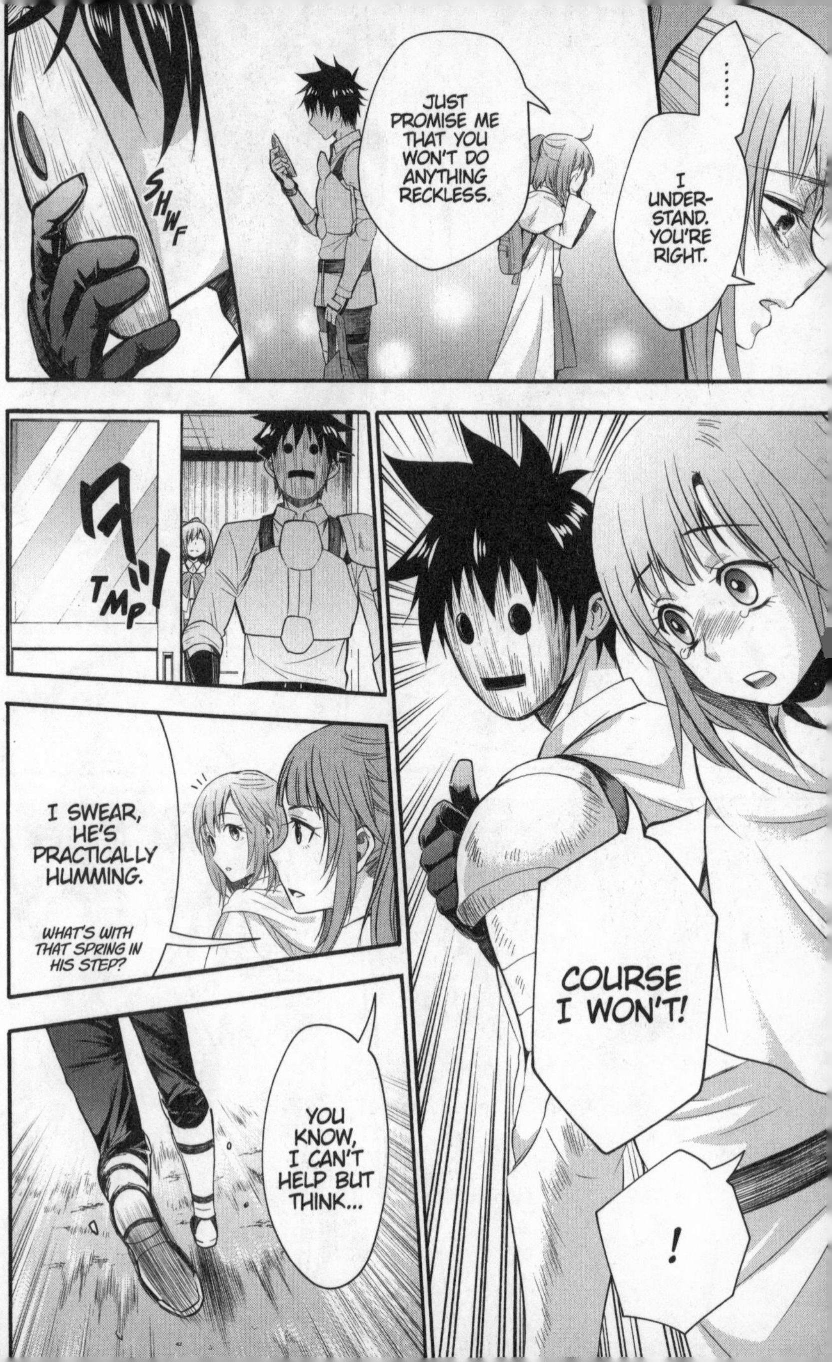
......
I UNDER-STAND. YOU'RE RIGHT.
JUST PROMISE ME THAT YOU WON'T DO ANYTHING RECKLESS.
SHWF
COURSE I WON'T!
!
タッ
TMP
I SWEAR, HE'S PRACTICALLY HUMMING.
WHAT'S WITH THAT SPRING IN HIS STEP?
YOU KNOW, I CAN'T HELP BUT THINK...

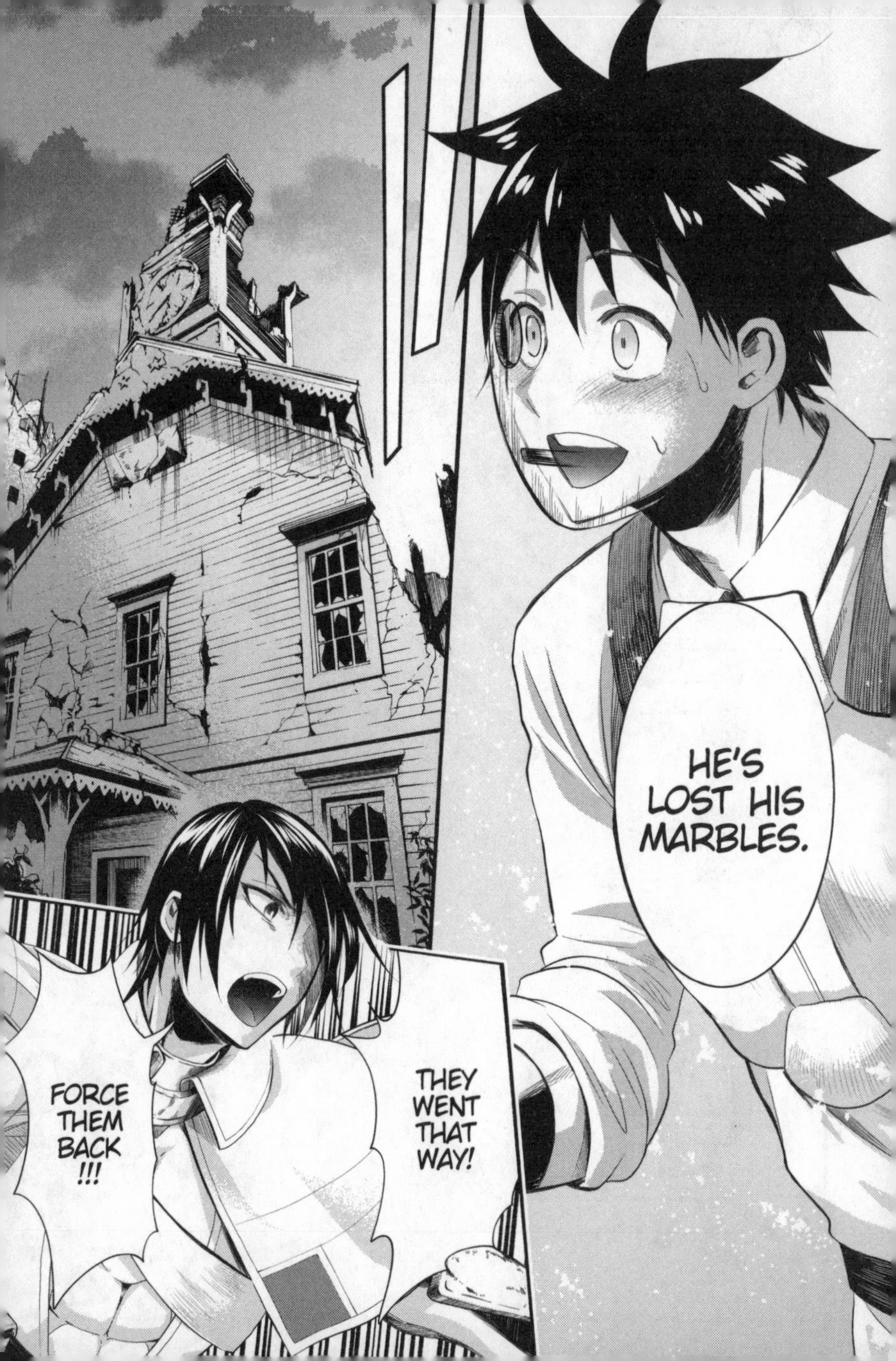
HE'S LOST HIS MARBLES.
THEY WENT THAT WAY!
FORCE THEM BACK!!!

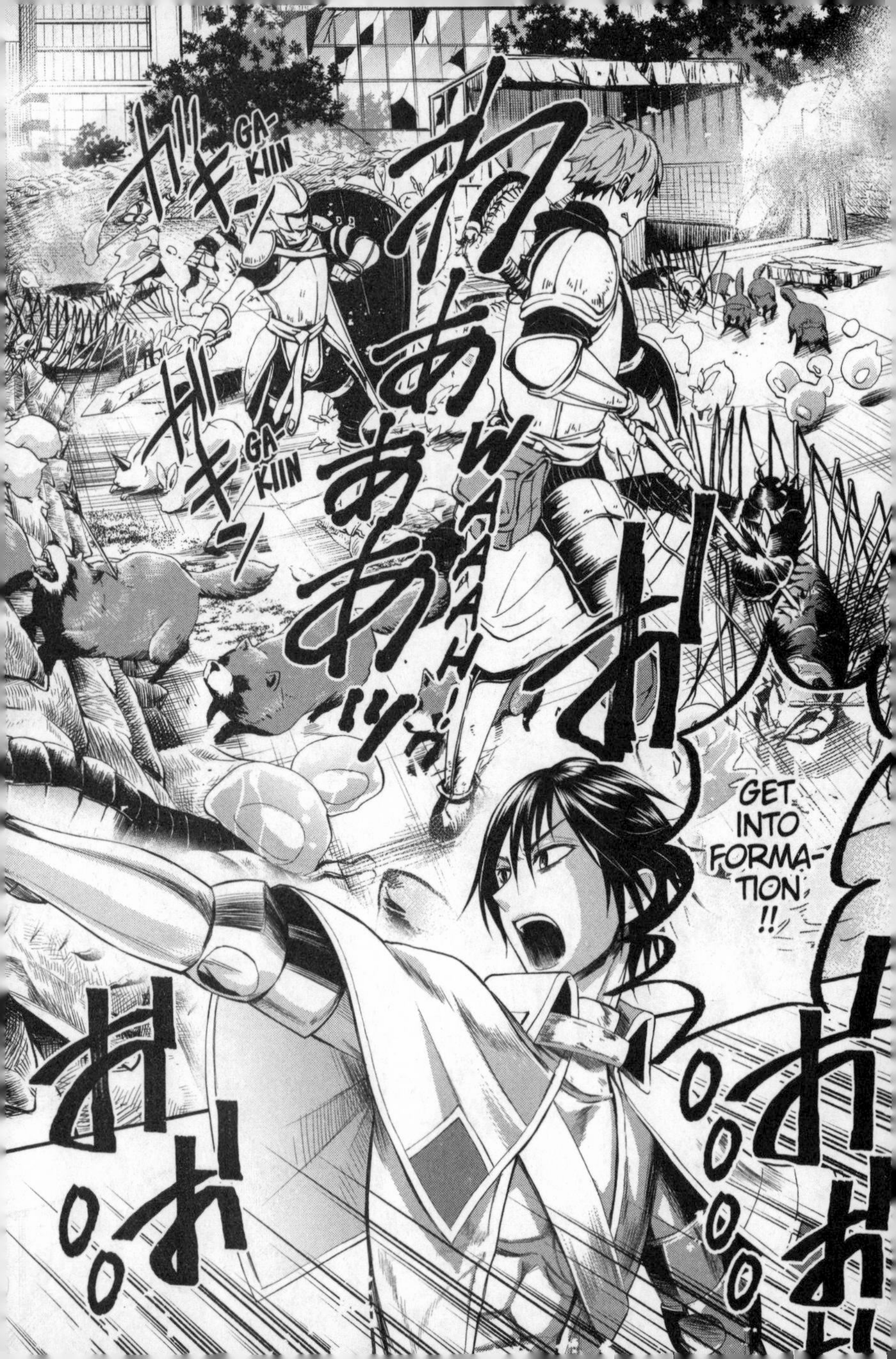
WAAAH!!
GA-KIIN
GA-KIIN
GET INTO FORMATION!!

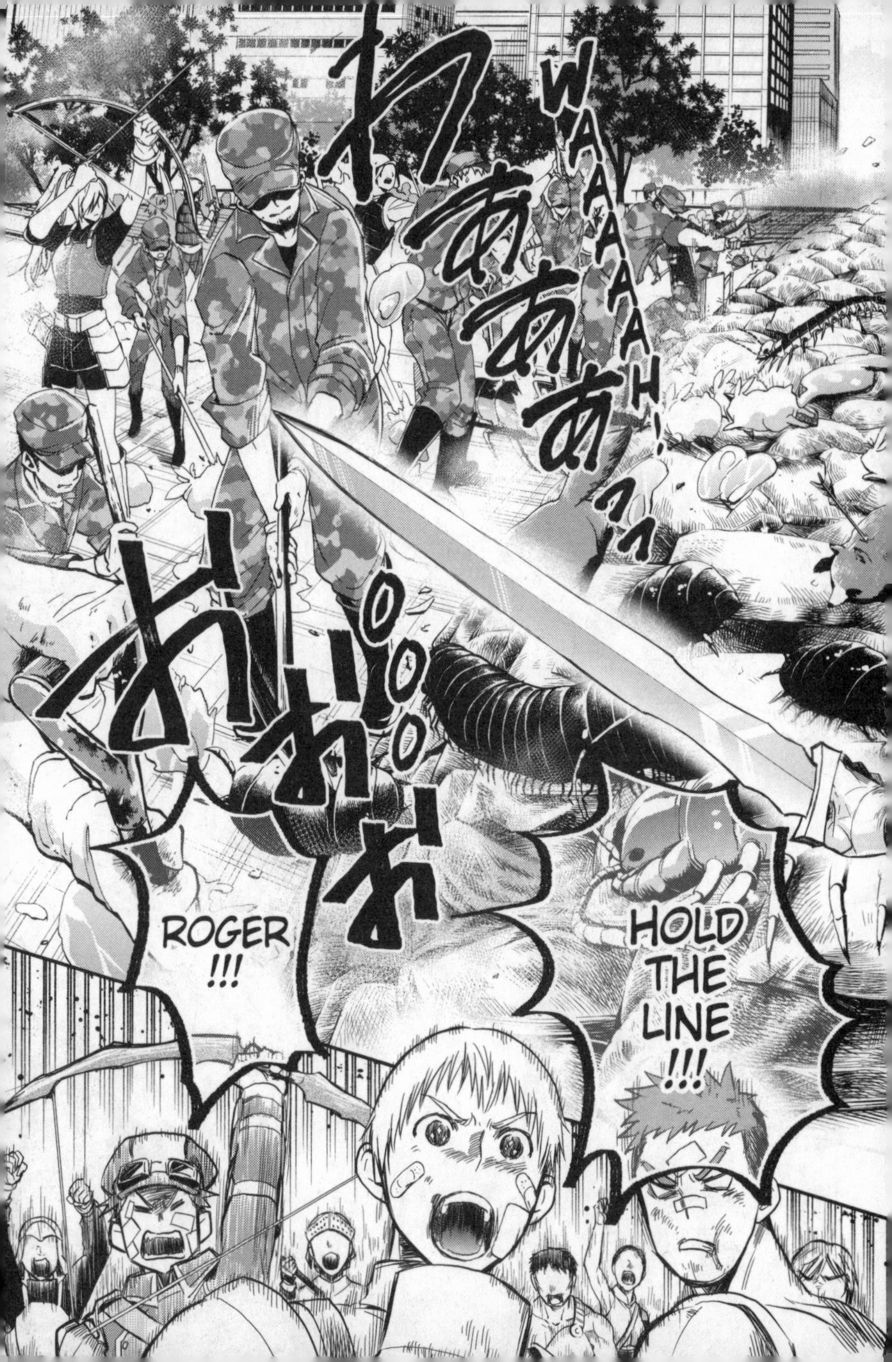

WAAAAAAH!!
わあああ
HOLD THE LINE!!!
OOOO
おおお
ROGER!!!

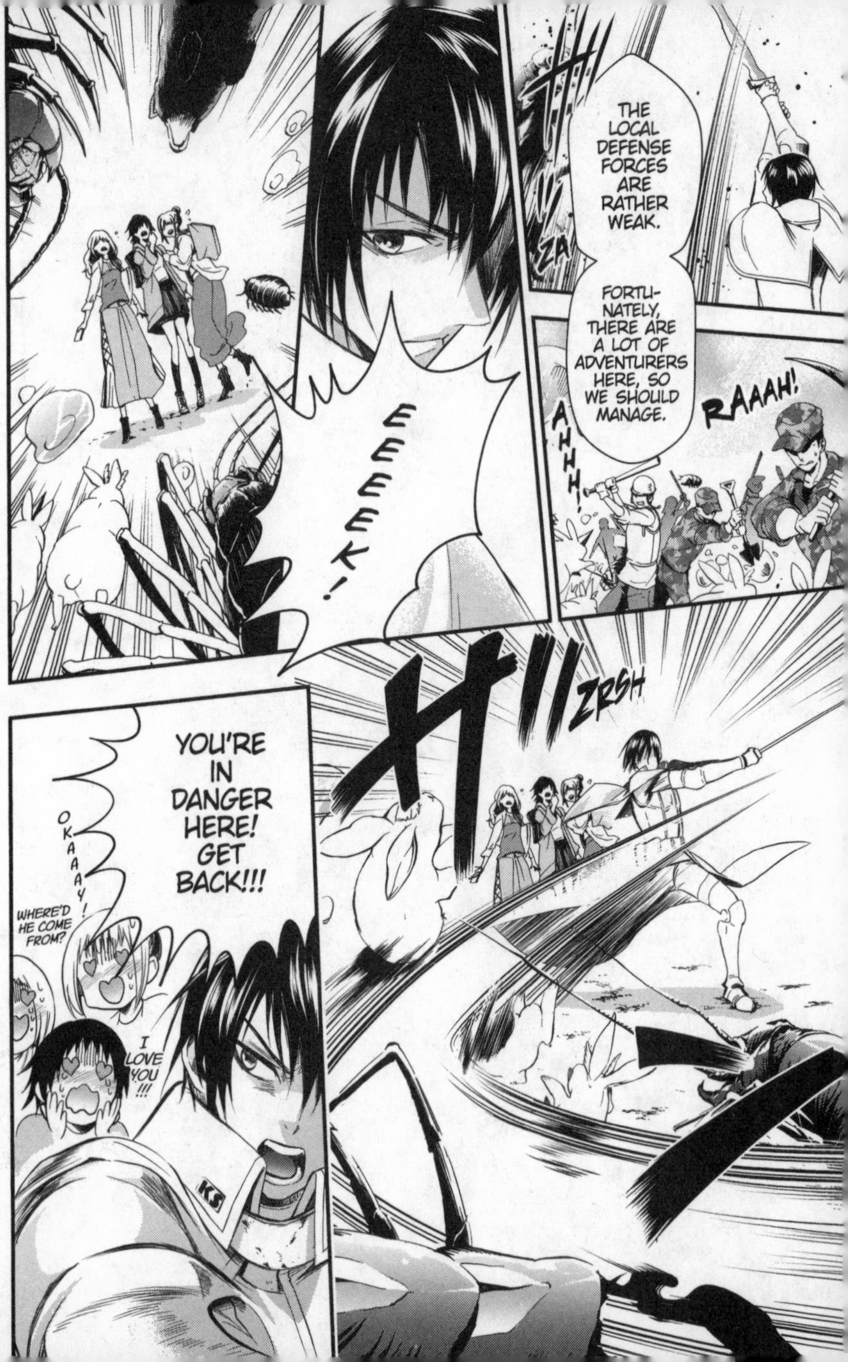
ZA
THE LOCAL DEFENSE FORCES ARE RATHER WEAK.
FORTU-NATELY, THERE ARE A LOT OF ADVENTURERS HERE, SO WE SHOULD MANAGE.
RAAAH!
AHHHH!
EEEEEK!
ZRSH
YOU'RE IN DANGER HERE! GET BACK!!!
OKAAAAY!
WHERE'D HE COME FROM?
I LOVE YOU!!!

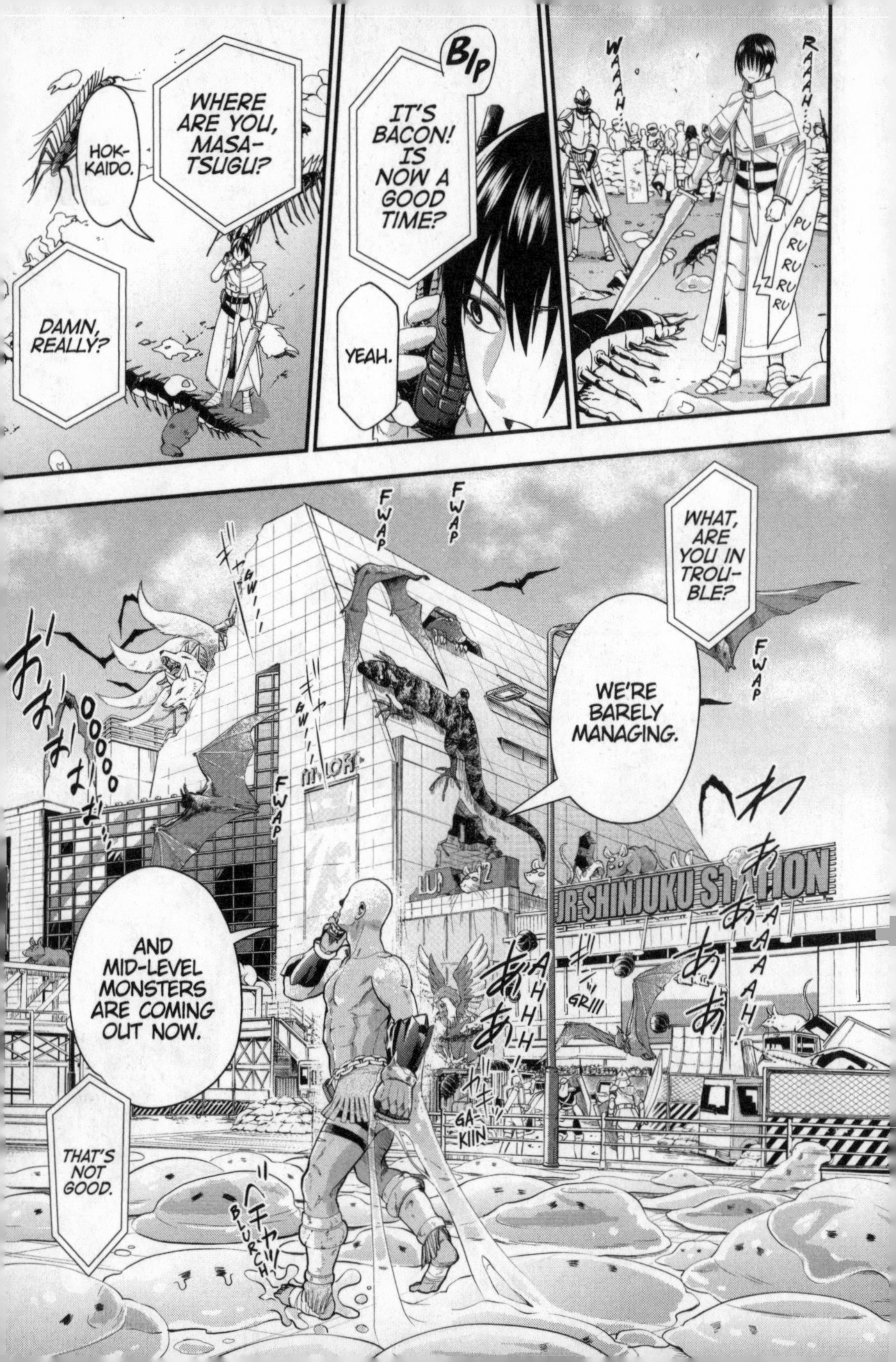
RAAAH...
WAAAAH...
PU RU RU RU RU
BIP
IT'S BACON! IS NOW A GOOD TIME?
YEAH.
WHERE ARE YOU, MASA-TSUGU?
HOK-KAIDO.
DAMN, REALLY?
FWAP FWAP
WHAT, ARE YOU IN TROU-BLE?
WE'RE BARELY MANAGING.
FWAP
GWI...
FWAP
OOOOOO
JR SHINJUKU STATION
AAAAAH!
GRIII
AHHHH!
GA-KIIN
AND MID-LEVEL MONSTERS ARE COMING OUT NOW.
THAT'S NOT GOOD.
BLURCH

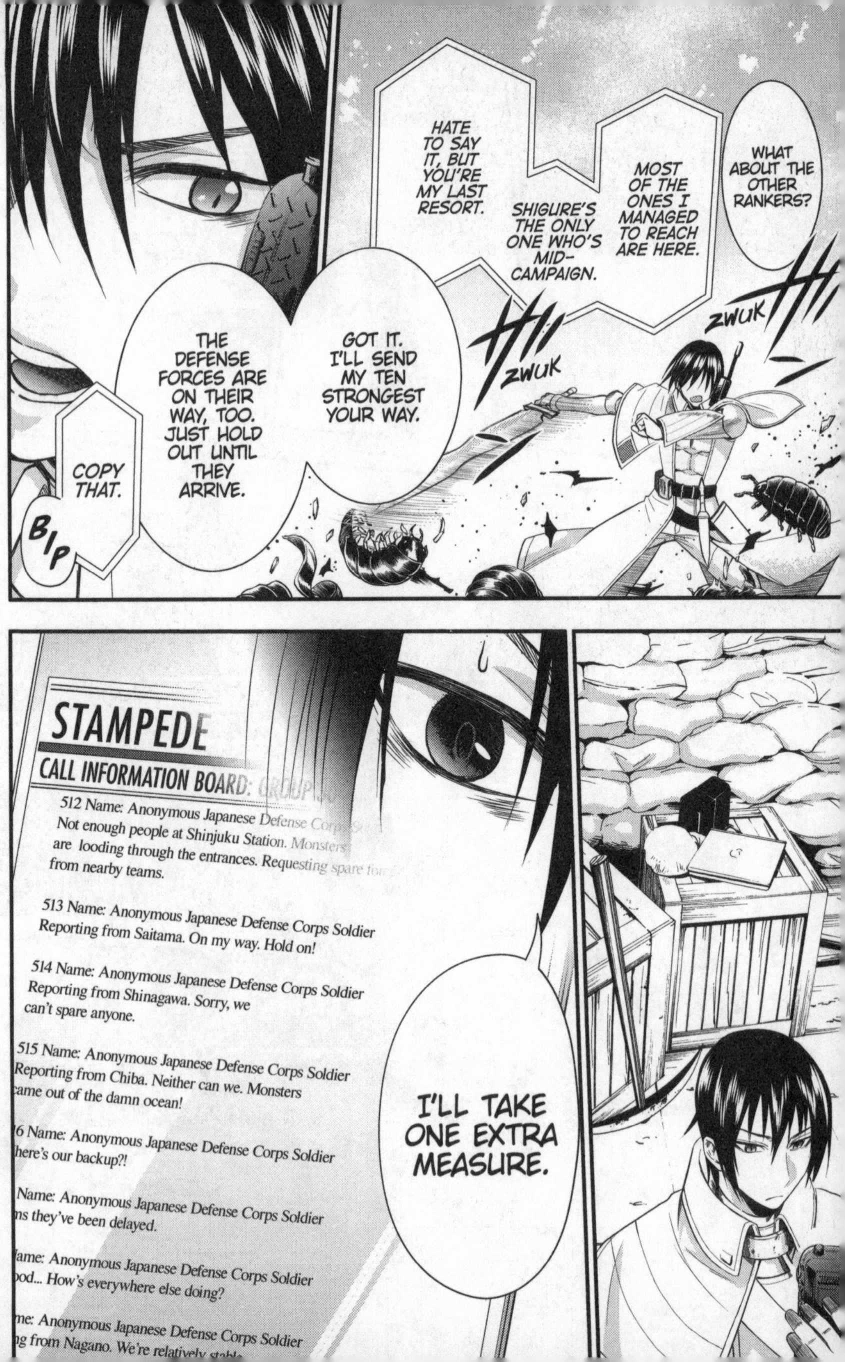
WHAT ABOUT THE OTHER RANKERS?
MOST OF THE ONES I MANAGED TO REACH ARE HERE.
SHIGURE'S THE ONLY ONE WHO'S MID-CAMPAIGN.
HATE TO SAY IT, BUT YOU'RE MY LAST RESORT.
ZWUK
ZWUK
GOT IT. I'LL SEND MY TEN STRONGEST YOUR WAY.
THE DEFENSE FORCES ARE ON THEIR WAY, TOO. JUST HOLD OUT UNTIL THEY ARRIVE.
COPY THAT.
BIP
I'LL TAKE ONE EXTRA MEASURE.
STAMPEDE
CALL INFORMATION BOARD:
512 Name: Anonymous Japanese Defense Corps
Not enough people at Shinjuku Station. Monsters
are looding through the entrances. Requesting spare
from nearby teams.
513 Name: Anonymous Japanese Defense Corps Soldier
Reporting from Saitama. On my way. Hold on!
514 Name: Anonymous Japanese Defense Corps Soldier
Reporting from Shinagawa. Sorry, we can't spare anyone.
515 Name: Anonymous Japanese Defense Corps Soldier
Reporting from Chiba. Neither can we. Monsters came out of the damn ocean!
6 Name: Anonymous Japanese Defense Corps Soldier
here's our backup?!
Name: Anonymous Japanese Defense Corps Soldier
ms they've been delayed.
Name: Anonymous Japanese Defense Corps Soldier
ood... How's everywhere else doing?
me: Anonymous Japanese Defense Corps Soldier
g from Nagano. We're relatively

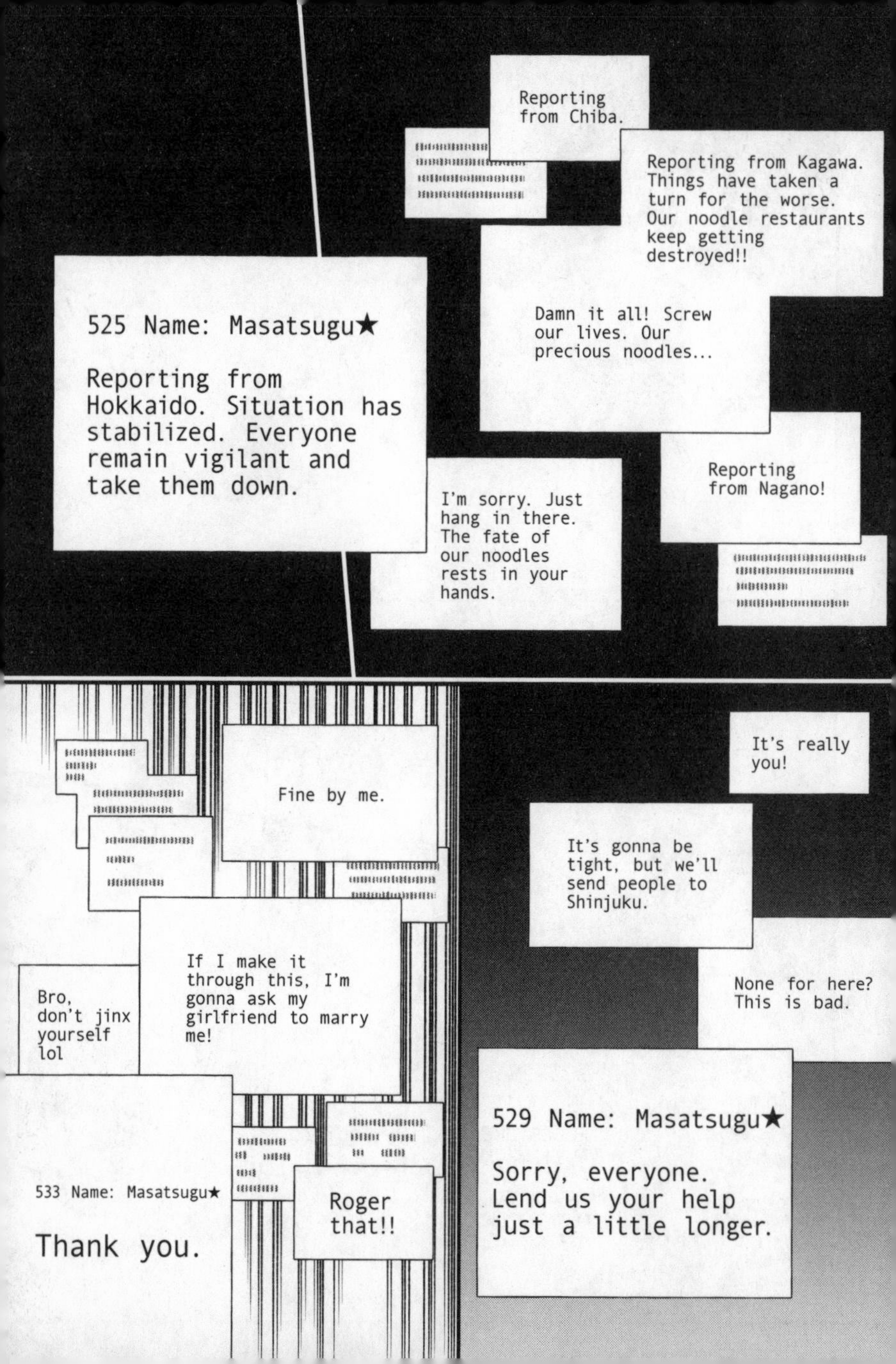

Reporting from Chiba.
Reporting from Kagawa. Things have taken a turn for the worse. Our noodle restaurants keep getting destroyed!!
Damn it all! Screw our lives. Our precious noodles...
525 Name: Masatsugu★
Reporting from Hokkaido. Situation has stabilized. Everyone remain vigilant and take them down.
Reporting from Nagano!
I'm sorry. Just hang in there. The fate of our noodles rests in your hands.
It's really you!
It's gonna be tight, but we'll send people to Shinjuku.
None for here? This is bad.
529 Name: Masatsugu★
Sorry, everyone. Lend us your help just a little longer.
Fine by me.
If I make it through this, I'm gonna ask my girlfriend to marry me!
Bro, don't jinx yourself lol
Roger that!!
533 Name: Masatsugu★
Thank you.

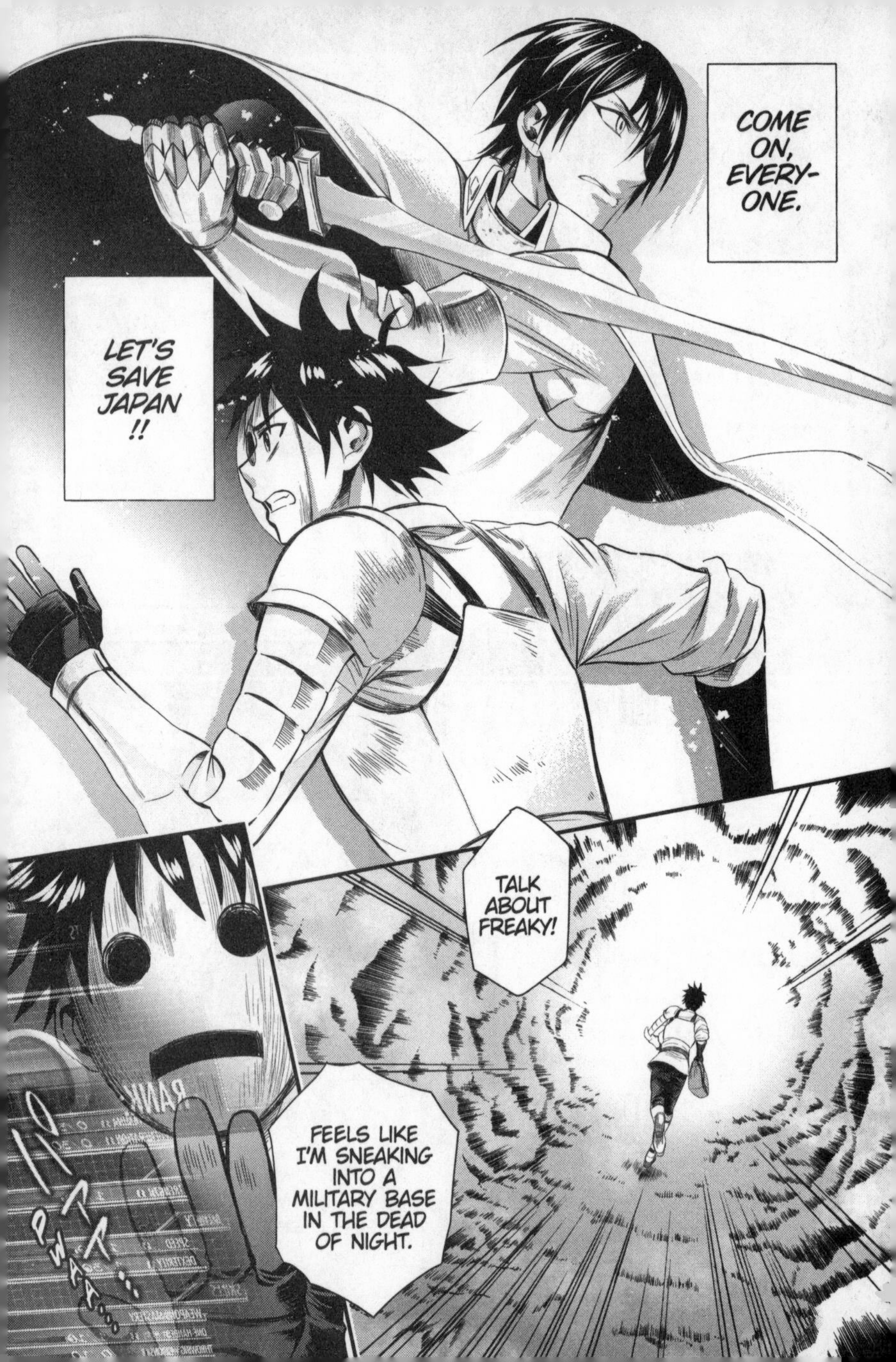
COME ON, EVERY-ONE.
LET'S SAVE JAPAN!!
TALK ABOUT FREAKY!
FEELS LIKE I'M SNEAKING INTO A MILITARY BASE IN THE DEAD OF NIGHT.
RANK

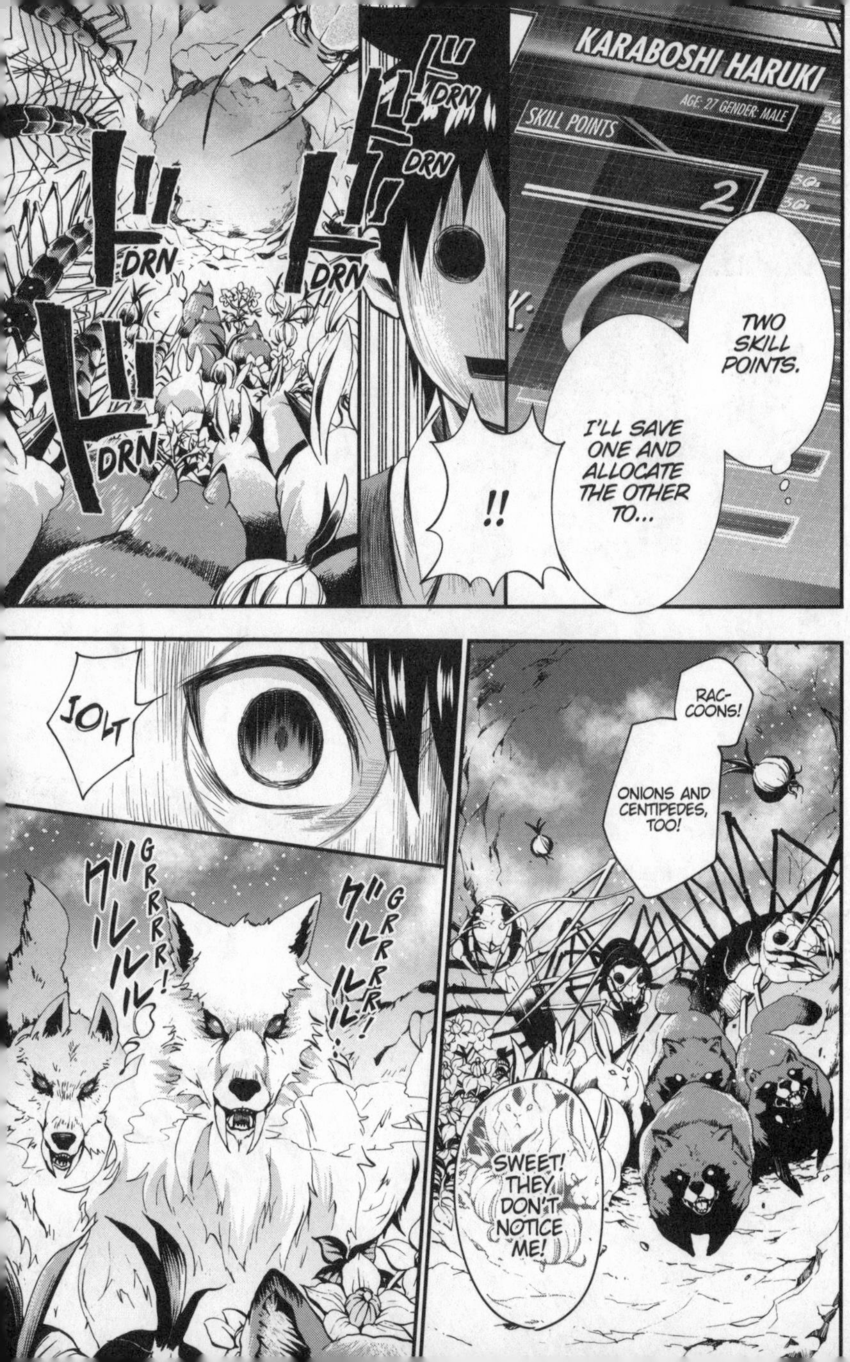
KARABOSHI HARUKI
AGE: 27 GENDER: MALE
SKILL POINTS
2
TWO SKILL POINTS.
I'LL SAVE ONE AND ALLOCATE THE OTHER TO...
!!
DRN
DRN
DRN
DRN
DRN
RAC-COONS!
ONIONS AND CENTIPEDES, TOO!
SWEET! THEY DON'T NOTICE ME!
JOLT
GRRRR!
GRRRRR!

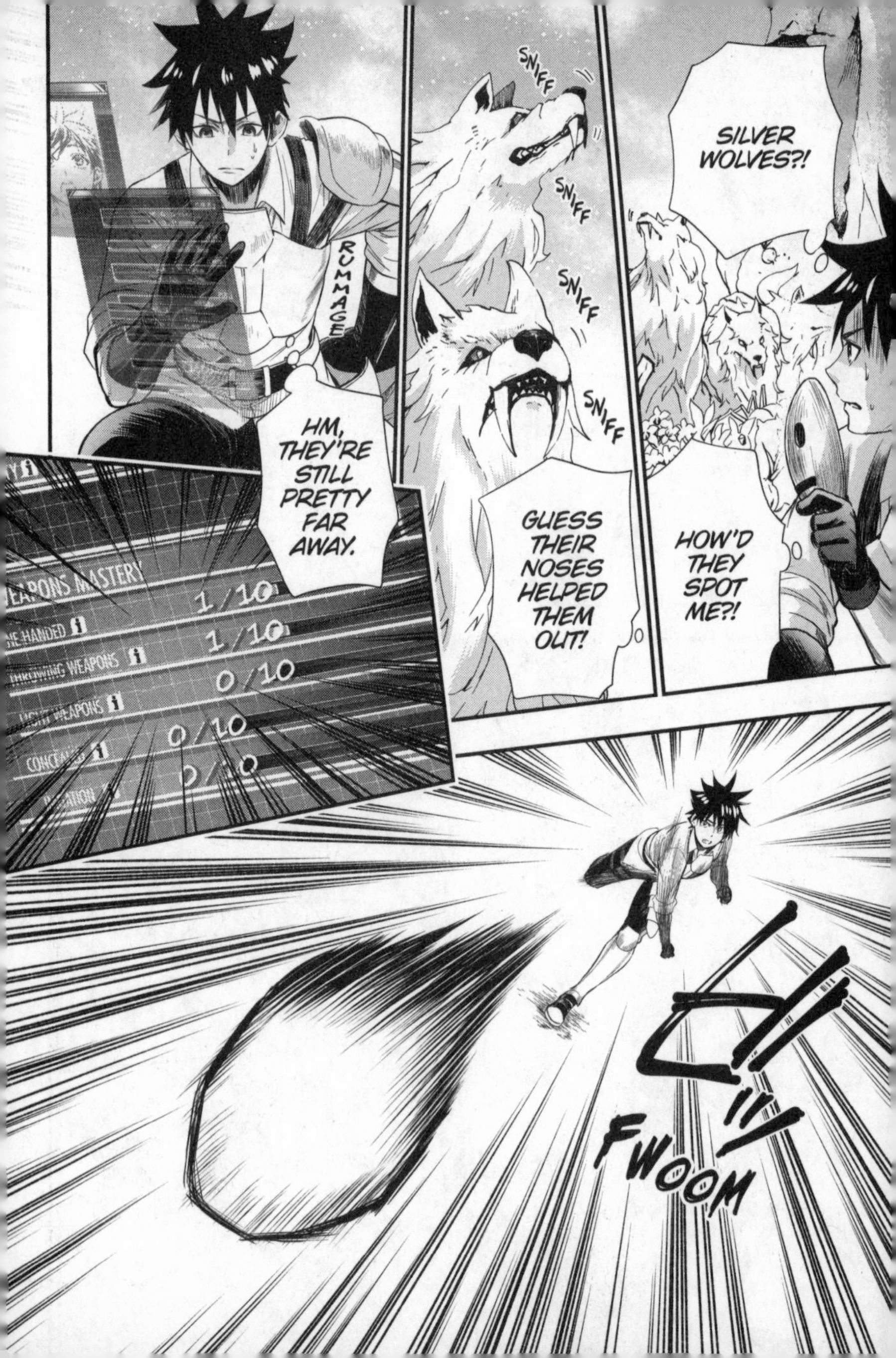

SILVER WOLVES?!
HOW'D THEY SPOT ME?!
SNIFF
SNIFF
SNIFF
SNIFF
GUESS THEIR NOSES HELPED THEM OUT!
RUMMAGE
HM, THEY'RE STILL PRETTY FAR AWAY.
EAPONS MASTERY
1/10
NE-HANDED
1/10
THROWING WEAPONS
0/10
0/10
FWOOM

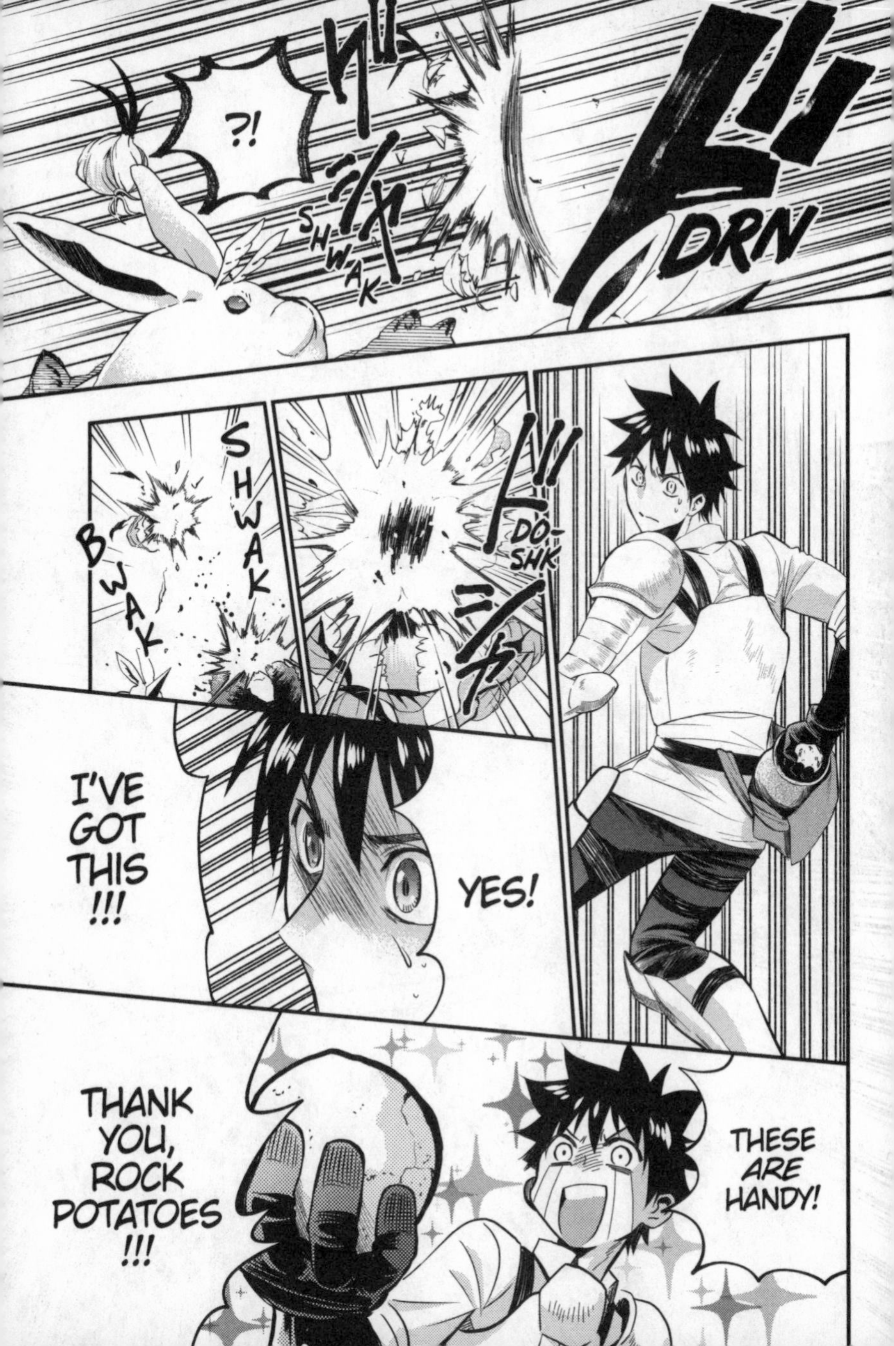
DRN
SHWAK
?!
DO-SHK
SHWAK
BWAK
YES!
I'VE GOT THIS!!!
THESE ARE HANDY!
THANK YOU, ROCK POTATOES!!!

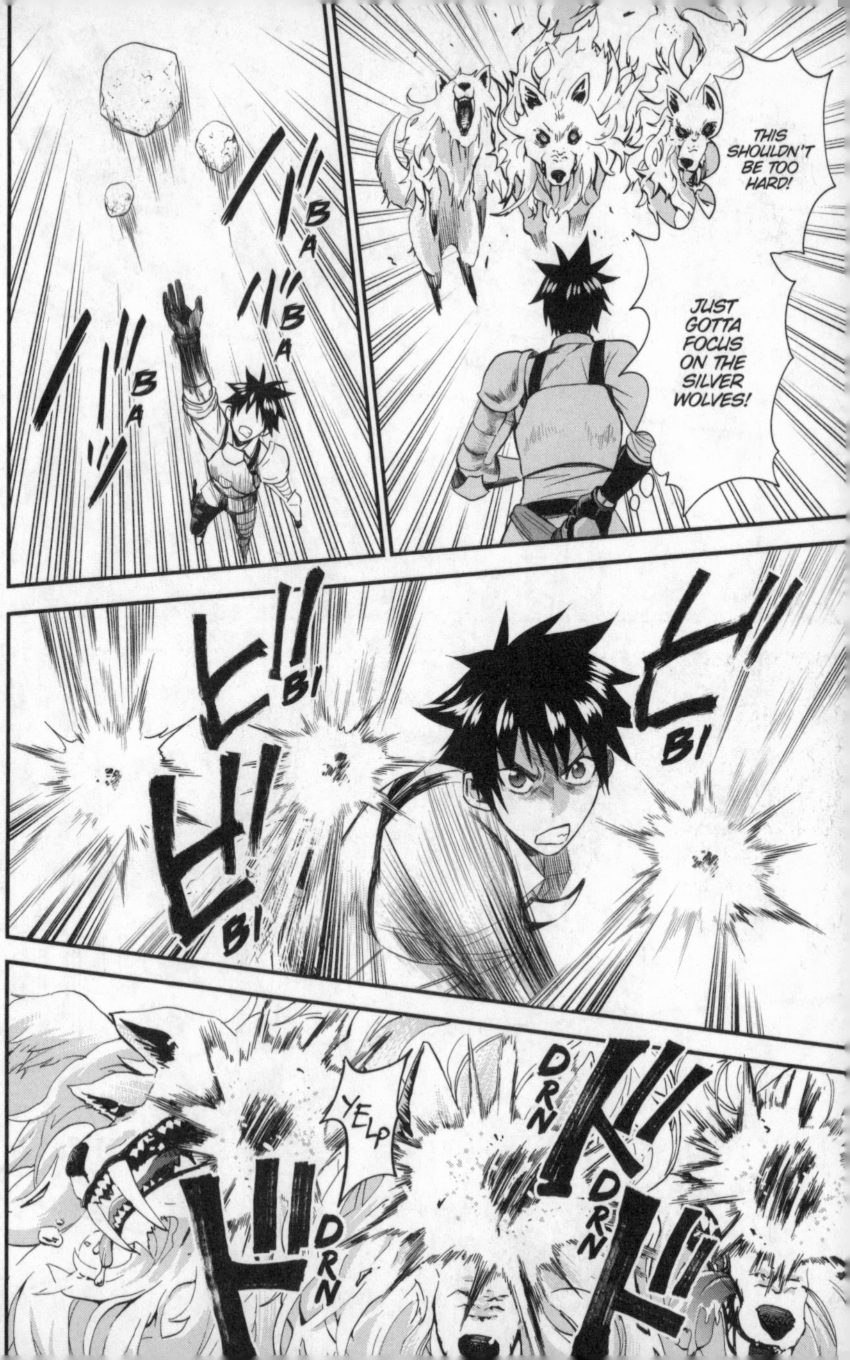
THIS SHOULDN'T BE TOO HARD!
JUST GOTTA FOCUS ON THE SILVER WOLVES!
BA
BA
BA
BI
BI
BI
DRN
DRN
YELP
DRN

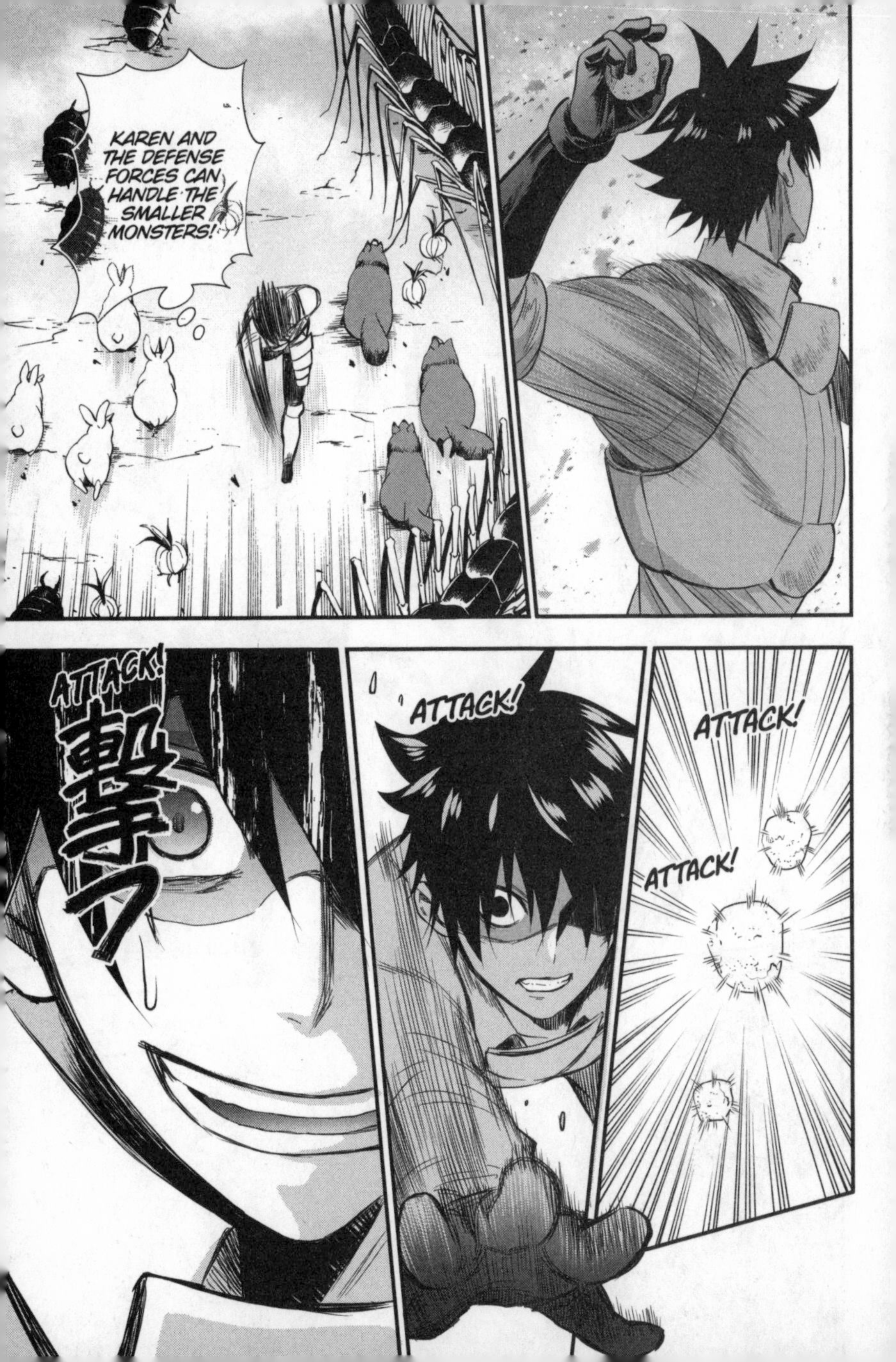
KAREN AND THE DEFENSE FORCES CAN HANDLE THE SMALLER MONSTERS!
ATTACK!
ATTACK!
ATTACK!
ATTACK!
撃つ

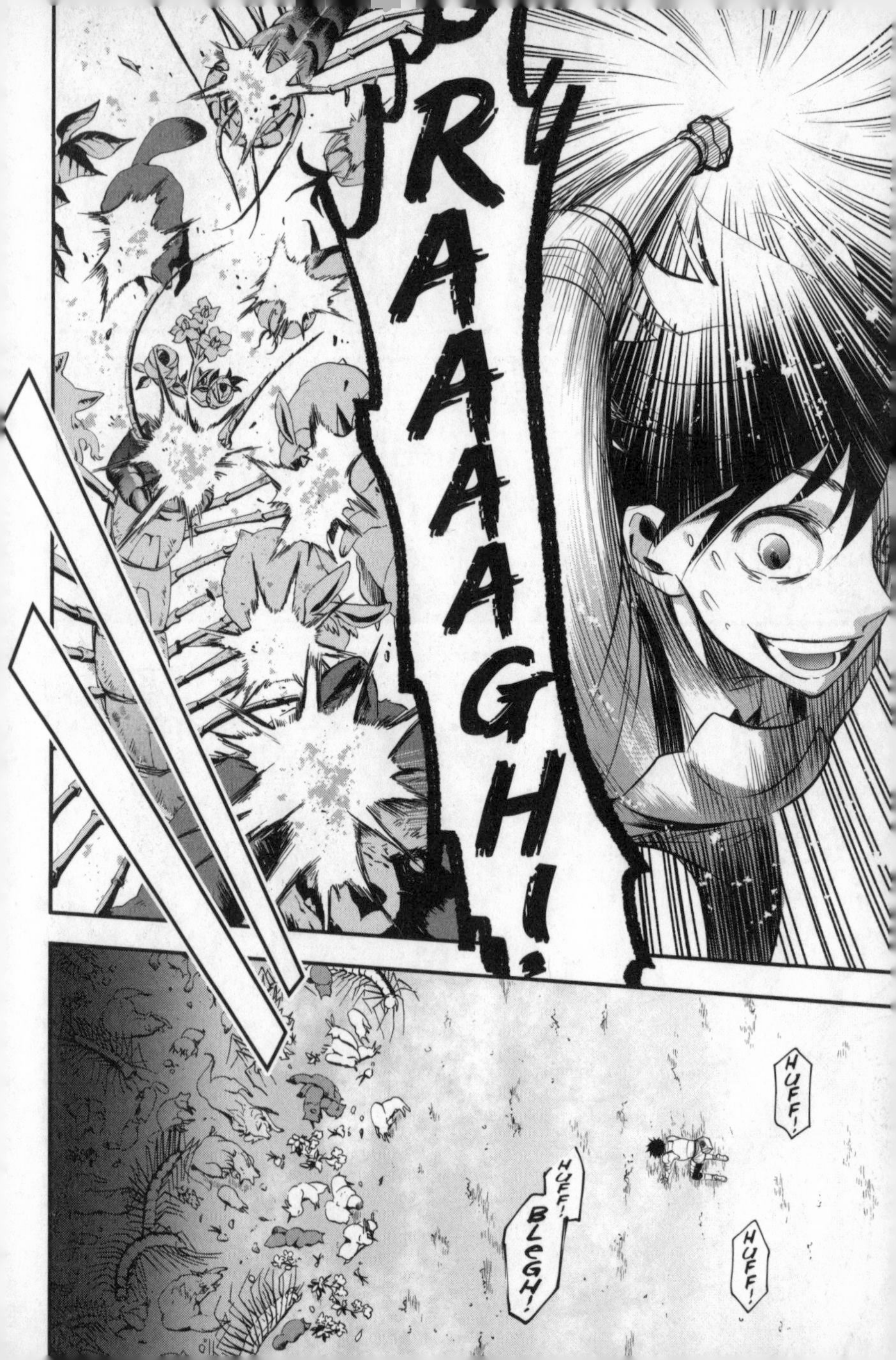

JRRAAAAAGH!
HUFF!
HUFF!
HUFF! BLEGH!

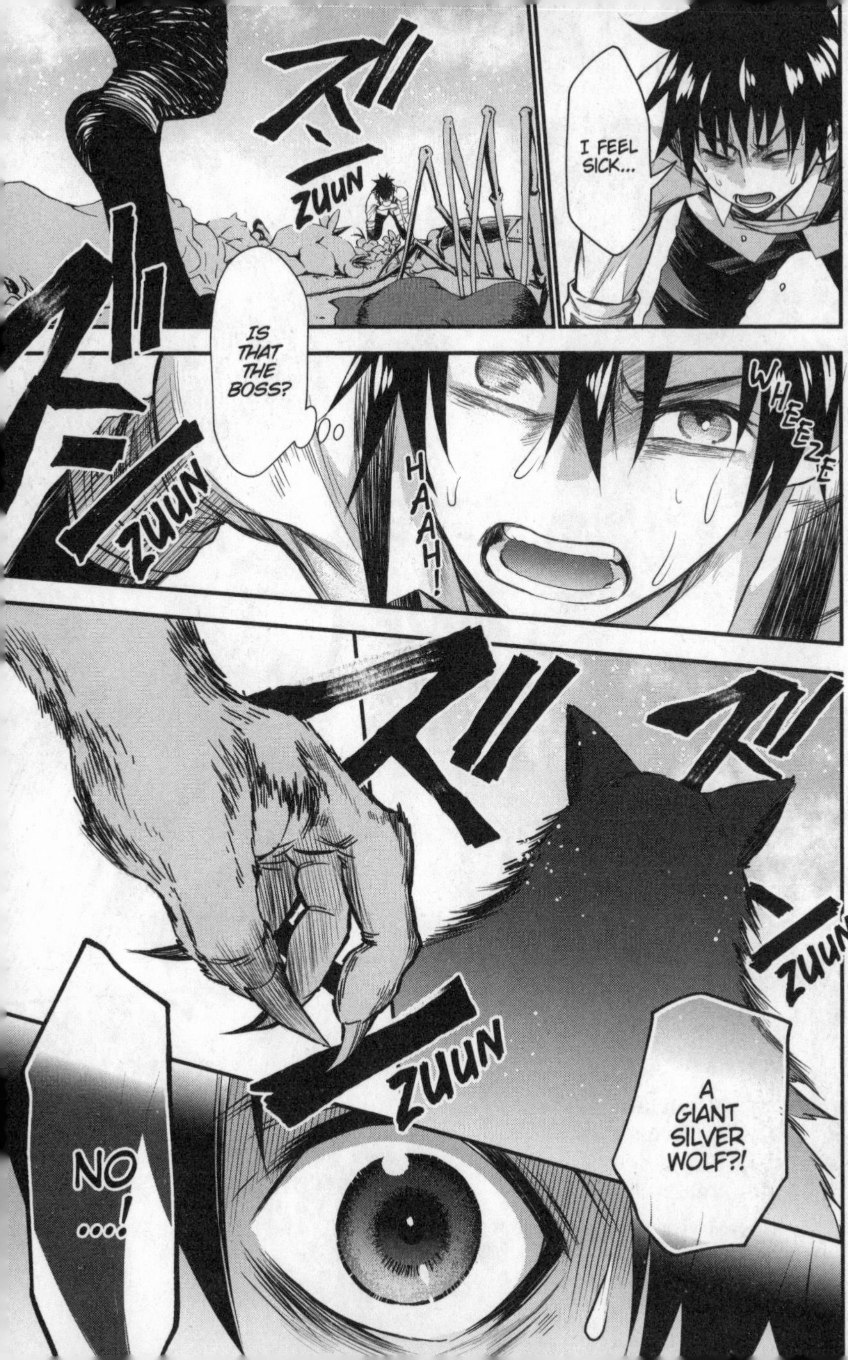
I FEEL SICK...
ZUUN
WHEEZE
HAAAH!
IS THAT THE BOSS?
ZUUN
ZUUN
A GIANT SILVER WOLF?!
ZUUN
NO ...!

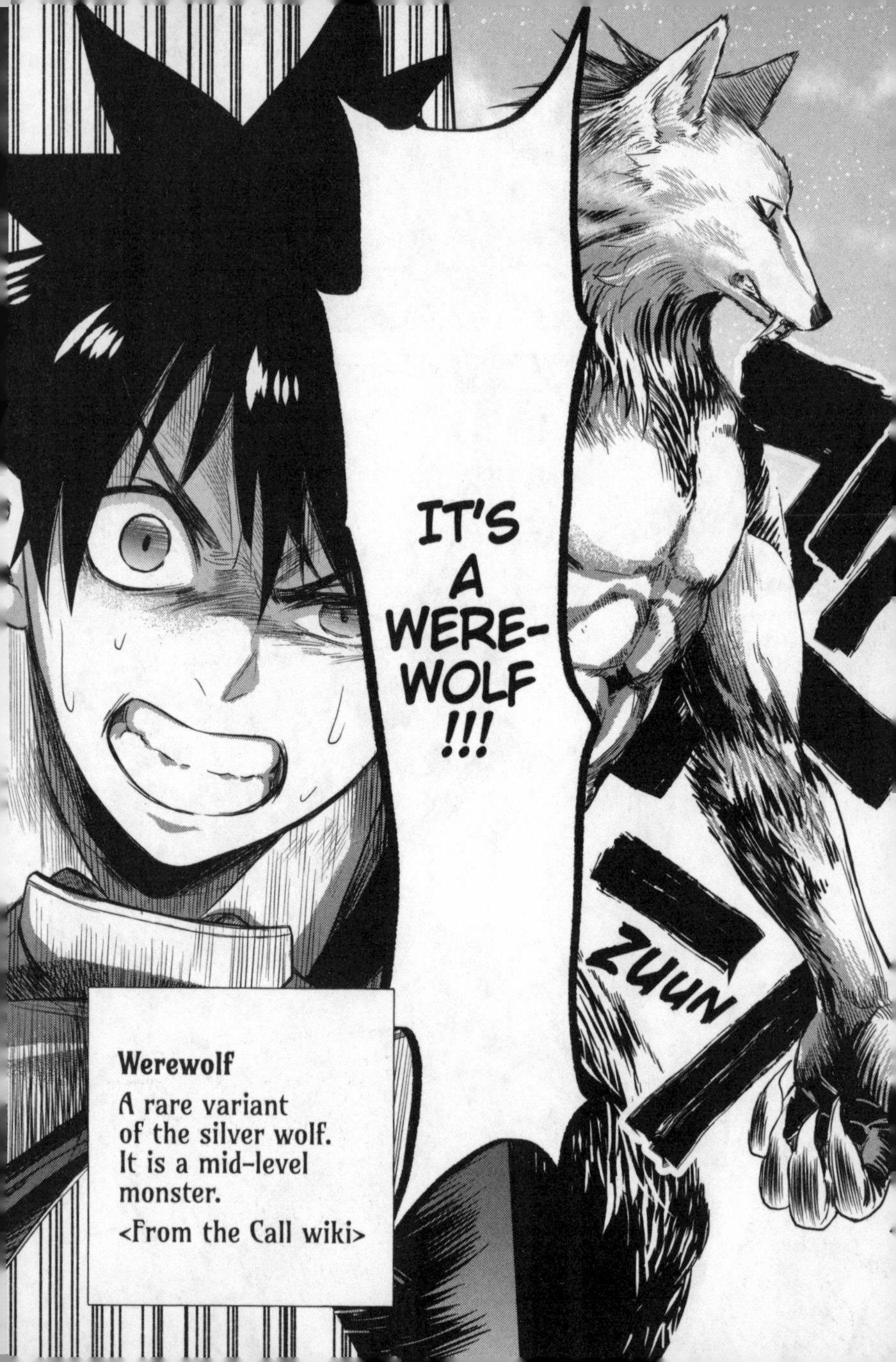
IT'S A WERE-WOLF!!!
ZUUN
Werewolf
A rare variant of the silver wolf. It is a mid-level monster.
<From the Call wiki>

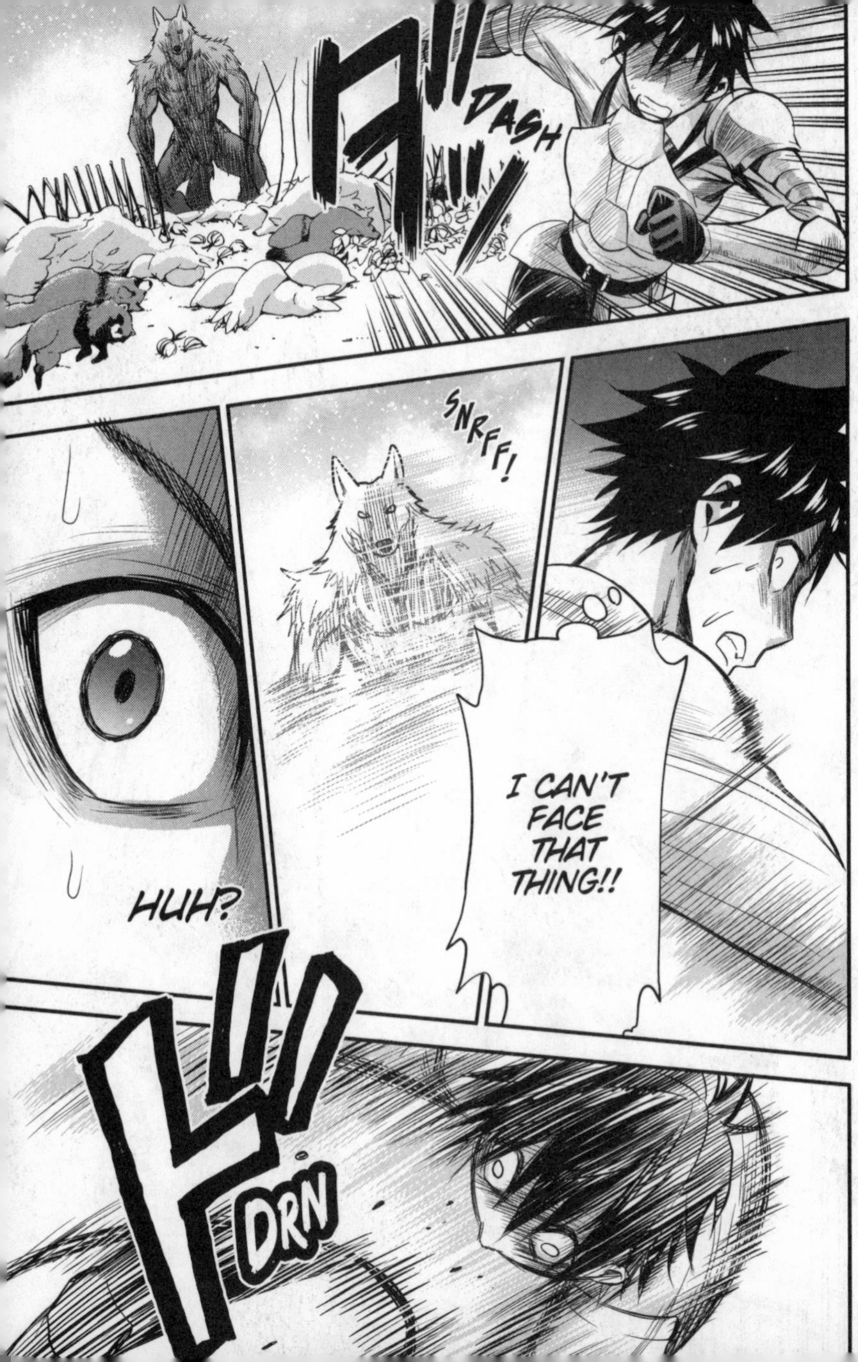
DASH
I CAN'T FACE THAT THING!!
SNRFF!
HUH?
DRN

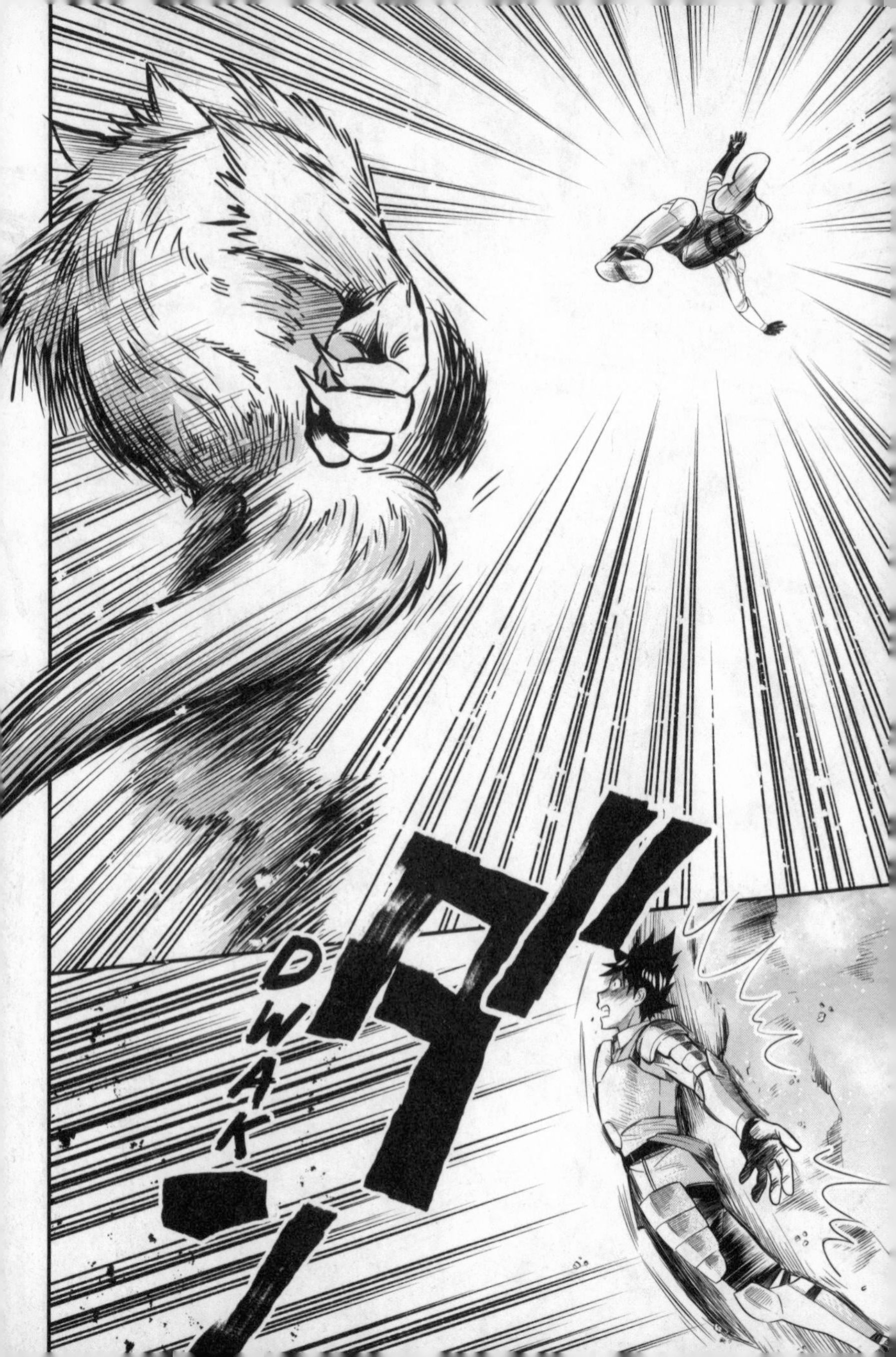
DWAK

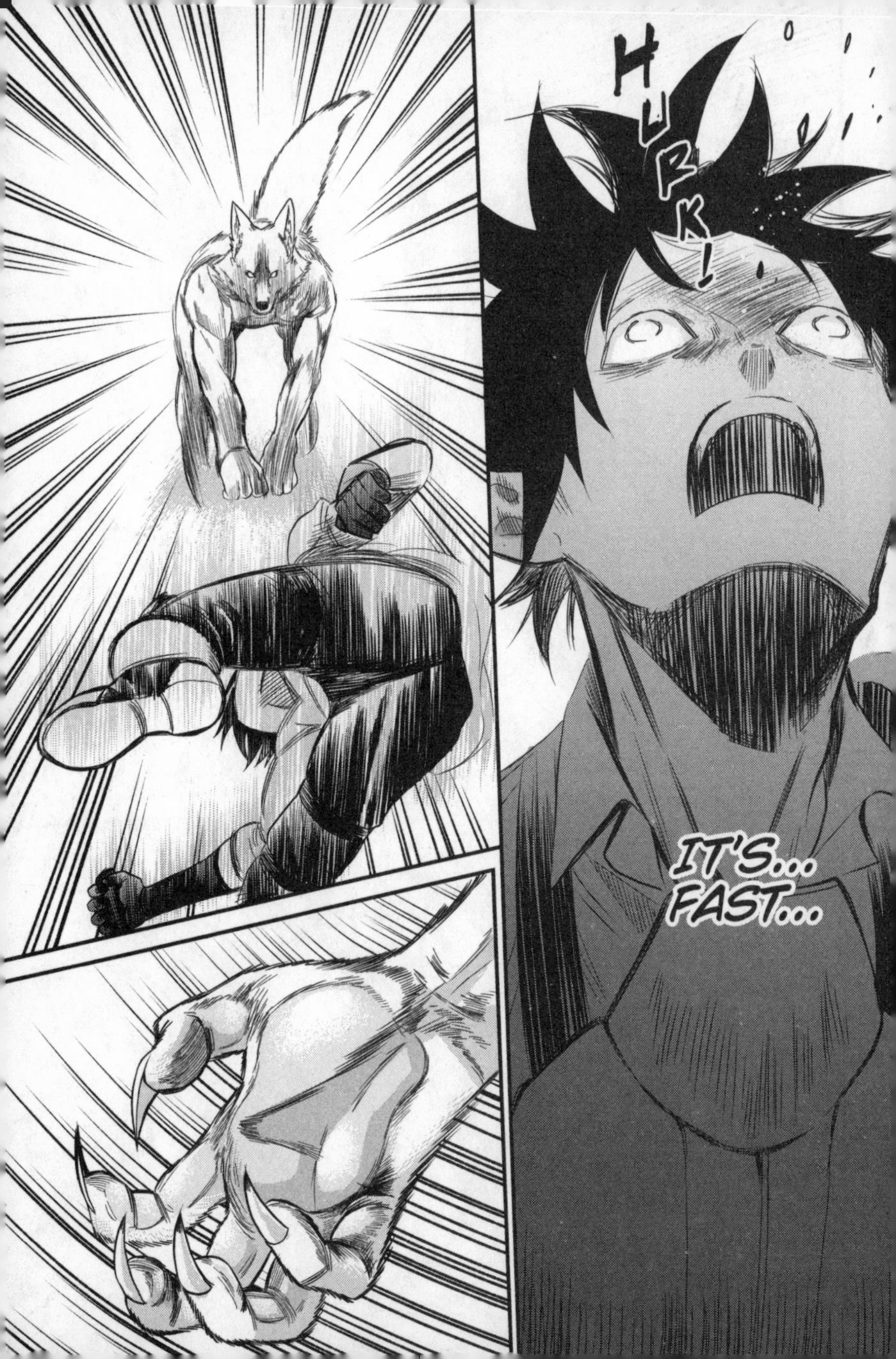
HURK!
IT'S...
FAST...

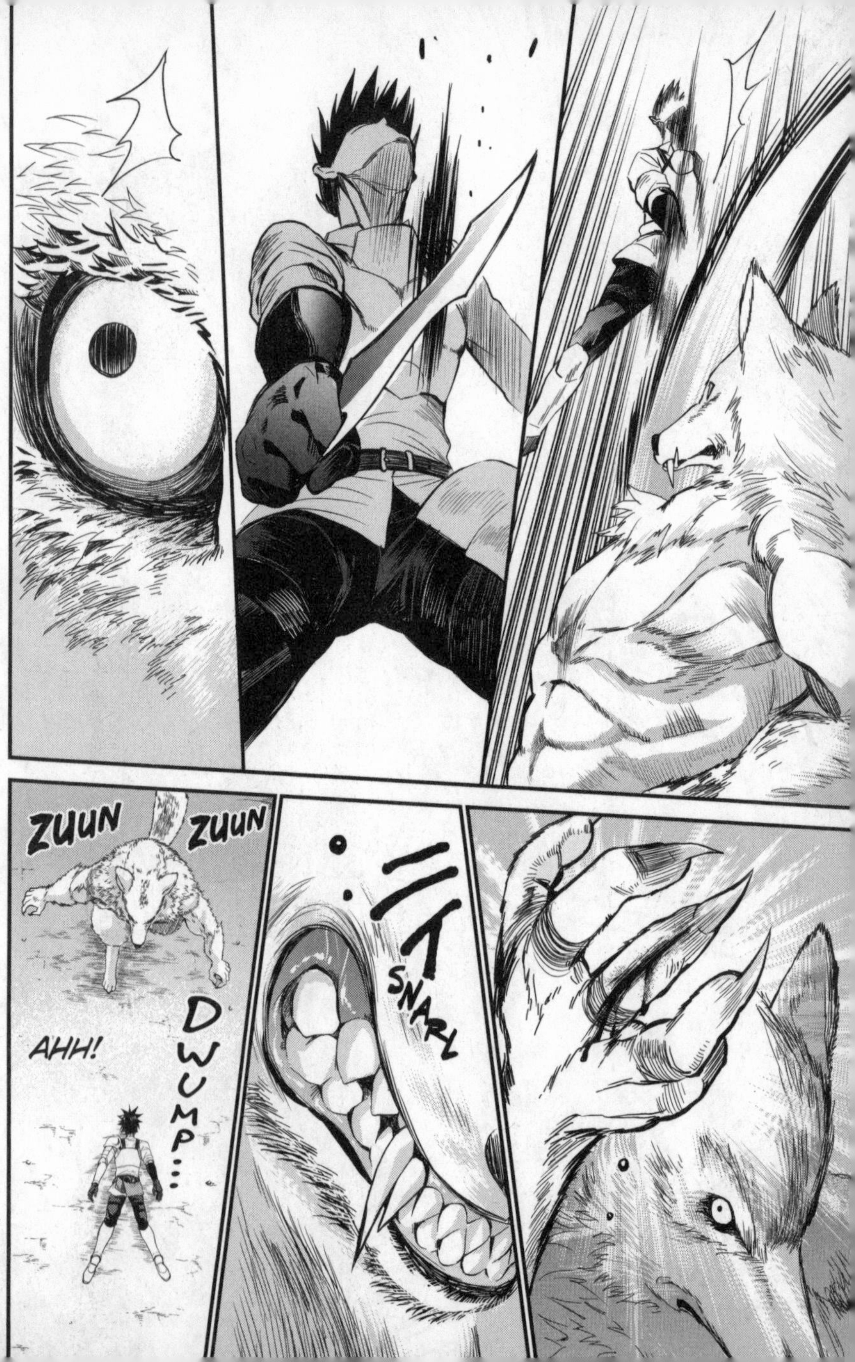
SNARL
ZUUN ZUUN
AHH!
DWUMP...

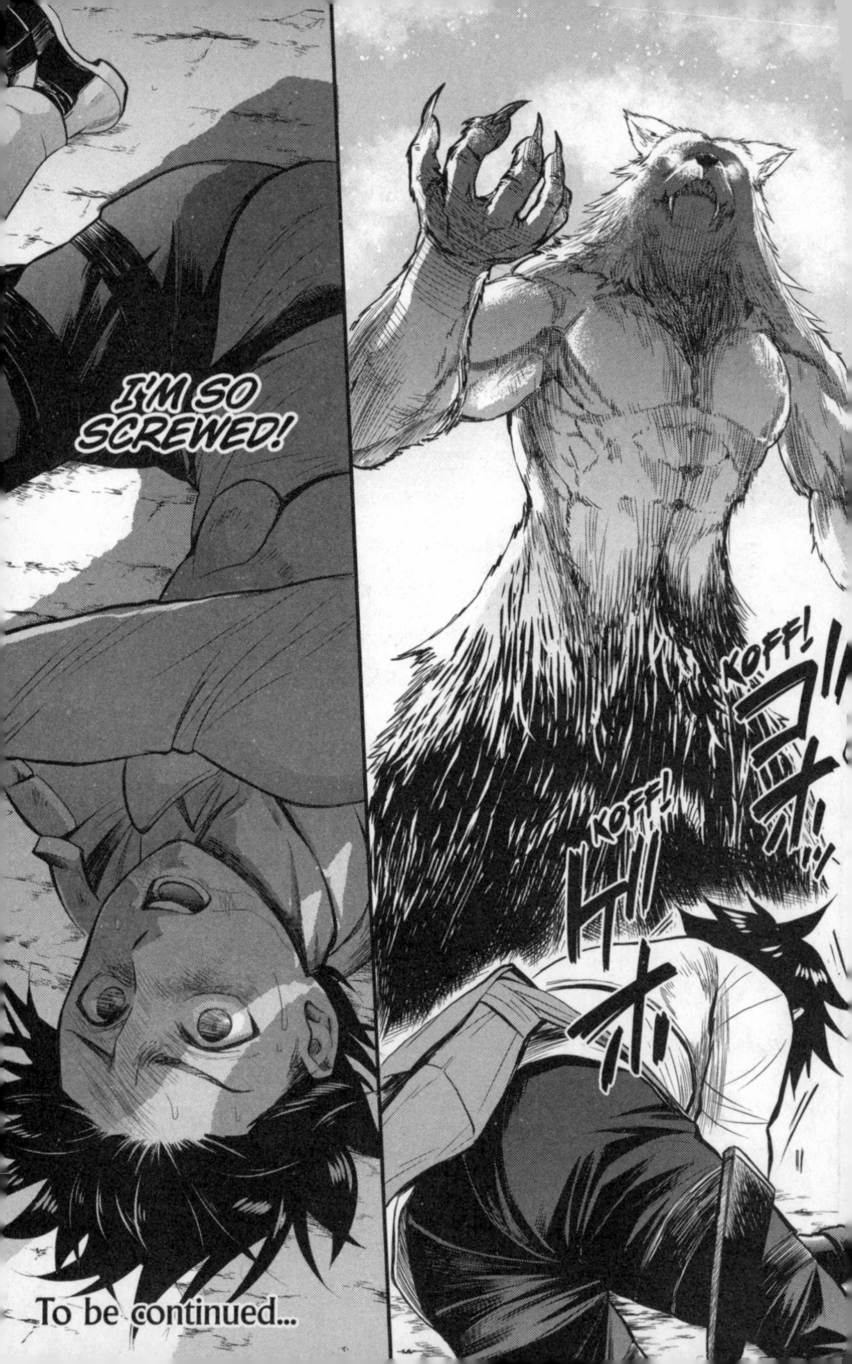
KOFF!
KOFF!
I'M SO SCREWED!
To be continued...

SEVEN SEAS ENTERTAINMENT PRESENTS

CALL TO ADVENTURE!
DEFEATING DUNGEONS
WITH A SKILL BOARD Vol. 2

story by **AKI HAGIU**   art by **RENJI KURIYAMA**   character design by **TEDDY**

TRANSLATION
Morgan Watchorn

ADAPTATION
Maneesh Maganti

LETTERING
Ochie Caraan

COVER DESIGN
Hanase Qi

LOGO DESIGN
George Panella

PROOFREADER
Kurestin Armada

COPY EDITOR
Dawn Davis

EDITOR
Jenn Grunigen

PREPRESS TECHNICIAN
iannon Rasmussen-Silverstein

PRODUCTION ASSOCIATE
Christa Miesner

PRODUCTION MANAGER
Lissa Pattillo

MANAGING EDITOR
Julie Davis

ASSOCIATE PUBLISHER
Adam Arnold

PUBLISHER
Jason DeAngelis

Seven Seas press and purchase enquiries can be sent to Marketing Manager Lianne
Sentar at press@gomanga.com. Information regarding the distribution and purchase of
digital editions is available from Digital Manager CK Russell at digital@gomanga.com.

Seven Seas and the Seven Seas logo are trademarks of
Seven Seas Entertainment. All rights reserved.

ISBN: 978-1-64827-614-9
Printed in Canada
First Printing: October 2021
10 9 8 7 6 5 4 3 2 1

READING DIRECTIONS

This book reads from *right to left*,
Japanese style. If this is your first time
reading manga, you start reading from
the top right panel on each page and
take it from there. If you get lost, just
follow the numbered diagram here.
It may seem backwards at first,
but you'll get the hang of it! Have fun!!

Follow us online: www.SevenSeasEntertainment.com